DATE DUE

AUG 1 7 2002		
SEP 1 2 2002		
OCT 0 8 2002		
OCT 0 8 2002		
OCT 2 6 2002		
DEC 0 9 2002		
DEC 3 1 2002		
FEB 0 5 2003		
MAR 1 8 2004		
APR 0 4 2005		

Demco, Inc 38-293

Gender & American Culture

Coeditors
Thadious M. Davis
Linda K. Kerber

Editorial Advisory Board
Nancy Cott
Cathy N. Davidson
Jane Sherron De Hart
Sara Evans
Mary Kelley
Annette Kolodny
Wendy Martin
Nell Irvin Painter
Janice Radway
Barbara Sicherman

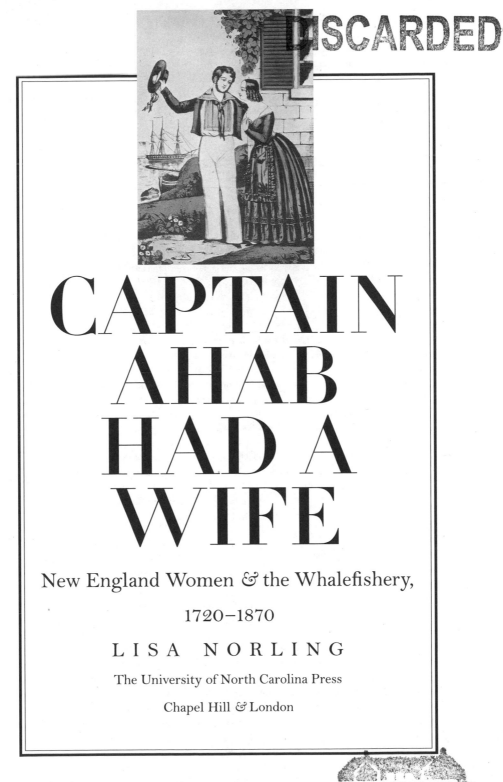

CAPTAIN AHAB HAD A WIFE

New England Women & the Whalefishery,

1720–1870

LISA NORLING

The University of North Carolina Press

Chapel Hill & London

© 2000 The University of North Carolina Press
All rights reserved
Manufactured in the United States of America
The paper in this book meets the guidelines for permanence and durability
of the Committee on Production Guidelines for Book Longevity of the Council on
Library Resources.
This book was set in Bell types by Tseng Information Systems, Inc.
Book design by Richard Hendel
Library of Congress Cataloging-in-Publication Data
Norling, Lisa.
Captain Ahab had a wife : New England women and the whalefishery, 1720–1870 /
Lisa Norling.
p.   cm.
Includes bibliographical references and index.
ISBN 0-8078-2561-1 (cloth : alk. paper) — ISBN 0-8078-4870-0 (pbk. : alk. paper)
1. Whaling—Massachusetts—New Bedford—History—19th century.
2. Women—Massachusetts—New Bedford—Social conditions—19th century.
3. Nantucket (Mass.)—Social life and customs—18th century.   I. Title.
SH383.2 .N67   2000
338.3'7295'0974485—dc21
99-088026

Portions of the book have been appeared previously, in somewhat different form,
in the following publications and are reprinted here with permission of the publishers: "Ahab's
Wife: Women and the American Whaling Industry, 1820–1870," in *Iron Men, Wooden Women:
Gender and Seafaring in the Atlantic World, 1700–1920*, edited by Margaret S. Creighton and Lisa
Norling, 70–91 (Baltimore: Johns Hopkins University Press, 1996); "Contrary Dependencies:
Whaling Agents and Whalemen's Families, 1830–1870," *Log of Mystic Seaport* 42, no. 1 (Spring
1990): 3–12; " 'How Frought with Sorrow and Heartpangs': Mariners' Wives and the Ideology
of Domesticity in New England, 1790–1880," *New England Quarterly* 65, no. 3 (September
1992): 422–46; "Judith Macy and Her Daybook; or, Crevecoeur and the Wives of Sherborn,"
Historic Nantucket 40, no. 4 (Winter 1992): 68–71; "The Sentimentalization of American
Seafaring: The Case of the New England Whalefishery," in *Jack Tar in History: Essays in the
History of Maritime Life and Labour*, edited by Colin Howell and Richard Twomey, 164–78
(Fredericton, N.B.: Acadiensis, 1991).

This volume was published with the generous assistance of the
Greensboro Women's Fund of the University of North Carolina Press.
Founding Contributors: Linda Arnold Carlisle, Sally Schindel Cone, Anne Faircloth,
Bonnie McElveen Hunter, Linda Bullard Jennings, Janice J. Kerley
(in honor of Margaret Supplee Smith), Nancy Rouzer May,
and Betty Hughes Nichols.

Frontispiece: "The Sailor's Adieu."
There were several versions of this extremely popular image, sometimes paired with
a second image titled "The Sailor's Return," including a widely distributed series by Currier
and Ives. This particular lithograph dates from ca. 1845 and was produced by Baillie and Sowle
of New Bedford, Mass. Courtesy of Old Dartmouth Historical Society–New Bedford
Whaling Museum (Trans. 785)

04 03 02 01 00   5 4 3 2 1

To my father,
Alfred Norling,
and the memory of my mother,
Kristin Norling,
with much gratitude,
appreciation,
and love.

CONTENTS

MAPS & ILLUSTRATIONS

ACKNOWLEDGMENTS

This book would not and could not have been written without the intellectual engagement, willingness to help, and friendship of dozens of people over the past decade. For the generosity and patience with which they shared their expertise with me, I am especially indebted to the former and current staff members of the archives and libraries I utilized: Paul Cyr and Tina Furtado of the New Bedford Free Public Library; Virginia Adams, Carol Juneau, Sienne Patch, and Judy Downey of the Old Dartmouth Historical Society–New Bedford Whaling Museum; Jacqueline Haring, Betsey Lowenstein, Gayl Michael, and Amy Rokicki of the Edouard A. Stackpole Research Center Library, Nantucket Historical Association; Betsy Tyler, Barbara Andrews, and Charlotte Maison at the Nantucket Atheneum; and Robert Webb, Stuart Frank, Mary Malloy, Sarah Hayes, and Ellen Hazen of the Kendall Whaling Museum. In particular, Judy Downey in New Bedford, Betsey Tyler on Nantucket, and Paul O'Pecko and Douglas Stein of the G. W. Blunt White Library, Mystic Seaport Museum, deserve special mention (if not Purple Hearts).

Also very helpful were Ann Allen and Marian Halperin of what is now the Martha's Vineyard Historical Society; Jane Ward at the Phillips Library of the Peabody Essex Museum; Florence Lathrop of the Baker Library at Harvard University; Todd Bryda at the Mattapoisett Historical Society; Rick Statler at the Rhode Island Historical Society; the staffs at the American Antiquarian Society, the Houghton Library of Harvard University, the John Carter Brown Library at Brown University, the Massachusetts State Archives, the Providence Public Library, the Newport

Historical Society, the Sandwich Historical Society, and the Schlesinger Library at Radcliffe Institute, and the friendly, if sometimes mystified, clerks at the city, town, and county offices in New Bedford, Nantucket, Dartmouth, Rochester, and Taunton, Massachusetts.

Many individuals in the communities I studied offered considerable hospitality along with their knowledge: Nathaniel Philbrick, Dr. Louise Hussey, Susan Beegel, Wes Tiffney, Helen Winslow Chase, Robert Leach, and Dr. Edouard Stackpole on Nantucket; Virginia Yans (and friends), and Marjory and Robert Potts on Martha's Vineyard. Marcia and John Anderson, Beth Schine and Pam McArthur, and Hillary Rettig and George Lewis welcomed me into their homes, usually on short notice and for extended periods of stay, during research trips. Pete Campbell's faith and friendship was a constant support. In Mystic, Katrina Bercaw and Guy Hermann, Ellen Anderson, Jim and Debby Carlton, Kate Sheehan Roach, Laurie Wilson, and Janie Wulff of the Williams-Mystic Program, and many other Mystic Seaport folks created an encouraging and challenging milieu in which I completed the dissertation on which this book is partly based.

During my stays in New Bedford, Mrs. Genevieve Darden, Mrs. Helen Radcliffe, Miss Ellen Howland, Mrs. Mary Bullard, and Mr. and Mrs. Robert Hardy all generously shared with me their own family traditions, stories, and materials. Brad Hathaway, Daniel Briggs, Mrs. Ella Sherberg, and Cynthia Dessen allowed me to examine manuscripts and books in their personal possession. Through the kind offices of Miss Howland, Mrs. Bullard, and Dr. John O'Toole, I also gained permission to explore the archival records of the still-active New Bedford Port Society and its Ladies' Branch. Joan Druett shared with me the fruits of her own indefatigable research into the lives of New England whaling wives at sea.

Over the course of my involvement with this project, I benefited greatly from the constructive criticism and counsel of many splendid scholars. Ava Baron, W. Jeffrey Bolster, Jeanne Boydston, Anne Boylan, Valerie Burton, Briton Busch, Catherine Clinton, Toby Ditz, Dianne Dugaw, Susan Eacker, Judith Fingard, Andrew German, Karen V. Hansen, Rhys Isaac, Carol Lasser, Jan Lewis, Kenneth Martin, Christopher McKee, Tamara Miller, Marcus Rediker, Barbara Sicherman, Judy Walkowitz, and other participants commented helpfully upon the various seminar and conference papers in which I developed many of the ideas of the book. Dorothy Sue Cobble, William Fowler, John Gillis, Glenn Gordinier, Ruth Herndon, Benjamin Labaree, T. Jackson Lears, Jennifer Reece, Edward Sloan, and

Daniel Vickers contributed extremely helpful commentary on the dissertation and other written work that became part of the book. My career as an historian has been tremendously enriched and enlivened by coconspirator Margaret Creighton's involvement and friendship.

I have been doubly fortunate to twice find myself, at Rutgers and again at Minnesota, in the midst of remarkably supportive and exciting intellectual communities. I owe a great deal to my graduate school colleagues Sharla Fett, Gretchen Galbraith, Jerma Jackson, Robert Johnston, Megan McClintock, Jacquelyn Miller, Jay Moore, Elizabeth Rose, Scott Sandage, Janann Sherman, Rus Uyeno, Pamela Walker, Tracey Weis, Susan Whitney, and Torun Willits. The book was much improved by the insight, generosity, and knowledge of participants in the University of Minnesota's Comparative Women's History and Early American History Workshops and of other colleagues, including Jean Allman, Sarah Chambers, Sean Condon, Andrea Foroughi, Robert Frame, Shari Geistfeld, Jill Gidmark, Jennifer Goloboy, Edward Griffin, David Hacker, Paisley Harris, John Howe, Rachel Martin, Elaine Tyler May, Robert McCaa, Katherine Meerse, Russell Menard, Brett Mizelle, Michelle Mouton, Matthew Mulcahy, Joanna O'Connell, Helena Polandt-McCormack, Carla Rahn Phillips, David Ryden, Lucy Simler, Jennifer Spear, Kathleen Thomas, Flo Waldron, Liping Wang, Barbara Welke, Leigh Ann Wheeler, Christy Whitfield, and Karen Woods.

The critique offered by Kate Torrey, Linda Kerber, and the readers for the University of North Carolina Press, especially that of Alfred Young, was particularly helpful. Andrea Foroughi, David Ryden, Karen Woods, Meghan Norling, and Patt Kelly rendered crucial service as research assistants extraordinaire, and the last-minute exertions of Patt, Mike Lansing, Cathy Fitch, Cassie Lucas, Matt Singewald, Susannah Smith, and Matt Sobek were memorable. I also much appreciated both the skill and the enthusiasm of UNC Press copy editor Kathy Malin.

I have also benefited from considerable institutional assistance. The original dissertation was supported in part by a Mellon Fellowship in the Humanities and by fellowships from the Rutgers University Graduate School and the Rutgers Center for Historical Analysis. I also held the Albion Post-Doctoral Fellowship in American Maritime Studies from Mystic Seaport's Munson Institute and the Williams-Mystic Program and, from the University of Minnesota, a two-year McKnight Land-Grant Professorship and several smaller research grants.

I owe my greatest debts to my wise and kind advisers, Mary Beth

Norton, Suzanne Lebsock, and Paul Clemens; my dear mentors and colleagues, Sara Evans, Mary Jo (MJ) Maynes, and Ann Waltner; and my superb partner-in-writing, Anna (Annette) Igra. Truly, without MJ, Ann, and Annette (all three of whom read the whole manuscript in various drafts), this book would never have been finished—their brilliance as historians and critics is surpassed only by their capacity for friendship. Of course, this book could never have happened at all without the love and support of my family. My deepest thanks to my parents, Alfred and Kristin Norling; to my siblings and their families, Jane Norling, Bob Lawson, and Rio Chavez, and Peter Norling, Barbara Dildine, and Meghan and Ginger Norling; and especially to my daughters, Abigail and Rebecca Norling-Ruggles, who may never know just how much this book dominated their first years, and to Steve Ruggles, my husband, who knows only too well.

CAPTAIN AHAB HAD A WIFE

INTRODUCTION
Captain Ahab Had a Wife

There are very few women in Melville's monumental 1851 novel, *Moby-Dick; or, The Whale*. Captain Ahab did, actually, have a wife. But she never appears in person, and she is mentioned only twice: once to signify Ahab's possession of "humanities" (warmer, softer, more nurturing and forgiving qualities) and once, by Ahab himself, in reference to his rejection of those humanities in his monomaniacal quest for the great white whale.[1] Of course, most of the action takes place at sea, and few women went to sea in the nineteenth century. So why remark on their absence from the book? I begin with Captain Ahab's wife because I think the way she is invoked in the novel sug-

~~ts~~ both the symbolic importance and the substantive

~~f~~ women from maritime culture then and from

~~tory~~ now.

~~tion~~ has focused largely on th

~~ualized~~ and almost wholly si~~n~~

~~ough~~ certainly not a "gen~~d~~

~~ng~~ has traditionally been ~~c~~

most strikingly gendered pursuits, an aggressively masculine world of "iron men on wooden ships" that marginalized and objectified real women while feminizing the sea, ships, and shoreside society. Women have served as the foil against which sailors and maritime culture in general asserted their rugged masculinity and demonstrated their estrangement from land-based society, as they "wandered," often "in exile," over "the trackless deep" on ships that were always called "she." In seafaring custom, song, and craft, women have featured more prominently as metaphor than as flesh-and-blood persons.[3]

In fairness, it was (and is) harder to see maritime women than it was to see sailors themselves because, though Jack Tar and Captain Ahab himself were immediately recognizable, their wives, mothers, and sisters did not look different from other women. These women did not walk with a rolling gait, their faces were not unusually weather-beaten, nor did they dress distinctively. They could not compare their hometowns to other ports around the world or tell from firsthand experience heroic tales of the beauties and terrors of the ocean or of the perils in hunting leviathan beasts. Very few women spent much time aboard ship. Their connection to the sea—what determined the rhythms and routine of their life—was through men.

For a century or more, a large popular audience of nautical enthusiasts has been moved by the poignancy of the women left behind onshore and been fascinated (and sometimes titillated) by the tales of the unusual women who broke with convention and went to sea. In contrast, most maritime historians have tended to dismiss as trivial and derivative the experiences and perspectives of Mrs. Ahab and her sisters. But recovering the stories of real maritime women enables us to move beyond the figure-heads and the chantey characterizations, the stiff and the stereotypical, and to restore crucial, missing dimensions of the social history of seafaring. Just as turning the lens of the telescope to a different magnification reveals a quite different picture,[4] broadening our vision beyond the ship to the shoreside community from which crews were drawn and ships were launched makes possible a more complete and more accurate history not only of maritime women but also of seafarers and of maritime enterprise. If maritime historians have neglected the female part of the landward sion, so too have other American historians largely overlooked the nt maritime elements in America's past. In particular, very fe of women have yet challenged the conflation of the coastal The oversight is unfortunate. Before the late nineteent e, after farmers, the second largest occupational

America, and for the preceding two and a half centuries our economy and society were fueled in major ways by maritime activities. As recent landmark scholarship in the social history of American seafaring has demonstrated, maritime enterprise and culture reflected, in some ways typified, and often influenced broad developments in American history from the seventeenth to the nineteenth centuries.[5] Sailors were neither atypical nor irrelevant. This study is intended to serve as a case in point: it aims to show how the particular interplay between economic, social, and cultural shifts in the whaling communities of southeastern New England throws into striking relief not only the conflicted development of liberal individualism for men (explored by Melville) but also the development of its female corollary, Victorian domesticity.

I began this study many years ago, as an undergraduate research project in my first women's history course. I had just been introduced to the Victorian "cult of True Womanhood."[6] At the time, I recall, I was both offended and deeply cynical. How could anyone have taken seriously the saccharine, sanctimonious pap pervading the period's popular literature, insisting that women were delicate, physically frail, intellectually incompetent, overly emotional, tending to the hysterical, and most appropriately relegated to the circumscribed female sphere of family and home sweet home? Surely, I thought, there had to have been women back then who had not knuckled under to the stifling cultural regime, who had not felt compelled to serve as the "Angel of the House," who were not necessarily pure, pious, submissive, and domestic. Remembering childhood summers on the New England coast and reminded of the capable, commonsensical women of Sarah Orne Jewett's *Country of the Pointed Firs*, I thought I would look in New England maritime communities for strong, independent women who had withstood the rising tide of Victorian domesticity along with their seafaring husbands' regular absences.

I did not find them. To my dismay, most of the sea-wives I studied (even the strong, independent ones) seemed to have subscribed just as wholeheartedly to pervasive ideas about female character and social roles as any other white, middle-class American women of the period. My d'covery raised a perplexing problem of interpretation. Here were w... familiar with the rhythms and risks of seafa... dic absences — three, four, even five years... f the nineteenth century — were compl... me from families where the men ha... randfathers, uncles, fathers, broth...

were all sailors and whose grandmothers, aunts, mothers, and sisters were all sea-wives. They were clearly forewarned by community tradition and personal experience about lengthy spousal separations and women's considerable responsibilities during men's absences. How was it, then, that these same women wrote letters to their husbands expressing such intense love, longing, and loneliness in such conventional sentimental language? How could they have possibly brought to their marriages such expectations of conjugal companionship and have felt so frustrated by the separations the women well knew were required by this particular form of deepwater work? How could they have adhered to an understanding of gender—the cultural meanings and values ascribed to biological sex differences, defining manhood and womanhood—that was so clearly dysfunctional in their particular circumstances?

Their stories were often poignant, sometimes downright heart-rending, and always deeply compelling. The stories of their lives raised a whole set of fascinating questions about the creation and power of cultural norms and the connection of these norms to both the lived experience of individuals and broader historical processes. In particular, they illuminate aspects of Victorian domesticity that we still do not clearly understand, even after the thirty-some years of vigorous women's history scholarship since Barbara Welter first identified and described the "cult of True Womanhood."[7]

We now recognize that domesticity was a particular set of closely related assumptions and ideals about gender, family, and home that saturated American culture in every conceivable form and medium from about 1820 to at least the end of the nineteenth century. According to the pervasive norms and values, men were supposed to be producers and providers who went out to work to support their families, which they understood to mean primarily their wives and children. Women's complementary responsibility was to create a home in which husbands were loved, sustained, and renewed, and children loved and nurtured. The home was envisioned as a private and spiritualized haven, isolated from the harsh and stressful worlds of work and partisan politics. As a consequence, the work that women performed within the home in service to their families was reconceptualized as an effortless labor of love rather than any sort of productive labor of pay. These ideas became so deeply entrenched in the popular mind that, somehow, what had been *prescription* shaded over imperceptibly to *description* of "natural" or innate womanhood and manhood. Breadwinning and female domesticity became the common sense the age, setting the limits of the imaginable and erecting a set of standards by which individuals and groups could be measured and judged.[8]

All eras have their particular commonsense understandings, of course. Human beings universally rely on organizing concepts and categories to make sense of themselves and their world, to themselves and to others. Such assumptions are in part learned and in part arrived at through experience, worked out through interaction with others around us and the situations and structures in which we are located. Abstract ideas are made concrete through a range of performances, from the way we tuck our children into bed at night and the way we greet our coworkers in the morning to the more formalized rituals associated with going to church, celebrating Independence Day on the Fourth of July, getting married, voting, taking out a bank loan, getting a driver's license, and the like. From the un-self-conscious and mundane to the highly deliberate and ceremonial, such activities define and communicate our sense of who we are, our understanding of the world around us, and our belief about what is appropriate and what is not. These assumptions are not necessarily logical or consistent: people are eclectic, drawing on and applying ideas that may seem suitable or appealing at the time but which, to outside observers, do not appear particularly useful or even rational.[9]

These understandings, though so widely shared that they come to seem both self-evident and natural, are historically and culturally variable, differing substantially from place to place and changing dramatically over time. Definitions of gender, the assumptions about what constitutes manhood and womanhood, offer a particularly clear example. Women in Western Europe in the Middle Ages, for instance, were considered to be *more* sexual and *less* moral or spiritual than men—quite the reverse of the later, Victorian view. In the seventeenth century, European colonizers were shocked to find the women in many Native American groups solely responsible for tilling the fields of corn and building their dwellings. A century later, in West Africa, other Europeans were even more shocked to see well-trained troops of armed women guarding the King of Dahomey's palace and serving in combat.[10] The particular understanding of female domesticity expressed by the New England maritime women, described in this book, actually represents a set of what were really quite new ideas about women, men, and family that emerged rapidly in the late eighteenth and early nineteenth centuries in North America and Western Europe.

What is still *not* so clear is quite how and why domesticity appear◄ then and there. Ever since Welter raised the topic in its American cont◄

historians have linked domesticity to economic change, in particular to commercialization and industrialization. It has been variously argued that female domesticity was a consequence of, rationalized, supported, compensated for, shored up, and ameliorated the harshness of the economic restructuring that moved men's paid labor and productive work from households to factories, stores, and offices. Other scholars have suggested that domesticity was a "cardinal value," the "hallmark" of the new, professional middle class created by the economic transformations and anxious to consolidate its social and political power.[11] What all these explanations share is an assertion that domesticity was somehow useful or functional, for at least certain groups in certain ways, even as it imposed unrealistic, contradictory, and often oppressive demands on so many women.

More recently, historians have focused instead on how domestic concepts and practices were invoked and experienced by a range of groups in a variety of situations. Many of these studies are more interested in meaning than in causation and so largely sidestep the structural issues altogether, simply assuming a connection without trying to explain it. As one recent account puts it, "[t]he ascendancy of marketplace relationships, commodity consumption, and partisan politics in a liberal state were contemporaneous and complementary with the constellation of ideas and ideals of domesticity."[12] Although not the central point, the clear implication is again that domesticity was functional, that it made sense and served a purpose (somebody's purpose) in the broad economic and political transformations of the period.

The mariners' wives in my study suggest a somewhat different chronology and a more nuanced interpretation. Here, domesticity was clearly not a by-product or consequence of economic change. Maritime communities such as those in southeastern New England had already, for generations, been organized around a rigid sexual division of labor in which only men (particularly young men) left to work on the sea and women remained on land, responsible for maintaining home and family. Yet, in the eighteenth century, maritime women and men shared a vision of the world as one unified place, organized hierarchically, in which women were not so much different from men as they were simply weaker, less capable, and therefore properly dependent and subservient. The belief that adult men were properly in charge all the time and everywhere undergirded mariners' habits of command both on shipboard and on shore. Family relationships were not too strained by whalemen's absences, which were limited to three, six, or nine months in length and commonly extended only through early adulthood.

These understandings of gender began to erode not with changes in seafaring labor practices but rather with the local importation of new ideas about sexual difference that defined women and men as fundamentally different kinds of beings, properly belonging in two separate spheres: a female-controlled world of home and a male-dominated world of work. The apparent correspondence of the new ideas with the traditional division of seafaring labor was striking—and rapidly assimilated into local arrangements and assumptions.

But, as the local maritime industries expanded, these maritime women —and their husbands too—clung to the domestic ideas and values even as these developed in painful contradiction to the material circumstances of their lives and were stretched quite beyond plausibility. The fishery itself, though in some ways threatened by the domestic conceptualization of marriage, incorporated ideas about conjugal responsibility and affection into the social relations of work at sea and on shore. The fishery thereby reinforced the new commonsense understandings about gender, even though habits of command developed at sea now sometimes clashed with women's authority on land. At the same time, though, domesticity offered the real-life Ahab's wife, and Ahab too, a powerful and indeed the only available way of understanding themselves as wives and husbands and maintaining their relationships during separations that now lasted three, four, or five years, and were repeated well through midlife. Domesticity— despite its tensions and contradictions—became virtually inescapable for these women and men too, here as elsewhere in America.

The nature of the American whalefishery, the local community supporting it, and the rich historical sources they generated allow us to explore in great detail the ways in which people understood and experienced this fundamental transformation in the relationships between faith, duty, and love, work and home life, families and communities, and women and men. The book takes a community-study approach to the area of overlap between southeastern New England and the whalefishery. While American whalers (whaling vessels of which ships were just one kind) traveled into the far corners of the globe, nearly all of them hailed from southeastern New England. During the most important years of the industry, from about the 1720s to the 1880s, the major American whaling ports were all located within a sixty-mile radius of Newport, Rhode Island—from

Provincetown on the tip of Cape Cod to the northeast, to New London, Connecticut, to the west, and Sag Harbor on Long Island to the south. Newport was the geographic but not the economic or social center of the industry, though: that distinction was reserved for Nantucket in the eighteenth century and New Bedford in the nineteenth.

The American whalefishery initially developed from sporadic shore whaling into a full-scale deep-sea industry in the first few decades of the eighteenth century, led primarily by pioneering entrepreneurs on the small island of Nantucket off the southeastern coast of Massachusetts. New England whalemen quickly learned how profitable the pursuit of whales could be, with rising prices in an expanding international market for whale oil (a particularly high-quality illuminant and lubricant) and bone (actually a strong, flexible cartilage). By the 1720s, technological advances in equipment and techniques freed whalemen from shore, and they took to the open sea on larger vessels for voyages that ranged from three to six months in duration. By 1770, Yankee whalers were plying the South Atlantic on nearly year-long voyages, and whale products formed New England's second most valuable export, just after codfish. Nantucket alone accounted for over half New England's catch. The Revolution and subsequent depression devastated the fishery, but after some years of distress the industry recovered and expanded dramatically in response to rising demand, rising prices, and, in 1790, the discovery of rich Pacific whaling grounds around the hazardous Cape Horn at the tip of South America.[13]

Sometime around 1825, the industry's center of gravity shifted, as Nantucket passed the whale-oil torch to New Bedford on the mainland, which boasted a deeper harbor and better connections to supplies and markets. At the peak of the whaling fleet in 1846, over 400 of the 736 American vessels afloat came from the greater New Bedford area, and the New Bedford customs district was the fourth largest in the country, ranking behind only New York, Boston, and New Orleans. American whalers now roamed the world's oceans—the Pacific, Indian, and Arctic as well as the Atlantic— on voyages lasting multiple years, reprovisioning in a host of foreign ports and transshipping their catch home. Some 10,000 men were employed at sea and on shore in whaling and related activities that brought millions of dollars back to southeastern New England.

The boom was over by the end of the 1870s, curtailed in part by the depletion of whale stocks and the discovery of petroleum. The destruction of thirty-two New Bedford whaleships crushed in the treacherous ice south of Alaska's Point Barrow in September 1871 and another thirteen of the

Arctic fleet in 1876 did not cause but dismally encapsulated the American fishery's decline. What whaling continued at all was mainly from vessels launched from the west coast. By 1884, the whalers out of San Francisco outnumbered all those sailing from eastern ports put together. By that time, most of the whale money in southeastern New England had been transferred into manufacturing and other ventures.

The whaling community changed form and meaning over time in tandem with the development of the southeastern New England region and the fishery itself, developing from a more clearly geographic definition to one based more on occupational identity.[14] On colonial Nantucket and in a few other small coastal villages of the eighteenth century, virtually all the inhabitants belonged to the whaling community to some degree. Whether they themselves went to sea or not, virtually everyone was related to or had close interaction with men who did. By the mid-nineteenth century, especially in the larger urban centers like New Bedford, the whaling community represented only that segment of the population most directly involved in the fishery. Accordingly, the first half of this book explores the whole community on eighteenth-century Nantucket. In the second half, I shift focus to the nineteenth century and more broadly to the larger southeastern New England region centered on New Bedford, but more narrowly on whalemen and their families.

My focus throughout is on a particular group of women and men identified both by their nativity in southeastern New England and by their connection to the fishery, the "career" whalemen and their mothers, sisters, daughters, and especially their wives: Captain and Mrs. Ahab rather than Jack and Jane Tar. Over the century and a half that the whaling industry lasted, recruitment and employment patterns were basically two-tier, determined not only by gender but also race and class.[15] All of those who worked on shipboard were male, of course. The majority of the crew, from "greenhands" to the skilled boatsteerers (or harpooners), was filled out by men and boys who generally had few more attractive employment options. They tended to be young, ranging in age from 15 to 30, most often unmarried, and, if lucky, would retire from sea after just a few voyages to pursue some other line of work on land; whaling was not often a long-term career for them. They were also a diverse lot and became even more so in the 1800s as Yankee whaling voyages extended to the other side of the globe and industry conditions deteriorated. Melville's characters on board the *Pequod*—Ishmael (the restless, rootless white), Tashtego (the Cape Cod Indian), Daggoo (the African), and Queequeg (the South Seas

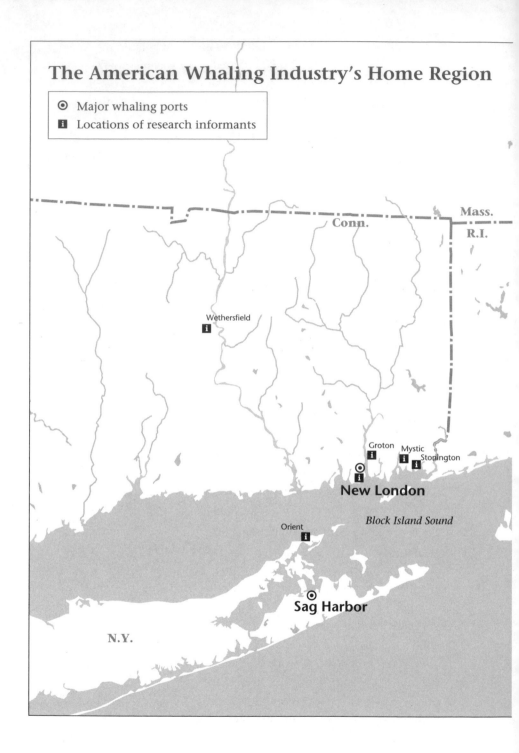

The American Whaling Industry's Home Region

⊙ Major whaling ports
ℹ Locations of research informants

Mass.

Conn.

R.I.

Wethersfield
ℹ

Groton
ℹ

Mystic
ℹ

Stonington
ℹ

⊙
ℹ
New London

Block Island Sound

Orient
ℹ

⊙
Sag Harbor

N.Y.

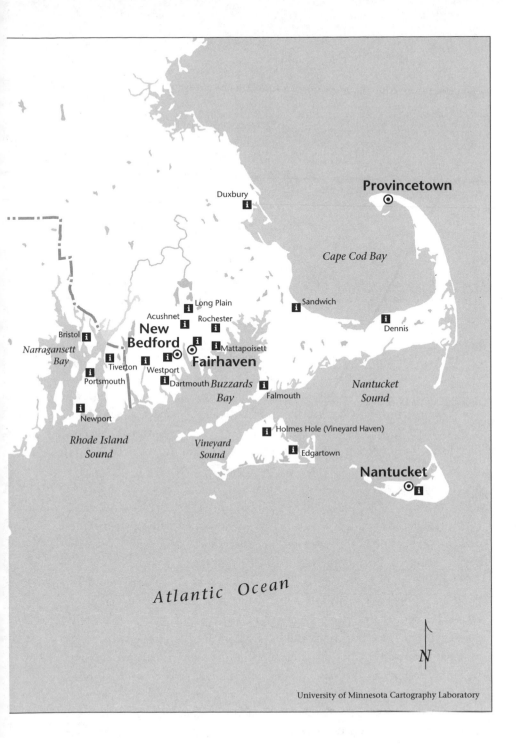

Provincetown

Cape Cod Bay

Duxbury

Long Plain
Acushnet
Rochester
New
Bedford
Mattapoisett
Fairhaven
Westport
Dartmouth
Buzzards
Bay

Sandwich

Dennis

Bristol

Narragansett
Bay

Tiverton

Portsmouth

Newport

Rhode Island
Sound

Vineyard
Sound

Falmouth

Nantucket
Sound

Holmes Hole (Vineyard Haven)

Edgartown

Nantucket

Atlantic Ocean

N

cannibal)—accurately reflected the multiracial and international composition of nineteenth-century whaling crews.

The highly responsible, skilled, and potentially lucrative positions of
captain and mate (second in command)—Melville's Ahab and Starbuck—
were customarily reserved for local, native-born, white men, who went to
sea in their mid-teens to learn the trade and quickly worked their way up.
They and their female connections came from family backgrounds that
ran the gamut from successful mariners, substantial farmers, and prosperous artisans to those in a quite precarious financial situation, and from the
highly literate and well-read to those who could barely write in an awkward scrawl. What they had in common was their place of origin (southeastern New England), their general religious affiliation (they were all
Protestant of one or another stripe), and, perhaps most significantly, their
race (with only a handful of extraordinary exceptions, they were all white,
primarily of English descent). These commonalities made possible considerable upward mobility within the industry for those men who demonstrated aptitude.[16]

These were master craftsmen, mariners skilled in the ways of the ship
and possessing sophisticated navigational ability and pronounced habits
of command, and at the same time specialists in the hazardous, disagreeable trade of hunting, slaughtering, and butchering whales at sea. This
homogeneous group, whom I call the "career" or "professional" whalemen, formed a stable core of the workforce on which the whaling agents
(the managers who were also usually the majority owners of their vessels)
largely depended, as the industry expanded, for the preservation of the
vessel and successful prosecution of the pursuit. These career whalemen
too were generally young, though, in growing contrast with the rest of the
crew, by the middle of the nineteenth century, successful captains would
often continue commanding vessels through midlife.

I was fortunate in finding in the archives of southeastern New England an astonishing wealth of sources, in particular many hundreds of
letters sent between women on shore and men at sea that have been largely
ignored by maritime historians and barely tapped by anyone else. Among
my most important bodies of evidence, summarized in the Appendix, are
the family papers of sixty-six families, encompassing two hundred individuals and ninety marriages in which the man was part of the fishery's
professional group. These families became my major informants largely
because of the abundant records they left behind. Much of this material,
of course, represents primarily those individuals who were literate, those

who cared deeply enough or needed to write, and those who chose to preserve their correspondence, journals, and other family records—in other words, those women and men with considerable emotional and, for some, also financial investments. But this was not true for all: even families of relatively modest means felt strongly enough to try to surmount the immense distance and time of separation the fishery demanded and attached enough value to their records to keep them.

A remarkable set of sources further extends the scope of my sample beyond those who saved their papers intentionally: a mailbag of 155 dead letters, addressed to but never received by men at sea.[17] Preserved among the papers of a midcentury postmaster in the New Bedford area, the letters date from 1841 to 1861; one is written in Portuguese, the rest in English. Forty-one of them were written by wives or sweethearts, ninety-two by parents or siblings, and twenty-two by apparently unrelated individuals, so the collection represents a range of relationships. Judged on the basis of handwriting, vocabulary, and grammar, the letters also reflect a range of educational and literacy levels and, judged by internal evidence that suggests occupations and residential patterns, a range in status from quite poor to middle class. Significantly, although they were saved quite by accident, these letters share much the same content and express much the same adherence to domestic ideals and values as the correspondence that was preserved intentionally.

The extensive industry records provided another, especially rich fund of information. In particular, whaling agents' correspondence, account books, and other business records supported the close examination of the interaction between the industry, whalemen's families, and the local community. Whalemen's shipping papers, crew accounts and lists, and logbooks enabled the reconstruction of men's careers at sea. Family papers and industry records were supplemented by published genealogies and vital records, censuses and city directories, and selected municipal tax lists and probate records, making it possible to understand the references in the personal and business letters and to flesh out the lives of my major informants more generally. To gain a more well rounded sense of the local context, I also turned to local and industry newspapers, other contemporary publications, and the records of local courts and government agencies, charitable groups, and religious reform organizations. Travel accounts and descriptions of Nantucket, New Bedford, and other coastal towns and villages supplied by observers from the 1750s to the 1870s offered additional information and insight.

I have quoted liberally from these sources in the pages that follow. I have tried to convey a sense of the original as much as possible and so have not standardized the often erratic spelling, capitalization, and abbreviation. Where I thought it necessary to clarify the meaning, however, I have added punctuation or inserted supplemental information in brackets.

The book is organized both chronologically and topically. The first two chapters explore the integration of colonial Anglo-American family and community life, religious principle and practice, and the early whale-fishery primarily on eighteenth-century Nantucket. Chapter 1 describes the content and complementary nature of men's and women's work, the local practice of patriarchal authority, and how these together fostered the emergence of the whaling industry. Chapter 2 explores how Quaker belief and discipline; understandings of love, marriage, and family; and the organization of social life on the island accommodated and cushioned the rhythms and stresses of the fishery. Chapter 3 examines the erosion of this way of life on colonial Nantucket and the introduction of new, revolutionary and romantic notions of sexual difference, love and marriage at the end of the eighteenth century. Chapters 4, 5, and 6 follow the whaling industry to New Bedford and the mainland for the peak era of the fishery, from about the 1820s to the 1870s. Chapter 4 examines the expansion and reorganization of the industry and its social relations at sea and on shore, identifying persistent patterns in the maritime gender division of labor that came into conflict with changing concepts about manhood and womanhood. Chapter 5 traces the consequences of the new ideas about conjugal passion and companionship for nineteenth-century maritime women's and men's experience of love, courtship, and marriage. Chapter 6, the final chapter, considers the organization and practice of maritime home life, exploring the multiple and conflicting meanings — and the high personal cost — of domesticity on land and at sea.

Ishmael, Melville's narrator in *Moby-Dick*, chose to go to Nantucket to begin his fateful voyage. He tells us, "my mind was made up to sail in no other than a Nantucket craft, because there was a fine, boisterous something about everything connected with that famous old island. . . . though New Bedford has of late been gradually monopolizing the business of whaling . . . Nantucket was her great original — the Tyre of this Carthage." [18]

We too will begin on Nantucket.

1

NANTUCKET & THE EIGHTEENTH-CENTURY WHALEFISHERY

In his tongue-in-cheek immortalization of Nantucket and its people in *Moby-Dick*, Melville linked the two elements of the island's society that rendered it so distinctive: its dominance by the Quaker faith and its dominance of the American whaling industry. Nantucket whalemen were "Quakers with a vengeance," he claimed. Melville, though having some fun at the expense of Nantucket society in his early chapters, was most interested in the character and experience of the island's men at sea. "Thus," he declared, "have these naked Nantucketers, these sea hermits, issuing from their ant-hill in the sea, overrun and conquered the waterworld like so many Alexanders."[1] Earlier observers had turned as much attention to the character of the island's society and governance as to the whalefishery itself. (It is notable that Melville did not actually set foot on Nantucket until well after the publication of *Moby-Dick*.)[2] Foremost among these early observers was the French social commentator J. Hector St. John de Crevecoeur, who visited Nantucket in the early 1770s and devoted a significant portion of his 1782 *Letters from an American Farmer* to detailed description of the island and its people. He too focused on the islanders' commitments to the whalefishery and the Quaker faith.

Generally the starting place for histories of eighteenth-century Nantucket, the *Letters* constitute one of the fullest first-hand accounts we have of the island's society in the pre-Revolutionary period. Crevecoeur's work is also a utopian vision, though not without its darker undertones: his lengthy and detailed praise of Nantucket enterprise and virtue forms a crucial part of his larger paean to American liberalism. "Though [Nantucket] is barren in its soil, insignificant in its extent, inconvenient in its situation, deprived of materials for building, it seems to have been inhabited merely to prove what mankind can do when happily governed!" Crevecoeur enthused. "[T]hey are permitted to enjoy a system of rational laws founded on perfect freedom. . . . I saw neither governors nor any pageantry of state, neither ostentatious magistrates nor any individuals clothed with useless dignity; no artificial phantoms subsist here, either civil or religious. . . . Idleness and poverty . . . are unknown here; each seeks in the prosecution of his lawful business that honest gain which supports them; every period of their time is full, either on shore or at sea. A probable expectation of reasonable profits or of kindly assistance if they fail of success renders them strangers to licentious expedients. The simplicity of their manners shortens the catalogues of their wants. . . . The sea which surrounds them is equally open to all and presents to all an equal title to the chance of good fortune." [3]

Unlike Melville, Crevecoeur gave equal credit for Nantucket's success to the island's women. He particularly praised how effectively the women and families onshore had adapted to the demands of the whaling industry. "As the sea excursions are often very long," Crevecoeur observed, "[the whalers'] wives are necessarily obliged to transact business, to settle accounts, and, in short, to rule and provide for their families. These circumstances, being often repeated, give women the abilities as well as a taste for that kind of superintendency, to which, by their prudence and good management, they seem to be in general very equal. This employment ripens their judgment, and justly entitles them to a rank superior to that of other wives." This female autonomy, though, did not disrupt the balance of authority within Nantucket marriages. Crevecoeur reported, "the men, at their return, weary with the fatigues of the sea, full of confidence and love, cheerfully give their consent to every transaction that has happened during their absence, and all is joy and peace. 'Wife, thee hast done well,' is the general approbation they receive for their application and industry." Indeed, the Frenchman wondered, "what would the men do without the agency of [their] faithful mates?"[4]

Though he was criticized for his overly rosy view,[5] much of Crevecoeur's description does appear on target. Eighteenth-century Nantucket women and men indeed appear to have perceived and acted out their familial and community roles in ways remarkably harmonious, or at least strikingly well adapted, to the flourishing of the whaling industry on which their economy primarily depended. Crevecoeur ultimately argued not for Nantucket exceptionalism but rather its representativeness as the distillation of American national character.[6] Here, too, Crevecoeur's assessment seems right: on close examination, it appears that despite superficial differences from other northeastern Anglo-American towns, gender roles and the character of the women on colonial Nantucket were not in the end unusual at all. Instead, certain typical features were actually enhanced and cast into greater relief. Crevecoeur's (and others') professed astonishment notwithstanding, Nantucket women belonged to the American mainstream too, and they can tell us much about the gendered nature of that mainstream in the eighteenth century. Crevecoeur stressed the importance to the fishery of Nantucket gender roles, family organization, and community life; unlike later chroniclers, he specifically made note of the women's contributions. His observations serve as our starting point for this study: the elements he identified are the focus of this chapter and the next.

Though whalers set off from many spots along the coasts of southeastern New England and Long Island, Nantucket was the undisputed center of the colonial fishery. Searching for a more diversified and successful subsistence than their barren sandbar of an island itself afforded, white Nantucketers had turned to the sea for their livelihood not long after English colonial settlement in the 1660s. Migratory patterns of certain species of whales brought them close to Long Island, Cape Cod, and Nantucket on a seasonal basis, and the coastal settlers soon discovered the profitability of the leviathan beasts. By the 1720s, Nantucketers had also initiated deep-sea whaling, enabled by technological advances and spurred by

This 1811 depiction of Nantucket shows the town buildings closely clustered on the southwest shore of the island's natural harbor, flanked by the long, low ropewalks on either side and the row of windmills on the rise above the town; note also the flock of free-ranging sheep on the point of land opposite the town. "The Town of Sherburne in the Island of Nantucket," engraving, 1811, Benjamin Tanner after Joseph Sansom. Courtesy of I. N. Phelps Stokes Collection, Miriam and Ira D. Wallach Division of Arts, Prints and Photographs, New York Public Library, Astor, Lenox and Tilden Foundations rising prices in a growing international market for whale oil, bone, and finished candles. By the mid-eighteenth century, the island's economy was dominated by whaling and its ancillary trades and businesses. Nantucket was "virtually a one-industry town, where, as the Massachusetts General Court recognized in the mid-1750s, the inhabitants' 'livelihood entirely depends on the whale fishery.'"[7]

Crevecoeur asserted that the Nantucketers' "confidence is so great and their knowledge of this branch of business so superior to that of any other people that they have acquired a monopoly of this commodity. . . . this is the greatest mart for oil, whalebone and spermaceti on the continent."[8] By the early 1770s, when Crevecoeur visited the island, 54 percent of the American fleet (by tonnage) were Nantucket vessels, which brought in 70 percent of the colonial catch; whale products were second only to codfish as the most important exports from New England.[9] In 1775, on the floor of Parliament itself, opponents to the act restricting New England commercial activity cited Nantucket, one MP reporting that "from the only harbour which this sterile island contains, without natural products of any sort, the inhabitants, by an astonishing industry, keep an 140 vessels in constant employment, [all but eight] in the whale-fishery."[10]

"Would you believe," Crevecoeur demanded of his readers, "that a sandy spot of about twenty-three thousand acres, affording neither stones nor timber, meadows nor arable, yet can boast of a handsome town consisting of more than 500 houses, should possess above 200 sail of vessels; constantly employ upwards of 2,000 seamen; feed more than 15,000 sheep, 500 cows, 200 horses; and has several citizens worth £20,000 sterling!" With the development of deep-sea whaling, the colonial settlement on Nantucket did indeed flourish. Although providing a significant portion of the seagoing labor for the early industry, Nantucket's indigenous population did not share in the prosperity it generated: already suffering from a century of exploitation and disease, the local Native Americans were virtually wiped out by a devastating epidemic in 1763. The English population on the island, however, boomed, growing from 917 people in 1726 to 4,545 by the time of the Revolution.[11]

Almost all eighteenth-century Nantucketers lived on the northern shore in the town of Sherburne, which occupied somewhat less than a mile along the southwest side of the island's large natural harbor and rose about a quarter of a mile up the gently sloping shoreline. Crevecoeur termed the town "handsome," but the more common off-island opinion held, as one visitor wrote, that the town "exhibits no marks of elegance or splendor." Many observers commented on the irregularly placed wood-shingled houses, a few dark red but most unpainted, and the meandering, unpaved streets "half-shoe deep" in sand, shaded here and there by cherry or peach trees. Around the fenced perimeter of the densely built town were planted a few vegetable gardens and cornfields, a row of wind-powered grist and fulling mills, and the ropewalks, the long narrow structures where hemp fiber was twisted into the miles of cordage needed to rig and operate ships. Beyond these stretched the bare, rolling expanse of heath, almost entirely denuded of trees by the early eighteenth century (many generations before Melville wrote that the islanders planted "toadstools before their houses to get under the shade in the summer time" and treated pieces of wood "like the bits of the true Cross"). The view was relieved only by a few areas of cultivated fields, some ponds and low-lying swamps (the latter quarried for peat by those residents who couldn't afford firewood imported from the mainland), and a couple of tiny villages, really seasonal fishing camps, along the southern shore. Most of the center of the island was held in common by descendants of the original English proprietors well into the nineteenth century and was occupied solely by a few horses, a couple of hundred cows, and several thousand sheep allowed to run at large all year long.[12]

Crevecoeur claimed that, on the arrival of the whaling fleet, "the bustle and hurry of business . . . would make you imagine that Sherborn is the capital of a very opulent and large province." Certainly by 1751, when the town's selectmen told the Massachusetts General Court that their "very sandy, barren land" was so worn out that it "would not support above sixty families in eatables with its produce," Nantucket's economy had become almost completely dominated by the whaling industry. Virtually all raw materials needed for basic subsistence as well as for supplying the whaling fleet had to be imported. Much of the commercial activity centered on the waterfront, where at the time of Crevecoeur's visit four sturdy wharves reached some 300 feet into the harbor. Thickly clustered nearby were the merchants' warehouses and countinghouses; tryworks and candleworks; boatbuilding and blockmaking shops; ships' chandleries and sail lofts; smithies, cooperages, and bakeries; taverns and grogshops. Scattered throughout the town, typically on the ground floor of residences, were dozens of other retail establishments and craft shops. In this regard, the town of Nantucket looked much like other seaports. (There being no other towns on the island, the name of Sherburne was officially changed to Nantucket in 1795.) But over the whole town, in a graphic reminder of the islanders' singular dependence, hung the stench of whale oil. Crevecoeur himself admitted that he "was much surprised at the disagreeable smell" and noted that "the neatness peculiar to these people can neither remove or prevent it."[13]

Sometime in the seventeenth century, Nantucketers, like their counterparts on Cape Cod and Long Island, established beachside stations from which lookouts watched for the spouting of right whales, which frequented the local waters from about November to March or April. When the huge beasts were sighted, six-man crews set off in small open boats across the treacherous shoals, their goal to harpoon a single whale at a time and tow its carcass back through the surf to shore for butchering, cleaning the bone and "trying" (rendering by boiling) the blubber into oil. This last part of the process was sufficiently noxious (from the stench of the rotting whale to the greasy smoke from boiling oil) that the authorities in Southampton (Long Island) passed legislation stating, "Where the trying of oyle so near the streets and houses, is so extreme noysome to all passers by, especially to those not accustomed to the sent thereof . . . the cort doth order that noe person after this present yeare shall try any oyle in this towne nearer than 25 poles from Main Street, under penalty of paying five pounds fine."[14] But the products were sufficiently valuable that the colonial authorities also mandated inspection, adjudicated disputed ownership, and taxed the proceeds.

The odor was not the only disagreeable aspect of whaling: it was notably dangerous, difficult, dirty, and exhausting. And it only became more so as the industry expanded in scale and scope. According to local legend, in 1712 a Nantucket boat commanded by one Christopher Hussey was blown by a gale far offshore, where he and his crew discovered and captured a sperm whale.[15] Spermaceti whales did not have the flexible bone of right whales, but they offered a much higher quality body oil, and the large cavity in their heads contained the most valuable "clear and sweet" oil of all. By 1715, Nantucketers sent some six sloops out in pursuit of "sparmacitys" on voyages of several weeks' duration. Each sloop carried a couple of small whaleboats, which were lowered when whales were sighted and from which the men would chase and harpoon their prey. Captured whales would be brought back to the whaleship, cut up alongside the vessel, and their blubber packed into casks and brought home for rendering into oil. By the 1750s, the installation on board ship of the tryworks,

"The Manner of Catching Whales," an English image depicting early-eighteenth-century whaling off Greenland, reproduced in *Churchill's Voyages*, Vol. 1 (London, 1744). Courtesy of Old Dartmouth Historical Society–New Bedford Whaling Museum (Neg. 16192)

large iron vats set into brick ovens on deck in which the blubber was rendered into oil, made feasible larger ships and longer voyages—and even more arduous work.

Sperm whales were smaller and faster than the right whales, but they were still considerably bigger than the men or the boats pursuing them; they also often put up more of a fight. In 1752, 19-year-old oarsman Peleg Folger recorded how a wounded whale "came at our boat & furiously ran over us and oversat us & made a Miserable rack of our boat in a moment: A Wonder & mercy it was . . . that we all Had our Lives Spar'd, tho the Whale Had Divers Warps after her [lines wrapped around her, connected to the boat], & Divers of us were Sadly puzzled under water." Crevecoeur speculated that "Were the whale armed with the jaws of the shark, and as voracious, [the whalemen] never would return home to amuse their listening wives with the interesting tale of the adventure," and he claimed, "if you attentively consider the immense disproportion between the object assailed and assailants, if you think of the diminutive size and weakness of their frail vehicle, if you recollect the treachery of the element on which this scene is transacted, the sudden and unforeseen accidents of winds, etc., you

"Stove boat," ca. 1840, watercolor by unknown whaleman artist. This image vividly depicts one of the dangers of the chase: having the boat "stove" or smashed by the whale. Courtesy of Old Dartmouth Historical Society–New Bedford Whaling Museum (Neg. 6772)

will readily acknowledge that it must require the most consummate exertion of all the strength, agility, and judgement of which the bodies and the minds of men are capable to undertake these adventurous encounters."[16]

The foremost recent historian of Nantucket's early whalefishery, Daniel Vickers, evocatively describes the capture and processing of two whales by the Nantucket brig *Polley* in July 1774:

> Every aspect . . . from the punishing stretch at the oars to bring the company within striking distance, through the hurried teamwork in maneuvering the frail craft clear of the angry victim, to the exhaustion of towing each gigantic corpse back to the ship—amounted to work on a scale that landsmen could scarcely imagine. . . . Even a successfully concluded chase, moreover, meant only the beginning of a longer task: that of trying the animal out. . . . [s]ecuring the whale to the side of the ship . . . ladling the pure spermaceti oil out of each animal's head, stripping the blubber off the two carcasses, boiling out the body oil, and pouring the cooled product into casks for storage. All told . . . from the

sighting of the whale until the last of thirty-seven barrels was sealed, the operation took the crew three solid days of strenuous labor. . . . [T]he peril and exhaustion that accompanied each stage of the process, not to mention the accumulation of soot and grease over every part of the vessel, must have caused some of the hands to question their decision to come along at all.[17]

But the profitability of the venture convinced them, and hundreds of other men on Nantucket and from coastal New England and Long Island too, that the possibilities for "quick and substantial returns" were worth leaving home for the risks, the toil, and the longer time at sea. The three-month summer cruises to the whaling grounds off Newfoundland—characteristic of the 1730s, 40s, and 50s—were supplanted in the 1760s by four- to five-month voyages farther north to the Davis Straits, east to the Azores, or south to the West Indies. In the final quarter of the century, nearly year-long trips to the African and South American coasts became common.[18] Vickers argues that, over the course of the eighteenth century, this "radical lengthening of voyages transformed the character of whaling as an occupation."[19] The dangers of the hunt and the processing of the catch increased proportionately—and so did the discomforts and the boredom of confinement at sea for extended periods.

The shift from shore whaling to the deep-sea fishery clearly had a major impact on women and the community onshore as well. Although it would be difficult to determine what percentage of men from Nantucket or another such community were actually at sea at any given time, contemporary observers remarked on their perceptible absence: the *Boston News-Letter* of 21 April 1737 reported that a dozen whaling vessels were being prepared in Provincetown (Cape Cod) for the Davis Straits and claimed that "so many were going on these voyages . . . that not more than twelve or fourteen men would be left at home." Some forty years later, Crevecoeur noticed on Nantucket that "the absence of so many [men] at particular seasons leaves the town quite desolate; and this mournful situation disposes the women to go to each other's house much oftener than when their husbands are at home: hence the custom of incessant visiting has infected every one, and even those whose husbands do not go abroad."[20]

Nantucket men's careers in whaling and other maritime enterprises were marked by an intermittency that was linked to season, to the availability of other economic opportunities, and to stage in life course. Like other seamen throughout the Atlantic world, most Nantucket seafarers

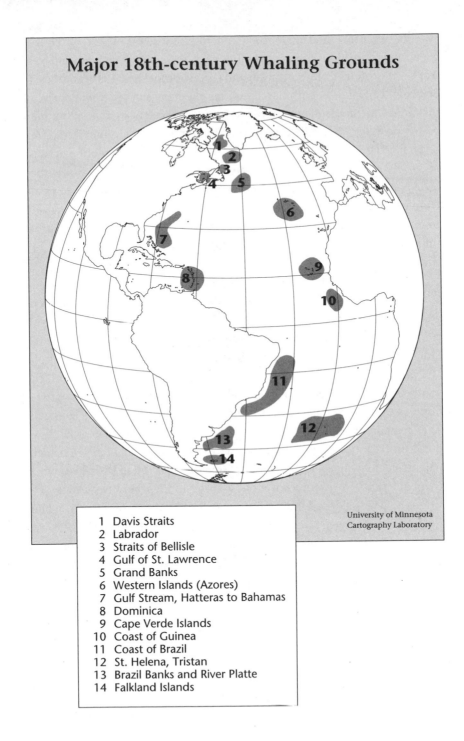

Major 18th-century Whaling Grounds

University of Minnesota
Cartography Laboratory

1 Davis Straits
2 Labrador
3 Straits of Bellisle
4 Gulf of St. Lawrence
5 Grand Banks
6 Western Islands (Azores)
7 Gulf Stream, Hatteras to Bahamas
8 Dominica
9 Cape Verde Islands
10 Coast of Guinea
11 Coast of Brazil
12 St. Helena, Tristan
13 Brazil Banks and River Platte
14 Falkland Islands

were between the ages of 15 and 30. Unlike those elsewhere, though—especially those in the major port cities such as Boston, Newport, and New York—the sailors from Nantucket and the neighboring areas of southeastern New England seem to have been for the most part relatively local in origin. As the maritime industries expanded, these boys and young men were simultaneously pulled to the sea by family or community tradition and pushed by economic necessity, as land shortages and depletion became acute and other opportunities on land were limited. Like the vessels they sailed on, not yet highly specialized in function, the seamen moved easily from one maritime enterprise to another, shifting from coastal carrying to international shipping or into whaling, as season permitted and market imperatives indicated. And most went to sea on just a few voyages, before they settled down on land to pursue some other field of labor.[21]

In his careful study of the colonial whalefishery on Nantucket, Daniel Vickers has identified the emergence of a two-tier system of recruitment and management after the technological advances of the mid-eighteenth century turned whaling into a much more expensive and complicated enterprise. The bottom tier was filled out by young men—blacks, Indians, and poorer off-island whites—who were drawn from throughout the southeastern New England region and who had few economic alternatives. Some of these young men may have chosen to go to sea, Vickers suggests, as a "temporary expedient . . . toward the eventual goal of personal independence," "a means of supporting themselves and their families, or perhaps even of laying aside some savings, during a period in their lives when their independent resources were at a minimum." Others were sons, servants, or slaves shipped out by fathers or heads of a household to whom the whaleman's wages would be paid at the end of the voyage, sent to sea as part of a family or household economic strategy in much the same way as daughters might be set to spinning, braiding straw bonnets, or stitching leather shoe parts.[22] Still others found themselves bound to sea as a consequence of their own indebtedness, "hands" supplied to the fishery by merchants and wealthy farmers who controlled their labor and thereby served informally as recruiting agents in the hopes of cashing in on the lucrative whale oil trade.[23]

In contrast to the limits on the young men disadvantaged by race, origin, or indebtedness, the highly responsible, skilled, and potentially lucrative officers' positions were reserved for a restricted pool of white, locally born, and well connected Nantucket men. As Crevecoeur asserted, Anglo Nantucket boys were first sent to school, where "they learn to read and write a good hand . . . they are then in general put apprentices to the cooper's trade" or some other landsman craft. Then, Crevecoeur continued, "at fourteen they are sent to sea, where . . . they learn the great and useful art of working a ship in all the different situations which the sea and wind so often require. . . . They then go gradually through every station of rowers, steersmen, and harpooners . . . and after having performed several such voyages and perfected themselves in this business, they are fit either for the counting house or the chase."[24] By way of example, Nantucket captain Benjamin Worth reported, "I began to follow the sea in 1783, being then 15 years of age, and continued until 1824. During this period of 41 years, I was a shipmaster 29 years. From the time when I commenced going to sea till I quitted the business, I was at home only seven years." Similarly, Captain George W. Gardner reported that he "began to follow the sea at 13 years of age, and continued in that service 37 years . . . [as] a shipmaster 21 years."[25] With these recruitment and career patterns, the dominant Nantucket families retained control of the whalefishery, and the whalefishery was assured of the most competent and loyal officers.

But, according to Vickers, "positions of command were the only ones with which young Nantucketers were satisfied. . . . Once it became clear to an individual that the heftier officers' lays were beyond his competence, he generally retired to ply a different trade on land."[26] Caleb Macy, the father of locally famed island chronicler Obed Macy, followed a career path more typical of the well-connected but less talented whalemen. Caleb, after first abandoning his father's line of work (farming, with milling and possibly some carpentry on the side) because, in son Obed's words, it was "in nowise congenial to his feelings, neither did it accord with his genius" and then abandoning a second trade (shoemaking), finally "concluded to follow the Sea." Caleb apparently went on several short whaling voyages and a few coastal trading trips as well. Unfortunately, though (again, according to Obed), Caleb "found his health incompetent to the hardships of a seafaring life, [and] therefore determined never to cross the ocean again." Happily for Caleb and his numerous progeny to come, at age 30 he managed to marry the wealthy and energetic widow Judith Folger Gardner. He thereupon became quite a successful entrepreneur, owning a shoe manufactory in which he employed a dozen men, as well as investing in a number of other profitable ventures, including real estate, one of the town wharves, and several whaleships.[27]

It is difficult to assess how the development of two-tier recruitment and distinct career patterns affected the social relations of work at sea.

The vicious intimidation and sometimes extreme cruelty that increasingly characterized labor discipline in the British navy and Anglo-American merchant marine in this period seem not to have extended to the colonial whalefishery. Deep-sea whaling was just as brutal work and was notably more hazardous than the shore fishery, but that brutality may have been inflicted primarily on the whales. In his shipboard journal, Peleg Folger described the dangers of the chase, the tedium of weeks at sea, and the sociability of his mates, but he did not mention any instances of discipline or violence. As on other sorts of ships, on whalers too the captain's authority was absolute, and the restrictiveness of life at sea was considerable. But potentially harsh treatment of the crew by the officers seems to have been mitigated by common local origins, relatively voluntary recruitment, the temporary nature of the occupation, and the shared opportunity to earn a substantial amount of cash.[28]

Whalemen were paid by the "lay" or share of the oil and bone at the end of the voyage, in a system stemming from early shore whaling and persisting in more elaborate and stratified form in the deep-sea fishery. Vessel owners claimed one-quarter or more of the value of the oil and bone taken on the voyage, with the remainder of the profits divided unequally between the members of the crew depending on their position. The actual value of each lay, of course, varied tremendously with the amount caught and the market price of oil at the vessel's return. Successful voyages at the right moment might yield substantial wages for all aboard. One Nantucket captain, Benjamin Hussey, spent a year in the South Atlantic in 1774, returned with a full ship, and netted £130 sterling. (By comparison, a Boston merchant captain could expect to earn about £3 per month in the early 1770s.) But voyages could also end in financial, if not actual, disaster: in 1771, another Nantucket whaling captain returned home from a six-month cruise having earned just £2.8. For the ordinary members of the whaling crew, the lay system instead of the straight monthly wage earned by merchant seamen might perpetuate their financial dependence: "The chance that [a whaleman] could come home with but little pay or even in debt could start a cycle of credit advances and voyages that did not quite meet the debts, followed by more advances and more voyages."[29]

Given the risks and separations of the fishery and the delay and uncertainty built into the lay system, the Nantucket whaling merchants were, as one of them, Christopher Starbuck, wrote in 1774, "obliged to trust an abundance of people in our connection with clothing and provisions for their families."[30] In other words, during the whalemen's absences, their families were supplied with the necessities of life or cash itself on credit extended by the managing shipowners. For example, in 1793 the owners of the ship *Edward* informed the captain, Micajah Gardner, that "thy Cooper is [paid] by the month and his wife Recieves Part of his wages Dailey."[31] Employment sometimes continued for many men over several voyages: both the "hand" and the master had an investment in a sustained relationship that implied obligations on both sides. One obligation on the part of the owners was their assumption of some measure of responsibility for the families of such men at sea on their vessels.[32] This sort of industrial paternalism on Nantucket was distinctive not in kind but rather in its density, its intricacy, and the extent to which it was keyed to the whalefishery. What the account books, correspondence, and other extant material seem to indicate is that on eighteenth-century Nantucket there existed a communitywide kind of paternalism that supported the local maritime industries, which involved many different individuals, participating in many different kinds of transactions and involving a variety of forms of exchange, on many different levels.

The account book of Walter Folger (1735–1826), recording transactions dating from 1764 to 1810, can serve as a case in point.[33] Folger's career illustrates the typical preindustrial pattern of male occupational pluralism as it occurred on Nantucket. Folger probably began as something of a carpenter and small boatbuilder.[34] By early in the account book, though, he seems to have evolved into more of a general merchant and provisioner of groceries, dry goods, and other sundries. Dozens of individuals are charged for a variety of commodities (nearly all of which had to be imported onto the small island): beef, fish, flour, rice, tea, coffee, molasses, butter, lard, salt, sugar, wine, brandy, rum, oil, candles, tin cups and plates, squares of glass, tools, boards, pins, thread, cloth, and articles of clothing. When the accounts were balanced, which occurred at any time from the moment of the transaction to five years later, Folger received in payment goods like corn, rye, wood, and ironwork; labor and services of various kinds (including washing, spinning, weaving, boarding "1 hand," carting, coopering, and carpentry); cash; and whalemen's lays in specific voyages. With the post-Revolution revitalization of Nantucket's whalefishery, Folger appears to have moved toward greater specialization as a whaling outfitter and owner of shares in vessels, an oil house, and a candle house.

With this range of activities and transactions spanning nearly half a century and involving well over a hundred different individuals, it seems likely that Folger would have been involved in extending credit to and helping sustain the wives and families of Nantucket sailors in the island's system of maritime paternalism. Yet women are conspicuous by their absence from his account book. Of the first fifty pages, which represent about a third of the volume and fifteen years of recordkeeping, there are reckonings with eighty-three men and just four women. Two of these women, Dinah Clark and Mary Clark, can be identified with some confidence as spinsters. The other two, Anna Flood and Mary Folger, cannot be identified with certainty, but it is probable that they too were either single or widowed.[35] (The only Anna Flood listed in Nantucket vital records died in 1789; her parentage, age and marital status is not listed. The same records show that there were several Mary Folgers alive and about at this time, some unmarried, some married. We cannot tell which particular women Walter meant, but certainly Walter knew, which suggests the face-to-face personal nature of these economic interactions.) All four of these women with their own accounts in Folger's book purchased primarily food items and cloth, which they paid for with their labor: washing, carding, days of unspecified "work", and, above all else, that archetypal occupation of single women: spinning.[36]

Only three of Folger's accounts in the first fifty pages refer explicitly to transactions made with married women, wives who are listed under their husband's names. Significantly, all three of these instances involved supplying the women with small amounts of cash on credit.[37] Only one of the three husbands, Walter's own brother Barzillai Folger Jr., can be positively identified as a mariner. In 1767 and 1768, Walter charged his younger brother Barzillai for mending a boat, a half ship boat, one cord of wood, eight lbs. of "spikes & Deck nails," "my Part of Building his house," and 1½ bushels of lime, for a total of £217 12s. In exchange, Walter received a service ("trimming old Cask"), one barrel of flour, four pairs of buttons, and two sizable payments in cash. In subsequent years, Walter continued to supply Barzillai with sundries and foodstuffs. More often, though, their transactions consisted of Walter advancing cash to Barzillai, to Barzillai's wife Miriam, and to their father, for which the older brother was paid back out of Barzillai's lays in his whaling voyages in the schooner *Seaflower* and possibly other vessels.[38]

Other accounts in Folger's book imply that the merchant supplied other whalemen's families with goods during the men's absences, but the recipients of the transactions are not specifically named. For example, during the first four months of 1792, Folger recorded in his account book seven

Facing pages from the "waste book" of Nantucket merchant Micajah Coffin, 1789–93. The account at the bottom of the pages lists, on the left, purchases of beef, flour, and other foodstuffs made by mariner Daniel Kelley's family during his whaling voyage in 1792 and, on the right, shows that these purchases were paid for out of Kelley's earnings from his voyage on the ship *Fox*, owned and managed by Francis Joy. Courtesy of the Nantucket Historical Association; photograph by Terry Pommett

transactions charged to another whaleman, Daniel "Killey," involving relatively small amounts of beef, flour, and molasses. On the "credit" side, with the date "1792" (day and month unspecified), Folger wrote: "This Acct Settled by Francis Joy out of Ship Foxs Voyage." Apparently Francis Joy, another prominent Nantucket merchant and managing owner of whaleships, including the *Fox*, had paid Folger the amount owed him by Daniel Kelley, out of what Kelley had earned as captain of the *Fox* during her 1792 voyage. Since Kelley had been at sea during the time the foodstuffs were charged, it was obviously some other member of his family who had actually obtained them.[39]

The "Waste Book" (daybook) and letterbooks of Folger's contemporary, Micajah Coffin (1734–1827), another prominent merchant on the island, substantiate the impressions gleaned from Folger's account book. As with Folger, the vast majority of Coffin's transactions are listed under male names, though he is likely to have been dealing with some other member of the men's families as well. For instance, the same Daniel Kelley apparently bought goods from Coffin as well as from Folger. On 3 January 1789, Kelley was charged by Coffin for a pound of tobacco which was, though, "Del[ivere]d his son Benjamin," and on January 16th he was charged for two pounds of "raizens" and another pound of tobacco supplied "to his daughter," all of which goods appear to have been paid for at some later date. Indeed, Coffin commonly extended credit to his customers: thus on 12 February 1789, he carefully noted that "John Wire" now owed him £1 12s. for a barrel of flour "del'd [on] his Order to his Daughter," for which "Wire" (Wyer) would pay "next summer."[40]

Coffin's willingness to wait until the summer to balance his accounts demonstrates how directly the Nantucket economy was linked to the whalefishery, especially the circulation of cash: most of the Nantucket whalers during this period were fishing the grounds in the South Atlantic and normally returned sometime between May and September.[41] Coffin used the seasonal rhythms of the fishery as an excuse when he explained to a New York supplier why meat remained unsold: "am Sorry it is such dull times have Sold but only ½ a barrel of thy beef as yet and no pork" but, Coffin added optimistically, "am in hopes to Sell thy pork in the course of the Summer when the money gets into the hands of the common people who are commonly the purchasers." Two years later his excuses must have sounded all too familiar: "one half and more of the Southern fleet we hear has faild of Voyages this Season and being no market for Sperm or whale oil there is no money in Circulation and we perceive the effects; not being able to collect in."[42]

This sort of maritime paternalism on Nantucket and in other communities along New England's southeastern coast more often took the form of credit than of cash. But the extent of the reliance by seamen's families on credit and other assistance is difficult to measure and, indeed, even to see at all, since women are noticeably missing from the sorts of accounts kept by Walter Folger and Micajah Coffin. Rather than representing any lack of involvement in the local economy, though, the absence of women's names in the merchants' record books reflects coverture, the legal status of wives, the great majority of all adult women. In most cases, under the English legal system brought over to the Anglo-American colonies, only single or widowed adult women (*femes soles*) were legally allowed to own property, own their own labor, enter into contracts, sue or be sued. Upon marriage, a woman's civil identity was "covered" or submerged into her husband's; she could no longer own property in her own name, nor keep her own wages, nor serve as legal guardian of her own children. As the preeminent legal authority in eighteenth-century England, Sir William Blackstone, explained, "by marriage, the husband and wife are one person in law, that is, the very being or legal existence of a woman is suspended during the marriage, or at least it is incorporated and consolidated into that of the husband: under whose wing, protection, and *cover* she performs everything, and is therefore called in our law-french a *feme-covert*."[43] In the surviving Nantucket records, transactions with married women or dependent children seem to have simply been listed under the name of the male head of household, the family patriarch, the person legally responsible for the debt.

The picture is clouded even further by the fact that maritime paternalism was not solely the responsibility of shipowners; it appears to have been diffused throughout the close-knit seafaring communities like Nantucket. In the preindustrial village environment within which the whalefishery emerged, organized within traditional networks of family and neighbors,[44] a permeable boundary between household and community allowed casual and reciprocal interaction whenever necessary. Kinfolk and neighbors stepped in readily and unselfconsciously to assist a wife and family during a seafaring husband's absence.[45]

Unfortunately, the surviving evidence is fragmentary. The clearest eighteenth-century example of the communitywide interactions that supported families during whalemen's voyages is supplied by a Quaker seawife living not on Nantucket but across on the mainland, though in very similar circumstances. Christopher Almy shipped out in 1797 on a vessel owned by the prominent Nantucket merchant William Rotch, bound for the Pacific whaling grounds. His wife Lydia and their two small children remained at home in Portsmouth, Rhode Island. In the diary she kept during Christopher's two-year absence, Lydia recorded both the activities and attitudes with which she supported their family. Lydia was in contact with her husband's employer at least once during Christopher's absence: "Had some conversation with William Roach concerning my dear husband," she wrote, adding "he said . . . I need not be uneasy."[46] The entry in the diary, though, suggests that she did not ask for nor receive financial assistance from Rotch. Instead, Lydia relied substantially on her own efforts—and the considerable assistance provided by her local community.

In September of 1798, her brother invited her to live with his family for the winter, an offer Lydia appreciated but did not accept. Her in-laws, who also lived in Portsmouth, stopped by often to visit and help out; on one such occasion, Lydia noticed, "Father Almy calls pritty often to se me and seams to be very happy and smileing perhaps it may be to cheer my drooping spirits[.] He talks encourageing about his sons." Two months later, she recorded that "my kind friend Edward Hall sent me word that if I wanted a pare of shoes he would make me some and wait till my husband came home for pay and if [Christopher] never should return he would give them to me." Another neighbor often sawed and split wood for her; Lydia confided to her diary: "I told him if my husband lived to return it would be made up to him. . . . [he] said he woud not take anything for it[,] further said he did it because he thought it was right for him so to do[,] said the sadisfaction he took in doeing of it was all the recompence he desired." Later Lydia remarked, "I am sensable how kind my friends are to me[.] It seems almost every body is willing to help me."[47]

In the most dire cases of distress, more formal relief structures had to step in: religious organizations and the town itself. Over the course of the eighteenth century, both the men's and the women's meetings of the Nantucket Society of Friends collected from their membership and disbursed assistance to other needy members, like the £3 cash given to Mary Newbegin, who had "made known her Necessities" in the winter of 1741–42, and the two cords of wood supplied to Eunice Guinn in 1761.[48] (By the second half of the century, the minutes of the Quaker monthly meetings regularly record the appointment of Overseers of the Poor but only rarely specify individual requests or payments.) The town's selectmen's journals also demonstrate that, like towns elsewhere in New England, Nantucket assumed some responsibility for its own indigent residents, providing provisions such as firewood, corn, and beef; paying boarding or nursing costs; arranging indentures for children; and, in extreme cases, removing people to the workhouse.[49] More often than not, those so assisted were women and children. Though any direct relationship to the maritime trades is difficult to trace on a case-by-case basis, historian Edward Byers finds that the number of Nantucket's dependent poor rose in the late eighteenth and early nineteenth century, which he correlates with expansion in whaling and merchant shipping. He found that in 1810, of the 6,807 residents of the island, there were 472 fatherless children and 379 widows (nearly a quarter of the adult women), and he claims that "many of these women, unable to care for themselves or their children, became a tremendous burden on the town." By 1821, more than half the households receiving some sort of assistance from the town were widowed or single women, most with children.[50]

The distinction between actual or virtual widowhood was of little consequence to some Nantucket sea-wives, particularly when they encountered the limits to their husbands' creditworthiness. Consider the case of mariner Zephaniah Pinkham and his wife Sarah. Zephaniah surfaces in the records of the Nantucket Inferior Court of Common Pleas as a defendant being sued by several creditors in 1763 and 1764. Merchants Joseph and William Rotch wanted to recover an advance made him of £15 18s 8d; spinster Anna Gardner needed the £15 10s she had loaned him, which he had contracted to repay at the return of the Sloop *Phenix* (under Pinkham's command) from "north carrolina and the Bahamas"; and merchants David Gardner and Timothy Folger sued to recover more than £200 "lawful money," the balance of accounts for "money and sundry goods" he had had from them for "sundry years past." No doubt a local response to the widespread commercial shocks of the early 1760s, Zephaniah's creditors had decided to call him to account—community paternalism and forbearance could not withstand the external pressures of credit crises.[51] A writ, executed 25 September 1765, directed that Zephaniah's personal and real estate be seized and conveyed to his largest creditors, David Gardner and Timothy Folger, and that the sheriff should "take the Body of the sd Zephaniah Pinkham & him Commit unto our Goal [*sic*] untill he pay the full Sums above Mentioned With your fees."[52] Did Zephaniah go to jail? For how long? How did he pay off his debts? And how did Sarah and their five children get by? Where did they go when their dwelling was seized by the town officials? The records are frustratingly incomplete; all we know is that Zephaniah was lost at sea in 1772. Sarah died six years later.[53]

The account books, the court records, and other such sources point to perhaps the most significant aspect of maritime paternalism as it existed on eighteenth-century Nantucket and in other coastal communities: whatever the goods and services supplied on credit to whalemen's families, these seem in no way sufficient to sustain households during the men's absences. As Zephaniah Pinkham's fate attested, in the maritime context, many of men's activities tied up large amounts of capital and labor for uncertain lengths of time and involved great risks, at the mercy of the tempestuous waves and dangerous currents of both the seas and the expanding boom-bust cycles of commercial capitalism. It was women's activities— predominantly local, daily, small in scale, often unrecorded, characterized more by barter and exchange than by cash transactions, involving services and goods that were ephemeral, consumed, used up and worn out—that kept family, household, and community going.[54] Crevecoeur was entirely on the mark when he asked rhetorically, "What would [Nantucket] men do without the agency of [their] faithful mates?"[55]

Whatever it was they actually did, women's efforts were not viewed as so much different from, and certainly not competing with, but rather as complementing men's activities. In fact, like wives throughout colonial Euro-American society, women married to seafarers routinely stepped in and served as their absent husbands' surrogates. As "deputy husband," a sea-wife could and did often perform tasks her husband normally would have, such as settling accounts in cash or goods with creditors or debtors, insuring cargo, and paying taxes.[56] Merchant captain Simeon Folger was one of a number of Nantucketers who expanded their maritime interests to include more trading voyages at the end of the eighteenth century. His wife, Phebe, frequently acted as her husband's junior partner at home— along with many other Nantucket sea-wives, judging by the Folgers' correspondence. Writing from Charleston, South Carolina, in February of 1788, Simeon informed Phebe, "I haive sent you twenty Pound of the Best Indigo in a [keg?] with Capt Parker and You will Git it of his Wife . . . I haive Sent Indigo to hudson [a New York settlement on the Hudson River founded by Nantucketers in the 1770s] By Capt bunker to git a Desk and 2 Tables and ½ Dozen Chairs and 2 Armed ones and I Expect you will Git them before I Git home. Rice will not Answer to Send." He was again in Charleston in March 1791 on a similar trading venture; he wrote Phebe, "I haive Shiped to Rhod Island by Capt Allen 87 lb Indigo[,] Capt Parker to haive half or 40 lb of it . . . & 7 [lb] for Capt Allen," and he cautioned her, "Dear Wife you must Weigh the Indigo before you Divid it for many times it falls Short." He continued by asking her advice on Nantucket market conditions: "I hope to hear from you Concerning Rice Wheather it will answer to Bring ther or no for I am in hopes it would be Cheaper . . . if it is a [Possible?] thing to Git me word Befor I sail for New York I wish you would So as I may no how to act in Regard to Rice & Indigo."[57]

Several years later, his trade routes had shifted, but his reliance on Phebe had not. Simeon was one of the many New England captains who found irresistible the possibilities for profit in supplying Caribbean and European markets during the Napoleonic conflicts.[58] In New York in 1798, Simeon was about to embark on a voyage to the West Indies even though, as he assured Phebe, "I was Determind [to come] home and left the Ship on that Intention." But his plans had changed, as he explained, "my Owner [of the ship, his employer] would not Consent my leaving the Ship" and offered Simeon an inducement to stay that the captain found compelling: "if I Go this Voige they are a Building a New ship for the Hamburg Trade and they [promise] it to me . . . and Likwise they Insure my wages and my Commissions of my Cargo Whether I am Taken [by privateers or hostile navies] or not." (We do not know if Phebe shared Simeon's enthusiasm at the prospects of a European voyage, despite his assurances, "I am in hops of Returning from this Voige in a Short time.") Although his homecoming was to be delayed, Simeon made arrangements to support his family from afar: he told Phebe, "I Shall Send by Daniel Barney Two hundred and Forty dollars one hundred to be Deliverd to [Peter?] Pinkhams Wife money he Sent from Philadelphia and you must Take a Recpt from his Wife when you Deliver the Letter & money. I shall Send you mor when I sail." [59]

Tellingly, despite Phebe Folger's evident competence and Simeon's confidence in her abilities, her subordinate status as a *feme covert* was clear: Simeon even addressed the letters he sent home to Nantucket to himself. Unfortunately, little evidence survives that explicitly documents how, throughout the eighteenth century, Nantucket sea-wives viewed themselves or their surrogate role. But the letter Judith Folger sent in 1768 to her "loving husband" Peter, then whaling near "ye Western Islands" (the Azores) suggests her deferential attitude as well as her competence and her activities. "I lack for nothing this world Afords but only your good Company," she began wistfully, and she hoped Peter had received the shirt and the "2 Pare of Stockings" she had sent by other outgoing Nantucket whalemen. Her choice in pronouns in the following passage is instructive: "I hear nothing Conserning your Venter [venture] yet," she reported, but added, "Walter hath got 1 Thousand Boards witch was £15 witch I gave him the mony for Carted and pild whare you ordered." She ended her short letter by assuring Peter, "I Remain your loving and honnest Wife until Death." [60] The lines of patriarchal authority were not tangled or stretched thin, it seems, even by mariners' extended and repeated absences, and their wives' prolonged experiences as deputy husbands.

Many Nantucket wives also sought, in classic "goodwife" fashion, to make an active contribution in their own right to their families' financial well-being. While her merchant-captain husband, Samuel, was at sea, Phebe Folger Coleman kept one of the many small private schools that comprised the Nantucket educational system until public schools were established in 1827.[61] In February of 1800, Samuel was apparently due into

Baltimore, where Phebe, his wife of just over a year, addressed a letter to him. Phebe was working to augment their income back home on Nantucket, as she informed Samuel: "I have kept school Days and evenings ever since the 16th of the 12th mo [December in Quaker terminology] and have above thirty schollars belonging to my school[.] The business is fatiguing but I think how much more [page torn; word missing] thou art to be beating [i.e., sailing] at this boisterous [i.e., rough] Season of the Year, And am willing to contribute my mite to accellerate that happy period when we shall not be obliged to separate." [62]

Lydia Almy also wanted to "contribute her mite." In the diary she kept during her husband's two-year absence, Lydia lamented that she was "in no way to due any thing towards earning my liveing which seems rather to distress my mind[,] knowing that my dear husband must be exposed to wind and weather and many hardships to indure whilst I am provided for in the best manner." [63] So, in addition to the daily round of child care and household tasks ranging from weaving and whitewashing to keeping livestock, preserving food, carting wood, and bringing in hay, Lydia also earned cash by taking in an occasional boarder and by tanning skins.[64] She also seems to have lent money on occasion: "received five dollars from Richard Arnold by the hand of Samuel Clark[,] it being money which I lent him," reads one such entry. It is notable that Lydia expressed no sense of internal conflict or inappropriateness concerning her forays into financial management and market production—even when one of her boarders apparently tried to shortchange her. "Have this eavening been setling with Isaac Lapham[.] Consider myself very hardly used by him," she wrote, admitting "it raised my temper a little for which I am very sorry that I had not power to govern." [65]

Phebe Coleman, Lydia Almy, and others actively contributed on their own account to their family's finances. But what they did was still viewed as just a "mite": in general, female labor was conceptualized in ways that largely sustained the underlying structures of patriarchal authority and the complementarity of men's and women's work. Just like their mainland sisters, most colonial Nantucket women were deputy husbands, goodwives, and mothers too, roles that all derived from the women's relationships to men and families. The precise and unquestioned chain of command on board ship, which demanded complete obedience as well as mutual interdependence and was absolutely necessary for survival on the ocean, was not alien or unfamiliar to the women and men on land either.

The same sense of order and acceptance of hierarchy prevailed at sea and onshore.

As on the mainland, the work that Nantucket women performed most often drew upon traditional female responsibilities and housewifery skills.[66] The kinds of activities women took on varied seasonally along with their age and family status, as well, just as did men's. Scattered throughout a range of sources—from the selectmen's journals and local court records to merchants' account books, family papers and correspondence, personal reminiscences, traveler's accounts, and local histories— are references to women's producing, preserving, and preparing food; spinning, weaving,[67] sewing, and washing; healing and nursing the sick, the very young, and the old; keeping boarders; running retail shops, inns, and taverns (of various repute); twisting twine; teaching school; and even making small loans and investments.[68] Though certainly considered less heroic and undoubtedly less risky than the men's pursuits at sea, women's work could sometimes be just as arduous, exhausting, and disagreeable.

Flexible interactions between households involving cooperative labor and exchange typified women's work on Nantucket as elsewhere in New England and were similarly crucial to family subsistence.[69] Crevecoeur had remarked on island women's "custom of incessant visiting," [70] and the local chronicler Obed Macy remembered in 1835 how the "nature of [colonial Nantucket women's] cares, and their common interests gave rise to the most friendly intercourse amongst them." [71] The scattered letters and rare diaries that have survived from eighteenth-century Nantucket document how extensive interactions based on shared work blended easily with broad-based sociability for the island's women just as for their mainland contemporaries. For example, the extant extracts from Kezia Coffin Fanning's diary document two instances of traditional "social childbirth." On 7 April 1779, Fanning recorded "Mama & myself called before sunrise to go to Tot Hussey's his wife in travel [i.e., travail or labor]—there was 20 women there—she was delivered before 8 o'clock of a large daughter—we breakfasted there got home before 9." In November of 1781, she similarly wrote, "Went to Abiel Barney's[.] She sent for the women— there were 15 women besides myself[—]at 11 o'clock she was delivered of a son." Fanning also described an equally traditional communal husking in the rural island neighborhood of Polpis in 1785: "All Polpis were there[,] as many as 40 persons—they finished husking by 9 . . . judged they husked 100 bu. corn . . . sang and danced till 12 & then we all came away."[72] The fragmentary diary entries from January 1799 recorded by young Nantucket sea-wife Abigail Drew demonstrate similar dynamics: while "Nabby" did laundry, salted mutton, and baked pies by herself, she knit and sewed "handkersheifs" and caps in company with other women, though when she did not feel well, she decided not to go to Mrs. Chadwick's to quilt.[73]

Across the bay in Portsmouth, Rhode Island, Lydia Almy similarly shared chores and responsibilities along with sociability. In December 1797, Lydia recorded in her diary, "Have been this eaven cuting up a pig Isac L [her boarder] helping me." The following month Lydia noted, "being invited to Pery Shereman's to dine . . . staid till night leaveing Salley Pearce to keep house for me . . . left my little ones at home." In May 1798, she recorded that she "spent a part of this afternoon down stares to nabour [neighbor] spensors, artermus fishes wife being their. went to nabour luthers about warping a peice [i.e., setting up a loom for weaving]." In March 1799, Lydia had lots of help as she prepared for an extended visit to her parents: "Moved my goods into nabour greeleys house[.] Had a number of yong men to assist me they offering to help . . . aunt sary and nany homes helped me whitewash." And she just as often returned such favors. In late 1797, she stayed two days with "nabour peckum," nursing a new mother and infant when both were ill. A month later she "kept house" for "nabour spenser" while the Spensers were away overnight.[74]

In Lydia Almy's diary, as in other contemporaneous Nantucket sources, child care seems just one duty, no more or less important among many. Reflections on motherhood are rare in the evidence surviving from the eighteenth century. In her short 1768 letter to her husband, Judith Folger mentioned the death of his brother's infant, her own brother's romantic interest, and reports of three other whalemen—but she did not write a word about their own three small daughters nor her advanced pregnancy.[75] The scrawled messages from Captain Joseph Wyer to his wife Margaret imply that her care for their young son was an important part of her life but by no means her only concern. In one such missive from 1797, Joseph explained the complicated problems he had encountered on his voyage and issued instructions to Margaret about financial matters; at the end he added, "My Brother Tim Informs me his Little nephew Is as Smart a Boy as Nantucket Produses[.] I Should be very Happey to Se him & be a Witness my Self . . . I hope he is a Good Boy & Minds his Scool."[76] Pious Quaker Lydia Almy cared deeply about her young children's spiritual well-being, but she felt just as comfortable leaving them in the care of men like her boarder Isaac Lapham or neighbor Mr. Baker as she did with women like Salley Pearce.[77] Though maternity was a nearly universal experience shared by Nantucket women and their mainland sisters [78] and primary care for young children their nearly universal responsibility, among these women motherhood was not yet highly sentimentalized nor singled out as a defining and unique element of female identity.[79]

Numbers of Nantucket women were not only mothers but also entrepreneurs, albeit primarily on a local and small scale.[80] (Some even combined the two enterprises: midwife Rachael Bunker was reputed to have delivered 2,994 Nantucket babies over her 33-year career, which ended only with her death at age 80 in 1796.) [81] For the pre-Revolutionary period, the Record Book of the Court of General Sessions in Nantucket listed those licensed to keep inns, sell liquors, and also to sell imported tea, coffee and chinaware; of the ten licensees listed on 4 March 1760, for example, two were women. Female involvement in such activities continued after the Revolution. On 5 October 1790, the town clerk recorded the people granted licenses to keep inns (one woman and three men) and retail "spirituous liquors" (thirteen people, three of whom were women). Eliza Barney remembered in 1826 how, when she was a child in the 1770s and 1780s, "all the dry-goods and groceries were kept by women who went to Boston semi-annually to renew their stock." [82] As in other contemporaneous seaports, some Nantucket women took advantage of the commercial opportunities created by the local maritime enterprises. In 1764, Mary Pinkham wrote to the Rhode Island merchants Nicholas Brown & Company, "I Have sent by Capt Duglus ½ blr Head Matter [high-quality whale oil][.] If you Have No good pouderd Shouger I Should Be Glad If youll Send What Is Due In New England Rum By the First oppertunity[.] Wee are out[.] I Expect the Whailmen Every Day[.] I must Have Sume To Wellcom Them." [83] Other female entrepreneurs no doubt offered unlicensed and considerably less respectable services to "wellcom" the "whailmen" and other sailors, as suggested by the occasional court cases charging women with "keeping a Tipling house," with "disorderly behavior" (sometimes associated with prostitution), or with bearing a child out of wedlock without an identified father.[84]

Although a few women may have stepped over the boundaries of legality or community moral norms, in general these "she-merchants" — even the married ones with husbands at sea *or in* residence — did not represent a transgression of traditionally female gender roles. The complementarity of women's and men's mercantile activities, rather than any subversiveness, is suggested by Crevecoeur's lavish praise of "Aunt Kesiah," Kezia Folger Coffin. "The richest person now in the island," Crevecoeur claimed, "owes all his present prosperity and success to the ingenuity of his wife . . . for while he was performing his first cruises, she traded with pins and needles and kept a school. Afterward she purchased more considerable articles, which she sold with so much judgement that she laid the foundation of a system of business that she has ever since prosecuted with equal dexterity and success. . . . [She and her husband] have the best country seat on the island . . . where they live with hospitality and in perfect union." [85] Kezia Coffin was an extreme case, of course; she became famous for her energy and financial acumen as well as notorious for her active Loyalist sympathies during the Revolution. It is possible that the extent to which women ran small commercial and retail establishments on Nantucket may have been somewhat unusual. But the fact that they did so at all was not; such efforts were typical throughout the towns and cities of colonial Anglo-America.[86] Perhaps the so-called "Petticoat Row" of shops on Nantucket's Center Street and the other female commercial involvement on the island represented a sort of communitywide, collective female assumption of the deputy husband role, which enabled the most prominent male merchants to concentrate effort, attention, and capital on the fishery and other maritime enterprises.

Historian Laurel Thatcher Ulrich has identified, in rural northern New England at this time, two distinct and semiautonomous family economies, one male and one female, within the typical household and linking households throughout the community. She explains, "female trade was interwoven with the [primarily male] mercantile economy and with the [sexintegrated] 'family economies' of particular households, but it was not subsumed by either." [87] The evidence from Nantucket suggests that, on the island too, there existed a similar pattern of male and female economies, integrated at particular points of overlap, operating within and between households. What may have been singular about the Nantucket case was the way in which the location and range of the overlap between the male and female economies ebbed and flowed with the contraction and expansion of the island's maritime industries.

Crevecoeur did not mention "Aunt Kesiah's" younger sister, Judith Folger Gardner Macy (1729–1819), but Macy, rather than Coffin, serves as the better illustration of the kinds of activities Nantucket women typically engaged in and the relationship of these to men's activities, within families and in the larger community. In 1746, less than two years after her father and eldest brother were lost at sea, the 17-year-old Judith Folger married James Gardner. James died of consumption just two years later. In 1749, Judith married again, taking as her second husband Caleb Macy, who was some eleven years her senior (and who had also, according to their granddaughter, wished to marry Judith even before her union with James Gardner).[88] Judith's and Caleb's marriage was a long and fruitful one: she bore ten children between 1751 and 1771, and they lived together another twenty-seven years after that, until Caleb's death in 1798. Judith herself died in 1819, a great-grandmother in her 90s. She outlived not only her husband but also all but four of her children.[89] As her son Obed described her, Judith was "generally healthy and of a strong constitution & remarkably industrious."[90]

Judith's strong constitution and industry appear to have been critical to her family's financial success. Acquiring Judith as a partner was clearly the turnaround for Caleb who, as described earlier in this chapter, had before his marriage moved fitfully between several occupations. Obed Macy recalled that his father "was not a workman of the first class, and his sickly complaints often prevailed and prevented his progress in business." But, at the advanced age of 30, Caleb married Judith. Now his shoemaking prospered; he eventually employed a dozen or so workmen and "engrossed the greater part of the shoes that was made and worn by the [Nantucket] Inhabitants, besides large quantities worn by Seamen and strangers."[91] He also began to invest in whaling voyages, wharves, and land, at one point reputedly owning one-thirtieth of the island's real estate.[92] Like virtually all Nantucketers, Caleb suffered some financial reverses during the Revolution, but he managed to conserve much of his property and recoup after the war. At his death in 1798, his estate was valued at over $17,000.[93]

Obed Macy wrote candidly that his father was "a weakly man" who "often called for his wife's assistance, not only in administering to his comfort in sickness but frequently in counseling together respecting his business." Judith's involvement with her husband's affairs and with his family began soon upon marriage. In early 1751, Caleb recorded in his account book that his father owed him £8 12s for "work dun by my wife." She again performed unspecified work for her father-in-law in 1754 and 1756. Judith also stepped in as her husband's surrogate on occasion; as Caleb's account book noted, for instance, in February 1753 Shubail Pinkham settled his debt for the two pair of pumps Caleb had made him with "cash paid to my wife."[94] Judith's domestic duties only grew more considerable as Caleb's shoe manufactory prospered: son Obed remembered that throughout his youth there were "frequently from ten to twelve workmen, besides the children & servants," which added up to a household of some twenty or more persons, for which Judith was responsible.

Judith began keeping her own account book, a daybook, in 1783, when she was 54 and her youngest child was 12. She continued it, erratically, to 1807.[95] Significantly, the great majority of the transactions she recorded were of small value, mostly in shillings and pence, and virtually all of the kinds of activities she records were traditionally female in association. Unfortunately, no record of Caleb's keeping has survived from the same years, so we cannot tell what the precise division of responsibilities and labor was between the wife and husband. Comparison of Judith's daybook with Caleb's earlier account book (covering mainly the 1740s through the 1760s) suggests, though, that by the 1780s Judith had assumed more autonomous responsibility for the household's food and clothing, while at the same time she took on small-scale income-producing activities.[96] Judith appears to have employed several women in spinning, including large quantities of shoe thread, probably for her husband's and later son Elisha's shoe manufacturing. She also paid in cash or kind both women and men to card wool fiber, dye and weave yarn, and full or dress cloth in the various phases of textile production. She sold quantities of raw wool and, later, quantities of milk as well; and she bought and sold or traded a variety of groceries and dry goods, sundries, and items of clothing. Among other less frequent transactions, she also listed charges to a couple of male boarders, and every once in a while she supplied some tallow to her sons Silvanus and Obed.[97]

By the time she began keeping her daybook, Judith was a substantial matron, still vigorous but well past her childbearing years, highly respected in the Quaker women's meeting and, it appears, the whole community.[98] Now, while her husband was overseeing his shoe operation and expanding real estate holdings, Judith was dealing on her own account with over a hundred other women and men on the island. Two of her sons (Elisha and the feeble Caleb Jr.) joined their father in the shoe manufactory; her other three sons—Barzillai, Silvanus, and Obed—formed a business partnership, increasingly active in the whalefishery and other maritime ventures.[99] At the same time, Judith's surviving unmarried daughters, Judith and Ruth, served as sort of junior partners to their mother. For instance, in 1792 Judith kept a running account with merchant George Freeborn in which "3 Days work by Ruth" was exchanged for lengths of "pershon" (i.e., persian, a kind of fabric) and sewing silk (thread). In contrast, Judith carefully recorded formal transactions with her sons, listing their full names: for example, "Obed Macy [debtor] to 4 lb of tallow for the Brig Polly." [100]

Judith Macy's extensive participation in wool, textile, and clothing production reflects the centrality of fiber and cloth to local female economies throughout Anglo-America as well as the importance of wool to the Nantucket economy. The earliest English settlers on the island intended to raise livestock from the outset; one of their first acts was to set aside much of their land to be used in common as pasturage, with grazing rights allotted by share. These grazing rights, known as "sheeps commons," were passed down to the proprietors' descendants and could be bought and sold.[101] (At the time of her death in 1819, Judith Macy controlled 30 sheeps commons inherited from her father and another 96 she had bought, and she owned 203 sheep.) [102] By the end of the seventeenth century, a fulling mill (where woven wool cloth was finished by scouring, shrinking, and pressing) was already in operation on the island, and by the early eighteenth century, Nantucket was recognized as one of the more important sheep-raising locations in New England. Thousands of sheep, each bearing the unique earmark of its owner, ran wild throughout the center of island, only occasionally penned in specific fields to provide manure. The immense flock of sheep was herded together as a whole just once a year, for a collective shearing. The town fathers designated one or two days in June for the shearing, which grew into a considerable annual festival, attended by virtually the whole island as well as professional shearers and "multitudes of hucksters and traders" from the mainland.[103] Crevecoeur commented that "the wool of Nantucket is of excellent quality. The . . . flock provides more than 50,000 pounds. . . . part of this they export, and the rest is spun by their industrious wives and converted into substantial garments." [104]

Sheep raising is a lot more prosaic than the heroic hunt of the leviathan whale, of course. It is no surprise that the commonplace sheep were almost completely ignored and that the whales and the fishery got most of the attention, then as now. The relationship between the two elements in Nantucket's economy and society is instructive, however. There, in plain view in the center of the island, were the dependable sheep. They quietly provided wool, mutton, and tallow—staples of everyday life, basic sustenance—the processing of which occupied hundreds of women, children, and some men too in various capacities, ranging from more formal, specialized work to the less formal household task squeezed in between countless other such chores. Then, hidden in the murky depths of the mysterious ocean, were the mighty whales. Their pursuit far at sea was the stuff of international commerce and high drama, strictly the preserve of young, strong men and highly skilled professional mariners, who might or might not survive the confrontation and return to their families. The contrast is striking. But, as historian Edward Byers suggests, Nantucket's wool production may in fact have served as an economic back-up when the whaling industry faltered.[105] So too did the island's local economy, through which women moved with ease and portions of which they dominated, unobtrusively coexist with and directly and indirectly support the much more famous whalefishery.

Nantucket women's support of the whaling industry extended beyond the material sustenance they supplied to their families during the men's absences. According to local legend, female concerns, preferences, and traditions also reinforced the values that ensured the fishery's success. Nantucket girls are supposed to have spurned the advances of any youth who had not yet "struck his whale," and wives condemned the husband who returned without a sufficiently "greasy ship." One Nantucket wife whose husband's earnings from his last voyage had about disappeared, reputedly remarked as she served a meager dinner, "Well, John, one or t'other of us has got to go round Cape Horn pretty soon, and I ain't goin."[106] The apocrypha, however suspect the specific details, appear to underscore not only a flintiness of female spirit but also the degree of female adaptation to the fishery that some more contemporary evidence bears out—such as the notable matter-of-factness with which one Elizabeth Chase Gardner (a Nantucket widow, mother, and mother-in-law of mariners) referred to the hazardous trip into the Pacific by way of Cape Horn as "a good voyage for the unstable youth."[107]

One Joseph Sansom, who published a detailed account of Nantucket in a Philadelphia magazine in 1811, described how "sea phrases . . . prevail in familiar conversation. Every child can tell *which way the wind blows*, and any old woman in the street, will talk of *cruising about, hailing an old messmate*, or *making one bring to*, as familiarly as the captain of a whale ship, just arrived from the north-west coast, will describe dimension to *a landlubber* by the span of his *gibboom*, or the length of his *mainstay*. If you have a spare dinner *it is short allowance*; if you are going to ride, the horse must be *tackled up*; or if the chaise is *rigged out*, and you are got *under way*, should you stop short of your *destination*, you are said to *tack about*, or *to make a harbour*."[108] An anonymous diarist who visited Nantucket in the early

1820s similarly observed (with considerable amusement) how the conversation of the "Nantucket beauties" he met "dwelt almost continually upon whales and whaling ... of the arrivals and clearances of port that day, of the hardships, miraculous escapes, fortunes and misfortunes, and everything else that appertains to a sailors life, which their fathers, brothers, friends, lovers and husbands had experienced, in their several voyages to the Brazill Banks or round Cape Horn."[109] Nantucket women did not themselves put to sea or pursue the whale. But their familiarity with the process and their easy use of the specialized language reflected their close connection and active contribution to the fishery.

The Nantucket whalefishery emerged within a local society that, as in the Anglo-American settlements on the mainland, was patriarchal, hierarchical, and corporate, held together by interpersonal connections of obligation and dependence. On colonial Nantucket, as elsewhere, there were no sharp boundaries between what we now consider public and private life, between the economic, the political, and the personal. Family, community, state, and church were seen as analogous in organization and function: families were "little commonwealths," and the commonwealth was the family writ large. Authority was firmly vested in the older male heads of households, the property-owning fathers of the towns, giving them power over all their dependents in a rather precise meaning of the term "patriarchy." Nantucketers, like other English colonists, were less concerned with abstract notions like "masculinity" and "femininity" than with concrete roles like husband and wife, master and mistress, which defined one's position on the social hierarchy relative to others and prescribed appropriate behavior. From this perspective, women were not understood to be so much a different sort of being than men; rather, they were seen as similar beings with less capacity, somewhat weaker, inferior, and dependent.[110]

As long as the hierarchical relations within the family, and in the community, remained stable, what women actually did varied considerably. The dominance of the whale fishery in the local economy (and its distinctive fragrance in the local atmosphere) should not blind us to the actual diversity in what most Nantucket men and women did on a daily basis or over the course of their lives. In both urban and rural areas throughout the colonial Northeast, a family's comfortable existence or even sheer subsistence required that individuals perform many different kinds of tasks, depending on the season and their age, sex, marital and parental status, and so forth. What historian Laurel Thatcher Ulrich has termed "occupational pluralism" characterized both men's and women's work lives.[111] As Nantucketer Walter Folger described in 1791, "It is no strange thing to see the same man occupy the station of a merchant, at other times that of a husbandman, of a blacksmith, or of a cooper, or a number of other occupations." [112] In general, men's and women's work was highly flexible and overlapping, exhibiting an interdependence and integration that were explicitly acknowledged.[113]

Boundaries located by law and custom circumscribed women's behavior and linked their identities to dominant men, fathers and husbands. Wives were cast as "goodwives" or "helpmeets," roles that stressed the wife's subordination to her husband, though within those broad limits there was some inherent flexibility. Seafaring labor was one of very few strictly sex-segregated occupations: as a rule, women simply did not ply the sea. On land, however, male and female labor overlapped in some areas and also generally shared the preindustrial rhythms of seasonality, task orientation, cooperative exchange, and life course.[114] Women were concerned mainly with domestic duties, but they could also take on tasks outside the home as long as their husbands approved, even acting in their husbands' behalf as "deputy husbands." [115] Nantucket too exhibited overlapping but semiautonomous men's and women's economies, porous boundaries between family and community, and lively patterns of interaction between households. Like men and women, "work" and "home" and "public" and "private" were not yet perceived as polar opposites, requiring quite different value systems and modes of behavior.

This organization of gender roles, family, and community life dovetailed neatly with the structure of maritime industries and the exigencies of seafaring throughout coastal New England, and especially on Nantucket, where they facilitated the rapid and successful development of the whaling industry. Men's absences of three, six, and nine months could be absorbed without too much difficulty when everyone's tasks were intermittent, relatively flexible, and often cooperatively shared. The rhythms of maritime and nonmaritime labor were not so different from each other. The hierarchical organization and exercise of authority on board ship corresponded to that on land as well. The smooth functioning of this way of life, though, depended in large part on the subordination of individual selves to their families and to the community as a whole.

Judith Macy died in 1819 at age 90. Her lifelong exertions, detailed above, enabled her to leave behind numerous descendants (four children, twenty-one grandchildren, and twenty-two great-grandchildren) and a substantial estate of over $4,300 to be distributed among them. It is illustrative, I think, that Judith drew up an addendum to her will in 1813 specifying that her prosperous merchant sons Silvanus and Obed manage her daughter Ruth's inheritance, so that Ruth's husband, whom Judith accused of unspecified "indiscreet conduct," should not gain control of the property.[116] In the end, her son-in-law predeceased her and the precaution proved unnecessary. This minor episode documents Judith's fiscal ken, her capacity to pass moral judgment on her son-in-law, and her close relationship with her daughter Ruth, with whom she seems to have lived the final few years of her life. But it also underscores the fact that her considerable agency and her maternal concern did not challenge the system of coverture and traditional patriarchal boundaries: she entrusted the care of property and her adult daughter to her sons.[117] Several years after her death, Obed Macy eulogized his mother in these words: "She . . . attended to her domestic concerns with that economy & exactness as becomes the ornament of her sex. . . . She was endowed with many excellent qualities, strictly honest & upright in all her dealings, kind and obliging to her neighbours, and the needy was not turned empty away. . . . She lived in peace with all mankind, careful to mind her own proper business." [118]

Judith Macy and her sister "Aunt Kesiah" Coffin were explicitly acknowledged as responsible for their families' considerable successes, as undoubtedly other less heralded women were for theirs. Given the exigencies and risks of seafaring, many more Nantucket women must have been simply the mainstay of their families' survival, as Crevecoeur pointed out. Neither the women themselves, nor their husbands or neighbors, viewed their activities or their considerable personal agency as subversive or even merely inappropriate. Female agency was critical to the men's enterprise, but its exercise did not challenge traditional hierarchies of authority, in which individual wills and interests were subordinated to the family and to the community as a whole. With the frequent and lengthy absences of so many married men and the importance of women's activities to the sustaining of household and community, Crevecoeur had noted an apparent danger in the married women's authority: "Those [men] who stay at home are full as passive in general, at least with regard to the inferior departments of the family. But," Crevecoeur cautioned, "you must not imagine . . . that the Nantucket wives are turbulent, of high temper, and difficult to be ruled; on the contrary, the wives of Sherborn, in so doing, comply only with the prevailing custom of the island; the husbands, equally submissive to the ancient and respectable manners of their country, submit, without ever suspecting that there can be any impropriety. Were they to behave otherwise, they would be afraid of subverting the principles of their society by altering its ancient rules; thus both parties are perfectly satisfied." [119] It is to "the principles of their society" I now turn, in Chapter 2, to examine the cultural dominance of the island achieved in the eighteenth century by the Society of Friends, or Quakers.

FAMILY, FAITH, &
COMMUNITY ON COLONIAL
NANTUCKET

In his 1782 *Letters from an American Farmer*, the French observer J. Hector St. John de Crevecoeur marveled that Nantucket whalemen did not fall prey to the "debauchery" and "foolishness" that characterized so many other seafaring subcultures. He attributed the islands' sailors' remarkable steadiness and gravity in large part to the stability of the island's family life. "Almost everybody here is married, for they get wives very young," Crevecoeur noted, "and the pleasure of returning to their families absorbs every other desire. The motives that lead them to the sea are very different from those of most other sea-faring men; it is neither idleness nor profligacy that send them to that element; it is a settled plan of life, a well-founded hope of earning a livelihood." He concluded, "the sea . . . becomes to them a kind of patrimony; they go to whaling with as much pleasure and tranquil indifference, with as strong an expectation of success, as a landman undertakes to clear a piece of swamp."[1]

Crevecoeur traced these attitudes back to the way in which Nantucket boys were raised, part ocean and part Quaker. He wrote poetically: "Those children born by the sea-side hear the roaring of its waves as soon as they are able to listen; it is the first noise with which they become acquainted, and by early plunging into it they acquire that boldness, that presence of mind, and dexterity which make them ever after such expert seamen."[2] Even more important, Crevecoeur thought, were the habits of "[f]rugal, sober, orderly parents, attached to their business, constantly following some useful occupation, never guilty of riot, dissipation, or other irregularities, [who] cannot fail of training up children to the same uniformity of life and manners." These lessons stemmed from the islanders' Quaker faith: "At their meetings, [the children] are taught the few, the simple tenets of their sect. . . . obedience to the laws, even to non-resistance, justice, good will to all, benevolence at home, sobriety, meekness, neatness, love of order, fondness and appetite for commerce. [Nantucketers] are as remarkable here for those virtues as at Philadelphia, which is their American cradle and the boast of that society [i.e., the Society of Friends]."[3] For Crevecoeur, Quaker values of sobriety, simplicity, self-discipline, and group conformity explained Nantucket success on shore and at sea.

Echoing Crevecoeur, professional historians in the twentieth century have also drawn connections between the island's dominant faith and its early dominance of the American whalefishery. Edward Byers recently postulated "a compatibility between the [commercial] inclinations and ethics of Nantucketers and the ethics of the Friends."[4] The maritime historian Elmo Hohman stressed the broader religious background to the industry, writing that

whaling demanded an unusual combination of qualities . . . and the Quaker-Puritan-Yankee stock of southern New England, through training, temperament, and cultural environment, possessed these traits in rare degree. . . . Courage, hardihood, skill, thrift carried to the point of parsimony, shrewdness, stubborn perseverance, ingenuity, sturdy independence, a cold lack of squeamishness in driving bargains, and a righteous scorn for luxuries,—these were characteristics . . . inculcated by the philosophy of Quaker and Puritan forbears and modified by several generations of struggle with a niggardly and often hostile

New World environment [which explains why] the leadership [of the industry] passed into the hands of Nantucket and New Bedford.[5]

Quaker and women's historians have suggested that the same Quaker ethos that enabled eighteenth-century Nantucket men to excel in whaling also enabled Nantucket women to develop an assertiveness unusual for the period. Like the Puritans and most other Protestant sectarians, Quakers advocated self-control, self-denial, and sobriety as much for women as for men. But the Quakers also heretically insisted on a spiritual equality among all believers. Anyone, even women, so directed by the inward light of God could speak the "Truth" publicly, serve as minister, and achieve a prominent position and a measure of authority within the Society. The Quakers' organizational form further contributed to women's developing a collective sense of authority and self-reliance, cultivated within relatively autonomous women's meetings for business that paralleled but were separate from the men's. Quaker historian Margaret Hope Bacon claimed that the Nantucket environment itself further amplified these characteristics: "Nantucket, with its isolation and frequent absence of husbands and fathers on whaling trips, became a training ground for the development of strong Quaker women: Lucretia Coffin Mott, Martha Coffin Wright, Phebe Hanaford, Maria Mitchell, and many other pioneer feminists came from Nantucket."[6]

These famous women belong to the nineteenth century, not to the mid-eighteenth-century heyday of the Nantucket Society of Friends. When we look more closely, it appears that at its height of local importance, the island's version of Quakerism may have promoted a considerable measure of female initiative and sense of personal competence—but, more significantly, it also promoted principles and practices that stressed "plain living" and self-restraint, spiritual self-negation, and group conformity. Crevecoeur described how "the wives of Sherborn . . . comply only with the prevailing custom of the island; the husbands [are] equally submissive to the ancient and respectable manners of their country."[7] Rather than fostering an unusual level of egalitarianism or individualism, the Quaker cultural synthesis on eighteenth-century Nantucket encouraged the subordination of individuals to family and community. It thereby channeled women's energies into sustaining families and a tightly knit community onshore that could withstand the demographic and social stresses the risky industry entailed.

Nantucket's distinctive association with the Society of Friends dated back to 1702 with the "convincement" (conversion) of the influential islander Mary Starbuck by visiting English Quakers. There had actually been a few Quakers among the early English settlers on the island, but, as the Quaker missionary (or "Public Friend") Thomas Story noted after his visit to Nantucket in 1704, "they had not been faithful, nor of good Report, but a Stumbling-block in the Way of the Weak; for they could not agree between themselves; and one of them was at odds with many of his Neighbours; so that they were set aside." [8] In general, the English settlement on Nantucket was marked by a relative measure of religious diversity and tolerance during its first several decades. Many of the original proprietors and their families were nonconformists: some Baptists, a few Quakers and Presbyterians, and several apparent "Nothingarians," so-called for their disinterest in religious observance. In the spring of 1660, the "first-purchasers" had moved from other Massachusetts towns to the island of Nantucket—conveniently remote and, until 1691, under the political jurisdiction of New York rather than Massachusetts—in part for economic opportunity but also in large part to escape the overly watchful and intolerant eye of the Puritan establishment during a nasty crackdown on religious dissenters and their sympathizers in the 1650s and 1660s.[9]

Despite repeated attempts by Puritan authorities to establish a Congregational church on Nantucket, the anticlerical islanders adamantly refused to call and pay for a minister. Thomas Story recounted in 1704:

> Several such, from time to time had made their Attempts upon this People . . . but were disappointed; for there was in this Island one Nathaniel Starbuck, whose Wife was a wise discreet Woman, well read in the Scriptures and not attached unto any Sect, but in great Reputation throughout the Island for her Knowledge in Matters of Religion . . . when at any time such Hirelings came to preach among them, and attempted to have a settled Maintenance, she always opposed it with solid Arguments, as being contrary to the Practice of the Apostles and Primitives . . . for Ministers of CHRIST ought to travel abroad in the World in that Calling, and not to sit down in one Place, unless they have Families to take Care of, and cannot leave them.[10]

Another visitor commented more cynically in 1755, after the Society of Friends had come to dominate the island's religious life, that although "the rightest part of the inhabitants embraced the principles of Truth from conviction, the others thought the expense of maintaining a priest would be too heavy for them and have turned to Quakers to save money." (Even the practicing Congregationalists refused to pay for a settled minister until 1767, when the First Congregational Church of Nantucket was finally incorporated.)[11]

This did not mean that the islanders were antireligious or disinterested in spiritual affairs. Several Quaker missionaries visited Nantucket in the late seventeenth and early eighteenth centuries, and many of them came away encouraged by their reception there. Audiences of two hundred or more islanders gathered to hear two Public Friends from Philadelphia, Thomas Chalkley and Joanna Slocomb Mott, who came on separate visits in 1698. Chalkley noted in his journal, "the people did generally acknowledge to the truth, and many of them were tender-hearted."[12] Mary Starbuck herself may well have been predisposed by way of family connection: Mary's husband's sister Sarah Starbuck Austin was already a Quaker minister on the New Hampshire coast, and Mary's youngest daughter Hephzibah had married an off-island Friend in 1694 and was also already an acknowledged minister in the Apponegansett Meeting just over on the mainland, in Dartmouth, Massachusetts.[13] But it was the powerful presence and persuasive preaching of English Friend John Richardson in 1702 that finally resulted in Mary's "convincement."

Mary Coffin Starbuck (1645–1717) was the youngest daughter of perhaps the most prominent of the original English proprietors, the "patriarch of Nantucket" Tristram Coffin and his wife Dionis.[14] In 1662, in the first English marriage performed on the island, the 17-year-old Mary wed Nathaniel Starbuck, son of another first-purchaser and brother of her brother's wife. A year later Mary gave birth to the first English child born on Nantucket, a daughter. In part due to her family's status and connections, in part certainly due to her own remarkable abilities, Mary Starbuck came to wield considerable influence in Nantucket society—more even, apparently, than her husband. John Richardson, the Quaker missionary who succeeded in converting Mary, remarked of the couple: "He appeared not a Man of mean Parts, but she so far exceeded him in soundness of Judgment, clearness of Understanding, and an elegant way of expressing herself, and that not in an affected Strain, but very natural to her, that it tended to lesson the Qualifications of her Husband."[15] Richardson referred to Mary as "she who was looked upon as a Deborah by these People," invoking the image of the Old Testament prophet and judge who led the

Israelites against the Canaanites.[16] Two years later another visiting Public Friend described her as "an Oracle among them . . . insomuch that they would not do anything without her Advice and Consent."[17]

Richardson and his traveling companions arrived at the island in late June of 1702 and "made bold" to go to Nathaniel Starbuck Jr.'s house for they "had heard he was a seeking religious Man." But Richardson was most impressed with Nathaniel's mother, Mary, then 57 years old, mother of ten children, and a highly successful "she-merchant." "At the first Sight of her," Richardson wrote, "it sprang in my Heart, To this Woman is the ever-lasting Love of God." Mary invited the group to join her family in attending the meeting of another "Non-Conformist Minister," but Richardson refused, suggesting that he would like to hold a meeting himself. Interestingly, Mary offered the use of her house, known locally as "Parliament House" for its unusually large main room, which was often used for town gatherings. The meeting was set for the following day.[18]

Richardson remembered that "the large and bright rubbed Room" was filled to capacity and "the Glass Windows taken out of the Frames" so that people outside could also see and hear. "It was not long before the mighty Power of the Lord began to work," he wrote, though others spoke first, while Richardson "sat a Considerable Time." Finally, as he recounted, "the Lord's heavenly Power raised me, and set me upon my Feet," and Richardson began to preach. Mary Starbuck was in the front row.

> The great Woman . . . for most of an Hour together, fought and strove against the Testimony, sometimes looking up in my Face with a pale, and then with a more ruddy Complexion; but the Strength of the Truth increased, and the Lord's mighty Power began to shake the People within and without Doors;. . . . When she could no longer contain, she submitted to the Power of Truth and the Doctrines thereof, and lifted up her Voice and wept: Oh! then the universal Cry and Brokenness of Heart and Tears was wonderful! . . . After some time Mary Starbuck stood up, and held out her Hand, and spoke tremblingly and said, All that ever we have been building, and all that ever we have done is all pulled down this Day, and this is the overwhelming Truth; or very near these Words. . . . and I observed that she, and as many as could well be seen, were wet with Tears from their Faces to the fore-skirts of their Garments, and the Floor was as though there has been a Shower of Rain upon it.[19]

Mary Starbuck's convincement suggests the appeal of Quaker belief to powerful women. Historians generally agree that "the climate of acceptance for women among the Quakers [was] virtually unique in European life in the seventeenth century."[20] Indeed, one of the assertions that more mainstream Protestants found the most offensive was Quaker advocacy of women's spiritual entitlement. "Quaking" or otherwise physically manifesting their direct experience of God's Truth, the first generation of Friends challenged both Anglican establishment and other, less radical Puritan reformers in belief and practice, frequently in open confrontation. In England and its colonies, Quaker women as well as men climbed into pulpits and disrupted church services. Some wore nothing but sackcloth and ashes or stripped themselves naked to prophesy in streets, town halls, and marketplaces; others sang and rejoiced aloud as they were whipped, imprisoned, or, like Mary Dyer in Boston in 1660, hanged.[21] Many of the earliest and most active Quaker preachers and proselytizers were women, including, in 1655, the first two missionaries to cross the Atlantic to North America, and also possibly in 1664 the first such Public Friend to visit Nantucket, one Jane Stokes.[22] Mary Starbuck undertook no such radically antiestablishment action herself. She was, after all, already an important figure in the Nantucket elite. But the force of her own conversion and the importance of her influence in converting Nantucket place her among the early Quaker women leaders.

Several theological tenets espoused by the first Quakers were particularly favorable to women and may well have been attractive to Mary Starbuck.[23] Most fundamentally, Quakers insisted on a spiritual equality among all believers, which derived from the equal possibility of experiencing God directly. Explicitly rejecting the concept of predestination, Friends argued that everyone was born with God's "seed" or the inward "light" within themselves. Furthermore, anyone could achieve rebirth and attain salvation spontaneously and without mediation if they sufficiently opened themselves to the "Truth." Expounding on the implications of this, founder George Fox asserted that all hierarchies, including that of gender, were the product of human sinfulness: it was Adam and Eve's disobedience that had made necessary social relations of subordination and oppression.[24] He explained, "For man and woman were helpsmeet, in the image of God and in Righteousness and holiness, in the dominion before they fell; but after the Fall, in the transgression, the man was to rule over his wife. But," he offered, "in the restoration by Christ into the image of God and

His righteousness and holiness again, in that they are helpsmeet, man and woman, as they were before the Fall."[25] Fox's notion of coequal, conjugal helpsmeets seems to correspond to the descriptions of Mary Starbuck's relationship with her husband, though it is not clear if it actually approximated her experience or instead shaped the Quaker missionaries' accounts. Perhaps it was both.

The Quakers also believed in continuous revelation, that God continued to speak to the regenerate with just as much force and authority as He had to the early Christians. Biblical injunctions such as those forbidding women to preach may have been appropriate a thousand years ago, they thought, but these had become obsolete by the seventeenth century. Such teachings could be updated or revised according to God's direction.[26] So anyone, even women, could publicly preach, write, and travel to proclaim the Truth if so moved by God, and an ordained clergy was unnecessary and wrong in claiming greater spiritual authority than laypersons. There were no prepared texts or sermons at Quaker meetings for worship; rather, groups of believers sat together in silence, waiting for the inward "light" to inspire one or more to speak. The early Quaker theologian Robert Barclay compared the gathering for worship to "many candles lighted and put in one place." The multitude of candles "greatly augment the light, and make it more to shine forth . . . to the refreshment of each individual; for that he partakes not only of the light and life in himself but in all the rest."[27] This focus on collective lay participation, along with the absence of ritualized worship and a professional ministry, broadened the possibilities for women's active participation and leadership.

Mary Starbuck was both active and indisputably the leader of the Quakers on Nantucket. Virtually every description of religion on the island, whether written by a Quaker or a non-Quaker from the eighteenth century to the twentieth, credits Mary Starbuck alone with establishing the Society of Friends there. In 1722, Nathan Prince, a native of Sandwich, Massachusetts (just across Nantucket Sound on Cape Cod), also a Harvard graduate and Congregational pastor, outlined the story:

> The Quakers are by far the prevailing part [on the island] . . . 'Tis strange how they have increased. Twenty years ago there was scarce one and now there are several hundreds, and all proceeded from a woman (one Starbuck) turning Quaker; who being a person of note for wisdom in this place became a preacher and soon converted so many as

that they formed themselves into a society and built a meeting house and became the prevailing profession of the island.[28]

The extant records corroborate the Reverend Prince's account. From 1702 to 1708, a few dozen Nantucket Friends met regularly for worship, often at the Starbucks' house. In April 1708, the Nantucket Quakers petitioned the New England Yearly Meeting in Newport, Rhode Island, for authorization to establish a regular monthly meeting on the island. Of the nine signatures on the request, seven were Starbucks by birth or marriage. And among the earliest acknowledged Quaker ministers on the island were Mary herself, her son Nathaniel Jr., and her daughter Priscilla Starbuck Coleman.[29] As it turned out, Mary's influence in the Nantucket Society of Friends extended well beyond her death in 1717 with the continued importance of her direct descendants through the midcentury high tide of Quakerism on the island. In fact, the dominance of Mary's family — combined with other theological tenets and institutional features of early Quakerism that powerfully emphasized collectivity and conformity — appear to have actually reduced the possibilities for non-Starbuck women's active participation and leadership. Mary Starbuck was clearly a motive force, but she did not necessarily model a role most women on eighteenth-century Nantucket could follow.

In 1708, when the Nantucketers petitioned to formalize their membership in the Society of Friends, the New England Yearly Meeting (itself an all-male body until 1761) was only empowered to authorize the formation of a men's monthly meeting. But at the island's first general meeting, held on June 28 of that year, the women cited "the power of the Lord as their authority" and established their own monthly meeting too.[30] The institutional form of parallel men's and women's meetings dated from the 1670s, when under the pressure of severe persecution and the centrifugal tendencies of their own theology, Quaker leaders George Fox and Margaret Fell (one of his earliest, most influential converts and later his wife) established a pyramidal organizational structure of local and regional meetings for business with authority over doctrine and members' behavior. Citing the distinctive needs of women, Fox and Fell had insisted on separate, parallel business meetings for men and for women.[31]

Some scholars have suggested that the experience of self-governance in their own separate meeting provided unusual opportunities for Quaker women to develop autonomous leadership skills, personal initiative, and a sense of competence.[32] That may well have been the case in other communities of Friends, but on eighteenth-century Nantucket these lessons were offered to very few women. The records of the island's monthly meetings for women (like those for the men's, too) show that the egalitarian implications of Quaker theory did not translate directly into democratic practice.

The men's and women's monthly meetings for business jointly formed the basic organizational unit in Quaker practice on Nantucket as elsewhere, serving administrative, parish-like functions. The monthly meetings sponsored open, joint meetings for worship on Thursdays and Sundays; raised and administered funds, including charitable assistance to needy members; built and maintained the meetinghouse; and corresponded with other meetings. They kept records of Quaker births and deaths, granted permission for couples to wed after establishing their "clearness" for marriage, and prepared permits for traveling or relocating Friends to carry to other meetings. In theory, anyone so moved by the inward light could speak out in the meeting for worship, and the authenticity of the inward light would assure that decisions made at the meeting for business would be reached by the consensus of the entire group. In practice, though, "weighty Friends" (especially worthy and pious members) identified those believers considered especially qualified to act as ministers and discouraged preaching by anyone else. And on Nantucket as elsewhere, the weighty Friends—those holding such positions as clerk, treasurer, elder, or overseer—wielded considerable influence in the meetings for business and in the local Quaker community more generally. Appropriately, these notables sat in front on raised benches during the weekly and monthly gatherings in the meetinghouse.[33]

What can only be called the oligarchic tendencies of the Nantucket women's meeting emerge unmistakably from the concise minutes carefully recorded each month by the clerk. During the meeting's first three decades, the minutes make note of 221 appointments to the offices of clerk, treasurer, elder, and overseer, and to serve other specific functions, such as to write reports to the regional quarterly meeting, to make the required regular visit to each Quaker family or to "treat with" transgressors, and (by far the most frequent appointment) to investigate young women's background and conduct before granting them permission to marry. Of the nearly one thousand members of the eighteenth-century Nantucket Society of Friends, there were almost certainly several hundred adult women among them.[34] However, just 29 women accounted for all

221 appointed positions between 1708 and 1740—and three quarters of this select few (a total of 23 women) performed only marriage inspections. In fact, for the first thirty years, two women dominated the meeting's activities, holding 80 percent of all appointments other than marriage inspections: Dorcas Gayer Starbuck and Dinah Coffin Starbuck, Mary's two daughters-in-law. As they aged and their activity waned, they passed the leadership baton to the next generation: Mary Starbuck's granddaughters Mehitable Pollard, Hephzibah Hussey, and Priscilla Bunker, and their cousin by marriage, Rachel Coleman. Leadership in the Nantucket Quaker women's meeting remained a family affair through two generations beyond Mary Starbuck herself.[35]

In fact, Nantucket's Quaker leadership was a family affair on several levels. Mary Starbuck's children also dominated the local men's meeting. Her son, Nathaniel Jr., served as clerk from 1708 until his death in 1753. His brother, Barnabus, served as treasurer from 1708 until 1718 when he moved to Newport, at which point Nathaniel Jr. took over that duty too. A third brother, Jethro, earned the distinction of being appointed to various committees and positions more often than any other single individual: seventy-eight times between 1708 and 1740. Overall, Mary Starbuck's sons, sons-in-law, and grandsons filled nearly half of all appointments made by the men's meeting for the first thirty years of its existence, as well as controlling the most important positions.[36] In some ways, their control extended over the women too, despite the separation of the men's and women's meetings for business. For the most important men were married to the most important women: Nathaniel Jr. was Dinah Coffin Starbuck's husband, and Jethro was married to Dorcas Gayer Starbuck. (Brother Barnabas never married.)

Given the family relationships of the leaders, it is not surprising that the women's monthly meeting tended to defer to the men's meeting and lacked final authority over its own members.[37] Just as historian Jean Soderlund found in her study of Quaker women's meetings in colonial New Jersey and Pennsylvania, the institutional and even physical separation of women's from men's meetings did not necessarily reflect female autonomy: "Quaker women held no power independent of the men, just as the men claimed no authority separate from the women." On Nantucket, as with their mid-Atlantic coreligionists, the leading women were often married to the leading men. Together, rather than with independent authority, "they watched over the congregations, just as husbands and wives together cared for and guided their own families."[38]

Enforcement of the "Discipline" was among the most important responsibilities of the weighty Friends of each local monthly meeting. In 1708 (the same year the Nantucket monthly meeting was formally established), delegates from the monthly and quarterly meetings gathered in Newport, Rhode Island, for the annual New England Yearly Meeting.[39] There, they approved the Discipline, a collection of rules to guide the subordinate meetings and govern Quaker conduct. Their goal was to recreate what they believed was the primitive Christian way of life by avoiding affectation or ornamentation in all things to avoid distraction from God's Truth.[40] The Discipline required members to manifest devotion to their faith through "right" or "holy conversation," by which they meant appropriate conduct and demeanor. "Holy conversation" extended from the characteristic Quaker "plain" speech, gesture, dress, and belongings to "plain dealing" or straightforward, transparent, peaceable behavior. Friends were also to follow Quaker rulings governing marriage within the faith, "tender" childrearing practices, and arbitration of disputes and were generally to submit to the collective authority of the meeting. The Discipline stipulated that monthly meetings appoint committees of "visitors" to inspect every household periodically and assure that the rules were being followed.[41]

Overall, the Discipline appears to have sat lightly on Nantucket Friends, at least for the first half-century. In "fourth month" of 1713, for example, the women's monthly meeting minutes noted laconically: "inquiry was made of the visiters how things are the answer is Reasonabley well." And at regular intervals for the next several decades thereafter, the visitors found "things indiffrant well." On the couple of occasions when the visitors found it "otherwise" they simply "[took] care to advise to a reformation," and few disciplinary "treatments" ensued.[42] There were only three disownments altogether before the 1750s, all three handled by the men's meeting and all three extreme cases involving repeat offenders whose conduct threatened their families' well-being.[43] Even those who married non-Quakers or committed other lesser breaches were forgiven after formally apologizing. In general, island Friends seemed to have few problems with the Discipline, the specific authority of the meeting, or the dominance of a small handful of "weighty" descendants of Mary Starbuck.

As it turned out, the meeting did not need to exercise strict discipline. With persuasive and prominent leadership, little organized competition, and birthright membership granted to the rapidly growing numbers of children born to Quaker parents, the Society of Friends flourished on Nantucket. By 1728, the island meeting numbered 359 adult members and had outgrown its original meetinghouse. The new "Great Meetinghouse," completed in 1732, offered a thousand seats and a sliding partition down the middle to separate the men's and women's monthly meetings for business (the partition was removed during the weekly meetings for worship, though women and men still sat separately). The building had to be enlarged in 1747 and again in 1764. Not all Nantucketers were Quaker. The Congregationalists claimed a significant minority, perhaps some three hundred adherents by midcentury, who were led by a cluster of prominent families descended from original proprietors as well. There were some Presbyterians and Baptists too.[44] Nonetheless, by the middle of the eighteenth century, the Society of Friends thoroughly dominated the island numerically, politically, and culturally.[45] Their ascendance would not be challenged until the Revolutionary era, and not eclipsed until a generation after that.

By all reports, the values, principles, and even aesthetic preferences of the Quaker majority became defining traits common to the whole island.[46] Crevecoeur described with approval the total lack of decoration or ostentation on the clothing and houses of even the most wealthy Nantucketers and asserted that, in general, "simplicity" was "their boast and their most distinguished characteristic." [47] Other travelers' reports agree. When the prominent Quaker reformer John Woolman visited Nantucket in 1760, he too greatly admired the "plainness of life" there, which he compared favorably to the conspicuous consumption of Philadelphia.[48] Crevecoeur and Woolman were, of course, using Nantucket as an example to preach from —but much surviving material evidence supports their accounts. Small, simple, and self-righteously unadorned buildings still crowd many of the town's narrow, crooked streets. Well into the nineteenth century, the insides of these structures were also characteristically "understated, sometimes severely simple," according to the scholars of American decorative arts Charles Carpenter Jr. and Mary Grace Carpenter. The Carpenters further suggest (as Woolman had two centuries earlier) that "Nantucket Quakers were probably more conservative than Quakers of Philadelphia and Newport [as] demonstrated by the comparative plainness of the surviving Nantucket houses and furnishings." [49]

Crevecoeur was particularly taken with the preferred mode of transportation on eighteenth-century Nantucket, the simple cart called a "calash," essentially an open wooden box set on a single axle and drawn by one horse. He related a telling incident:

"A Perspective View of part of the town of Nantucket taken from a north window in the house of Walter Folger," watercolor by Nantucket resident Phebe Folger, 1797. By permission of the Department of Printing and Graphic Arts, The Houghton Library, Harvard University (fMS Typ 245)

> A few years ago, two *single-horse chairs* were imported from Boston, to the great offense of these prudent citizens; nothing appeared to them more culpable than the use of such gaudy painted vehicles in contempt of the more useful and simple *single-horse cart* of their fathers. This piece of extravagant and unknown luxury almost caused a schism, and set every tongue a-going; some predicted the approaching ruin of those families that had imported them; others feared the dangers of example; never since the foundation of the town had there happened anything which so much alarmed their primitive community.

Crevecoeur concluded, with evident approval, that on Nantucket, Quaker custom had "acquired the authority of law." [50] Who needed overt discipline when the pressure to conform was such a powerful force?

The flourishing of the Society of Friends on eighteenth-century Nantucket provides the cultural framework in which, as Crevecoeur claimed, island wives were in no way "turbulent, of high temper, and difficult to be ruled," despite men's absences at sea. On Nantucket, as elsewhere, colonial Quakers' doctrinal emphasis on direct individual revelation and lay governance did not, in practice, actually promote much in the way of female autonomy or individualism. What Crevecoeur termed "the ancient and respectable manners of their country" encouraged Nantucket women to "submit" (his term seems apt) to the collective imperatives of faith, family, and community.[51]

Rather than in the separate space of the women's meeting, most Nantucket women found recognition of their importance within marriage, family, and community life. As Jean Soderlund observed of mid-Atlantic Quakers, on Nantucket, too, "though the women were not independent, they did have power. They held authority and responsibility within the Quaker community as protectors of the well-being of women and children and as supervisors of female behavior." In particular, "Quaker women were vital partners in the activities of their faith. The central focus of the women's meetings was on the family: their business concerned marriage, courtship, education of the young, morality, and simplicity in dress and behavior. Traditionally, these concerns were the primary business of the Society as a whole. . . . To Friends, the family was paramount, and the Quaker community was the extension of the family." [52]

Crevecoeur remarked upon the unusually high incidence of marriage among the island's whalemen compared with other deep-sea mariners and upon the young age at which they married. His observation is borne out by a more recent investigation of Nantucket demography: Edward Byers found that between 1740 and 1780 the native-born, white, Nantucket whalemen married at an average age of under 23 years and after 1780 at an average of about 24 years. A rare early census of Nantucket dating from 1800—a listing of over 1,900 individuals by household, which represents about a third of the island's population—substantiates and extends Byers' findings. The median age at marriage for men listed in this census was just 24 years, and for women 22.5 years; over 70 percent of Nantucket men and nearly 80 percent of the women were married by age 25, and over 90 percent of the men by age 30.[53] Eighteenth-century Nantucketers, then, married on average about two years earlier than their counterparts on the mainland, and fewer of them remained single.[54]

Crevecoeur attributed the prevalence of youthful marriages to Nantucketers' love of family life and Quaker patterns of sociability, while Byers stresses the opportunity afforded young men by whaling to acquire enough money to marry at an early age.[55] Crevecoeur and Byers are both right: the young age at which Nantucket men married indicates that not only could they afford to do so on their whaling profits but also, clearly, that they wanted to. Like Quakers elsewhere, Nantucket men viewed spousal companionship and women's activities as necessary to their own and their families' spiritual and material well-being, but marriage and the functions performed by wives took on even greater importance given the stresses and uncertainties of the whale fishery.

Perhaps earlier and to a greater extent than other Protestants, Quakers encouraged voluntary marriages founded on mutual attraction between the potential bride and groom and accomplished through relatively relaxed and informal courtship.[56] On Nantucket, when the ships returned from a season of whaling, Crevecoeur wrote, the young men

> easily find out which is the most convenient house, and there they assemble with the girls of the neighbourhood. Instead of cards, musical instruments, or songs, they relate stories of their whaling voyages, their various sea adventures, and talk of the different coasts and people they have visited. . . . [The young men and women] whisper to one another their spontaneous reflections: puddings, pies, and custards never fail to be produced . . . they often all laugh and talk together. . . . This lasts until the father and mother return, when all retire to their respective homes, the men reconducting the partners of their affections.[57]

Conjugal affection was not supposed to be animated by passion but rather to express a moderate love that both reflected and was firmly subordinated to one's love of God. In general principle, Quakers agreed with the description of appropriate marital relations offered by a prominent Puritan minister: "the indisputable Authority, the plain Command of the Great God, required Husbands and Wives, to have and manifest very great affection, love and kindness to one another. They should (out of Conscience to God) study and strive to render each others life easy, quiet and comfortable; to please, gratifie and oblige one another, as far as lawfully they can." The most important element in a truly Christian marriage was spiritual: the godly husband and wife would be improved by loving God in the image of their spouse. But Puritan authorities also warned of the dangers of idolatry in loving any human being too much. This was an even greater potential problem for Quakers: the doctrines of the inner light and direct revelation made it both more difficult and more crucial to prevent conjugal love from being confused with or even displacing love of God.[58]

Catharine Phillips, an English Public Friend who visited Nantucket in 1754, counseled young, single women "to guard their own minds, lest they admit of any pleasing imagination, and stamp it with the awful name of revelation; and so slide into a familiarity and freedom of conversation and behaviour, which might tend to engage the affections of young men." Phillips acknowledged the difficulty occasioned by the Quaker lay ministry: "When we are singularly made instruments of good, in the hand of Providence, to any soul, there is a natural aptitude to lean a little to the instrument, and to prefer it above others. . . . The Lord, leading the mind by gradual steps from the love of other objects to the entire love of himself, the one only pure, eternal Excellency, may permit it for a season to lean to an instrument; in which case a prudent reserve is necessary, as well as a tender regard to the growth of the party thus visited." But it was important not to conflate or confuse mere affection between two mortals with the divine love of God shared by believers in Truth: "I confess, it is sometimes a nice point, to be ready to be of service to such, and preserve the unity of the Spirit, free from mixture of natural affection." Phillips was sure that divine guidance would prevail: "Truth, if adhered to . . . will also direct to steer safely between these dangerous extremes." [59]

Given the importance to the Quaker community of the appropriate form of godly love, marriage, and family life, the wiser heads of the meeting's elders ostensibly held veto power over marital choice. This was the rationale behind the most frequent activity by far undertaken by the Nantucket women's monthly meeting for business—the investigation of prospective brides. Pairs of "weighty" matrons were appointed to "inspect the clearness" of each woman who appeared with her prospective husband in front of the meeting, as required, to "declare their intentions of marriage"; the men's meeting similarly investigated each man. This did not prove any sort of meaningful obstacle: for the first several decades, only very rarely did the committees identify problems or recommend withholding permission. Marriages to close relatives or even to non-Quakers, though both officially proscribed, were tolerated more often than not. So many couples were allowed to "proceed in marriage" that in 1722 the Nantucket meeting wrote to ask if they could hold weddings at the Thursday meetings for worship as well as on Sundays. Sixty-five marriages were held in the first quarter-century of the meeting's existence (1709–34), another 63 in the following decade (1735–44), and 102 the decade after that (1745–54).[60]

Individual parents may have been less indulgent or more watchful than the Quaker elders. In 1768, Judith Folger wrote to her whaling husband of her brother's dashed romance: "Jonathan went up in Town a most Every Night[.] He would have been marryed before he went a way [but] father would know [i.e., not] consent to it." [61] Judith did not mention why her father objected to Jonathan's interest nor did she identify the young woman in question (presumably her husband was already familiar with the details), but her comment suggests that at least occasionally some Nantucket parents might exercise their own veto over their children's marital choice. But just given the sheer number of marriages recorded by the Quaker meeting and the demonstrated tolerance by its leadership of many infractions of Quaker marriage rules, such obstructions seem to have been rare.

In the complacent midcentury atmosphere, the elders of the men's and women's meetings were quite willing to make allowance for the exigencies of seafaring. In 1738, sailor Christopher Worth and his intended, Dinah Paddack, asked the men's and women's meetings to speed up the process of being cleared for marriage. The women's monthly meeting minutes recorded, "he being a seafareing man & on his passage from boston could not reach ye last monthly meeting but fel short of ye same (by reason of Contrary Winds) & not knowing how soon he might take a voyg asks frds [friends'] condesention." Just two weeks later instead of a full month, the meeting found "nothing butt yt they are clear" and so granted the couple permission to proceed with the marriage.[62] On colonial Nantucket, Quaker practice was sufficiently flexible to accommodate the rhythms and demands of maritime life; indeed, it cushioned them.

Once married, Nantucketers "cease to appear so cheerful and gay," Crevecoeur reported. "The title of master of a family necessarily requires more solid behavior and deportment; the new wife follows in the trammels of custom, which are as powerful as the tyranny of fashion; she gradually advises and directs; the new husband soon goes to sea; he leaves her to learn and exercise the new government in which she is entered." Obed Macy's nostalgic 1835 description of colonial Nantucket explained why: "The husband was a great part of his time at sea, and when on shore his calling was such as to allow him little time for his fire-side." Indeed, Macy claimed, "the Nantucket whaleman, when with his family, is but a visitor there. . . . He is in the bosom of his family weeks, on the bosom of the ocean years." Therefore, "on the mother devolved almost every family care, both those of the immediate household and those of a more general nature."[63]

The island's maritime gender division of labor resonated with Quaker tradition in ways that may have validated both for Nantucketers. In her analysis of the writings of the seventeenth-century founding generation of Quakers, historian Phyllis Mack found that the women typically were more preoccupied with issues of integration than were male Quakers, who were more preoccupied with issues of separation and breaking away from family. Mack points out, "fortunately for these zealous male Friends, Quaker women were there to mediate between the world of flesh and that of the spirit. The romantic heroism of the male seeker and prophet was sustained by the somewhat less romantic heroism of the benign, reassuringly stationary (but no less dedicated) mother in Israel." [64]

In the journal he kept on several short, midcentury whaling voyages, young whaleman Peleg Folger conveyed a colorful sense of some of the parallels between Quaker "seekers" and "mothers in Israel" and the men and women of Nantucket. At sea in the spring of 1752, the 19-year-old Folger had reflected that "[w]e poor Seamen are many times in Jeopardy of life by Storms, tempests, Rocks, Shoals, Pirates, Whales and many unhealthy Climates . . . the Creator to whom I trust is able to deliver out of all Danger forevermore." But with the unsinkable high spirits of youth, on a fine August day at sea in 1754, Folger wrote cheerfully, "if the weather is so Pleasant at home it is a charming day for the Young Ladies to go to meeting & if they do but Get any Good by it it will be very well: So Remembring all at Home . . . & wishing them all well & a happy & prosperous Meeting . . . while we are Drinking Flip [i.e., punch] & Chasing Whales." [65]

Later in life, after he had retired from sea and perhaps after he had been appointed clerk of the men's monthly meeting, Folger memorialized the two terrifying times he had gone overboard in a poem titled "Dominum Collaudamus" ("Let us praise the Lord"). After rather generic mention of God's wonders in the natural world, Folger got specific:

> Thou didst, O Lord, create the mighty whale,
> That wondrous monster of a mighty length;
> Vast is his head and body, vast his tail,
> Beyond conception his unmeasured strength.
>
> But, everlasting God, thou dost ordain
> That we, poor feeble mortals should engage
> (Ourselves, our wives and children to maintain,)
> This dreadful monster with a martial rage.
>
> And though he furiously doth us assail,
> Thou dost preserve us from all dangers free;
> He cuts our boat in pieces with his tail,
> And spills us all at once into the sea.

I twice into the dark abyss was cast,
Straining and struggling to retain my breath;
Thy waves and billows over me were past;
Thou didst, O Lord, deliver me from death.

Great was my anguish, earnest were my cries—
Above the power of human tongue to tell;
Thou heardst, O Lord, my groans and bitter sighs
Whilst I was lab'ring in the womb of hell.

Thou savedst me from the dangers of the sea,
That I might bless thy name for ever more.
Thy love and power the same will ever be;
Thy mercy is an inexhausted store.[66]

Though he does explain whale hunting by parenthetically referring to men's responsibility to maintain their families, Folger's ocean-based revelations focus narrowly on his own confrontation with the whale, the sea, and God's power and mercy. In contrast, Nantucket founding mother Mary Starbuck reputedly combined her spiritual seeking and forceful intellect with a sensitivity to others. In John Richardson's description of the pivotal meeting in 1702 at which his persuasive preaching converted Starbuck, she is cast as the very model of a Quaker mother of Israel, one who could integrate "spiritual intensity, moral integrity, and attentiveness to the human needs of Friends."[67] Richardson remembered that, despite herself experiencing God's presence so intensely that it reduced her to weeping, Starbuck still noticed his own exhaustion and dizziness after feeling and speaking the Truth so powerfully: "Mary, that worthy Woman said to me, when a little come to consider the poor State that I was in, Dear Child, what shall I do for you? I said, a little would do for me; if thou canst get me something to drink that is not strong but rather warm, it may do well: So she did."[68]

The "mother in Israel" figure drew her authority in large part from the Quaker identification of the household as a crucial site of spirituality and their investment of all family relations with spiritual import. Marriage was supposed to be based on a pure religious love, a unity of spiritually equal souls to be assured by strict examination by the meeting. The fruit of these unions, children born with both God's seed and the capacity to sin within themselves, were to be raised "tenderly," nurtured into the community of believers, protected from corrupting worldly influences. Historians

"Portrait of Mrs. Judith Macy ca. 1799" by W. Ferdinand Macy, 1878, oil on canvas. Courtesy of the Nantucket Historical Association; photograph by Terry Pommett

of seventeenth- and eighteenth-century Friends in the Middle Colonies argue that the Quaker definition of marriage and the stress on "tender" childrearing enhanced women's status and authority.[69] This seems to have been even more the case on Nantucket, where seamen's regular absences placed greater family responsibilities on wives' and mothers' shoulders.

John Woolman, the Quaker reformer from New Jersey, acknowledged the influence and responsibility of the island's women when he visited in the spring of 1760. "I was concerned to speak with the women Friends in their Monthly Meeting of business," he recorded in his journal, "and in the fresh spring of pure love to open before them the advantage, both inward and outward, of attending singly to the pure guidance of the Holy Spirit, and therein to educate their children in true humility and the disuse of all superfluities." He also pointedly "remind[ed] them of the difficulties their husbands and sons were frequently exposed to at sea, and that the more plain and simple their way of living was, the less need of running great hazards to support them in it." So Woolman was led to "encourag[e] the young women in their neat, decent way of attending themselves on the affairs of the house, showing . . . that where people were truly humble . . . and were content with a plain way of life, that it had ever been attended with more true peace and calmness of mind than those have had who, aspiring to greatness and outward show, have grasped hard for an income to support themselves in it." [70]

The goal of unity and love among Friends was underscored by frequently invoked familial metaphors,[71] which on Nantucket took on flesh-and-blood reality. George Fox energetically advocated the self-definition of Quakers, those within the boundaries of the faith, as "the family and household of God." [72] On eighteenth-century Nantucket, family and community were very nearly the same thing. The tribalism that characterized other colonial Quaker communities found perhaps its ultimate expression in Nantucket's English founders' pronounced habit of endogamous marriage.[73] Crevecoeur observed that "the majority of the present inhabitants are the descendants of the twenty-seven first proprietors who patented the island . . . they are all in some degree related to each other." He further noted that "they always call each other cousin, uncle, or aunt, which are become such common appellations that no other are made use of in their daily intercourse; you would be deemed stiff and affected were you to refuse conforming yourself to this ancient custom, which truly depicts the image of a large family." [74] (Certainly the labyrinthine coils of Nantucket genealogy bear out his impression, as will attest anyone who has tried to sort out the multiple connections between Starbucks, Coffins, Macys, Folgers, Gardners, and the rest.) Native son Walter Folger Jr. similarly testified, "The inhabitants live together like one great family, not in one house, but in friendship." As he told the readers of the *Massachusetts Historical Society Collections* in 1791, "They not only know their nearest neighbors, but each one knows all the rest. If you should wish to see any man, you need but ask the first inhabitant you meet, and he will be able to conduct you to his residence, to tell what occupation he is of, and any other particulars you may wish to know." [75]

The small, fragmentary journal of young sea-wife Abigail Gardner Drew provides graphic documentation of family extension on Nantucket, and the fluid overlapping of kin and community in island socializing, as in the shared work described in Chapter 1. "Nabby" turned 22 years old on the tenth of January 1799, the year her record begins; she had been married to whaleman Gershom Drew for almost four years but had not yet borne her first child.[76] On 3 January 1799, Nabby wrote: "Hannah [her older, unmarried sister] and myself with Mr D [her husband] up to Mrs Longs have a very socible evening[,] am much pleased with an acquaintance who comes in at 8[.] We stay till ten and have some new songs." On January 15: "This afternoon to Mrs Swains where there is Mrs E Cary & Miss L Coffin & Mary Barnard, play cards in the eve[,] get home at 10." January 16: "Suky comes here this eve to go to aunt Ruths[.] We go to a dance to Captn Pollards. Mr H come in here & Mrs E Long comes in a while but we go and stay till half past 12[.] Suky comes home with us stays all night." January 20: "The eve spend at Miss H Dilano and very agreeable[.] Mr Drew come after me at 9." Winter weather didn't keep Nabby at home: on January 25, she recorded, "Very wet and stormy to day[.] Mr Drew Hannah & myself to Mr E Drews [probably her husband's brother] to dine[,] comes up a thick snow at 12[,] we ride there . . . Mrs S Dilano & Mrs P Chadwick &c [there] have a very agreeable day & eve Mr & Mrs Drew [likely her husband's parents] comes in at 8 to sup with us." That month she also went regularly to religious services, attended two funerals, and witnessed her sister-in-law Polly's wedding.[77]

The young married couple did have some sort of base they termed "home," possibly one or two second-floor "chambers" they rented.[78] What is striking is the lack of spatial privacy or really any sense of conceptual differentiation of their home from the rest of the community, especially in contrast to the highly sentimental ideal of a private home that would develop by the mid-1800s.[79] In January 1799, at the beginning of the diary, Nabby's sister-in-law Polly (the same age as Nabby and soon to be married) appears to have been living with Nabby and her husband, and "Suky" (obviously a close friend and possibly also a relative) stayed overnight on more than one occasion. Nabby remarked, "We have considerable of a company with comers & goers all the time." [80]

Nabby was Congregationalist, not Quaker, and she later converted to Methodism. Pious Friends certainly frowned on the music, dancing, and card playing she so enjoyed, though even among the younger generation Quaker discipline was breaking down by the end of the eighteenth century, as we will see in Chapter 3. Nonetheless, the dizzying round of activities and dozens of names (relatives, neighbors, friends) inscribed in Nabby's diary underscores how widely and deeply the local Quaker-influenced tribalism pervaded island society. The flow of individuals around the neighborhood to work, play, eat, and stay together is constant. Nantucket women as well as their men moved around the community with great ease and frequency, going in and out of each other's households naturally and without second thought. For Nabby and Gershom, as for virtually all other Nantucketers, Quaker and non-Quaker alike, family and community life were nearly the same thing.

The majority of names Nabby recorded in her diary are female. Even when Gershom was home between voyages, Nabby's socializing, like her work, only partially overlapped with her husband's. Yet, significantly, hers seems no rigidly exclusive "female world of love and ritual"; rather than a strictly sex-based segregation, an informal and flexible independence characterized both Nabby's and Gershom's activities.[81] This flexibility, along with the expansive understanding of kinship in practice, made it easier for both the women who remained on land and the men who came and went to survive their periodic separations and for the community at large to adapt to the regular absence of so many young men.

Late in 1801, Nabby Drew made an extended stay with her surviving parent, her widowed mother. Gershom was then whaling off the coast of Brazil on a ship commanded by Nabby's brother. The ship had sailed in August, and Nabby expected the men would be gone a total of ten months. Meanwhile she, now with her first child in tow, a son then 13 months old, temporarily moved back into her mother's household. "I have given up housekeeping & board with my Mar for the present as I am not fond of liveing alone," she explained in December, in a letter to her off-island aunt. Nabby also wrote that another young woman, Nancy Jarwood, who was herself just 18 and married only ten months, was boarding with them for the winter as well.[82]

These sorts of flexible arrangements were common, on-island as off. In 1790, Kezia Coffin Fanning had made note of a similar arrangement: "Elizabeth Long & her two children & her sister Sally goodwin moved into the E[ast] room of this house we live in, the two women belong to Portland down East. Long married Elizabeth there & brought her here." Crevecoeur had observed that "some of [their houses] are filled with two families, for when the husbands are at sea, the wives require less house-room." The households might not always be completely harmonious, though. Edmund Gardner informed his brother Charles, who was then somewhere in the South Pacific on the ship *Thames*, that another family "now live in the west room & our parents in the wrest part" of the house and commented ruefully, "Some times I think myself Next to Socrates for commanding My temper."[83]

A surviving 1800 household census enumeration for Nantucket, which includes about a third of the island's population (but not, unfortunately, Nabby and Gershom Drew or Kezia Coffin Fanning), attests to the extent of combined and extended households and corroborates Crevecoeur. Almost half of young married women aged 20 to 24 years are listed as residing with their parents. A fifth of young husbands in the same age group lived with their own parents and almost a third with their in-laws. One in six of all the households described in the census contained married children. In fact, almost a third of the families were extended either laterally or vertically; that is, they contained kinfolk beyond the nuclear unit of parents and their children—a surprisingly high proportion, given the general rate of about 10 percent found in eighteenth-century England and the only three locations in colonial America with comparable data. One in six of these Nantucket households also counted non-kin among its residents.[84]

Very little is known about this rare census, begun in August 1800. The record does not indicate who wrote down the information or why, on the tiny handwritten pages that simply record names, ages, and birthdates, lines drawn between apparent household units, double lines between houses. But the information, corroborated and extended by genealogical data from the Nantucket vital records, testifies to the complexity and variety of Nantucket residential arrangements. For example, the dwelling numbered 59, headed by the widowed Laban Gardner, age 37, included his three daughters, aged 10, 5, and 3; his married sister Hephzibah, age 26, her husband Thaddeus, 28, and her 2-year-old daughter Eunice; his sister Elizabeth, age 19, and her husband David, 24. (Were Laban's brothers-in-law at sea much of the time? Did Laban invite his young married sisters to live with him and help care for his own young daughters after his wife died?)

Dwelling number 36 contained a similarly extended family: in one part of the house lived the elderly widow Lydia Coffin, age 78, with her youngest child, Labbeus, a 38-year-old bachelor. In another part of the same house, Lydia's widowed daughter-in-law Abigail (age unknown) shared quarters with two of *her* daughters, Abigail, age 17 and still single, and Lydia, 29, along with Lydia's husband Andrew, 31. (Did the elder Lydia and her daughter-in-law Abigail lose their men to the sea? Did the younger Lydia stay with her grandmother, mother, and sister while her own husband shipped out?) Thomas Starbuck, age 58, and his wife Dinah, 57, shared dwelling number 100 with their widowed daughter Rachel, 33, and her two children, aged 5 years and 6 months, respectively; their newly married 19-year-old daughter Dinah and her husband; their 5-year-old grandson (son of their son Simeon); and two unrelated boarders, a 13-year-old motherless boy and a 23-year-old single man from Falmouth. (Were these multiple generations and individuals brought together in this household by whaling or other maritime pursuits?) The census listing is as eloquent in the stories it hints at and the questions it raises as in the documentation it provides about the island's household structure.

A range of Nantucket sources suggest that the islanders subscribed to widely held Anglo-American notions that a family encompassed everyone, kin and non-kin, living together under the authority of a household head. Throughout the British colonies in North America, boundaries between households were porous and continuously reconfigured as people moved around their communities and region according to need and preference. Adolescents and young adults often lived and worked in households other than those of their parents, and families themselves combined or hived off with a fluidity and ease we would find surprising, even unsettling.[85] The poignant individual stories and the broader patterns documented on Nantucket thus represent the local adaptation of widespread contemporary practices to the pronounced rhythms of the fishery, in particular the periodic absence of so many men at sea.[86] The island's dominant Quaker culture extended, reinforced, and legitimated common patterns of kin and community overlap and highly malleable residential arrangements, which became crucial to withstanding the personal, familial, and community stresses of whaling.

Little direct evidence has survived that illuminates how Nantucket sea-wives themselves felt about their conjugal roles, family responsibilities, and community relationships. Again, Lydia Almy, the Rhode Island Quaker whaleman's wife introduced in Chapter 1, makes it possible to assess the personal implications for women of the local Quaker cultural synthesis during its eighteenth-century heyday. Throughout the diary she kept from August 1797 to June 1799 during her husband's whaling voyage "round cape horn" and into the Pacific, Lydia made frequent reference to her husband Christopher and to her emotional and spiritual state, as well as recording many of the quotidian details of her life. The diary itself seems to have been inspired by her husband's absence, in part as a means by which she could continue to share her life with her husband during their separation and in part a record to share with him after his return. In an early entry she wrote that she was "feeling myself in duty bound to write a little[,] that my dear husband may know how it fares with me if he should live to return which if should be would afford me grate satisfaction[.] Think I cannot omit any thing that would give him any pleasur or comfort at our meeting." [87] Though many entries document how often she thought of Christopher, they rarely describe the content of her thoughts, and not once are they retrospective, but instead focus on immediate circumstances and events.[88]

The diary provides much evidence that Lydia, like her coreligionist contemporaries over on Nantucket, was deeply enmeshed in a community that was at once both intensive and extensive. In the twenty-two months that Christopher was away, Lydia shared living quarters with relatives, boarders, and neighbors, for an afternoon, overnight, a few days, or several weeks at a time. About half of the time her husband was at sea, Lydia lived in what she called her "habitation," part of a house she rented from "nabour Shearman." After Shearman moved, she "got the promas of part of nabour Grales house," into which she "moved her goods" some weeks later. In both sets of rented rooms, she shared her space with her two small children and an intermittent boarder, Isaac Lapham. Sometimes Lapham's wife and child also joined them, as did Lydia's sister Elizabeth and other relatives and friends. Lydia also regularly shared work and socialized with the other adults in the houses and in the neighborhood (she was particularly pleased that Christopher's father came to call and offered help so often). Lydia herself moved easily around the region—with or often without her children—walking, riding on borrowed horses, or getting rides in other people's carts, "shases," and "slays," or taking a "paccat" [packet] or "feary" across Narragansett Bay or the Sakonnet River. She went into nearby Portsmouth on day trips or made more extended stays there with her Uncle Job, including most of February 1798 and parts of February and March in 1799. She also spent most of the summer and fall of 1798 in her inland hometown of Smithfield, splitting her time between her father's, her brother George's and her brother Samuel's houses. Much of her movement was religiously inspired. Lydia went to meeting as often as she could: weekly, monthly, quarterly, and even the yearly meeting in Greenwich across the bay.

Despite her wide social circle and frequent interactions with others, Lydia deeply regretted the absence of Christopher. Significantly, it was his companionship she missed most, rather than his labor or his authority. "O that my Dear husband may be returned to me again in the Lords time[—] missing his agreeable company very much," she recorded, and reminded herself firmly, "I ought not to comeplain or think my lot was hard. . . . I have everything to make me comfortable and happy and want for nothing of this worlds goods except the company of my dear husband." On only a handful of occasions over the nearly two years that he was gone did she miss having him home specifically to chop wood, bring home the cow, or help nurse a severely ill child. Much more often, she missed having him there to confide in, to comfort her, and to share her concerns. He was her "companion," her "endeared friend," her "kind husband," her "beloved," the "dear partner of my breast," the "nearest connection in this life" and "my dearest treasure in life." Ten months after Christopher had shipped out, Lydia summed up her conjugal ideal: "if we equally set our sholders to the wheel and prye forward in the fear of the Lord . . . we shall be supported comfortable through life without our ever being parted nor in such a manner as we now are."

Separation was the greatest challenge Lydia felt she faced. Not surprisingly, given his emotional importance to her, she worried about Christopher. "O the lonesome moments I must now and then endure," she mused sadly, "often doth fears arise lest some misfortune hath hapned to my beloved husband that is to[o] near and dear to me tho so far Distant wheare money will not purchase news from him." A neighbor stopped in and recounted "descriptions of a voige round cape horn" which only raised Lydia's "anxious cares" even further, though on other occasions returning seamen delivered good news of Christopher and at least twice the owner of his ship reassured her that she "need not be uneasy." Lydia took comfort in the company of other mariners' wives: "have had the agreeable company of Elisabeth Cockshell," she recorded, "which was of grate satisfaction in my lonely state[.] She said she knew how to share with me [as] she had many trials to pass through her husband being at sea." Lydia rued the "intrest" that enticed Christopher to ship out from a community where, unlike on Nantucket, there were other options available, and she wrote, "If we are ever sufered to meet again I due believe it must be for contience [conscience] sake and not intrest that will avail for me to give my consent for the like again." Another neighbor "like one of jobs comforters" told Lydia that if Christopher "should make any thing [i.e., a profit] he will certainly go again." Lydia replied, "If thou thinks so I wounder thou will speak it, for it creates a very disagreeable feeling in me when any one say so[.] He said I shall go with him next time so his wife and my self had a lovely time a sheding tears." [89]

Only once did Lydia's worries bubble over into resentment explicitly aimed at Christopher himself. When her sister-in-law received a letter from her husband, Christopher's brother, who was on the same ship,

Lydia's disappointment in not hearing from Christopher himself sharp. She griped in her diary, "My father . . . said Lydia this is the comfortable news thou hast had yet from thy husband it doth certify it not troubled but is content about his famaly . . . I have no desire he should be troubled about me only that he might think of me so much as to imbrace every Oportunity that I might here from him. [I] believe he is not nor ever was sensable of my cares and trobles for him." She was much pleased when she did hear from Christopher, eight months later: "Receivd a letter from my dear husband dated more than a year since, not withstanding we have had much later news there was grate satisfaction in peruseing of it." In February of 1799 she thought he was headed home until she received a letter in which Christopher raised the possibility of staying out longer. "The dissapointment seemed to be more than I could bare," Lydia confessed, but still, after reading the page "over and over many times," she "could not blame him in the least." More often than not, she put aside her concerns and was certain that, compared to others, she "had one of the best of husbands." [90]

Throughout her diary, Lydia tried to subordinate her love and fears for Christopher to her faith. In several entries she worried that "too much of my time is taken up with the thoughts of my Endeared Friend"; at times "the rains [reins] will sometimes git loose and my mind gits far beyond the bounds where it ought to be," and she feared "lest I sin therein." She was comforted by occasional dreams of Christopher until the night she explicitly went to bed with "a grate desire that I might dream of my dear husband" but suffered a frightening nightmare instead. The next morning she reflected that "it was not right for me to eaven to desire to dream of my husband." In January of 1798 she tempered her delight on receiving a letter from Christopher by writing "think I injoy grater favours than I am worthy of O that I may keep my plase and not be too much overjoyd at such seasons." She was proud of her 3-year-old son's precociousness when he spoke of his father, such as the morning "he saith mommey due get up and make a jonneycake for Dear Dadey for he will come by and by," but she also regretted that her "little prattler's" conversation so often "put [her] in mind" of Christopher and caused her "to shed tears." Again and again she wished that she might "become more reconsiled to my alotments" or be "indued [endowed] with patience to wait the appointed time." [91]

Lydia found considerable solace in her frequent religious devotions. She prayed for her husband's welfare: "O Father be pleasd to draw near the partner of my breast, doe for him as thou has done for me[,] hold him ne hollow of thy holy hand."[92] The weekly meetings for worship ght her much relief: on one typical occasion, she wrote that she had very comfortable [meeting] my husband was brought as it were very ear to me"; at another, she "felt the love of god flow into my heart." The local fellowship of Quakers supported her efforts in other ways as well. One winter's evening, she carded wool while her boarder read aloud from the Bible, the second chapter of Titus. (This chapter prescribes proper godly behavior for different social groups, and calls on "aged women" to "teach the young women to be sober, to love their husbands, to love their children, to be discreet, keepers at home, good, obedient to their own husbands, that the word of God be not blasphemed." The chapter continues by demanding that all believers deny "ungodliness, and worldly lusts" and "live soberly, righteously, and godly, in this present world; Looking for that blessed hope, and the glorious appearing of the great God, and our Saviour Jesus Christ.")[93] Lydia found this "very instructing." At the end of an informal gathering for worship "downstares" on another evening, Elizabeth Cockshell (who seems to have been a minister in Lydia's meeting) "came to me takeing me by the hand [and] saith if thou hunger and thyrs [thirst] after righteousness thou shalt be filled[,] if thou cast thy care of the lord he will be thy support through all those trying senes." Lydia reflected, "O such opportunities as these surely it must be on my part if I due not improve by them, believeing they come from that power who seeth not as man seeth."[94]

Lydia found fellowship, affirmation, and a necessary strength in the particular sort of religiously inspired submission that Cockshell recommended to her. "May I be kept low and humble in the sight of my maker is the desire of my heart," Lydia wrote, and chided herself, "saith my soul be still[,] there is a voice that the muffling waves must obey." She prayed "O may I give thanks to the allwise disposeer of all things who hath seen meet thus to point out this lonesome situation for me[,] may thou O Lord be with me as thou hast heretofore been[,] wilt thou be pleased to keep my mind stayed according to thy good will and pleasure that I go not astray[.] Make cleane my heart[,] let not thy hand spare nor thine Eye pitty till thou has performed the work."[95] To those who asked if she worried about losing her husband, she responded stoutly, "I have never been uneasy on that account believeing their is a protector who if he pleaseth can bring them safe back again." She was quite sure that "it was the lords will that we should be thus parted" in order, she wrote, "to ween our affections from this world and fit us for his own servis."[96] Overall, Lydia's response to her seafaring husband's absence was shaped into a some[what] tense but nonetheless clear resignation by the forces of her Quaker fa[ith] and custom.

Melville wrote in *Moby-Dick* that Nantucketers "in general retain in an uncommon measure the peculiarities of the Quaker, only variously and anomalously modified by things altogether alien and heterogeneous." He further pointed out (with considerably more irony and double entendre than Crevecoeur) the contradictions between Nantucket's dominant faith and dominant industry: "[T]hese Quakers are the most sanguinary of all sailors and whalehunters. They are fighting Quakers; they are Quakers with a vengeance." Melville's character Captain Bildad, one of the managing owners of the whaleship *Pequod* and former whaleman himself, served as a prime example: he "refus[ed], from conscientious scruples, to bear arms against land invaders, yet himself had illimitably invaded the Atlantic and Pacific; and though a sworn foe to human bloodshed, yet had he in his straight-bodied coat, spilled tuns upon tuns of leviathan gore. How now in the contemplative evening of his days, the pious Bildad reconciled these things . . . I do not know. . . . For a pious man, especially for a Quaker, he was certainly rather hard-hearted, to say the least."[97]

Any potentially corrosive consequences of Bildad's inconsistencies were made up for by the efforts of his sister Charity, a fictional Quaker "mother in Israel" with a Melvillian twist:

> a lean old lady of a most determined and indefatigable spirit, but withal very kindhearted, who seemed resolved that, if *she* could help it, nothing could be found wanting in the [ship] Pequod. . . . At one time she would come on board with a jar of pickles for the steward's pantry; another time with a bunch of quills for the chief mate's desk . . . a third time with a roll of flannel for the small of some one's rheumatic back. Never did any woman better deserve her name, which was Charity — Aunt Charity, as everybody called her. And like a sister of charity did this charitable Aunt Charity bustle about hither and thither, ready to turn her hand and heart to anything that promised to yield safety, comfort, and consolation to all on board a ship in which her beloved brother Bildad was concerned, and in which she herself owned a score or two of well-saved dollars.[98]

it was startling," Melville's narrator tells us, "to see this excellent hearted Quakeress coming on board, as she did the last day, with a long oil-ladle in one hand, and a still longer whaling lance in the other."

Ultimately, though, Melville, like Crevecoeur before him, portrayed Nantucket as representative rather than fundamentally different from the American mainstream. And both Melville and Crevecoeur ultimately recognized that the role of Quakerism on the island was as hyperbole, exaggeration of the norm rather than unlikeness. We should pay attention. Like the stench of whale oil hanging over the town, the vision of gray-skirted figures moving busily around its narrow, crooked streets, sprinkling their speech with "thee" and "thou" along with offhand references to "parmicetty" whales and voyages around Cape Horn, have encouraged us to view colonial Nantucket and its women as unique. But this is misleading. As in Aunt Charity's character, on eighteenth-century Nantucket and (perhaps to a less pronounced extent) elsewhere in southeastern New England, Quaker tenets and practice did not run counter to but rather enhanced features of colonial Anglo-American culture in a way that successfully channeled women's energies into sustaining families and their community, both necessary to support the developing whalefishery and to survive its personal and social stresses.

As it turned out, the mutually reinforcing qualities of Nantucket's religious belief and practice and the fishery did not last out the century. As we shall see in Chapter 3, what disrupted the relationship came not directly with the expansion of the industry itself, nor with related changes in men's and women's work, nor even with the considerable depredations and turmoil brought on by the American Revolution, but rather in the areas of religion and romance. The spearhead of change was less economic pressures or political events than spiritual and emotional expectations, unleashed by a sequence of events beginning with a generational shift in the women's meeting leadership in the 1760s, the arrival on-island of an aggressive Quaker reform movement in the 1770s, and ultimately the erosion of Nantucket's Quaker cultural synthesis. By the turn of the nineteenth century, the shifting relationship between faith, family, and community on Nantucket (and indeed throughout the coastal region of southeastern New England) would render men's seafaring even more difficult, not less, for women to endure.

THE IMPACT OF
RELIGIOUS REFORM, REVOLUTION,
& ROMANTICISM ON NANTUCKET

In 1797, Phebe Folger began to keep a commonplace book. With elaborate calligraphic flourishes and the date in Roman numerals, she titled her book: "Un Recueil [a collection or a miscellany] Containing Painting, Penmanship, Algebra and Pieces selected from various Authors in Prose and Verse, with a few Pieces in French with their Translation / By Phebe Folger of Nantucket."[1] And it was just that, an eclectic mix of accomplished watercolors (many with verse captions) and alphabets in different styles; mathematical exercises, including "Extraction of Cube Root," "Quadratic Equations," and even "Promiscuous Questions in Arithmetic and Algebra"; sermon excerpts and biblical aphorisms, leavened by selections from classics by Ovid, Homer, and Seneca and more contemporary authors Pope, Swift, and Voltaire. There is evidence of much erudition throughout the large volume: Folger must have been something of a bluestocking, one of those famed women of letters alternately celebrated and reviled in the eighteenth and early nineteenth centuries. The first three pages of her book contain pen-and-ink sketches of several famous men—including, among others, explorer Captain James Cook, South Carolinian statesman Henry Laurens, Benjamin Franklin, and George Washington—which correspond in seriousness of purpose with topics like "Panegyric on the Scriptures, extracted from Hunter's Lectures" and the "Beneficial Effects of a Taste for the Belles Lettres." But the dominant themes are pastoral and romantic: still lifes of vegetables, fruit, and flowers; poetry and prose extracts titled "The Happy Pair," "The Four Lessons of Love," "The Four Seasons," "On the Fair Sex," "Conjugal Affection," "Sensibility," and "Adelaid, or the Lovely Rustick."

Most of the content of Phebe's "Recueil," even in its eclecticism and contradictory juxtapositions, seems not too unusual for any such well educated, well-to-do, genteel, young Anglo-American lady of the late eighteenth century, even with Folger's evident bluestocking tendencies.[2] There are a few clues, though, to her less typical situation, such as the portrait of English Quaker leader John Fothergill (who had visited Nantucket in 1737),[3] the verse tribute to the "Noted & Celebrated Quaker Mary Drummond," a poem titled "The Sailor, an Elegy," and the two watercolors of prosaic Nantucket town scenes, accurate even down to the cabbages and manure pile. Folger was a member in good standing of the Nantucket Quaker meeting; she was also daughter of one of the more prominent Nantucket families. (Her older brother, Walter Folger Jr., with whom she studied French and no doubt other subjects, would go on to much acclaim as an inventor, astronomer, mechanical engineer, judge, state senator, two-term congressman from Massachusetts, and builder of a remarkable clock.)[4] But there seems something incongruous in the idea of this Phebe Folger, 25-year-old spinster, dressed soberly in Quaker gray or brown, sitting in a modest wooden house on the small, barren island of Nantucket, carefully copying French phrases in Italianate calligraphy and drawing the likeness of American heroes and English duchesses, bucolic swains and sweethearts, gamboling "lambkins" and discreetly naked cherubs.

The incongruity is all the more striking because by this point, the Quakers on Nantucket had put themselves through more than two decades of a rigorous self-purification movement, enforcing much stricter adherence to Quaker discipline and faith. As it turned out, these reform attempts were of only limited success. Phebe Folger's commonplace book

Un Recueil

Containing

Painting, Penmanship, Algebra
and Pieces selected from various Authors in Prose and Verse; with a few
Pieces in French with their Translation

By

Phebe Folger of Nantucket

And you, ye works of art, allur'd mine eye,
The breathing picture, and the living stone:
Tho' gold, tho' splendor, heaven and fate deny,
Yet might I call one Titian stroke my own!
Smit with the charms of Fame whose lovely spoil,
The wreath, the garland, fire the Poets pride,
I trim'd my lamp, consum'd the midnight oil
But soon the paths of health and fame divide!
But now 'tis o'er the dear delusion's o'er!
A breezeless stagnant air becalms my soul:
A fond aspiring candidate no more,
I scorn the palm before I reach the goal

MDCCXCVII

serves as just one indicator that the tide of genteel culture rising through the Atlantic world over the course of the eighteenth century had finally reached even the shores of Quaker Nantucket.[5] Bringing in its wake new ideas about gender, love, and marriage, the sweeping cultural shift had as profound an influence on Nantucket women and the whaling community as did the specific disruptions of the American Revolution itself. This chapter explores how the dominance of Quakerism in local culture and its support for Nantucket's whaling and other maritime industries, described in Chapters 1 and 2, eroded under both internal and external pressures of religious reform, revolution, and Romanticism.

Nantucket historian Edward Byers dates the decline of Nantucket's Society of Friends "back to the 1770s, the period of Quakerism's overwhelming preeminence." He claims that "[a]t the very moment that Quaker culture had its greatest power to shape Nantucketers' values and beliefs, the seeds of its own decline were being sown"[6]—ironically, in the attempt to reinvigorate Quaker piety. From nearly its seventeenth-century beginning, there had existed a fundamental tension in American Quakerism between the more worldly Friends, who tended to be more active and ambitious politically and economically, and the more devoutly religious Friends, who rejected a secular orientation and who insisted on the rigorous application of Quaker precepts, including humility, self-denial, and devotion to God. The worldly Friends generally held the upper hand until the Seven Years War brought the Quaker government in Pennsylvania to crisis in the 1750s. The Quaker "peace testimony" declared that to take up arms or support those who make war is a fundamental denial of Truth. The conflict between Quaker belief and the demands for war taxes, military service, oath-taking and the like opened the door for the more pious Friends in Pennsylvania, who undertook an aggressive reform movement to purify the Society of Friends by enforcing Quaker discipline much more strictly. By the 1770s the reform movement had reached full swing in New England, including Nantucket.[7]

The groundwork for the Nantucket meeting's reform activity of the 1770s was laid in the preceding two decades, beginning with the passing of the founding generation. Catharine Phillips, who visited Nantucket in 1754, described the "many worthy professors of Truth" who established Quakerism on Nantucket early in the century but noted that "most of these being removed to their eternal mansions, and their offspring not generally walking by the same rule, our Society was in a state of weakness, although the meeting was yet large." In particular, she thought, the youth "having been left much to themselves, and the work of the discipline having been neglected, they were unprepared for it, and ignorant of its weight and necessity; so that the meeting seemed in a dwindling condition, as to the life of the Truth."[8] Nantucketer Sarah Barney, writing to a Philadelphia connection in 1763, also complained of the "declension and backsliding in our Society," citing the "many pretenders to religion . . . but very few humble walkers and truely living members."[9]

As the older generation passed away, reform-minded leaders like Sarah Barney took over the women's meeting. For its first half-century the women's meeting was dominated by the small number of most prominent female Friends, most of them direct descendants or in-laws of founding mother Mary Starbuck herself. Under their leadership, the women's meeting generally deferred to the authority of the men's meeting, which was led in large part by their husbands, brothers, and brothers-in-law. Late in 1759, though, the clerk of the women's monthly meeting recorded in the minutes that "several who were formerly chosen visitors have declined it by Reason of Infirmity of Age."[10] The leading matrons who had served on the committees enforcing Quaker discipline were passing the torch to a younger generation. Some had already died, others would shortly; of the founding women, Dorcas Gayer Starbuck died in 1747, Dinah Coffin Starbuck in 1750, and Priscilla Starbuck Coleman in 1762. And in 1764, the two most important positions changed hands: long-time clerk Mehitable Pollard stepped down after serving the meeting since 1737, and equally long-time treasurer Hephzibah Hussey, whose first appointment was in 1726, also resigned.[11]

As the old guard faded from view, the women's meeting became considerably more active and autonomous. In December 1759, in fact at the very next monthly meeting after the aging visitors had declined reappointment, the women's meeting instituted its own preparative meeting to set the monthly meeting's agenda and take care of other business (the men's preparative meeting had first met in 1723). Nantucket women served as representatives to the regional Quarterly Meeting in Newport for the first time in 1764.[12] And the women's meeting began disciplining its own members and deciding who could and could not join the meeting. For example, in August of 1763 the women had referred the problem of Abigail Myrick's marrying out of meeting (i.e., marrying a non-Quaker) to the men's meeting, as they had done for decades. But two years later, after "treating with" Eunice Guinn for the same infraction but receiving "no satisfaction," the women went ahead on their own and disowned her.[13] In a striking indication of the extent to which female independence developed over that decade, in 1770 the men's meeting protested, writing to the Rhode Island Quarterly Meeting to ask whether the women's meeting had "proper authority to receive members and condemn offenders without the concurrence of or advice of the men's meeting." The male Friends must have been disappointed when the Quarterly Meeting upheld the women, replying that "it is the right of the women's meeting to receive or disown [its own] members."[14]

The assertiveness of the new women's leaders reflected in part the effects of an earlier shift in the leadership of the men's meeting. Until the 1740s, the same men who dominated the Quaker meeting were married to the women who dominated the women's meeting—and they were also the men occupying the key political positions in the town. But, after 1740, Byers tells us, as "the demands of the institutions increased, it was no longer possible for the same men to lead both institutions effectively," so a sort of specialization in town leadership developed.[15] At the same time, the conjugal correspondence between the men's and women's meeting diminished. Many of the leading matrons of the women's meeting were often related to but not necessarily married to the leading male Friends; other leaders of both meetings (notably Peleg Folger and Sarah Barney) never married at all.[16] Further splintering the dominance of the original Quaker oligarchy, factionalism erupted within the meeting itself in the 1750s over the disownment of three members and charges against a fourth for overstocking the island's common lands with more sheep than they were allotted shares for. The fifteen-year conflict was passed all the way to the London Meeting for Sufferings, the highest authority of the transatlantic Quaker community, which reversed the disownments and ordered the Nantucket meeting to avoid adjudicating property issues. The bitter Commons case eroded the consensus and harmony that the monthly meeting strove for, though it apparently did not threaten the broad Quaker cultural hegemony pervading the island as a whole.[17]

Another factor that may well have affected the balance of power between the men's and women's meetings was demographic. As in many other churches throughout New England for decades, it appears that the women in the congregation began to outnumber the men. Catharine Phillips had found in 1754 that on Nantucket "our Society was in a state of weakness," but she described how "[s]ome of the youth, *especially of our own sex*, appeared hopeful."[18] By 1781, George Churchman noted that the sex ratio of women to men was about three to one "among the youth" because, he explained, as the men were "mostly brought up to the seas, since the troublesom times & the declining of the whale business [during the Revolution], many of them have left this Island & gone elsewhere."[19]

There are hints that the numerical imbalance extended to the raised benches at the front of the meetinghouse where the ministers and elders sat, too. Unlike those in many other New England churches, women here may also have been disproportionately represented among the ministers. According to a mid-nineteenth-century account:

> In the latter half of the 18th century, a certain Quaker minister on the island had displeased some of the members of the meeting. A visiting Friend told the meeting in his testimony that as a sign and witness of God's displeasure of their attitude "the Lord would send a famine of the Word." The offending minister died in 1789 and . . . "there have been since that time but three men ministers who continued to reside on the island, one of whom never spoke, or but once or twice, except in meetings of business, after he was recommended. Exemplary, devoted, and in some cases able women, have mostly furnished the spoken word."[20]

Quaker women on Nantucket, it seems, had finally realized the potential for female initiative and authority implied by Mary Starbuck's example and more generally by Quaker theology and practice.

Heeding the exhortations of the numerous pious and reform-minded Friends visiting Nantucket from the Philadelphia region and elsewhere in the Quaker world, the leaders of the women's meeting channeled their new empowerment into a local self-purification movement. The men's meeting joined in the holy cause of rigorous self-scrutiny and reinforced discipline. By the 1770s, "local criticisms would fuse with a reform movement centered in Philadelphia to bring forth a radical transformation of the Nantucket meeting."[21]

The records of the Nantucket women's and men's monthly meetings reflect the new orientation: there were just 90 cases of Quaker discipline on the island between 1708 and 1770, but a whopping 602 cases from 1770 to 1795. Those cases included past as well as current offenders; the Nantucket Quaker leaders even pored through their records to identify transgressors who they thought had not been sufficiently admonished by their more tolerant predecessors.[22] Before the 1770s, almost three-quarters of those members charged with breaches of discipline were required only to acknowledge and condemn their actions in front of the meeting (an embarrassing enough proceeding but one without lasting repercussions), but the new generation of reformers was much less likely to forgive offenses. In 1774, the process of disownment was streamlined, and a formal "Book of Disownments" was begun in the following year; by the 1780s, over 80 percent of those disciplined were expelled outright. From 1770 through 1779, fully 130 men and 97 women were disowned by the Nantucket Society of Friends.[23] A small but telling number of other members, dismayed by the policy shift, even took the initiative to resign their own membership. At the same time, in response to wartime disruptions, dozens of Friends were also leaving Nantucket and the monthly meeting to settle elsewhere.

By 1796, when English Friend Martha Routh came to Nantucket, only a minority of the islanders (one historian calculates 18 percent, another estimates 30 percent) actually belonged to the local monthly meeting. Routh found that "the life of Truth was mournfully low" and reported that the number of "living members" was "so small as to be scarcely able to bear the weight of the dead." [24] Ironically, the new assertiveness and voice of the new Quaker women's leaders only contributed to rendering them and the ways of the Society of Friends irrelevant to the majority of Nantucketers, for the reformers' efforts decimated the membership and diminished the cultural force of Quakerism on the island.[25]

The Revolution itself both strengthened the resolve of Quaker reformers and ended up contributing to their ultimate irrelevance by the end of the century.[26] The conflict between England and its American colonies put all of Nantucket, Quaker and non-Quaker alike, in a peculiar and difficult position. Religious principle sharpened and justified economic self-interest and the realistic sense that the island itself was vulnerable to attack from either side, all of which combined in Nantucket's leadership's attempt to maintain neutrality. Though a few Nantucketers were active supporters of the patriot cause and another small group was avowedly Loyalist, it seems that most islanders followed suit and simply tried to wait the war out. It was a difficult balancing act, inviting hostilities from both sides, and it had catastrophic consequences.[27]

The island's prosperity depended almost entirely upon the whaling industry, most of the products of which were sold directly to London merchants. Most Nantucketers saw no reason to disrupt their profitable commercial relations or protest against the imperial mercantilist policies under which the local economy flourished. They generally ignored all the agitation leading up to war, opting not to join in the protests, consumer boycotts, and nonexportation pacts that so many other Americans found compelling. Nantucket's aloofness from the patriot cause was cast in bold relief by the dramatic events in Boston Harbor on 16 December 1773, when "Indians" boarded three ships and dumped the cargo of tea overboard; two of those ships belonged to Nantucket merchants (and prominent Quakers), brothers William and Francis Rotch. Nantucket was supposed to have been included in Parliament's 1775 Restraining Act, restricting American trade and commerce and prohibiting the New England colonies from carrying on their North Atlantic fisheries. However, thanks to testimony on the island's behalf from London merchants and no less a distinguished advocate than Edmund Burke, the prominent member of Parliament, Nantucket's whalefishery was specifically exempted.

Added to Nantucket economic self-interest—and to the suspicions of many mainland patriots that the islanders were "rank Tories," like their coreligionists in Philadelphia—was the Quaker "Peace Testimony," which required pacifism and forbid oath taking. In 1774, Nantucketer Joseph Mitchell, serving on the "Epistle Committee" of the New England Yearly Meeting, put his signature to the group-issued statement declaring that "the commotions rising in the British Dominions as they are in their consequences outwardly calamitous, may be feared as marks of Divine Displeasure."[28] In 1775, after the outbreak of the war, the Nantucket Monthly Meeting read aloud an epistle sent out by the Philadelphia meeting that termed patriot authority "a usurpation of power."[29] Over the course of the war, forty-six Nantucket men were disowned for violating the Quaker peace testimony, mainly for going to sea "in an armed vessel." Memorials sent from Nantucket to the Massachusetts authorities invoked religious principle as well as the island's vulnerability in their pleas:

placed on an Island, detach'd at least Thirty miles from any part of the Continent, whose production is insufficient to support one third part of its Inhabitants with the necessaries of life, and laying open to any Naval power, to stop all supplies with a small armed force by sea, the only channel by which we can receive them; The Inhabitants are the greater part, of the people call'd Quakers, whose well known principles of Religion, will not admit of their taking up arms in a military way in any case whatever; all these circumstances consider'd we hope will influence you, to advise us to pursue such measures, as to avoid giving any just occasion of offence to our fellow subjects this, or the other side of the Atlantic.[30]

But revolutions do not admit of neutrality. The American patriots on the mainland and the British who dominated the surrounding seas both demanded that Nantucket choose sides or suffer the consequences. The islanders were forced to confront the war almost immediately when, following the battles at Lexington and Concord in April 1775, dozens of loyalists and other mainland connections sought safety by fleeing to Nantucket. Others on-island predicted the future more accurately and chose instead to head inland to escape the hostilities. In May, a hundred provincial soldiers arrived to commandeer whaleboats and other supplies for the patriot army. (Sixteen-year-old Tory sympathizer Kezia Coffin Jr. recorded in her diary indignantly, "them rebel Low lived fellows have been exercising by the mills to-day—Drumming & fifeing!" and "God save George the King!" Some weeks later, she greeted news of the Declaration of Independence with the exclamation, "Horrible!")[31] In the ensuing months, British warships stopped in for provisions or protection from stormy weather. Suspicious, the Continental Congress ordered a complete boycott on trade with Nantucket as early as July 1775, although that September the Massachusetts Provincial Congress responded to Nantucketers' pleas and began to allow them to bring in provisions and send out whaling voyages by applying to the Falmouth (Cape Cod) Committee of Safety for permits.

The island managed to scrape by for the first three years of the war, launching whaleships and importing supplies, with—or often without— the requisite permits. Coffin recorded in her diary several smuggling trips to Long Island made by the man she would marry, Phineas Fanning, including one he made in November of 1775, when he arrived "after going through everything but death."[32] With audacity on a grander scale, some Nantucket shipowners operated their whaleships directly out of London during the war. In October 1778, Benjamin Franklin and John Adams reported that the British whaling fleet in the south Atlantic was manned by "at least 450 of the best seamen . . . almost all being from Nantucket and Cape Cod."[33]

But in 1778 severe weather caused extensive damage to island crops and livestock; the winter of 1779–80, which islanders called simply "the hard winter," was worse yet.[34] Perhaps more damaging, the American-French treaty of May 1778 brought the British navy into the waters surrounding the island, to intercept the French fleet and also crack down on colonial privateers operating in the area. In September 1778, British forces laid waste to much of the village of New Bedford and then plundered the island of Martha's Vineyard. The panicked Nantucketers feared (rightfully) that they were next, but in the nick of time the British troops were ordered back to New York. Another attack was threatened in 1779 and occasioned much confusion and distress; this time, though, the island was apparently saved by contrary winds. Despite assurances from British commanders in Newport and New York (agreements that prompted the Massachusetts authorities to charge Nantucket with attempting to negotiate a separate treaty), Loyalist privateers as well as American ones continued to roam the area, capturing and burning Nantucket vessels through 1780 and 1781. Nantucket ships, laden with profitable cargo, were inviting targets, and Nantucket sailors were captured, imprisoned, or pressed into service by both sides.

Obed Macy, who had witnessed the Revolution as a young man, wrote later that he "might fill a volume in enumerating the various vicissitudes and embarrassments, to which the people of this devoted island were subject during the war." In his *History of Nantucket*, published in 1835, Macy described how "[t]he seafaring people, whose necessities exposed them to the casualties of war, suffered very much," reporting that by war's end the "inhabitants [were] driven from their wonted line of business into a state of inactivity" and that "[t]he town exhibited the appearance of a deserted village rather than of a flourishing seaport." Describing the vessels lining the shore "stripped to their naked masts" and the "losses by plunderers, the almost total stoppage of all business," he concluded, "At the commencement of the war, there were more than an hundred and fifty vessels belonging to the place; at its close there remained only two or three old hulks." Despite the islanders' politically suspect attempts at the time to stay neutral, in hindsight Macy insisted, "It will not be doubted that Nantucket paid as dearly for the independence of our country as any place in the union."

Macy's accounting enumerated at some length the human, in particular the familial, costs of the war. "Many were cut off, in the prime of life, by the prison-ship, by disasters at sea, in battle, or by other causes produced by war," he recorded. "Many bereaved and aged parents were left to mourn over their offspring, snatched from them by violence or disease in distant parts and under distressing circumstances. . . . The war had made many widows and orphans, who had now to endure the miseries of famine, in addition to the poignant grief occasioned by the loss of their dearest relatives. . . . Many mourning families were thus driven to beg their bread." In the revolutionary crisis, the contribution of Nantucket's women was as crucial as it was characteristic. With "rigid economy," "patient endurance," and home manufactures, Macy wrote, "the female part of families . . . frequently supported the whole domestic circle; evincing the strength of their attachment and the value of their services to those, on whom they themselves were wont to depend for protection and support." In 1835, looking back from his early Victorian vantage point, the Revolutionary upset in the Nantucket gender order seemed to Macy a world turned upside down indeed.[35]

Macy may have exaggerated slightly in claiming that "only two or three old hulks" survived the war, but Nantucket's whaling industry was indeed devastated by the Revolutionary conflict. At least 85 percent of the island's fleet had been captured or destroyed by war's end in 1783. Peace did not immediately bring prosperity: the devastating loss of capital, exclusion from the British imperial system, and weak domestic demand for whale oil slowed recovery of Nantucket's economy. A Boston merchant reported to John Adams in 1785 that the Massachusetts whalefishery was "almost at an end" and predicted that "another season will probably finish it." Events proved him wrong, but the war's effect was certainly catastrophic: economic historian Gordon Bjork judged that "the whalers of Nantucket were probably a group of people more hurt by the aftermath of the Revolution than any other group."[36]

Distress inspired desperate measures, including, for significant numbers of Nantucketers, even abandoning the island and seeking opportunity elsewhere. It was not the first time: Crevecoeur had described the removal of several families to North Carolina and Maine in the 1760s, remarking that "emigration is both natural and easy to a maritime people."[37] Other islanders had left the island earlier in the century as well. Those expatriates usually took up farming, lumbering, and other land-based enterprises on the mainland, keeping in close touch with and even acting as "peripheral suppliers" to their island relatives. Now, in 1785, several whalemen, shipowners, and their families relocated to pursue the fishery from the village of Hudson in New York state, about a hundred easily navigable miles up the Hudson River, which had been settled a few years earlier by other Nantucketers. Another group (less reconciled to the new American nation and

"New Bedford, 50 years ago," 1855 lithograph by Charles Taber and Co. after the oil painting "Old Four Corners, New Bedford," ca. 1855, by William Allen Wall. The figure seated in the one-horse chaise in the center foreground is the prominent whaling merchant William Rotch Sr., originally of Nantucket, who moved to New Bedford in 1795. His son, William Rotch Jr., is the portly figure directly under the flagpole. Courtesy of Old Dartmouth Historical Society–New Bedford Whaling Museum. (Neg. 13522)

less optimistic about non-English markets for whale products) took themselves, their ships, and their whaling expertise to Nova Scotia. Still others were lured to Milford Haven, Wales, by the promise of subsidies and protected access to the lucrative London market, offered by an English government anxious to expand its share of the international fishery. Perhaps the single most important Nantucket whaling merchant, William Rotch, was disappointed in his negotiations with the Board of Trade in London and moved on to France in 1786, where he tried to establish a whaling outpost in Dunkirk. Though supported by the French government, the experiment only faltered along until another revolution put an end to it and sent the Nantucketers home in 1793. In the end, perhaps the most significant removal was also the shortest when, in 1785, William Rotch sent his son, William Jr. over to New Bedford to restart the mainland branch of the family whaling business begun there by his father twenty years before. Rotch himself would follow in 1795, his partner and son-in-law Samuel Rodman in 1798.[38]

Not everyone left the island. Reluctance to give up on either Nantucket or the industry so "peculiarly suited" to local "genius" (as Macy put it) finally paid off, as the island's fishery and other maritime enterprises began to pick up toward the end of the 1780s, assisted by government subsidies and the development of new markets for whale oil, candles, and bone. Island whalemen plumbed the rich whaling grounds in the South Atlantic and, in 1790, rounded Cape Horn and began exploring (and exploiting) the wealth of the Pacific—greatly extending the length of their voyages as a consequence. Along with their seafaring brethren from Salem, Boston, New London, and other New England ports, some Nantucket mariners also found that independence freed them to pursue speculative ventures into the far reaches of the world, from Sumatra to St. Petersburg, Smyrna to San Salvador, as the Napoleonic wars tied up European fleets. "Neutral trading" was competitive and risky but the possibilities were great—until shut down again by Jefferson's Embargo in 1807 and another war with England, the War of 1812.[39]

According to Obed Macy, by the end of the 1780s there were not enough men on Nantucket to fill the crews of the growing number of whaling and merchant voyages, so "it therefore became necessary to resort to the continent for a considerable portion of each crew, whence there were brought some Indians and a great number of negroes. Many of the latter took up their residence here, and became the heads of families."[40] By 1790, there was actually a net increase in Nantucket's population, a trend that continued for some decades. Importantly, though, many of these newcomers to the island were not old-stock Yankees. Maritime laborers and small-scale artisans attracted by employment opportunities, Irish, Portuguese, African-American, and by the early nineteenth century even South Sea islanders, they were a mixed and largely impoverished group. And hardly any of them were Quaker. By 1830, in fact, no more than 10 percent of Nantucketers belonged to the monthly meeting, the rest worshipping instead (if they chose to do so at all) at one of the Congregationalist, Methodist, Universalist, or African churches.[41] As one result of the forty-some years of war and economic and political disruptions, Nantucket's population and island society became considerably more diverse.[42]

The Quaker cultural synthesis had already begun to fracture from within, even before the Revolution began. Wartime privations and dislocations both exacerbated that process and, in the aftermath of the conflict, added new external pressures. At the end of the Revolution, Obed Macy remembered,

> Blest with the enjoyment of peace, all were glad to turn their attention from the distressing scenes of the late conflict to the pursuits of peaceful life. But the effects of the war on the manners and customs of the inhabitants yet remained. Coming from various parts of the world, where they had been detained as prisoners, or whither they had wandered as exiles from their native home, many had brought with them the fashions and the morals of other nations. The change was observable in their dress and mode of living; it added materially to their expenses, and sometimes led to permanent injury. The great [post-war] success in whaling, though it pretty generally overbalanced the increased expenses in living, had no tendency to lessen the immoralities which were unhappily introduced into society.[43]

Nantucket's whalefishery and other maritime industries rebounded vigorously, if erratically, after the Revolution. However, Quaker cultural dominance did not make a similar comeback, and its diminution had significant consequences for the emotional lives of Nantucket's maritime women.

The spearhead of change, it seems, was as much cultural practices and preferences as economic pressures and political events. The end of the century brought to the island a broadening of cultural resources, which reflected in part the broadening of the local community through both out-migration and immigration and in part the diminishing impact of Quaker discipline and erosion of Quaker influence throughout Nantucket society. The preoccupations of the Quaker reformers and the infractions for which the Nantucket Monthly Meeting disowned members in the last quarter of the eighteenth century help us identify the new attitudes and practices they found so alarming—rightfully so, for these attitudes and practices fundamentally altered the local cultural landscape.

When John Woolman visited in 1760, he had greatly admired the "plainness of life" on Nantucket, as did Crevecoeur a decade or so later.[44] But, at the Revolution's end, the men's monthly meeting unhappily assessed the situation and found an alarming "shortness" on the island in the "education of children, attendance at our religious meetings, and [in maintaining] a strict care in keeping to plainness of language, behavior, and apparel."[45] In 1781, visiting Friend George Churchman noted in his journal that he and his companions "dropt" a "few words" of caution to a Nantucket woman "concerning a large gilded Looking-glass with a curious scolloped frame, & touching some other delicacies." He was pleased that "the woman friend . . . took the hints kindly."[46] Another off-islander, Elizabeth Wilkinson, similarly criticized Nantucketers' dress and jewelry.[47] Numbers of Friends were "treated with" informally on occasions that did not make it into the official records, such as when Kezia Coffin Jr. recorded in her diary in January of 1777 (when she was just short of 17 years old) that a delegation of Quaker matrons advised her "not to dress so fashionable."[48]

Consumer temptations were certainly available on the island by this point. Until the outbreak of Revolution, Nantucket had been prospering and commercially well connected, and at least a few of the non-Quaker elite liked to display evidence of their success. Thomas Brock, whose rise from "mariner" to "merchant" to "Esqr." (i.e., gentleman) is documented in the town registry of deeds, became one of the richest men on Nantucket, worth £16,192 when he died in 1750. The inventory of his estate listed an impressive £338 worth of silver, including seventeen serving spoons, a dozen teaspoons, and a set of silver breeches buttons. The stock of dry goods he carried in his store was also impressive: linen imported from Holland or Germany, fine handkerchiefs from England, and striped "Bengal" silk from India. The wardrobe of another Nantucketer, John Clark, enumerated on his death in 1768, included among many other items two beaver hats, silver shoe and sleeve buckles, and a waistcoat of "fine red Broad Cloth, Gold lace."[49] The experts on Nantucket arts and crafts, Charles Carpenter Jr. and Mary Grace Carpenter, attribute the "conservative predilection of most [colonial] Nantucketers" to "maritime tradition and Quaker preferences." But they also caution that it would be a mistake to "carry this idea of a Nantucket plain style too far." By the middle of the eighteenth century, they report, "quite a few Nantucketers [owned] the best of personal and home furnishings in the latest style. . . . Nantucketers may have been isolated and insular, but they knew what was going on in Boston and Philadelphia and London."[50] A 1769 letter from Benjamin Franklin to his "Loving Cousin" Kezia (Kezia Coffin Sr.), for example, described "a pair of very nice snuffers" along with "some very neat candlesticks . . . with a pretty contrivance to push up from the bottom" that he planned to send to her from London.[51]

However, just seven cases of the ninety-seven women disowned in the 1770s, the most intense and busiest period of reform on the island, involved material possessions. Five of these disownments were for outright theft (e.g., "unlawfully covetting and taking her neighbors goods"). Only two women were expelled from the meeting for violating Quaker rules of "plainness" with material goods: Franklin's cousin Kezia in 1773, not for her candlesticks but rather for a spinet; and Susanna Folger in 1777 "for her dress and address, and her children wearing gaudy apparel." [52] Just two men were disowned for parallel offenses: Jethro Pinkham for "keeping a violin to play upon" and Tristram Coffin for his "appearance in dress & address" (as well as his "frequenting the meeting of another society").[53] Given the relatively few charges concerning "plainness," it appears that, despite the occasional verbal hand-wringing, even reform-minded island Quakers were willing to overlook minor indulgences in the good things in life made possible by Nantucket's commercial success. In this they resembled the reformist Quakers in the Mid-Atlantic states, who also rarely prosecuted members for only these sorts of consumer offenses.[54]

Behavior was another matter altogether. A few young Nantucket Quakers were charged with "fornication" or having a child too soon after marriage, a few others for being inoculated for smallpox. Still more were charged with "disorderly walking" (which could refer to any kind of non-Quaker behavior) or, more specifically, with playing cards, frequenting places of diversion or attending "frolics," excessive drinking, violent or abusive behavior, profane swearing, defaulting on debts, theft, or taking up arms during the Revolution. Several women and men were disciplined for simply "being at a marriage [not their own] performed by a priest," and two men were charged with insulting the Quaker elders who were routinely inspecting their clearness for marriage. Kezia Coffin's offense was not just acquiring a spinet, but for what she did with it: "Teaching her Daughter or Causing her to Bee Taught To Play Thereon Contrary to the advice of Friends." [55] Coffin's disownment, though, did not put a stop to the behavior nor protect the daughter in question. Kezia Coffin Jr. recorded in her diary several months later, "Kezia [Starbuck] and I went to Esqr. Hussey's. Mrs. Hammatt & Lucy were there. Messrs. Fanning & Hammatt & Peleg Coffin came . . . Capt. Thatcher came afternoon & played on the Spinnet. My spinnet is at Esqr. Hussey's carried there because the [F]riends were displeased with its being at Father's. Thatcher plays tolerably well. Eve Mr. Johnson & Burton & Eben Calif were there[,] they danced play'd on the violin &c. . . . We had a variety of music — spent a very agreeable afternoon & eve." [56]

Music and dancing posed particular problems for pious Friends on-island as elsewhere. In the 1770s, fifteen women and at least nineteen men were disciplined for "frequenting places where Fiddling and dancing were carried on" or the like; some were "partakers" of the entertainment, too.[57]

As Englishman Thomas Clarkson explained in 1808, "[Friends] are of the opinion that, if instrumental music were admitted as a gratification in leisure hours, it would take the place of many of these serious retirements and become very injurious to their interests and their characters as Christians."[58] Thus, on her deathbed in 1804, Nantucketer Sarah Coffin Barker told her husband that she had "been disturbed by some People dancing," which had "afflicted" her "much." She declared, "Poor Creatures I would not exchange my situation (a Bed of languishing) for theirs & the whole World."[59]

Barker was "thankful" that in her youth she had been "left under the care of my dear Aunts, who were concerned to keep me in plainness of Speech & Apparel, and restrain me from idle, rude company," although she admitted that "at times I have thought it hard I could not go out in Company; but I have had to see they knew what was best for me." Now, with the moral authority of imminent death, Barker tried in turn to convey what she thought best for the "precious Lambs commited to my care" (four sons, a niece, another young woman who had lived with her for several years). She repeatedly exhorted them and the others attending her bedside to attend meeting, keep to plainness, be sober, seek retirement, avoid bad company, "forsake the World & all its lying vanities," "read good Books & not bad ones, as they will steal away the mind from that which is good," and in particular "read the Holy Scriptures."[60]

According to the account of her final two-week ordeal, recorded by her devoted husband, Barker seems to have distributed her counsel fairly indiscriminately upon both her male and female relations. However, there was clearly a gendered pattern to the assessment of offenses and discipline leveled by the Nantucket Monthly Meeting to which Barker belonged.[61] In the decade of the 1770s, twice as many women as men were disciplined for fornication (ten vs. five). Men only were charged with drunkenness, profanity, joining the Freemasons, refusing to pay debts, and, during the Revolution, privateering or going to sea on armed vessels.[62]

This gender differentiation in breaches of Quaker discipline is also suggested in the off-island Friend George Churchman's account of a visit with one Nantucket family during his stay on the island in 1781. Churchman recorded in his journal how "at one place a young woman who had married out of the Order was much tender'd & broken at the expressing of a few sentences which touched her Condition; and her brother, who came into the room whilst we were sitting, (appearing in a libertine way, & lately come from sea), the propriety of trying to cleanse his Ways by taking heed to the inspeaking word, was mention'd to him; . . . at which he seemed struck, & his countenance fell."[63] Here the young woman, charged with loving unwisely, is portrayed as passively sitting inside a room; she is "tender'd & broken" by the minister's admonition. Her brother is described in much more active terms and with a greater range of opportunities (even for misbehavior): he has just "come from sea" and into the room; he is accused of "libertinism"; and when cautioned, he is "struck" and his countenance "falls." Quantitatively and qualitatively, Quaker discipline and description seem to have reflected newer concepts of sex differences then spreading in the eighteenth-century Anglo-American world—ideas that associated women with passivity, delicacy, and emotion and men with activity, strength, reason, and choice.[64]

What bothered the reforming Friends on Nantucket by far the most, again like their coreligionists elsewhere, were violations of the Quaker rules regarding marriage. Both women and men were miscreants in this, but it was proportionately more of a female offense. Five women and two men were disowned for marrying first cousins, which violated the Quaker ban against marriage with near relations. Most significantly, over half of those ninety-seven women disowned in the 1770s (fifty-nine of them, or 61 percent) were expelled for marrying non-Quakers, as were sixty-six (51 percent) of the men.[65] Kezia Coffin Jr. herself, despite being warned by the matrons of the women's monthly meeting in January 1777, went ahead with her plans and that April married her non-Quaker suitor, Phineas Fanning (who was also an off-islander, and a Long Island lawyer to boot), for which rebellious act she was promptly disowned.[66] Kezia Jr., like so many other young Nantucket women and men, followed her heart right out of the Quaker meeting.

Quaker reformers on- and off-island alike were so insistent on marriage to other believers in the Truth only because they were convinced that the future of the Society of Friends depended on children being raised properly in the faith in Quaker households. (Some Nantucket Friends were even disowned for placing their sons in apprenticeship to non-Quakers; in one 1778 case, the men's meeting cited "the danger and great disadvantage that must attend the education of our youth when under the tuition and influence of those who are of different sentiments in religion from us.") Hindsight shows that the reformers' concerns were not misplaced. A rising rate of exogamous marriages did threaten Quaker family life, in part by ending the generous practice of conferring birthright membership on children born to even one Quaker parent. In 1774, the New England Yearly

Meeting answered queries from Nantucket and other monthly meetings in the region by deciding that children would be automatically considered Quakers only if *both* parents were members.[67] Given the importance of marriage to the Society's generational continuation as well as its help in ensuring the daily practice of piety, the new leaders seemed to have raised the standards and attempted to exert even more control over the personal life of youthful Quakers.

The flood of marriages out of meeting serves as striking notice that the more strict application of Quaker discipline failed. Martha Routh met on Nantucket with a "very comely young woman," then near death, "who, about eleven months before, contrary to her mother's and friends' advice, had gone out in marriage with one not of our Society. When so ill that her dissolution appeared near, she requested to see me. . . . [W]e went, and sat by her; an affecting time indeed it was; her near relations were in great distress, and her own was almost insupportable, begging earnestly in a plaintive language, that seemed almost to pierce my soul, for a little longer time, that she might be favoured to feel a hope of reconciliation to the Almighty, and to her friends; saying, she was afraid she had been deceived, in thinking she had a right to choose for herself, in the step she had taken."[68] In the end, though, very few Friends returned to the fold. Almost none of those disowned for marrying out of meeting, it seems, came round to thinking, as did this young woman, that they did not have a right to choose for themselves.

But why did so many of the Nantucket Quaker youth choose to flout this particular rule, which was so important to their birthright faith? For some young men and women, the "plain" speech, the "thee" and the "thou," became irksome, the old-fashioned, sober dress unappealing, and the prohibition against music and other diversions oppressive to their spirits. But these offenses were more often secondary charges tacked on to the major breach of discipline: marrying out of meeting. Many of the miscreants—especially the young women—chose to express their rebelliousness primarily by exercising marital choice, which by the final decades of the century virtually guaranteed their expulsion from the Society. (A choice it clearly was: the relatively equal numbers of women and men disowned for this offense suggest that demography was not directly responsible. Presumably those women and men could have married each other.) Much historical research has documented how, in the late eighteenth century, lots of young people were not listening to their parents, their ministers, or their elders of all sorts. Indicators such as a dramatic rise in premarital pregnancy and in the number of daughters marrying out of birth order demonstrate just some of the forms and range of a widespread revolt in generational relations that accompanied the political revolt, part of what literary historian Jay Fliegelman has aptly termed the revolution against patriarchal authority.[69] Here, the major preoccupation of the Nantucket monthly meeting with punishing exogamous marriage, combined with the increasing frequency with which the island's young Friends were marrying non-Quakers, serve as indicators not only of the threat that such marriages posed to the local Society of Friends and of the extent of youthful rebelliousness; it also signals the arrival on Nantucket of new and revolutionary understandings of love and marriage.

For all its being a rather small and barren island, Nantucket was no backwater. The scale and importance of its whalefishery ensured its centrality in the eighteenth-century North Atlantic economy and the regular arrival and dispatch of hundreds of vessels a year. Its vitality as a Quaker center also sent "Public Friends" on and off the island in a steady stream. Nantucket's involvement in the American Revolutionary war, disruptive as it was, highlighted its location right in the thick of things. Nantucket was vitally linked into Atlantic-wide networks of commerce, religion, and politics; those channels to the outer world delivered all sorts of people and printed materials to the island. It might seem surprising that such a prosperous town would not publish its first local newspaper until 1816 (and that one failed; it was not until 1821 that Nantucket had a reliable, regular local newspaper).[70] But this gap serves as further evidence of the island's cosmopolitanism: there was no local paper earlier in part because the islanders found newspapers, magazines, books, and the like from Boston, New York, and London both of interest and readily available.[71]

With the erosion of Quaker influence, more and more young islanders were susceptible to the radical new ideas about love and marriage expressed in much of the imported print material. Not coincidentally, this was exactly when dramatic reassessments of family relationships, gender differences, and emotional life became issues in widespread political and intellectual debates, part of the multilayered, transatlantic struggle over the fundamental issues of authority, vulnerability, freedom, equality, and obligation in human society that marked the Age of Revolution.[72] Relationships between wives and husbands, children and parents, reason and feeling, duty and love, virtue and corruption, individualism and interdependence were all being reconsidered, in part through what literary historian Cathy Davidson calls a "reading revolution," the combined effects of an unprecedented flood of publications and rapidly rising literacy rates. Traditional religious literature and the classics were losing readers to newer genres, especially widely read conduct books and enormously popular sentimental novels and poetry.[73] Poor dying Sarah Barker's pleas that her children avoid "bad books" [74] now appear all the more poignant when we understand the broader context, because in one sense she was right: the incursion of this literature on Nantucket did indeed irrevocably subvert the religious principles and the way of life in which Barker so ardently believed. The new preoccupations and themes are clearly discernible in the writings of three young, late-century Nantucket women: Eunice Swain, Abigail Gardner Drew, and Phebe Folger.

In the manuscripts collection of the Nantucket Atheneum (now the island's public library), there is a tantalizing document identified only as "Journal/Poetry 1776–1788," a somewhat ragged assemblage of large sheets of paper sewn together. In it, someone (almost all of it appears to be in the same handwriting) transcribed bits of poetry, one piece dated 1784; lists of marriages, funerals, and ship arrivals in 1788; copies of two personal letters, both dated 1776; extracts from the "Journal of the brigg lark" from its 1781 whaling voyage; and random notes. Three of the poems are signed "Eunis Swain," and internal evidence suggests that, of the two Eunice Swains living on Nantucket in the late eighteenth century, the author was the one born in 1765, who married James Hussey in 1786. She would have been only 11 when the two letters were written (assuming the dates refer to when they were actually composed), which seems a bit youthful for their content, but, as described in Chapter 2, Nantucket girls did sometimes marry young, even in their early or mid-teens.[75] This Eunice Swain married James Hussey in August of 1786 and had her first child in 1787, which might explain why the collection breaks off in 1788. Despite all the uncertainty surrounding its provenance and author, though, this document is rich and revealing.

One of the two letters, the one dated London, 25 July 1776, seems like an attempt at epistolary fiction, particularly given the absence of any personal detail and the male narrator. With almost comic precision, it recapitulates what historian Ruth Bloch has identified as pervasive themes in the popular fiction of the period: objections to "oppressive patriarchal authority," here represented stereotypically through the "cruelty of authoritarian, status-seeking fathers forcing their sacrificial offspring to reject true love or to accept odious suitors against their will," and at the same time challenges to "corrupt and artificial manners associated with aristocratic fashion and foreign taste."[76]

Written in a male voice, the letter tells "Dear Sister" a romantic and harrowing tale: "The tears flows from my Eys to think my parents was so Cruel and hard hearted to Turn there Backs upon mee because I loved A girl that was Disagreable to them." In an explicit critique of class snobbery, the narrator's beloved exemplifies humble, modest virtue to a divine degree: "O Could I be in her Company an hour it would be more to mee than thousend Elce Whare[,] for she is like some goddes or Angel[,] she is worthy of any lord . . . My parents slighted her Because She was poor But She hath that that will go Before Beauty or treasure." Separation from this celestial being has forced the narrator's fall from grace into the restless, profligate, solitary life of a sailor: "O how Can they [i.e., his parents] lay their heads Down in peace . . . They have a Son Rambling in the Wide World Spending As he goes and is Becom A poor hermit upon Earth. . . . once I had Negros to wait on mee But Now the Best of my liveing is Salt Beaf And hard Bread. . . . I am obliged to make the seas my home whare the Billows are a foaming over my head whare I can find No rest." The letter ends with a conventional appeal to God's mercy, but the religious framework invoked is markedly different from the pious submission and resignation Lydia Almy tried to achieve, described in Chapter 2. Here, the narrator attributes the lovers' separation and suffering not to a divine mandate but to parental tyranny. "It is my parents that has Brought me to this," the narrator explains to his sister, and predicts, "You Never will see mee Again for I am to beat the Seas As long as I Live and I Expect they will prove my grave." The letter ends on a somewhat perfunctory note of piety: "I hope he that Made mee will Carry mee through this troublesome world and land mee Safe in That Desired Port whare all tears may be wiped Away and trouble Shall be No more So I remain your Affectionate Brother untill Death. . . . Finis."[77]

On another page of the journal, Eunice wrote (or copied) a short, unattributed poem that described the kind of love the (probably) fictional young sailor felt for his sweetheart:

> Love is the most tender passian of the Mind
> The Safest refuge Inocence Can find
> The Safe Director of ungarded youth
> Armd with Strong Virtue and Securd by truth

Heaven into our Cup this Drop has thrown
To make Natures Draught of life go Down

Eunice here expresses faith that, rather than competing with love for God,
human love (that "most tender passian") can be divinely granted, protec-
tive of virtue, and morally uplifting.

But, in a distant echo of the Christian narrative combining love and
martyrdom, Eunice also finds that even divinely authorized love entails
suffering. The second letter transcribed in the journal, dated "Nantucket,
March ye 30 1776," amply demonstrates the risks in graphically physical
language:

> My Dearest and best beloved . . . I was Glad to hear of your Arival for
> it was 3 months and 8 Days before we heard of you In which time my
> poor Soul was overwhelmed with Sorrow for you and my heart Was
> greived When I found Every body was Doubtfull of you. . . . O my
> Dear you Are Not Sensible of it[.] I often Pourd my Soul to God on
> your behalf all bathed in tears[.] I prayed heartily to god with a Sin-
> cear heart that if it was your misfortune to be Cast Into the Devouring
> waves . . . that when your Departing Soul might leave your mortal body
> that he Would be pleased to receive you Into the arms of his mercy that
> you might be Ever happy. . . . wee Are att a Distance and the foam-
> ing billows a roreing betwixt us but my heart is Allways with you for
> my love is such that rivers Cannot quench for you are all Ways with
> me though I Dont See your person you are allways within my heart
> Which makes mee so Discontented and will make me forever unhappy
> and misarable.

The bottom of the page is torn off. It is not clear to whom Eunice might
have written this letter (it was dated a full decade before she married), or
even for certain if it was fictional or intended for a real recipient, although
the inclusion of some details about an upcoming trip to the mainland hint
at the latter. Nonetheless, the letter eloquently testifies to the notion that
love entails an ecstatic union of two hearts, to a newly acceptable intensity
of passion in human love, and to the sharp, even surgical, sense of misery
in separation and potential loss.[78]

Like many of her contemporaries on both sides of the Atlantic, Eunice
Swain clearly felt that "sensibility," the capacity or tendency to be strongly
affected by emotion, was no bad thing. In a late-century reaction against
the Enlightenment emphasis on order, moderation, and reason, the Ro-

mantic writers and thinkers validated unfettered emotion and imagination, awe, and even terror, as essential to creativity, authenticity, personal
freedom, and their ultimate goal, to experience the transcendence of the
"Sublime," the infinite and unfathomable power and chaos of the universe.[79]
For women like Eunice Swain, the local diffusion of Romantic sensibility
set in motion a subtle but unmistakable reordering of the relationship between secular and religious feeling.[80] The way in which Lydia Almy subordinated human love to her religious faith no longer worked for the countless young women who celebrated emotional intensity, granted it divine
sanction, and located it in love for another human being.

Abigail (Nabby) Gardner Drew's diary, written circa 1799–1818, even
more poignantly attests to the effect of sensibility on courtship and the
potential for its frustration in marriage. Like Eunice Swain's journal, Nabby's diary is a fragmentary compilation probably sewn together long after
it was written. In Chapter 2, extracts from the diary demonstrated the
sociability that was characteristic of eighteenth-century Nantucket, the
interaction with family members, neighbors, and friends in and out of each
others' households many times a day. Interspersed with those predominantly cheerful listings of daily activities are passages of much more intense retrospection.

One such reflective section seems to be a reminiscence of Nabby's
courtship with Gershom Drew, the young man she eventually married.
The account sounds all the bell notes of the new passionate kind of human
love that literally took control over her body and even haunted her dreams:

> The summer after I was Thirteen I had the Happiness to fall again in
> the Company of Gm. Drew, but so far was he from takeing any notice of
> me that he even paid his [word heavily crossed out] to another young
> Lady at the same time. It was then I was oblig'd to have Recourse to
> my sisters advice to keep me from betraying a Passion which I had long
> with difficulty laboured under — ... I used often dream of him at my feet,
> then would start out of my sleep & speak out in Raptur he is come, then
> perceive myself & fall asleep & dream of his being with me at a house
> where wee were both to Reside, talking in the most tender manner ...
> from them [i.e., the dreams] I should derive considerable comfort, &
> reflect at times why I should dream of him and flatter myself at one day
> or other haveing the happiness to find my Dreams come true. ... I was
> on the point of despairing & Mr D— says permiting another jentleman
> to share my heart when he suddenly slipt in & took his place. But I will

not allow that, for I thought my affections too much fixed on another to give any encouragement to Mr B.

The emotional communication of soulmates promised by this sort of total love even transcends language and renders it unnecessary: Nabby remembered how "Mr D. was to[o] respectfull, or too bashfull as yet, to make an express declaration of his passion. However, wee converced by a language much more inteligible, & more to be credited than that of words; & when wee come to express our sentiments found that wee had nothing new to tell." [81]

Nabby married Gershom on 16 April 1795; she was 18, he was 21. Their first child was born on 28 October 1800; they would have five more. Gershom's father is identified in various town records as a blacksmith or a trader. When he died in 1809, he had risen to become one of the wealthiest men on Nantucket, with an estate valued at $15,934.93. Gershom, the oldest son, was named one of the two administrators of his father's estate and is identified on those documents as a mariner. Gershom and at least four of his six brothers went whaling out of Nantucket and, later, New Bedford, Gershom on a ship commanded by Nabby's brother at least once.[82] Gershom probably made at least one merchant voyage as well, because he died in August of 1826 from yellow fever in Port au Prince, a frequent destination for New England merchant mariners in the Caribbean. Nabby never remarried and lived until the ripe old age of 91.[83]

Theirs was not a perfect romance. On 31 March 1802, Nabby jotted in her diary, "A very serious evening this[—]what will not malice & envy do[.] But why should I muse on such things[?] Have I not found long ere this that the world is all deceit—O how awful is the State of Sinner, then let me try to become the Immortal part within." And on July 2 that same year, "O! if wee could but know how many bitter disappointments wee are like to encounter by trusting too much to the flattering Syren[,] wee should certainly be more cautious & avoid the snare."

Nabby never specifies the particulars of her distress. Several undated entries, though obscure, hint at its extent and its location within her marriage. "To be chained to the oar is a blessing in comparison with what I endure," she proclaimed darkly, continuing,

O how much do we undergo with pleasure for those wee esteem and how many trials and difficulties we entertain even with rapture for the one wee love. [B]ut to be sepperated from them & compeled to live (or waste ones day I may say) with a person whom you cannot love or esteem and at the same time wear a mask of tenderness so forren from the heart for the sake of keeping peace and to blind the world, is wretchedness itself—how many hours is spent in reflecting on my unhappy situation . . . that might be improved to form the soul anew to happiness & life, were it not for a continual fiend in my bosom that robs my home of ev'ry enjoyment. People in general find most comfort at home, but for me if I have any it must be sought else where.

In her unhappiness, Nabby here highlighted several elements of the new conception of marriage: the notion that conjugality should involve reciprocal rapture, the misery of enforced separation from one's true soulmate, the demand for intimacy that inspired fear of deception. Nabby's ruminations also offer evidence of another novel and important ingredient of the emerging Anglo-American culture of domesticity: an understanding of "home" as the geographic center of emotional life, envisioned as a place of comfort and personal authenticity.[84]

At one particularly conflicted moment, Nabby reflected,

Nothing can give me more satisfaction than to find I am not wholly despised by the one who in spite of all the command I have over myself possesses my heart. I look on myself intirely free as to any engagement with those who by their own conduct & behavior have forfeted all title to my probation and regard and should think myself intirely at liberty to act myself in every sense but never will I do a thing which will hurt my Child or my own Honour no I would sooner commit suicide than by runing from one evil (like a Coward) fall in another much worse—

The line between Nabby's understanding of her own life and the plot of so much contemporary fiction seems blurred here indeed. The ubiquitous plot in much of the new sentimental fiction turned on courtship and seduction, in which pure, innocent young women underwent often violent challenges to their chastity and virtue while seeking love and marriage. A number of historians have argued that such story lines held direct political resonance; as Jan Lewis put it, "the young woman's quest for a suitable husband and her attempt to navigate between the eighteenth century's Scylla of overweening power and its Charybdis of seductive liberty was the nation's plot as well."[85] Through such stories of implicit or sometimes explicit challenge to patriarchal tyranny and aristocratic decadence, this literature generally "upheld the freedom of individual choice," but it also "sanctioned the authority of truly loving parents and husbands and celebrated the virtues of emotional interdependence within a family life that was deemed the foundation of the social order itself."[86] To Nabby, free choice and the authority of true love were deemed the essential foundation of a personal happiness to which she felt entitled. Her personal dilemma was being caught between maternal obligation, spousal betrayal, and extramarital love. In her formulation, her own life was a variation on the sentimental fiction's main themes.

One particularly significant aspect of Nabby's testimony is her explicit (if eclectic) allusions to literature to help her work through her personal dilemmas. She transcribed in her diary all sorts of extracts from prose and poetry that offered solace or explanation. "Seek in love for aught but love alone," she quoted on one page, and later, "All our disappointments are proportion'd to the warmth of our expectations, and when our fears and apprehensions are once alarm'd, the effect is as painful to us as the Passion of Jealousy, when once set on float by never so trifleing a Cause (Trifles light as air are to the Jealous Confirmations strong as proof of holy writ)." At one moment she copied out a breezy stanza she attributed to Swift: "Whence proceeds this weight we lay, / on what detracting people say. / Their utmost malice cannot make / Your head or tooth or finger ach, / Nor spoil your [illegible] your face / Or put one feature out of place." At other moments she was equally likely to cite the Biblical texts of sermons she found particularly meaningful, such as 12 Romans 9: "Let love be genuine; hate what is evil, hold fast to what is good" (though until her conversion to Methodism in 1807 or 1808, the religious references in her diary seem a little sparse). The way in which bits and pieces that Nabby heard or read are interwoven in her diary with entries describing her own activities and memories suggests that literary themes not only particularly resonated with her life but also provided her with a concrete script. She drew on the themes not only because they reflected her experience but actually to shape it.[87]

Phebe Folger's 1797 commonplace book offers especially rich confirmation that the broad cultural revolution had arrived on Nantucket—even among the remaining Quakers, among most of whom the fire of reforming zeal had, by the end of the century, died down. Through her transcriptions of literature that she admired and in her own writing, Folger reworked nearly all the themes and concepts tentatively expressed in Eunice Swain's modest, awkward efforts and in Nabby Drew's tormented diary entries.

Phebe would marry the following year; perhaps it is no surprise that much of the content of her collection addresses the nature of love and marriage. On one page, in one typical instance, she copied out a substantial portion of American author David Humphrey's 1786 epic poem titled "The Happiness of America." The excerpt Phebe selected included the following lines:

> O thou sweet passion whose blest charm connects
> In heav'n's own ties, the strong and feebler sex!
> Shed thy soft empire o'er the willing mind,
> Exult, adorn and purify mankind! . . .
>
> To love submits the monsters of the main,
> And ev'ry beast that haunts the desert plain;
> But man, alone, the brightest flame inspires,
> A spark enkindled from celestial fires.
>
> Hail, hallow'd wedloc! purest, happiest state!
> Thy untry'd raptures let my song relate:
> Give me, e'er long, thy mysteries to prove,
> And taste as well as sing the sweets of love!

Literary critic Jay Fliegelman explains that Humphrey's poem paraphrases John Milton's widely read "Hymn to Wedded Love" in a "national affirmation of the sacred character of affectional and voluntaristic marriage," in order to "extoll a nation in which lovers listen to their hearts." Phebe would certainly have understood the political import of Humphrey's epic. No doubt the influence ran the other direction as well: the overlapping political and religious references must have reinforced the idealization of mutual passion in marriage on a personal level too. Here, again (even in the writings of a pious young Quaker woman in such good standing with the Nantucket Monthly Meeting that it had just appointed her mistress of the newly organized Quaker school), we can trace the subtle displacement of love for God by love for a human being, a view in which the two are understood not as competing but rather as reinforcing each other.[88]

In what may be her own skillfully constructed poem, "The Sailor, an Elegy," Phebe translated the new Romantic ideas about a passionate and sacred human love into a maritime context specifically appropriate for Nantucketers:

> The Sailor sighs, as sinks his native shore,
> As all its les'ning turrets bluely fade;
> He climbs the mast to feast his eye once more,

And busy fancy fondly lends her aid.
Ah! now, each dear, domestic scene he knew,
Recall'd and cherish'd in a distant clime;
Charms with the magic of a moonlight view,
Its colours mellow'd, not impair'd by time.
True as the needle, homeward points his heart,
Thro' all the horrors of the stormy main;
This, the last wish with which its warmth could part,
To meet the smile of her he loves again.
When morn first faintly draws her silver line,
Or Eve's grey cloud descends to drink the wave;
When sea and sky in midnight darkness join,
Still, still he views the parting look she gave.
Her gentle spirit, lightly hovering o'er,
Attends his little bark from pole to pole;
And, when the beating billows around him roar,
Whispers sweet home to soothe his troubled soul.
Carv'd is her name in many a spicy grove,
In many a plaintain-forest waving wide;
Where dusky youths in painted plumage rove,
And giant palms o'er arch the yellow tide.
But lo, at last he comes with crowded sail!
Lo o'er the clift what eager figures bend!
And hark, what mingled murmers swell the gale!
In each he hears the welcome of a friend.
'Tis she, 'tis she herself she waves her hand!
Soon is the anchor cast, the canvas furl'd;
Soon thro' the whitening surge he springs to land,
And clasps the maid he singled from the world.

There is much going on in this poem, but three elements seem especially relevant here. First is the nature and purpose of the sailor's relationship with "her he loves." She is the one individual "he singled from the world," which signals how exclusive as well as how intense their connection is. Their love is capable of transcending vast distance, time, and the ocean, "lightly hovering o'er" land and sea, "attend[ing]" his little bark from pole to pole," and most importantly, soothing his soul when troubled by stormy seas both literal and figurative. In exotic foreign lands, the sailor withstands the threats (and temptations?) offered by "dusky youths in painted plumage" by invoking his beloved and their love through the act of carving her name into "many a spicy grove" (which also legitimates American imperialism by inscribing American gender ideals onto foreign landscapes, but that is another story).

The second point, closely related to the first, is the recasting of gender definitions accomplished in the poem. Conspicuously, the elegy is for the sailor alone, and he is the poem's protagonist. Until the final seven lines of the poem, his beloved is nothing more than a disembodied "gentle spirit," a "parting look," a "smile" and a "murmur." She is, in effect, the essence of their love itself. The maid herself and her life on shore are both notably absent, portrayed throughout the poem merely as projections of the sailor's desires, needs, and destiny. This is a strikingly male-centered formulation of love that is as narcissistic as it is romantic. At work here are new ideas about sex differences emerging in the late eighteenth century: the association of women with a set of qualities and values that included modesty, sympathy, tenderness, piety, charity, and self-sacrifice, while men and reason became more exclusively associated with rationality, bravery, activity, and self-interest. In Phebe's poem, it is to "clasp the maid" whom the sailor loves, an act of possession, that brings him back to home and stability ("springs to land"), which also suggests a third aspect of the poem that is relevant here: the linking of the sailor's heart and "her he loves" with "sweet home" and, through the image of the compass, purposeful direction.

In November of the following year, 1798, Phebe Folger finally married and put these ideas to the test of experience. She was then 27, and she took for her spouse Samuel Coleman, a Quaker sailor some three years her junior. As a young boy in 1779, Samuel had moved from Nantucket to the village of Hudson, New York, with his parents and several other island families; he returned to the island to get married with full approbation of the Nantucket Monthly Meeting. Early in 1800, Samuel was off commanding a merchant vessel when Phebe wrote to inform him, "I have kept school Days and evenings . . . and have above thirty schollars . . . the business is fatiguing but [I] am willing to contribute my mite to accellerate that happy period when we shall not be obliged to separate." She continued, "I want to know whether thou thinks of coming home directly from New York or of getting a Freight for some other place[.] I hope thou wilt pursue the path most for thy honour and advantage, tho I should be willing to sacrafice almost every other advantage to see thee." She signed her letter, "thy loving Wife." [89]

Nearly a decade and three children later,[90] Samuel was still going to sea—and Phebe was still holding onto her ideals of conjugal love and companionship. She told Samuel "I am very lonesome . . . thy absence grows more insupportable than it used to be," though she reported, "I want for nothing but thy company." Asking rhetorically "Why should so much of our time be spent apart? . . . Is the acquisition of wealth an adequate compensation for the tedious hours of absence?" she supplied her own answer, declaring firmly, "To me it is not." [91] Phebe's complaints may have had some effect, as Samuel appears to have seen the force of her argument. (Whether he shared her sentiments, we do not know.) At any rate, less than a year after Phebe wrote that letter, Samuel informed the Nantucket Monthly Meeting that they were moving to Hudson. He requested and was granted a certificate of removal for himself and family.[92] They took their by then four daughters to New York State and seem to have begun a life together on land, farming, running a gristmill, and raising sheep.[93]

In her correspondence with her husband, Phebe portrayed herself as the protagonist of her own life. She was not willing to serve merely as the reflection of her husband's needs and interests; she expressed her own needs and desires along with a sense of entitlement to their fulfillment. But the way Phebe defined those needs and desires—as can be seen in the writings of Eunice Swain and Nabby Drew as well—reflected the erosion of traditional Quaker values and the incursion of new Romantic ideas. Human love was now, even on Nantucket, a "sweet passion" and "a spark enkindled by celestial fires" that could "exult, adorn and purify mankind!" when contained within marriage, "hallow'd wedloc! purest, happiest state!"

As a consequence of the crumbling of the Quaker cultural synthesis under the pressures of reform, revolution, and Romanticism, the particular accommodation between seafaring and society developed on colonial Nantucket broke down by the end of the century. Nantucket women—like other women in the region and, indeed, on both sides of the Atlantic— were turning to new cultural forms and literary models to make sense of their lives. Their strength and assertiveness, so celebrated by Crevecoeur, was now diverted into a Romantic idiom that set a higher priority on intense feeling than on competence in the prosaic affairs of daily life. As it traditionally had, the ideal conjugal relationship was supposed to include companionship and partnership. But now it additionally required reciprocal rapture, exclusive possession of each other's hearts, and a divinely

Mrs. Phebe Folger Coleman, ca. 1850.
Courtesy of the Nantucket Historical Association

sanctioned, transcendent unity of souls. If based on "true" love, marriage also promised comfort, moral uplift, even a kind of salvation, blended with intimacy and personal authenticity that were best achieved at home. No longer held in check by Quaker discipline, recast and reinforced by broad political resonance, and inflated by Romantic sensibility, personal expectations and the emotional stakes in marriage were rising high.

The American whaling industry would also, in the new century, expand exponentially in scale and scope, sending tens of thousands of men on hundreds of ships into the farthest reaches of the globe on voyages that lengthened to three, four, even five years at a stretch. Maritime women were increasingly caught between growth and change in the whalefishery and the spreading ideals of Romantic conjugality. As we will see in the following chapters, the fundamental reworking of the relationship between religious faith, love, and marriage initiated at the end of the eighteenth century would deprive nineteenth-century maritime women of the perspectives that had enabled their colonial foremothers to accommodate the female share of the risks and costs of seafaring. The emergence of an even newer ideal of female domesticity, one centered on an intact nuclear family comfortably ensconced within a private and pious home, would even further complicate the experience of the "Cape Horn widows" whose husbands rounded the tip of South America and plied the Pacific, the Indian, and the western Arctic Oceans.

As the whalefishery expanded, Nantucket's dominance would be challenged and, by the 1820s, eclipsed by the mainland port of New Bedford, the beneficiary of the transferred capital and experience of Nantucket émigré William Rotch and his family partnership. Crevecoeur observed that Nantucketers often "emigrated like bees, in regular and connected swarms."[94] We too will follow William Rotch, Phebe and Samuel Coleman, and Nabby Drew's husband Gershom and his seafaring brothers over to the mainland, to continue our exploration of the interaction between the whalefishery and local gender practices as these developed in uneasy tandem.

NEW BEDFORD &
THE NINETEENTH-CENTURY
WHALEFISHERY

In 1832, the New York author Joseph Coleman Hart (who had island connections through his mother) visited Nantucket. Two years later, he published a novel entitled *Miriam Coffin; or, The Whale-fishermen*, which drew on what he had seen, heard, and read about the island and its whalefishery (including, apparently, Crevecoeur's *Letters*). For the epigraph on the title page of his novel, Hart chose an excerpt from Edmund Burke's 1775 romantic testament to Nantucket whalemen's bravery and energy:

> Whilst we follow them amidst the tumbling mountains of ice, and behold them penetrating into the deepest frozen recesses of Hudson's Bay and Davis's Straits—whilst we are looking for them between the Arctic Circle, we hear that they have pierced into the opposite region of Polar cold—that they are at the Antipodes, and engaged under the frozen Serpent of

the South. Falkland Island, which seemed too remote and romantic an object for the grasp of national ambition, is but a stage and resting-place in the progress of their victorious industry. Nor is the Equinoctial heat more discouraging to them than the accumulated winter of both the Poles. We know, that whilst some of them draw the line and strike the harpoon on the coast of Africa, others run the longitude, and pursue their gigantic game along the coast of Brazil. No sea but what is vexed by their fisheries—no climate that is not witness to their unceasing toils![1]

Early in the first chapter, Hart himself praised "that sort of *half quaker—half sailor* breed, to be found nowhere else on earth" in similarly romantic terms, describing Nantucket men as "fishermen upon a grand scale, [who] pursue and conquer the monarch of the seas in distant and remote waters." "The females of the island," Hart told his readers, "are modest, virtuous, and agreeable, and thrive with commendable industry at home."[2]

Despite his benign introduction, Hart focused much of the book's energy on decrying the dangers of women's assuming power during the absence of their husbands. The title character, Miriam, was recognizably based on Nantucket's Loyalist female merchant Kezia Folger Coffin. But where Crevecoeur had lauded "Aunt Kesiah" sixty years before, Hart now described her as "ambitious to the last degree," with "volcanic fires . . . smouldering in her bosom." The fictional Miriam dupes her husband into granting her power of attorney over his affairs just before he boards ship, saying to herself,

> "Must we, because we are women, for ever be confined to the distaff and the spinning-wheel—to the nursery and the kitchen? Pshaw!—I will assume such a front and presence as may become a woman with a masculine spirit. Men shall point to me, and cry out as I pass—'*That is Miriam—Miriam Coffin!*'—and children shall remember my greatness. . . . Let me but be firmly seated in the saddle, and I will ride such a race as shall make men—ay, the boasting men—stare with unfeigned wonder!"

Her ambitious plans, predictably, do not work out the way she intended. According to Hart's story, Miriam Coffin dissipates her husband's hard-won fortune on unnecessary luxuries and unsound speculations while he is away at sea. At the same time, she alienates her neighbors with brazen profiteering during Revolutionary War shortages. She even coerces her daughter into marrying her ally, an unscrupulous lawyer from off-island. At the end, when Miriam's husband returns to find his affairs in a state of utter disaster, he upbraids her, " 'thy unchastened ambition, not content with reasonable gains, hath ruined thy husband stock and flock!—Get thee gone to thy kitchen, where it is fitting thou should'st preside:—Go, go to thy kitchen, woman, and do thou never meddle with men's affairs more!' " [3]

Though well received in 1834, Hart's novel did not make it into the canon of great American literature; the work is remembered now mainly as one of Melville's sources of information for *Moby-Dick*. But Hart's tale of old Nantucket can be instructive to us, too, for the half-century voyage from Crevecoeur's praise to Hart's melodramatic criticism marks a sea change in the way in which women's relationship to the whaling industry and community was conceptualized. The Nantucket Quaker sea-wife, recognized in the eighteenth century as strong, competent, and vitally involved in the whalefishery, was by the 1830s disparaged in the popular imagination: *Miriam Coffin* dramatizes a new worry about women's capacity for destructiveness when left alone on shore. At the same time, the bold, brave whalemen of the Burkean epigraph triumph over climatic extremes and their leviathan prey without any acknowledgement of women's shoreside support of the industry. The novel reflects how real maritime women were increasingly caught between dramatic expansion in the whaling industry and new domestic ideas about women's work and place in society.

By the time Hart visited Nantucket, New England's whaling industry had recently undergone an important transition in location and scale. Though Nantucket was still heavily dependent on the fishery, the industry's center of gravity clearly shifted to New Bedford in the mid-1820s. An unfortunately placed sandbar prevented the larger whaleships from entering Nantucket harbor even when assisted by "camels," flotation devices affixed to their sides. More basic yet, the island lacked the resources of the mainland: it was more expensive there to outfit vessels and ship crews and to disperse the whale products at the end of the voyage after the domestic market developed. By 1823, New Bedford's fleet and its output exceeded Nantucket's, and the town on the Acushnet River became the nation's leading whaling port until the industry's precipitous decline near the end of the century.

The fishery's movement from the island of Nantucket to New Bedford on the mainland corresponded to a complicated transformation in the ways in which the industry and its community were organized. The numbers of men employed, the number and the size of vessels in the fleet, the distance and the duration of voyages—all rose exponentially after the conclusion of the War of 1812. Rather than restricting themselves to the Atlantic on trips lasting less than a year, more and more Yankee whalers were rounding Cape Horn or the Cape of Good Hope and spending three, four, even five years exploiting the rich whaling grounds in the less familiar and often even more hazardous Pacific, Indian, and western Arctic Oceans. This expansion and the related restructuring in the industry's organization gradually altered the material conditions and rhythms of life within the maritime communities of southeastern New England.

At sea, the pursuit of whales became increasingly a specialized activity, with vessels specifically built for the purpose and crewed by men considered different from other sailors. By the middle of the century, the global extent, much longer voyages, competition and cost-cutting measures in the industry, and availability of other employment options on land combined to render whaling a considerably more unpleasant, harsh, and exploitative occupation for the bulk of the crew and exacerbated the division between the foremast hands and the officers. Vicious intimidation and violent discipline became much more commonplace. Recruitment at home became more difficult and, abroad, desertion became rampant; the agents and captains had to ship new men to replace those lost in ports around the world. The agents also reached beyond the immediate Nantucket and New Bedford areas to find skilled career mariners to command their ships, recruiting from all of southeastern New England and the Northeastern coastal region. In contrast to the high turnover rates and instability of much of the crew, the officers—skilled specialists in the capture and processing of whales—now tended to prolong their careers over much more of their adult lives.

The anarchic tendencies, strains, and fissures developing in the fishery were counteracted, in part, by a common understanding of gender roles and family responsibilities that was shared by the agents and owners and the professional whalemen on whom they depended. For centuries, seafaring had been strictly the preserve of men, with women left behind on shore, and whaling was certainly no exception to the rule. But in the nineteenth century this particular sexual division of labor—men at sea, women on shore—became associated with the new concepts of sexual difference that, as described in Chapter 3, had emerged during the Revolutionary era. The new Romantic ideas about manhood and womanhood were grafted onto economic and social organization in a particularly geographic conceptualization of gender, which defined men as rational actors, producers, and providers operating independently in a wide public world and women as emotional dependents located in a private home—the classic tenets of domesticity. Joseph Hart's description of Nantucket whalemen and their women at home in his novel *Miriam Coffin* demonstrates how easily the domestic conceptualization of gender seemed to fit the local arrangements.

A number of historians have documented how preindustrial patterns of social and economic organization centering on the family and household broke down rapidly in the fifty years after the Revolution. Economic expansion and reorganization physically severed residences from manufactory, warehouse, and retail shop in commercial centers, while urbanization, migration, and increasing population diversity shattered traditional forms of authority and fragmented community. Nineteenth-century Americans tried to make sense of the transforming world around them by means of a whole host of new (or newly sharpened) conceptual categories that set in opposition public and private, work and home, production and consumption, head and heart, active and passive, male and female.[4] This chapter examines how these evolving gendered assumptions were incorporated into the social relations of work within the American whalefishery and in the regional community, now centered on New Bedford, that supported it.

Although relatively young among New England's seafaring towns, New Bedford rapidly became one of the most prominent in the nineteenth century. It originated as the small settlement called Four Corners, on the banks of the Acushnet River within the township of Dartmouth, a farming community established back in the 1650s by Quakers driven out of the Plymouth and Massachusetts Bay colonies, who were later joined in the area by a number of equally dissident Baptists. Joseph Russell (1719–1804), a prosperous Quaker farmer and landowner in Dartmouth, may have begun as early as 1755 to send out one or two small vessels from the fine natural harbor at the mouth of the Acushnet River for short whaling voyages; a decade later he had four at sea. In 1765, the energetic Nantucket merchant Joseph Rotch selected Four Corners as an advantageous site for pursuing the whalefishery on a large scale. Under the impetus of Rotch's capital, experience, and enterprise, the industry took off. The little settlement, renamed Bedford and later New Bedford, flourished. By 1775, some fifty whaling vessels and a few merchant ships were sailing from the village, which now numbered over a thousand residents and claimed its own candleworks, ropewalks, warehouses, and wharves.[5]

The Revolution devastated New Bedford along with much of the rest of the region. In retaliation for the American privateers' operating out of Buzzard's Bay and taking shelter in New Bedford's harbor, on 5 September 1778, some four thousand British soldiers and sailors burned more than seventy ships and much of the town. In a measure of the extent of local distress, the General Court of Massachusetts appropriated £1200 for New Bedford's relief in 1780. The economic depression following the war compounded the difficulties. In 1786, Massachusetts's total exports amounted to only one-quarter of what they had been twelve years before, and by 1789 only one-third of the whaling fleet of 1773 had been restored.[6]

But the chilling effects of the war on maritime enterprise did not last long. The total whalefishing fleet owned in Massachusetts almost doubled between 1794 and 1802 and increased another 50 percent by 1810.[7] New Bedford, already a third larger than its parent community Dartmouth, was incorporated as a separate town in 1787, and according to the 1790 census, 3,313 inhabitants claimed residence there. By 1792, they could read their first local newspaper and, the following year, could get their mail direct via a weekly stagecoach from Boston. By the beginning years of the nineteenth century, they could put their money in the Bedford Bank, choose between three schools, and worship with Methodists or Unitarians as well as Quakers, Baptists, or Congregationalists.[8]

President Jefferson's Embargo Act of 1807 and especially the War of 1812 again wreaked havoc on the maritime activities of New England in general and of New Bedford in particular. Eighty years later, local historian Leonard Ellis described the effects of the hostilities on his town:

Bedford village was in a sad condition when the second war with England was brought to a close. The wheels of industry had long since ceased to move, and her fleet of vessels that had brought wealth and prosperity had been driven from the ocean. Her shops and shipyards were closed, the wharves were lined with dismasted vessels, the port was shut against every enterprise by the close blockade of the enemy, and the citizens wandered about the streets in enforced idleness.[9]

Again, the idleness did not last long. The end of the war ushered in a period of remarkable growth and prosperity in New England's maritime enterprises. Coastal trading, deep-sea trading, and whaling all rebuilt and gathered momentum in the late teens and twenties, and surged in the 1830s, 1840s, and 1850s. In particular, New Bedford boomed as the value of the American whalefishery's output rose, from about $1.2 million per year in the 1820s to a peak almost ten times that total in the 1850s. Whaling and manufacturing of whaling products ranked right behind shoes and cottons in the Massachusetts economy. Returns of over 100 percent profit were not uncommon. The size of the fleet expanded proportionately, both in the size and the numbers of vessels. Crews ranged in size from eighteen men on the smaller schooners to an average of twenty-five men on the barks and twenty-nine men on the ships. In 1855, some 466 vessels from New England (over 300 of them from New Bedford alone) hunted in fifty-one different whaling grounds, covering six of the seven seas. The most lucrative grounds were in the Pacific, Indian, and western Arctic Oceans, and the oil and bone was often transferred and sent home on merchant ships, so that the whalers could stay out on voyages that now averaged almost four years (forty-five months) in length.[10]

New Bedford grew by leaps and bounds, its population climbing to 7,592 in 1830 and to 16,443 in 1850. Capping the period of rapid expansion and development, it was officially designated a city in 1847. Neighboring villages scattered through the scrub oak and pine forests, rocky hills, salt meadows, and along the numerous inlets, coves, bays, and marshes of the southeastern corner of Massachusetts—Tiverton, Russell's Mills, Westport, Smith's Mills, and Padanarum to the west; Acushnet, Long Plain, and Freetown to the north; Mattapoisett and Rochester to the east; even to some extent the towns on Cape Cod and the islands—came to depend on New Bedford (and Fairhaven, just across the river) as their main commercial center. In return, these communities supplied the city with capital for investment, lumber for building ships, food to provision them with, and more than a few farmboys (potential captains) anxious to go to sea.

New Bedford easily betrayed its whaling connection and testified to the fishery's prosperity. Shipowning families like the Rotches, the Rodmans, the Swifts, and the Grinnells displayed the wealth they made from the industry in the fine houses built along County Street, "beautifully shaded with ancient elms," along Cottage and Sixth streets, and in the neighborhood known as Acushnet Heights—all up on the hill overlooking the bustling town, the harbor filled with ships, and "magnificent views of country, river, bay and islands."[11] Melville was only slightly exaggerating when he proclaimed, "nowhere in all America will you find more patrician-like houses; parks and gardens more opulent, than in New Bedford. . . . In

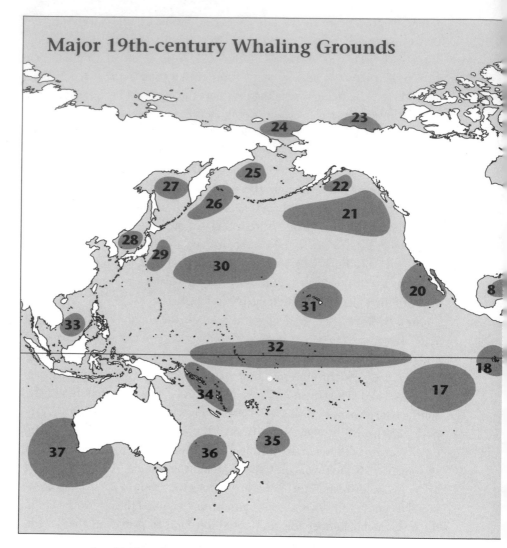

Major 19th-century Whaling Grounds

1   Hudson Bay
2   Cumberland Sound
3   Commodore Morris
4   Western
5   Western Islands (Azores)
6   Madeira
7   Cape Verde
8   Gulf Drop
9   Twelve forty
10 Carroll
11 Saint Helena
12 Pigeon
13 Tristan
14 Falkland Islands
15 Coast of Chile
16 Callao
17 Offshore Grounds
18 Galapagos
19 Bay of Panama
20 Coast of California
21 Northwest Coast
22 Kodiak

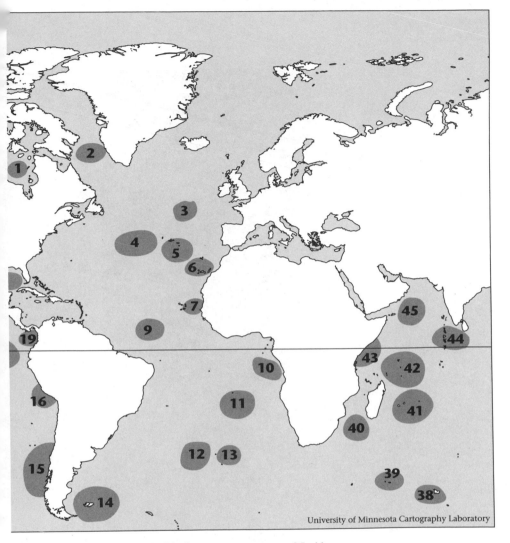

"View of New Bedford from Fairhaven" ca. 1845. Created by prominent local artist William Allen Wall, this painting conveys the bustling, burgeoning nature of New Bedford, which was soon to be incorporated as a city. Courtesy of Old Dartmouth Historical Society–New Bedford Whaling Museum (Neg. 5535)

"View of the River at Russell's Mills [Dartmouth]," ca. 1870, also by William Allen Wall, depicts the more bucolic character of the rural areas around New Bedford. Privately owned, reproduced by permission (New Bedford Whaling Museum Neg. 5510)

summer time, the town is sweet to see; full of fine maples—long avenues of green and gold. . . . So omnipotent is art; which in many a district of New Bedford has superinduced bright terraces of flowers upon the barren refuse rocks thrown aside at creation's final day." He pointed to the "iron emblematical harpoons round yonder lofty mansion" as proof of the source of New Bedford's success, and explained "All these brave houses and flowery gardens came from the Atlantic, Pacific, and Indian oceans, harpooned and dragged up hither from the bottom of the sea."[12]

Native son Llewellyn Howland remembered, many decades later, as a child walking down the hill from County Street into the city. Looking down the main thoroughfare leading to the harbor, Union Street, he saw "etched on the sky" a forest of "masts and yards of ships." Howland recalled how, as he and his father descended, the buildings became smaller and older, "the intervals between cross-streets shortened, and the flagstones underfoot, and the beach-cobble paving, became more worn and irregular." With the vivid impressions of a small boy, Howland remembered that "every block of buildings had its own particular smell—dry goods, millinery and apothecary shops to start with—followed by coffee, molasses and food frying; then liquor, tobacco, fruits and vegetables, and at the end as we came out onto broad Front Street, running north and south across the wharf-heads, the soft hazy air was heavy with a pungent reek of whale and sperm oil expressed by the hot June sun from the tiers of casks lined up along the wharves. Sharpening rather than blunting this prevailing odor there came a whiff of Stockholm tar as we passed north by one of the [sail lofts] where . . . we caught sight of a rigger at work. . . . A few steps farther on, it was the acrid flavor of white oak shavings drifting out from a cooper shop that tickled our noses." [13] Howland's redolent memories provide a striking contrast to Crevecoeur's account from a hundred years earlier (quoted in Chapter 1); the stench of whale oil that had hung over all of colonial Nantucket was now confined just to the waterfront district in New Bedford, a pungent indication of increased specialization within the industry and differentiation in the supporting community.

New Bedford offered not only a variety of scents but also a variety of human beings. In the eighteenth century, the seasonal departure of the fleet had left the colonial whaling ports disproportionately female. In mid-nineteenth-century New Bedford, however, perhaps only 10 percent of the city's male residents were actually at sea at any one time. And the comings and goings of ships periodically brought in waves of additional men from around the World. Melville, for one, relished the city's startling diversity. Even allowing for artistic license, his evocative description may not have been far off the mark:

> Any considerable seaport will frequently offer to view the queerest looking nondescripts from foreign parts. Even in Broadway and Chestnut streets, Mediterranean mariners will sometimes jostle the affrighted ladies. . . . But New Bedford beats all Water Street and Wapping. In these last-mentioned haunts, you see only sailors; but in New Bedford, actual cannibals stand chatting at street corners; savages outright . . . it makes a stranger stare. But besides the Feegeeans, Tongatabooars, Erromangoans, Pannangians, and Brighgians, and, besides the wild specimens of the whaling-craft which unheeded reel about the streets, you will see other sights still more curious, certainly more comical. There weekly arrive in this town scores of green Vermonters and New Hampshire men, all athirst for gain and glory in the fishery. . . . Many are as green as the Green Mountains whence they came. [14]

But the mingling described by Melville did not imply that New Bedford was a melting pot. The social geography of the booming city reflected trends in the social relations of work within the fishery, in particular the sharpening distinction between the career mariners who commanded the ships and most of the rest of the crew. A local booster and publicist,

New Bedford's commercial district, looking down the hill toward the waterfront: "View looking east down Union Street from Purchase Street," ca. 1870, stereograph by Stephen F. Adams. Courtesy of Old Dartmouth Historical Society–New Bedford Whaling Museum (Neg. 12232)

A typical New Bedford waterfront scene, with casks of whale oil lining the wharves: "Bark *Massachusetts*, drying sail," 1868, stereograph by Stephen F. Adams. Courtesy of Old Dartmouth Historical Society–New Bedford Whaling Museum (Neg. 2316)

the Reverend Frederic Denison, wrote in 1879, "Ah! no one can know New Bedford outside and inside without visiting the Tars' Retreat or Seamen's Senate at Kelley's on Union Street, and being introduced to the Chronometer Club when in full session. There you will get your latitude and longitude made up from lunar observations and dead reckonings that are sure to put you on your prosperous voyage. Every member of this Club, in tongue and memory, moves on gimbals and so keeps a level head. . . . Every member . . . has harpooned the North Pole, and can try out of Arctic fogs and ice floes." [15] Denison's cozy account highlights the two elements that distinguished the professional whalemen: their exclusive knowledge of navigation and ability in shiphandling and their specialized skill and success in producing profitable cargoes of oil and bone. In particular, the experience of command at sea marked a man as a "master" and conveyed a great deal of social capital back on land in "Sperm City."

Rev. Denison conspicuously did not describe, in his *Illustrated New Bedford,* the "low-gabled taverns" named Cape Horn Inn, the Spouter's Friend, the Greasy Luck Inn, Crossed Harpoons, the Trypot Inn, and the Homeward Bound.[16] But, in a 1930 speech commemorating the hundredth anniversary of the evangelical New Bedford Port Society, a subsequent local eminence, Zephaniah Pease, described the more notorious areas of the waterfront a hundred years before, the "hideous and abhorred and unhallowed spots," precincts which, he claimed, "were shunned by the natives." Pease alluded to

> the locality known as "the Marsh" at the foot of Howland Street, "Chepachet" where Buttonwood Park is now located, "Hard Dig" on Kempton Street, "Dog Corners" at Allen Street. . . . Here were boarding houses where sailors were robbed, saloons dealing out delirium and death, dance halls and houses where female harpies reigned. . . . Respectability avoided these districts. . . . Even the constabulary left the dwellers in these precincts to their devices, and human life was not safe there after dark.[17]

Pease's obvious biases, along with the coordinates he lists, demonstrates the class-based understanding of respectability that differentiated both rank within the whalefishery and the social mapping of nineteenth-century New Bedford. Although it was not his point, Pease's rhetoric also makes clear that the prosperity that whaling brought to New Bedford was not equally shared.

Between the Revolution and the War of 1812, maritime enterprise expanded within familiar colonial patterns of organization. In the New Bedford area, as on Nantucket and elsewhere, masterminding the far-flung activities were general merchants who carried out all the basic commercial functions, serving as exporters, wholesalers, importers, retailers, ship-owners, bankers, and insurers. The family constituted the basic unit of commerce; the merchants knew personally most of the individuals with whom they dealt, and business relationships and combinations of capital were often cemented by marriages. Since merchants relied heavily upon the captains or shipboard business agents to handle transactions in distant ports, most preferred to have family members or men of long acquaintance command their vessels. These captains usually supplemented their cash wages with "privileges," their own share of the ship and cargo. Many of the wealthy merchants of the eighteenth and early nineteenth centuries were retired master mariners who had made good on such ventures.[18]

By way of example, Captain Isaac Cory and his sons were the lead-ing merchants in the village of Westport Point (to the west of New Bed-ford) from the 1760s to the mid-1800s, variously involved in shipbuilding, coastal and West Indies shipping, fishing, and whaling; they also oper-ated the local general store and, briefly, a cottage weaving venture. In the Corys' account with a James Manchester from 1780 to 1800, listed on the debit side are charges for goods and usages like bread, candles, pork, old spectacles, "shugar" and "1 turn with my scow." On the credit side are entries such as "By part of days work onloading Brig Boards &c" and "By your son James wages to Burmuda as per Portage Bill."

James Jr. served again on another West Indies voyage, this time on the Corys' schooner *Rhoda*, from December 1801 to March 1802. When the *Rhoda* was converted for whaling in 1803, many of the crew, including James, converted as well; James went on at least two whaling voyages on the *Rhoda*, in 1803 and 1804. In the following decades, as the Corys trans-ferred more of their capital into whaling, the patterns of family and com-munity employment appear to have persisted. Fourteen men, all of local origin, set sail in July 1822 in the Corys' schooner *Polly & Eliza* for a year-long whaling voyage "to the Western Islands [the Azores] & elsewhere." Among the fourteen, there were two pairs of surnames that probably indi-cate kinship: the captain and an "oarsman" (foremast hand), who may have been his son or nephew; and the cooper and a boatsteerer (both skilled positions, here at the same lay), who may have been brothers or cousins. During the voyage, the wives of the captain and one mate and a female relative of the other mate (at least she had the same surname) requested and received advances; at the end, two seamen's fathers were paid their sons' wages. One of the fathers was paid another crew member's wages, too. The request from the mate's wife conveys the flavor of the small community and her familiarity with the agent: "Sir I inform you that I am at present In want of a little meet and can have a nice Pig for the Cash the man is in want of the money by the 25 of this month to settle his rents . . . you sent me word . . . that you would send to the North River this spring and purchase me some Porck but it will acomodate me much better to have this Pig."

The Corys appear to have adopted the same familiar style of paternalism as practiced on eighteenth-century Nantucket, providing goods or money as advances charged against the seamen's earnings. They also provided less tangible support, especially in the form of information about the men at sea. Both are illustrated in a letter to Isaac Cory, circa 1800, from a seaman's wife: "Sir, perhaps you will think it strange my sending to you for money again so soon . . . [torn: something about a bill for carpentry, which took most of her supply of cash] . . . if you could let me have 02 [dollars] more I hope I shall make out. I have my childrens shooling to pay every 3 months & many calls for money that I am obliged to pay." At the bottom of the note, she added, "if you hear from the brig do send me word." [19]

Just as their sisters on Nantucket had done for decades, sea-wives on the mainland also typically acted as their husband's junior partners or surrogates while the seafarers were absent. Thaddeus Pickens of Fairhaven commanded merchant ships that traded along the American seaboard and to Europe at the turn of the nineteenth century. He seems to have been an entrepreneur fairly typical of his time and place, having somewhat uncertain success juggling several ventures at a time.[20] His wife, Peace Bennett Pickens, handled many details of her husband's business while he was away. Thaddeus's letters to Peace were filled with instructions to pay debts, make purchases, and secure documents. Although his father and other connections were also available, Thaddeus preferred to have his wife act for him. Peace joked to Thaddeus in 1804, "I shall very soon think that I am intitled to a small premium for doing business here as well as thou in New York." It was both sad and appropriate when Peace was appointed administratrix of his estate when Thaddeus was lost at sea in 1811.[21]

Although New England ships plied many of the same trading routes and whaling grounds, significant changes occurred in the organization of the maritime industries within a generation after the War of 1812. Economic expansion and increased complexity forced the replacement of family-based operations of general merchants by less personal networks of jobber, importer, factor, broker, and commission agent. Less personal market forces supplanted personal contact in the management of the growing volume of trade, as increasing numbers of businessmen turned from partnerships to incorporated joint-stock companies. Increased scale in business and stepped-up competition spurred the development of bigger and faster vessels. In turn, their prohibitive initial cost and maintenance expenses tended to separate owner from importer: shipowners carried freight for others rather than investing in speculative cargoes on their own account. Regularly scheduled packet ships took goods and passengers between designated ports. Enterprises grew more specialized, concentrating on a specific commodity, while certain seaports gradually dominated one or another branch of commerce. Boston absorbed most of the general shipping of Massachusetts, for example, while New Bedford gained control over whaling.[22]

The two-tier recruitment pattern established in the colonial fishery persisted and intensified throughout the antebellum period. The career whalemen filling the officer positions now came from all over the coastal Northeast, and the foremast hands literally from all over the world. A federal law of 1817 stipulating that two-thirds of the crew on every American ship be American citizens was generally ignored by the 1840s as shipowners learned the advantages of cheaper, more easily exploited immigrant and foreign labor. The new patterns of recruitment were reflected in the remarkable diversity in New Bedford's population, which so struck Melville. Portuguese from the Azores, Cape Verdeans, Polynesian "Kanakas," Irish and other European immigrants, and free blacks mingled with the descendants of the original Quaker, Baptist, and Congregationalist settlers and indigenous Native Americans.

Fewer Yankee boys went to sea as opportunities in manufacturing, railroads, and westward expansion became more attractive. But any local white man who displayed energy and talent on board ship was virtually assured of rapid promotion. Now, though, rather than retiring from sea by their early thirties and taking up some other line of work, as preceding generations had done, successful mariners found it less easy or less profitable to switch to other pursuits and so tended to prolong their careers in the fishery for a greater portion of their adult lives. The managing agents preferred to fill the forecastle with inexpensive, inexperienced men, including many foreigners, with the expectation of rapid turnover, rather than developing a pool of reliable, skilled whalemen who would demand higher pay. (Some agents even instructed their captains to encourage desertion near the end of a voyage.) As a consequence, the agents depended even more heavily on the stable core of career whalemen to command their ships, in order to counteract the anarchic tendencies inherent in global geographic dispersal, severely limited communications, and especially the heterogeneity, inexperience, and proclivity to desertion among the foremast hands.[23]

Remuneration as well as background widened the gap between officers and crew: as the century progressed, wages for captains and mates rose while the ordinary seaman's wages dropped. At the turn of the century, lays ranged from $1/15$ of the net proceeds for the captain to $1/75$ for foremast hands and $1/120$ for cabin or ships' boys. Occasionally, charges accrued during the voyage were deducted from the seamen's earnings. After 1830 or so, however, lays began to stretch from $1/8$ for the most favored captains to $1/200$ for "green hands" and $1/250$ for boys. And all but the captain were now also assessed for a share in the risks and costs of the voyage as well as its profits: subtracted from the lays were a variety of charges for fitting out the ship and discharging the cargo, outfitters' bills and other costs incurred in port, cash advances for themselves and occasionally for family members, their "slops" (supplies purchased on board ship)—plus interest charges of up to 25 percent on many of the charges. In sum, most whalemen walked away from their voyages with pitifully small amounts. According to one study, "no matter what price index is chosen, the real wages of all 'enlisted' whalemen appear to have declined by more than the most pessimistic of the onshore estimates [for unskilled workers]."[24]

Equally appalling as the extortionate system of lays were the conditions in the industry, which deteriorated substantially as voyages lengthened. The tools and techniques of whaling did not change dramatically between the middle of the eighteenth century and the middle of the nineteenth: the large whaleships cruised the grounds (sometimes for tense but tedious days or weeks) until a whale was sighted, whereupon the small boats were lowered and sent in chase, rowed usually by six-man crews (or, if sufficiently distant, sailed for part of the way) right up next to the beast. The harpooneer hurled a harpoon at the whale, hoping to fasten a stout line to the beast and tire it as it attempted to escape, dragging the boat behind it—or worse, fought back. When the whale finally stopped moving, the boat would again pull up close and the boatheader (usually one of the ship's officers or the captain himself) would kill the whale, plunging a spear-like lance into its body, aiming for the vital organs.

The hunt itself was sometimes heroic but always extremely hazardous. Accident and injury were commonplace, and death not infrequent. Much

"South Sea Whale Fishery, No. I, a representation of the method of attacking the sper-macetti whale, also the mode of cutting them into the ships and boiling the oil on deck," 1835, colored aquatint by Ambroise Louis Garneray. Courtesy of Old Dartmouth Historical Society–New Bedford Whaling Museum (Neg. 16086)

less exhilarating and even more arduous work began after the kill, as the boat towed the animal back to the ship for processing. The whale would be fastened to the side of the vessel, and the men, balancing on a lowered stage and trying to avoid the sharks attracted by the whale's carcass, would cut off the head and strip off the blubber (much like peeling an orange). Huge strips of flesh and fat were hoisted aboard for cutting and then mincing into smaller pieces suitable for boiling down in large iron vats set on brick fireplaces. Rendered oil would be cooled and then poured into barrels and stored in the ship's hold. Sperm whales carried additional pure oil in their heads, which had to be bailed out, and their ivory teeth were extracted. The valuable baleen (bone and cartilage) from the right and bowhead whales was carefully stripped, cleaned, dried, and bundled. The whole process could take two or three days, with men working in shifts round the clock. It was filthy, exhausting, dangerous, and disgusting work,

conducted on vessels pitching and rolling on the open sea, tryworks billowing noxious smoke, deck awash with grease, grime, and gore.[25]

While the work itself did not change dramatically, several new factors made the occupation significantly more miserable in the nineteenth
century. Voyages now sailed even more dangerous waters in the Pacific,
Indian, and Arctic Oceans and stayed out much, much longer—now for
years at a time. At the same time, shipboard violence and brutal discipline
became much more commonplace in the whaling fleet. Even as a public
campaign to abolish flogging and other forms of corporal punishment was
gathering steam on land, the forceful application of fists, kicks, whips, be-
laying pins, bricks, or anything else ready to hand became depressingly
frequent at sea. Some captains put men in shackles, strung them up in
the rigging, or confined them in lockers or trypots. In only slightly more
subtle forms of coercion, they might employ punitive bread-and-water
diets, assign unnecessary work, or in their usual role as ship's doctor, assign particularly nasty medical "treatments" for men suspected of feigning
illness. Not surprisingly, desertion was rampant; whaling vessels rarely
returned with the same crew they had shipped. (Melville himself deserted
from his first whaling voyage after a year and a half, in 1842, and shipped
only briefly on other whalers. He eventually made his way home from the
South Pacific by signing up for a short hitch in the U.S. Navy.).[26]

In port, the hapless seamen were often victimized by those sailortown
suppliers of specialized goods and services colorfully known as "land
sharks": exploitive boardinghouse keepers, grog dispensers, prostitutes,
outfitters, and shipping agents paid by the head. To complete their crews,
agents turned to the notorious practice of "shanghaiing," forcibly induc-
ing sailors to ship out by resorting to trickery. Green farmboys were enticed to sign up with all sorts of illusory promises. Vagrants, drunkards,
and criminals were hired with no questions asked. Foreign crew members
were picked up in ports around the world to replace deserters.[27]

Overseeing the whole enterprise were the whaling agents, usually
prominent local merchants who owned the major share of the vessels they
managed. As they had in the eighteenth century, agents supervised the
initial fitting out of each vessel, hired the officers and the crew, and over-
saw (as best they could from shore) the voyages through correspondence
with their captains and representatives in foreign ports. At the end of each
voyage they calculated the current market value of the returned oils and
bone and distributed the net proceeds to the investors and the crew. As the

industry developed in the nineteenth century, however, the agents tended to rely on others to supply much of the initial capital, build the ships, recruit and outfit the foremast hands, provision the vessels, and process the products returned from the voyage.[28]

The intimate connections between the managing owners and whalemen's families in the local community, which had characterized the colonial and early national whalefishery, were supplanted by the middle of the nineteenth century by a more narrowly focused kind of paternalism. The agents' relationships with the families of the foremast hands diminished markedly, in contrast with their intensified relationship with the officers' families. The diverging relationships between the owners on shore and the men at sea drew on more general, emerging notions that implicitly assumed a separation between work and home, which in this case took two distinct forms. The agents tended to downplay the common seamen's connections to family economies, and they cast the wives and parents of the career whalemen as dependents only.

The new distinctions between the more transient "hands" and the career whalemen were apparent even before they first set foot aboard a whaler. Seamen typically began their careers in their teens; the crew lists and shipping papers show that whalemen were no exception. The legal requirements involved in employing minors, however, were probably honored more often in the breach than in the observance. Josiah Holmes Jr. & Brother, well-respected shipbuilders in Mattapoisett who also served as agents for four of the whaleships they built, carefully preserved parental permissions with the other records of each voyage. "This certifies that I am wiling that my Son can go a voige a whaling in the ship Oscar from Mattipoiset," read one such typical agreement.[29] But the scrupulousness with which the Holmeses, quite small-scale operators, preserved this and similar agreements only serves to accentuate the general absence of such permissions in the records of the larger agencies based in the bigger ports, like Swift & Allen and J. & W. R. Wing of New Bedford.

It is possible that the recruiting agents, on whom many whaling agents relied for the majority of their crews during the industry's peak years, obtained the agreements rather than the whaling agents themselves. It is more likely, though, that with the increasing shortage of labor in the industry and the concomitant rise of various unscrupulous methods of recruitment, the formalities were most often ignored. As whaling became a less attractive form of employment, agents preferred to fill out their crews with more tractable greenhands and men with few complicating connections to shore.[30] It is significant that the few surviving parental permissions are all for local boys, perhaps on route to a future command and, more immediately, whose parents were close on hand. The most distant ones obtained by Josiah Holmes Jr. & Brother of Mattapoisett were from Fall River, about twelve miles away. The general trends were indicated in a letter from Jonathan W. Ketcham, superintendent of the New York House of Refuge, inquiring of Swift & Allen in 1849 about the possibility of finding berths aboard their whalers for some of the boys under his care. "If you take the 3 young men," he wrote, "I will give you such as have no parents. and if they have I will obtain their written consent so that you shall have no trouble with law suits from them."[31]

It is not clear just how troublesome to the agents such lawsuits actually were. The ledgers demonstrate that although it became less common for fathers to receive the balance due their sons at the end of a voyage — probably due largely to the shift to nonlocal men — it was not uncommon for the balance due to be paid to a lawyer, though it is impossible to tell whether it was at the behest of the sailor himself, his parents, or from some other cause. There is some evidence that fathers, wives, and other heirs from as far away as the Azores did receive, at least some of the time, the earnings and other effects of seamen who had died during voyages. But this process of recovery was made possible largely through the agency of attorneys, public administrators, U.S. and foreign consular representatives, and even the pastor of the New Bedford Seamen's Bethel, all of whom (except perhaps the pastor) occasionally advanced heirs' claims in return for a cut of the proceeds.[32] One father from Hoboken, New Jersey, having just learned that after all the various deductions, his deceased son's share came to just $20, wrote bitterly to the agents, "I think it is rather a small sum for 18 months hard laibor." He threatened to "hier a loyer" if the matter weren't settled in a more satisfactory manner, but there is no indication of the outcome.[33] Overall, it appears that the agents' withdrawal from any relationship with the families of foremast hands may have drawn in other bureaucrats and private charitable efforts.

For parents and other relatives from Hoboken or other faraway places, often the only contact with the agents — in the rare instance of contact at all — was in the form of anxious requests for information about their seafaring sons. A letter from upstate New York to the Nantucket agents Charles and Henry Coffin is typical even in its pathos:

To C & H Coffin—owners of Ship Constitution of nantucket Jentlemen
I have A Son A Bord of your Ship . . . I Should like to here from you
wether you have herd from the Ship And wen you Expect her We have
had no word of our Son Sence he Sailed from your Port And if you have
hurd from the Ship I Should like to here from you where & what She was
A Doing If my Son Should return I Sould Like to here from you And
Advise him to Com and Se us for the time Appears very Long . . . Dear
Isaac Van Hagen remember that you have A father & Mother Brother
& Sisters And they All think of you and the time you went Away . . .
Jentlemen wright as son as Convenient Yours with Respect

John J. Van Hagen [34]

Nearly all such inquiries were from parents or siblings, which suggests
that the seamen who had established conjugal relationships were perhaps
more punctilious in trying to maintain those ties than were adolescent
boys with their parents. (The boys probably did not care about obtaining
parental permissions either.) After all, for the youthful "greenhands," the
experience of shipping out was part of their break from their families of
origin, a rite of passage toward male adulthood.[35] For the young local men
beginning a career in the whalefishery, shipping out was also the first step
toward a professional identity in an occupation that was associated with
their place of birth but which also required that they leave it repeatedly—
a push-pull rhythm of movement between land and sea, home and work.

For the group of career whalemen, *continuing* to go to sea was often linked
to their eventual marrying and starting families of their own. To many
of the young men in southeastern New England, whaling represented a
way to earn the cash they considered necessary to begin married life, even
though three- and four-year absences obviously complicated courtship.
Alonzo M. Taber told his brother in an 1852 letter, "if we do well in her
[the vessel] this season I think I shall come home next winter and get
married." Ezra Goodnough recorded similar sentiments in his shipboard
diary in 1847, noting (in appropriately nautical terms) that he looked forward to "getting spliced from the strength of this voyage." [36]

"Getting spliced" served to bind mariners more firmly to their home
community, a process in which women played an important metaphorical
role since mariners' primary emotional tie to their home communities was

"The Proposal," scrimshaw carving. Courtesy of Old Dartmouth Historical Society–
New Bedford Whaling Museum (Neg. 14294)

anchored in their wives. Henry Beetle, for example, told his wife Eliza,
"without you this world would be a wilderness to me," and George Bowman wrote to his sister that "the only thing that will bring me home is that
Little Wife of mine." [37] This kind of romantic attachment reinforced the
economic and legal strings that pulled men back to the home port. As Melville colorfully explained, "the young girls breathe such musk, their sailor
sweethearts smell them miles off shore, as though they were drawing nigh
the odorous Moluccas instead of the Puritanic sands" of Massachusetts.[38]

Flushed with young love, Captain Leonard Gifford explained in 1851
to his fianceé Lucy Roberts the difference she had made in him: "Had you
not have learned me to love you with all the devotion that my heart is
capable of feeling," Leonard claimed, "I might still have been the careless
happy go luckey dog that I have been for the last six years, for Lucy before I became acquainted with you . . . all places were alike to me, and I
felt that thear was as much happines for me on board of a ship, even in
the middle of the ocean as I could find on my native land." He confided,
"I must confess that I have for a long time labored under the impression
that money was the only foundation of happyness in the world [but] now

I feel that all the wealth of the Indies and the gold of Callifornia combined cannot in the least repay me for the loss of your society . . . so soon as we meet," Leonard promised, "we will take the earlyest opportunity to have the silken cord wound around us, that binds two willing hearts in the holy bonds of matrimony." [39]

But Captain Gifford also felt the pull of occupational pride and the pressure for profit, which mandated that he stay out until his ship was full. [40] At stake was his reputation within the industry at large and also back at home in New Bedford. In 1853, two years after his passionate avowal, Leonard told Lucy, "if I am not fortunate I shall be shure to take another year for if I live to reach home no man shall be able to say by me thear goes a fellow that brought home a broken [i.e., losing] voyage." [41] He meant it too: Gifford's problem-plagued voyage lasted nearly six years. He and Lucy were married two weeks after he returned.

Gifford would learn that man's financial needs only increased after the wedding. Mariners, like their land-based peers, subscribed to the male breadwinner ethic that linked a husband's and father's manhood to his ability to provide financially for his family. [42] So, despite the pain of separation from the loved one, marriage served also to send the mariner out to sea again. Captain Samuel Braley shipped out on the *Arab* of Fairhaven just two weeks after his marriage in 1847. During the three-and-a-half-year voyage, especially after learning of his wife's delivery of their first child, he meditated in his journal frequently on his duties as a husband and father. In one entry, he reflected, "If I had no one but myself to care for; I would not care if I never had a dollar more than enough for the present use; but . . . there are two beings whome I love dearer than self that are helpless as it were dependent on me for subsistence." After successfully capturing a whale, he noted, "The whale made a little more than a hundred barrels [of oil] . . . the procedes of [which] will buy the child a frock and the mother too." At another point in the voyage, though, not having seen a whale in some time and consequently feeling less sanguine about his familial responsibilities, he wrote glumly: "What a great fool I was to marry—if it was not for that Wife and *her* boy I would curse the whales and go cod-fishing." [43]

First mate Charles Peirce, forced to leave a New Bedford whaler midway through a Pacific voyage due to illness, was set ashore in Australia. He worried frantically about his family's support; as he wrote to his wife, "The cold I got before sailing from home I have not got clear of yet [so] I have been obliged to leive the ship . . . if their is any prospect for me [here]

I shal stop a while longer, & . . . send you some money soon. dear wife I have not forgotten you neither shal I . . . my family is what I am working for, trying to live for." By December he had improved enough to ship out on another whaler, and assured his wife, "Dont think because I am sailing out of Sydney that I have forgotten that I am a Husband & Father. I am in hopes to be able to send you some Money from this Voyage, if I cant send for you [to join him]." He sailed out of Australia off and on over the next three years, but his condition again took a turn for the worse. In early 1874 he reported, "My health is very poor, too bad to go to sea any more, but my dear and *good wife*, my mind has troubled me the most to think I have not been able to help you. sometimes . . . my brain is almost turned, when I look back and see how much better it would have been if I had not left home at all. . . . it was the fartherest from my thoughts, when I left you, for you to support yourself and the Children, all this time." (Unable to whale, or work at all, Peirce did eventually make it home to see his family in late 1874. Within two years he was dead of tuberculosis.)[44]

Their sense of duty and concern for their families factored into the career mariners' relationship with their employers, the agents. To command the mariners' loyalty and, implicitly, their assumption of responsibility for the ship, the managing owners offered assurances that the female dependents left at home would be protected and provided for in a kind of exchange of obligation.[45] Managing owner Matthew Howland, after informing his distant relation and captain Philip Howland of a robbery in the house where Philip's wife was boarding, assured the absent mariner, "In this and all other things that may occur during thy absence thy Wife & family will be just *as well cared for* by us and thy friends as thee could do."[46] Accustomed to this sort of attention, Philip was considerably aggrieved several years later by the neglect he felt from his new employers, Thomas Knowles & Co. In September 1866, over two years out, he wrote bitterly to them, "I see by your letter . . . that you complain of my not writing. The fault is all your own. My family are only nine miles from you and the Mail Stage runs by the door every day, it would be very easy for you to ascertain the state of their health and mention it to me when you write. Capt. Cash, Capt. Coffin and others of my acquaintance are in the frequent receipt of news from their families by letters from their owners. . . . [I]t seemed to me," he added pointedly, "that you cared little about us and that being the case I felt that I cared as little for you."[47]

On a lighter note, George Richmond, managing owner of the New Bedford ship *Hope*, wrote to Captain Leonard Gifford in 1854, "I expect I may have affronted your sister a little. She sent over for two Hundred Dollars to buy a piano-forte . . . I sent the money[,] gently hinting it would be cheaper to hire than to buy. I dont know but that I done wrong, but I done it for your interest." In his reply, Gifford advised the agent: "If you and my spunkey sister are not in good terms you had better make your peace as soon as possible. When I write to the old folks I shall tell them to turn her over to you every time she calls and should you be unfortunate enough to be out of funds when she is expected you had better get Ezra or some of the Boys to lock you up in the fire proof safe and I canot insure your safety even then unless you stop up the key hole, for gass lamps and old maids are develish dangerous things when they explode." [48]

Richmond also tried to persuade Gifford to prolong his voyage by assuring him that the owners would protect the absent captain's interests in love as well as property. Referring to Gifford's fianceé Lucy Roberts, Richmond wrote, "That *Young Lady* up to the Corner . . . will be all the better for waiting another year. If you will agree to stay [on the ship, in the Pacific] . . . Ezra & myself will see that no young fellows are allowed to trespass upon your grounds or pluck the *blooming Flower* but will keep everything 'all right' until you arrive." [49]

The expectation of reciprocity was clearly articulated from the other side of the exchange as well. Gifford wrote to Richmond in a more serious vein: "I see by your letters and account current that you had had to advance my mother more money than I expected they would nead when I left home . . . I will now assure you if I have not before done so, that it gives me more sattisfaction to know they have had all they wanted from you than any other course you could have taken for . . . I alwais intend that my mother shall enjoy all the comforts of life, and you cannot please better than by continueing to advance her any reasonable amount." [50]

Wives and mothers themselves sometimes referred to the exchange of male responsibilities in their negotiations with the owners for cash advances against the whalemen's wages—and the women often found the agents less than helpful. In 1846, when John Codd was in the Pacific on the Nantucket ship *Columbia*, his pregnant wife wrote to the owners, "Sir will you please advance me 50 dollars and charge the same to my Husband['s account.] John told me you would advance me two hundred pr year during his absence." A year later, with the baby undoubtedly on her mind if not her lap, Mrs. Codd wrote, "I am obliged to call on again for money, and must say I do not feel that you have treated me well; My Husband did not think you would let his family suffer for the necessries of life, when he shipp'd in your employ. I am out of Food and Fuel, and unless you can do something for me must write by every Ship for him to return and take care of his family." [51]

Sophia Brown, the wife of one seaman and mother of another, seemed especially resentful of the upper hand the agents held over the men at sea and their dependents ashore. "Mr Coffin sir," she began her request. "I hope you good men will Excuse me for looking upon you at this time for a litle asistance . . . I no Moses his out fit bill was veary hy and do not expect the Oil that has Come will meat it. still," she pointed out, "their is enough on board to pay you all." She added, "i have Labord veary hard to git a Longe sins my husband sail . . . my health has fail me now and i am not able to work as i have dun[.] theirfore if you Could let me have 15 or 20 dollar it would enable me to git a Long till i am better able to work agane[.] five dollar would be a grate releaf to me if you Cant not spair eny more[.] I should feal veary gratefull to you for so doing." A few weeks later, she informed the agents, "if it is in your power to settle with me now it would be a great relief[,] for I am sick and suffering for want of means to make me comfortable." With legitimate complaint, she continued bitterly, "it is very hard to have what belongs to me by law and certainly in justice witheld from me so long when I am in need of it so much[.] you that have a plenty little know the feelings of those that are in want of every comfort of life." [52]

As Mrs. Codd and Mrs. Brown found to their distress, the image of reciprocity diverged from the substance: the exchange of responsibilities between men at sea and men on land seems to have been more often rhetorical than actual as the industry reorganized (in the economists' optimistic term, rationalized). By mid-century, the owners' responsibility for the mariners' families had been markedly reduced, particularly in its most concrete, financial form. Any cash or credit received before the final accounting were considered advances and deducted from the whaleman's total earnings, usually with a steep interest charge tacked on. Mindful of the high interest charge attached, Sarah Church actually turned down assistance when offered by the owners, who were responding to her husband's request from sea, because, she explained, "I do not like to draw on his voyage any more than is necessary." [53]

Despite the interest charges, some whalemen occasionally arranged for the payment of installments of money to dependents at home during the voyage. For example, in 1852 the owners agreed "to pay the wife of Thomas R. Oakman [probably first mate] as order Fifty dollars at the ex-

Swift & Allen account with third mate Daniel A. Delany on the ship *Gratitude* on its August 1851 to June 1854 voyage, indicating that the shipowners provided Delany's wife cash advances of $25 at regular intervals during her husband's three-year absence. At the end of the voyage, these and other charges were deducted from Delany's share ($933.70) of the total proceeds, so that he ended up clearing $202.21. Courtesy of Old Dartmouth Historical Society–New Bedford Whaling Museum (Neg. 16193)

piration of six months from the sailing of Ship Saratoga and also every succeeding term of six months that the said Oakman shall remain on board said ship." [54] Hannah Ashley, the wife of the first mate of the *Governor Troup* on its 1862–67 voyage, picked up $30 every two months from the New Bedford agent E. C. Jones.[55] The account for William Troy, second mate of the bark *Harvest,* in Swift & Allen's ledger book indicates that before he left New Bedford in 1847, Troy arranged for the agents to pay $8 per month to a local merchant, to cover his wife's bills. Orlando H. Houston's wife assured him, "The owners are very kind to me[—]i have no troble in getting my money." [56]

But such regular arrangements seem to have been more ad hoc in the whaling industry than in other maritime trades, negotiated on an individual basis with only the most trusted career officers. With the wild fluctuations in prices of whale products and the uneven success of the fishery, agents could not predict their profits or the eventual amount of a seaman's lay, and they were often reluctant to supply funds on such a regular basis. The climbing desertion rate undoubtedly discouraged them as well; the ledgers show that advances were occasionally paid to relatives of men who later deserted, which may (depending on what point during the voyage the sailor jumped ship) have meant a loss to be absorbed by the agent and outfitter.[57] In the end, no more than a quarter of even the career whalemen's families actually received cash or credit during a voyage.[58]

The characteristically erratic timing and random amounts listed in many of the shipowners' accounts suggest that these sorts of advances could not have represented the families' sole source of financial support. Harriet Allen routinely experienced cash shortfalls during the delays between her requests and when the agent of her husband's ship, Andrew Hicks, finally supplied the advances. Phebe Cottle felt compelled to justify her appeal for help on the grounds of extreme hardship: "I am sorry to be obliged to again call for assistance but my rent has become due and my wood is out and I am in need of manny articles for my family that I cannot do without," she explained. "I have tried to get along as sparingly as possible but mother is very sick and I am obliged to give up my work in some measure . . . I want you should let me have 30 or 40 dollars and hope not have to call again[.] It is no pleasure to me I will assure you[,] but my family is truly in need." [59] And other women simply did not bother to ask at all. "I hav not troubled mr Rodman nor dont think I shall," Emeline Parsons told her husband William. Sylvia Leonard similarly mentioned to her husband John, three years after he had shipped out, "I have not seen the owners since you went away and do not feel as though I could go to them now." [60]

Ultimately, it seems clear that the industry discussion characterizing females as dependents mattered more to the men, those at sea and those on land, as a means of cementing their own relationships.[61] With the expansion and greater specialization of function within the industry, the paternalism of the managing shipowners became more narrowly focused, limited only to the families of career officers and, indeed, limited more to rhetoric than substance. Assistance to families was viewed more as charitable aid than as entitlement to a just share of the proceeds. That rhetoric increasingly depicted women and families onshore as the dependents of men at sea—but, on closer examination, it appears that the direction of dependency actually ran in the opposite direction.

As whaling voyages stretched to three years and more, the professional mariners increasingly depended upon their wives and other women at home in both direct and indirect ways. The men at sea, the industry, the community, and governmental authorities continued to rely on wives' traditional "deputy husband" services in representing seafaring men, who were now absent for longer periods. Maritime women also served as intermediaries between the fraternity at sea and the community on shore, a role that was increasing important to the smooth functioning of the fishery as it reorganized and expanded in scale and scope.

As they had done for generations, mariners at sea routinely relied upon their wives' ability to represent them and look after their interests in their relations with the managing owners. Now, however, with structural changes in the economy and rationalization in the industry itself, these responsibilities were less directly involved in the production end and more often took on the nature of family cash management. During their husbands' voyages, both Harriet Allen and Caroline Gifford communicated with the shipowners about insuring their husbands' shares of the oil and bone. Eliza Beetle, on Martha's Vineyard, frequently served as agent for her husband Henry. On one occasion in 1851, he wrote to her, "[The owners] hold my note for 200 dollars or a little over . . . to be paid when I get home," and he advised, "if you have the money to spare and pay it, it will stop interest [from accruing]." Later that voyage, he asked her to insure his share of the cargo against loss. Off again in a hurry in 1854, he instructed her, "I had so little time in New Bedford I could not get [my employment] agreement in writing. . . . Dont rest until you get it."[62]

Other women acted on their own initiative—though still on their husbands' and families' behalf. Caroline Gifford not only managed a farm, she also decided when to invest in land and how to dispose of funds in the bank. In one letter, she told Charles, "The Sherman land . . . was put up at auction about 3 months ago . . . I thought you wanted it & I wanted it & Brother Sherman seemed to think it would [be] a great advantage to this place . . . I got him to bid it off[.] He give 331 dollars for it . . . & I think it was very cheap." Another time, she collected a note due Charles from the whaling agent whose ship Charles had commanded and decided what to do with it: "There was about 5000 dollars due you at Philips after your voyage was settled . . . of what I didnt use, since you wrote about putting it on the Bank of Fall River . . . I told Philips I wanted about 800 put in your name & 800 in mine. I didnt know what better I could do [because you] cant put in but 1000 [per person] . . . write me if I shall put more in in the childrens names." [63]

Some mariners preferred to have other men act for them: in 1855, Philip Howland officially granted a power of attorney to his friend and associate Charles Tucker so that Tucker, rather than Philip's wife, could look after the captain's affairs for the duration of his absence.[64] And sometimes wives expressed distress or a lack of confidence in their own ability to manage. Harriet Allen, despite her husband's granting her an official power of attorney over his finances and affairs, worried continuously about high prices and making ends meet, fretting, "I cannot help feeling troubled when I think how much it has cost me to live & for other expenses since D. has been gone. I know he will be surprised. I have tried very hard to economize but there are so many to care for." [65] Nonetheless, wives' involvement in their husbands' affairs was frequent and considered natural and necessary. Both men and women assumed that a husband's and wife's interests were identical: as Sylvia Leonard told her seagoing husband, "everything I do . . . is more for you than for myself." [66]

The same assumptions also assigned to men's families rather than to their employers the duty of representing them to the governmental authorities during their absences. By state law and by local custom, young single men were usually considered resident in their parents' households, and husbands were always considered resident wherever their wives and children lived. It was to the domiciles, rather than to the shipowner's offices, that the tax collector went—unlike the outfitters and other creditors more closely connected to the industry, who would go directly to the men's employers. Henry H. Crapo, the New Bedford town clerk and tax collector in the late 1830s and early 1840s, kept an unofficial "Memorandum Book of Tax Delinquents" in which he carefully noted in 1838, "Job Taber. family lives in old brick house on S. Water St. with [wife's father] Tailor Davenport. [Taber] is in ship Alexander. wife can't pay." A few pages later, Crapo recorded ruefully, "John Adams, was in ship Benj. Rush of Warren, has left her, has been gone 4 years. father says I shan't get [the tax]." Other typical entries include: "Amos S. Churchill . . . in ship Sarah Frances of F[air] Haven. Mrs. C. may send the money bye & bye," and "Benjm. B. Dunlap, wife lives with [illegible] Reynolds & is his daughter, [Dunlap] is in ship Wm. Hamilton, Capt. Swain, she will pay 1st of March." [67]

The managing agents of the industry itself also regularly turned to the mariners' families for information about the men and ships at sea. With the unpredictability of the fishery, the managing agents needed as much information as possible to make vital decisions about when and where to sell cargo or how much insurance to buy.[68] To add to their sources, they consulted whalemen's family members too. During the *Hope's* voyage under Leonard Gifford's command, the New Bedford firm of Wilcox & Richmond was in touch with the captain's mother, sister, and fianceé; they also wrote to the father of the first mate and the wife of the second mate for news. Mrs. Eliza Lewis, wife of the second mate, passed along what she had heard, writing from Nantucket: "Sir I have Recieved the money you cent . . . you Rote to Me to know About the ship and how they git a long[.] he Rites me Word . . . to Give my self no uneasiness for all Things look promising for a prospours Voyge and a Lucky one. You may expect News when I git my letter from cros land . . . they ware a doing well 5 month a gow." [69]

Communication between sea and shore was not easy or straightforward, but with the dramatic nineteenth-century expansion of the industry over time and space, it became increasingly important both to the industry and to the sailors' personal connections. Families, friends, and business associates would send letters by every vessel setting sail for that part of the world where the intended recipient was believed to be. Men at sea sent letters by every ship they met, in port or passing in the ocean, that seemed likely to reach home before they did. Santa Maria, an uninhabited island in the Galapagos group that was a favorite port of call for vessels in the Pacific whaling fleet, boasted a container, covered with a giant tortoise shell and nailed to a post at the head of a cove called Post Office Bay, where mail was dropped off and picked up by passing vessels. Such means of communication were generally tenuous and uncertain, for all too obvious reasons. One wife reputedly sent over a hundred letters to her husband over a three-year period, of which he received only six.[70] By midcentury, development of more regular postal services to major ports such as Honolulu and San Francisco (augmented by regularly scheduled steamships and a railroad line crossing the isthmus of Panama, among other advances)[71] helped but did not completely overcome problems. It was never certain where or when a given whaler would put into port.

To guard against a breakdown in communication between the shipowners and the ship, Captain William Loring Taber regularly enclosed news for the whaling agent in letters to his wife Susan. In one, he instructed her to "please write Mr. Thomas giving him the date, & Lattitude,

& Longitude, health, & quantity of Oil, & bound South . . . I havent time to write [him];" in another he asked that she "write to Mr. Thomas evry time that I write to you . . . for he might not get his [letter]." [72] Requesting an advance from her husband's employers in 1849, Mrs. Charles G. Clarke of Pawtucket added a crisp postscript: "I have heard from my husband and the glittering prospects of obtaining Gold has induced them to stop to Pannama and take a Cargo of 2 legged Whales to Sanfrancisco." [73] Mrs. J. E. Chase wrote with emphatic underlining to agents Swift & Allen, "My long *patient* waiting has been rewarded by two long letters from *Capt Chase* . . . He has taken no oil since August and has seen whales but twenty eight times this voyage . . . He keeps from five to twelve men on the lookout from daylight to dark. *He is discouraged.* I am sure I am. He will *never* come *home at this rate.* He received *no letters* from you." [74]

The useful involvement of the women and other family members on land in facilitating the vital flow of information was taken for granted with little remark, although *The Whaleman's Shipping List,* (the industry newspaper first published in 1843), did express its appreciation of the efforts of those captain's wives who accompanied their husbands. In a brief 1853 article about the women at sea, the editor noted enthusiastically, "The enterprising ladies not only preserve unbroken the ties of domestic life . . . [they] not only cheer by their presence the monotony and discomfort of long and perilous voyages; . . . they [also] make capital correspondents, and through the female love of letter-writing, keep us well posted up in the catch and prospects of the season." [75]

The shipowners were quite willing to facilitate the flow of mail in both directions, too—for the sake of industrial discipline as well as information. Agent Robert Greaves wrote to Mrs. Cornelius Marchant of Martha's Vineyard, "Dear Madam, Captain Soule of 'Milo' sent in a boat under charge of your good husband on the 22nd of last month to see if there were any letters for the ship. . . . All hands [are] well and in good spirits." It had been almost two years since the *Milo* had left New Bedford on 5 November 1855. Greaves explained, "I have written you these few lines to re-assure you on the subject of your letters to him. I received two for him ten days after his recent visit, which he will not probably get until the ship comes in in August next." He also informed her, "Letters from home give men great satisfaction & keep them from listening to the many solicitations & overtures they receive from bad people [causing] them to run away & a happy contented crew will [illegible] make a better voyage than the contrary." [76]

Women at home also served as social surrogates on their absent men's behalf. The social relations of work at sea were informally affirmed and extended, occasionally at the career mariners' explicit requests, through the interactions of the female community onshore. Philip Howland asked that Patience, his second wife, "tell Thurza Howland that Josiah is a good Boy and will make something . . . [also] please inform Mrs. Easton that her husband is well . . . tell her that I will take good care of him." A year and a half later, Philip requested that she "write to Mrs Easton[,] Mrs Frederick A Easton[,] request a visit from her and return it[—]she is a very fine woman[.] tell her that Mr Easton is well . . . he is one [of] those who merit my approbation and tell her that he shall not go anybodies mate again and that when he goes she shall go with him" (in other words, with Howland's recommendation, Easton will be promoted to captain and thus will be able to take his wife to sea with him).[77]

Somewhat more ingenuously, first mate Charles Peirce wrote from the South Pacific to his wife Eliza: "I like the Capt. very much so far, he has treated me so far like an equal, and he shal loose nothing by it. I would go a long way to serve him. we have some grand good times talking about our wifes at home, he says he hopes his wife and you will be neighborly, while we are gone." He felt equally enthusiastic about the second mate, as he told Eliza, "I like him much, we have some real good times talking about home . . . when we get home we are going to have our friends to visit each other." [78]

Such extensive patterns of sociability—the same sorts of neighborly interaction remarked upon by Crevecoeur back in the eighteenth century—continued to be a crucial way in which women wove their community together and maintained a place in it for their men. Sharing information about the men at sea formed an important component in the shoreside networks. Surviving evidence provides a particularly clear demonstration of the grapevine in the little village of Acushnet, just north of New Bedford. In 1862, William Ashley shipped out of New Bedford as the first mate of the *Governor Troup*, a whaleship commanded by his older brother Edward. Another Acushnet boy, Benny Wilson, went too, at a greenhand's lay. Two years later, William wrote back home to his wife, Hannah: "Tell Mr. Willsons Folks that Benny is as fat as a Cub and is a prety good boy." The Wilsons returned the favor on at least one occasion: Hannah recorded in her diary, "Called at Mr. Wilson's and heard Bennies letter read." Still another Acushnet neighbor, 13-year-old Amelia Keen, passed on news about William Ashley to her older brother, then at sea in another New Bedford whaler, the bark *Vigilant:* "Mr. Ashleys folks have received a letter from Wm. Ashley. He wrote to the boys that if they could find any stones to pick they had better stay at home and pick them rather than to go to sea." [79] In Acushnet, as in villages and neighborhoods throughout the region, news of the whalemen was passed from household to household, and letters from sea were read aloud to assembled companies.

Absent now for longer periods and over more of their lives, the career mariners relied upon their female connections to keep in touch with events and people both at home and at sea. Two months out from New Bedford, Captain William Loring Taber wrote his new wife, Susan, "I . . . hope you will write by every ship that comes around Cape Horn sperm whaling, & as soon as you receive this, please to write to me at Talcahuano, & at Paita." In his next letter, he proclaimed rather grandiloquently, "I perfectly long to have some of those endearing epistles that you are so famous for writing—I know what they are as a lover, but not as husband, but I live in hope, that the time is not far distant when the epistolary effusions from my dear wife will gladden the breast of her affectionate husband." [80]

William wanted to hear from her, of course, but he wanted to know about the others at home too: "How is father, & mother . . . you will always remember me to them with much kindness, you will also send my love 'way down East' or anywhere else that Rebecca [Susan's sister] may be—How does Mary Ann B. & Crandel get along, How is M. M. Barstow, is she married yet[?]" On occasion William asked for more mundane information ("how much was our tax this year—who are our tenants?") and for news about other Mattapoisett men at sea ("I wish you to write me particularly about Father, [brothers] Alonzo & Edwin, how they are getting along [at sea] & when they expect to come home, & if they were successful—Do you hear anything from Richard Barstow . . . where is David Dexter?") [81]

None of Susan's answering "epistolary effusions" has been located, but the correspondence from shore to ship routinely contained news of courtships and marriages, births and deaths, successes and failures. In almost comically concise prose, Phebe C. Sisson wrote:

Dear husband i take this opportunity to write you a few lines to let you know that all are in good health at present and i hope these lines find you the same. Miss brownnell and her children has divided, and the little house has fell to [illegible] and i am in it yet and ann eliza has got married to luther daton and george to caroline gifford. stephen has got home rhoda has got a boy Bill has moved to his new house. and the old folks is well . . . they have had another reformation to the head river and made business of winter religion but when it comes warm weather it wore off i dont think of any more to write and i will close.[82]

Even as terse as it was, a letter like Phebe Sisson's served dual integrative functions.[83] With their conversations, with their actions, and with their recording of both in letters then sent to sea, Susan Taber, Phebe Sisson, and all the other wives like them mediated and maintained their husbands' place within family and community.

Women also helped furnish, in ways both tangible and intangible, their men's place on the ship and within the shipboard community. Harriet Allen of New Bedford meticulously recorded in her diary the preparations made before her husband David went to sea as captain of the *Sea Fox* in 1865. David took care of some financial arrangements, paid some outstanding bills, and made a few large purchases, all probably with an advance from the agent. He also had a lawyer draw up a power of attorney for Harriet; perhaps he was inspired to do so because, during his previous voyage, Harriet had had to enlist the help of David's brothers when it came time to pay his taxes and when she requested that the shipowners insure his share of the cargo. Now, in the weeks before he was due to ship out again, Harriet made sure David's seagoing wardrobe was in order, mending his coats "&c." She also made his bed covering, helped him pick out books for the voyage, and sat for an ambrotype for him to take to sea (their children sat too). Right before he left, she also "cut a curl from Nellie's head & [took] one of Henry's . . . & tied them together with a blue bow & put them into a box in D.'s drawer on board." [84]

Harriet's efforts were typical: wives and other family members routinely prepared clothing, bedding, preserved food, and other useful and comforting items for the men to take to sea. When John Leonard left New Bedford in October of 1854, his wife Sylvia packed for him sweetmeats and cider, shirts and socks. Ruth Barker Post asked her husband, Captain Francis Post, "do let me know if your butter and cheese and dried fruit turned out well." [85] Samuel Braley told his wife, Mary Ann, that "Grandmother Douglas['s] cotton stockings ware well, but then there is not more than half enough for the voyage; I wish you would send me a dozzen pair more." Mary Ann also made up some medicines for Samuel; at one point, he calls her "my Apothicary," though later he sounded less than grateful for her efforts: "I have taken three Lobelia pills (large ones what great awkward things you and Kate made: they are enough to gag a horse)." [86]

Particular items and services may have further distinguished the officers from the foremast hands, not merely in health and comfort, but also in their relationship to the industry. The women's efforts and skills at least partially eliminated the need for a relationship with the most extortionist of the land sharks, the outfitters. The agents' account books show that about 85 percent of the foremast hands saw much of their earnings siphoned directly off to the outfitters to pay debts incurred for room, board, and supplies before the sailors had even left port. But such charges, for generally smaller debts, were assessed against just over a third of the officers, mainly the younger third and fourth mates, who were more likely to still be single.[87]

The actual fruits of women's labor, however, were now, by midcentury, often unacknowledged, devalued, or obscured by their symbolic associations. First mate Charles Peirce wrote to his wife Eliza, "you spoke of my shirts, never mind the shirts, those will do at present." Charles was much more grateful for the mementos she sent on to him, especially the picture of her with the son he had not yet seen: "last Saturday Night I was made very glad by receiving my Box, that you sent. . . . My darling Eliza I thank you a thousand times for such a handsome Boy. really, he is a fine loocking Child . . . your Picture you said was not a good one. I thought so to[o] when I first received it but the more I loock at it the better I like it . . . how I should like to kiss the original. I have to kiss the Picture. you do loock so good, with the little fellow in your arms, & he seems to be loocking me right in the face."[88] Peirce clearly valued the emotional content of his wife's efforts more than the practical.

Another whaleman described in his journal the effect a quilt had on one of his shipmates: "He was discovered sitting upon his chest bathed in tears, weeping excessively over a bed quilt which he informed [us] was the gift of his Grandmother, who was upwards of ninety years of age and in all probability he would never see her again." For his emotional display, the unfortunate sailor was labeled the "ship's fool."[89] Samuel Braley's request for more of Grandmother Douglas's socks was followed by his nostalgic idealization of his wife's own work: "I cannot ware those that you knit; it seems sacralage: how much I prize evry thing that is the work of thy dear hands." Some months later, Captain Braley recorded in his journal that he had knocked a man down "three or four times." Though he knew that corporal punishment was "contrary to the precepts and example of the Holy Jesus," Braley found it to be the most effective form of discipline. "The laziest, most stubbornly uncooperative men in the ship," he wrote, were now "the most attentive and active men. . . . Such is the effect of giving one man a pounding."[90] The cruelty of their work and the harshly authoritarian structure of shipboard labor stand in stunning, if not surprising, contrast to the whalemen's highly sentimentalized family relationships.

The sentimentality was not, however, irrelevant to the prosecution of the whalefishery. The symbolic content of the clothing and quilts, other necessities, comforts, and mementos provided by the women at home was crucial in helping sustain at both ends intimate relationships over the thousands of miles and many years that separated husbands from wives, sons from mothers, and brothers from sisters. Providing these things—and their emotional associations—was important to the industry as well. For some men, the loving relationships represented by the items may have helped in some small measure to compensate for the inherent brutality of the fishery and, especially for the captains isolated in the aftercabin, the pressures of their position. In making concrete the ties of career mariners to their families, the objects also reaffirmed the responsibilities as provider that in part sent men to sea in the first place and thus strengthened their commitment to the industry and a successful outcome of each voyage. Ironically, though, the emphasis on the sentimental meaning and associations of the goods and supplies ended up masking the substance of women's labor and reinforcing the notion of female dependency, through the process that historian Jeanne Boydston has termed "the pastoralization of housework."[91]

Women's direct contributions to the whalefishery were multiple and varied, though not everything they did was equally acknowledged. But by far their most important contribution was indirect: their taking responsibility for family and community onshore during the men's absences. The rhythms of migrant labor that were built into the industry's growth and expansion into distant seas simply and fundamentally assumed the continued willingness and ability of those left on shore to care for the young, the sick, and the old; to oversee property, manage budgets, maintain households, integrate networks of kinship and neighborhood; and generally to do whatever was necessary to support families during the men's absences.

As in the eighteenth century, what women actually did on a daily basis depended on their family status, their age and access to resources, and whether they found themselves in (or took themselves to) more rural or more urban settings. Other historians have suggested that the broad process of industrialization over the nineteenth century brought with it an increasing differentiation between men's work as specialized, spatially segregated, cash- and time-oriented, and women's work as less specialized or segregated and persisting in its task orientation.[92] Within the whaling community, though, the extent of specialization, segregation, or task orientation of men's work aboard ship and the intermittent nature of seafaring did not change fundamentally, any more than did the nature of women's work onshore. What did change was the lengthening of voyages and of professional whalemen's careers and the narrowing of their occupational identities accordingly. In contrast, nineteenth-century women's work lives continued to display the same sort of diversity and occupational pluralism as did that of their colonial forebears, both male and female.

In 1840, Jared Gardner wrote from aboard ship to his wife Harriet, back at home on Nantucket: "When I turn in [to sleep] and hol that camfiter on me that our sweet sister gave me I think of the patch work that she pointed out to me that was of your dress. It seams allmost as though I can sea you with it on. . . . Pleas give my love to all our friends and brothers and sisters and that dear one who lade asside her own work and assisted in making my clothes for they are as well as hands can make them."[93] Jared was reminded of a whole community of loved ones when he held his emotionally laden quilt close to him; his quilt, and the homesick reminiscing it inspired, reminds us of the fundamental continuities in the work of maritime women like Harriet and her sisters. As was the case in the eighteenth century, malleable households, geographic mobility, extensive community interaction, and a sense of sisterhood enabled nineteenth-century women to share their domestic responsibilities and tasks. This flexibility proved especially important in the context of the whalefishery, where the division of labor between wives and husbands was increasingly measured in years and hemispheres.

With the stirrings of industrialization in the region, along with demographic and economic growth due in part to the booming whalefishery, the kinds of work available to women and their opportunities for earning cash wages expanded.[94] In the whaling region, as in the rest of the antebellum Northeast, young women were a bit more independent and mobile before marriage, just like their brothers setting off for sea — only on a much reduced scale, and only if their kinfolk could spare them. In 1850, Ruth Grinnell told her sweetheart, whaleman James Sowle, that she thought of going from Westport up to Fall River for work, though she didn't specify what kind.[95] "Sister Sally" filled in her brother Horatio, at sea on the bark *Mattapoisett,* on the activities of their unmarried siblings and peers: "Sarah lives to home [in Westport] this summer . . . Mary is over here [New Bedford] learning a trade Albert has gone out West . . . I still board to Charles & work in the shop." Similarly, Perry Lawton informed George Allen, his friend at sea, of the whereabouts of the Westport "girls" they knew: "Mary Ann Brownell keeps school down here and Hannah at the Sandford schoolhouse, Elizabeth keeps with her mother . . . Hannah Tripp and Beck live single yet, Almeda King works at the tiverton four corners . . . your beloved Sarah C. Tripp is going next week to learn to be a tailoress."[96]

Marriage appears to have reduced women's independence but not necessarily the scope of their activities. The broadest responsibility for sustaining their families and households and, by extension, the stability of their communities, fell squarely onto the married women's shoulders, as it had for generations. In the more urban areas of the region, barter was increasingly replaced by transactions involving cash. With the increasing interpenetration of the market and the household economy, married women often found themselves short of necessary cash during their husbands' absences: "I *must* have more money," Harriet Allen worried.[97] With the evolution of the "lay" system and the limitations in industry paternalism, wives had to find other ways to support their families. Women in New Bedford or other urban centers earned money by accepting various kinds of piecework, especially sewing, or by taking in boarders or purveying many different kinds of goods in small retail shops.[98] Centre Street, part of the business district in Nantucket, was even called "Petticoat Row" for its female shopkeepers.[99] Many women in the maritime communities certainly participated in other, less licit income-raising activities in the grogshops and brothels that so horrified Zephaniah Pease, but, significantly, the kinds of work taken on by the women who were connected to the career whalemen remained clearly within the bounds of middle-class respectability.[100]

The whalefishery itself expanded the opportunities for women to use their needles and their housewifery skills. Over a three-year period Eliza Stanton earned $27.17 sewing shirts for sailors for the New Bedford outfitters Cook & Snow. In 1837, the Ladies' Branch of the New Bedford Port Society for the Moral Improvement of Seamen opened a nonprofit clothing store for sailors, hiring as seamstresses seamen's wives and daughters, at wages somewhat higher than average; it is not clear from the surviving records why the store closed a few years later. Opportunities for piece-work, though perhaps at lower wages, continued: Sarah Cory wrote her husband, "I have so much sewing all the time I dont hardly know what to do some times but they wont take no for an answer so I am obliged to do it."[101]

Taking in boarders may have tied or surpassed sewing in women's income-producing possibilities. The practice ranged from the small-scale, informal, and occasional to large-scale commercial enterprise. Sylvia Sowle of New Bedford casually took in four ships carpenters as boarders for a few months, reporting to her absent husband, "they are very good bords i like the buisness much beter than i expected to." In contrast, while Captain Silas Fisk commanded whalers in distant seas, his wife Julia back home in Groton, Connecticut, ran a seaside resort–style boardinghouse that accommodated dozens of guests at a time, among them the famed sentimental poet Lydia Sigourney.[102]

In rural areas, women like Hannah Blackmer of Acushnet, Mary Ann Braley of Rochester, Caroline Gifford of Dartmouth, and Caroline Omey of Westport typically kept farms going with their own labor and that of their children, other relatives, neighbors, and hired help. In addition to helping out on her parents-in-law's farmstead, Hannah Ashley gave piano lessons to two neighboring girls and also utilized her apparently consider-able dressmaking skills (cutting out, fitting, gathering, and pleating) for several local women.[103]

Abby Grinnell of rural Tiverton, Rhode Island, told her husband, Stephen Grinnell, then commanding the Westport ship *Barclay*, on 6 Sep-tember 1845: "Your baby is fat and she grows like a weed. You little man Philip and Stephen go to school and they learn very fast. Your daughters remember their love to their respected father." Abby was equally fortu-nate with their crops and livestock: "Our corn is very large and the barley is very good. We have thrashed that in the corner lot and in the lot by the house and we got sixty bushels . . . Gideon's corn is not near so large as yours. I gues that there will be more weeds in the orchard than potatoes. I have bought me a cow to fat and I gave eleven dollars for her. Your oxen have done very well this summer and they are fat enough for beef. The carrot is as thick as white weed down below Gideon's corn and we want you to hom to be a pulling it. . . . I hope that you will be so lucky that you will come next spring and as much sooner as you are a mind to."[104] Abby's choice in pronouns is telling. With her attributions, she not only included her absent husband in the family activities, she also downplayed her own obvious decisiveness in deference to his authority within the family.

Sarah Wilkey, of the neighboring town of Westport, sat down just a day later to write to her husband Alden, who seems to have been serving as mate under Captain Grinnell on the *Barclay*. But Sarah had less fortunate news to report: "We had a heavy hail storm across here this summer which cut the corn & vegatables to peices . . . some of the stones were as large as hens eggs." Moreover, adding insult to injury, "the worms have eat up most all the corn." But she resolutely "went a claming and caught a good fare," adding, with a touch of humor, "& hope you will doo as well as I did."[105]

In both urban and rural areas throughout the region, informal sharing and exchange between households of food, household necessities and luxuries, and reading material persisted. Harriet Allen, who worried so about cash shortfalls, was also involved in frequent exchanges of household goods. She sent a bag of flour to one Ellen (probably her sister) on 6 June 1863; a week later her sister-in-law Phebe Ann loaned her some tubs. Other equally typical notations in Harriet's diary recorded on 10 February 1863 that "Sylvia brought two numbers of the 'Little Pilgrim'" and on 14 February, "Mary Nickerson came. Let her have one of my [illegible] shells & received a few in return."[106] Susan Snow Gifford wrote her husband John, "I am going to carry that boul and saucer home that you brought those scraps from Mrs Stephens in you forgot to carry them home and she will certainly think she has lost them."[107]

Whether they worked for wages or by the piece in town, carefully managed a family budget and supplemented cash resources with neighborly sharing and exchange, or kept a farm going in an outlying area, women did whatever they could—and had to—in support of their families, most importantly their children. As elsewhere in America at the time, being a wife was inextricably linked to motherhood, even here where the spacing between children corresponded more closely to the length of whaling voyages than to female biological rhythms.[108] It was assumed without question that the mother bore the major responsibility for the children. She was, after all, the one left onshore with them, from the very moment of conception.

One Alexander Hathaway, lately retired from sea, wrote descriptively in 1843 to his "Dear Brother," Captain Henry Brightman: "I will draw along down Bridge Street where a young woman lives upstairs, over a

Baker Shop. She shows her good keeping very much and in your letter you caution me about introducing new members, but people that lives in glass houses should not through stones, if I am not mistaken in my calculation between the 15th and the last of July will be an interesting period in said house and you will be permitted to have the honnor of a new title say for instance *PA*." Brightman had left New Bedford in command of the brig *Solon* in late October of 1842; Hathaway observed that the pregnancy "must be news to you." But he assured his whaling brother, "Katherine has been up and spent a week with us. . . . She appears to be quite reconciled to her situation though it does not agree with her very well yet I think she will wether it first rate . . . she has plenty of friends and comforters which makes such cares more pleasant than they otherways would be."[109]

Many maritime mothers certainly cherished and delighted in their children, now much more explicitly and intensely than their eighteenth-century foremothers had done—in a reflection of the increased importance accorded motherhood in society at large as well as due to their husbands' longer absences.[110] Selina Coffin reported to her husband, "Jethro Frank . . . is a darling boy just as good as he can be."[111] "Between you & me," Caroline Gifford confided to her husband about their toddler son, "he is the smartest & hansomest boy that I ever see."[112]

But many other sea-wives found that maritime motherhood could be a both burdensome and compromised role. Betsey King, for one, found the maternal responsibilities particularly heavy. In 1850, she told her husband, Captain James King Jr., that their youngest daughter, also named Betsey, was "a real little chatterbox." The harried mother confessed (or complained), "I get along very well when the other two are at school but when they come home it seems sometimes as though I should go crazy." Their son James, she wrote, "is a pretty good boy but you know that he is a very great talker and he loves to hector the other children . . . Matilda will not bear a might from him." Not surprisingly, Mrs. King noted, "It is a task to bring up three children," and she added humbly, "I feel the responsibility more and more every day and my deficency in doing my duty to them, I know that I can do nothing without the help of the holy spirit and I do pray to my heavenly father that he would guide and direct in the right path."[113]

Myra Weeks, who noted that "I have to write with one hand and rock the cradle with the other," apparently found the duties downright onerous. She was less willing than Betsey King to assume the properly humble and pious posture; nor did Myra acknowledge either the delights of motherhood or of a privatized home. She wrote somewhat acidly to her whaling husband in 1842, "I think it is rather lonesome to be shut up here day after day with 3 little children to take care of. I should be glad to know how you would like [it]." [114]

For some twenty-five years after her marriage in 1849, Caroline Gifford ran the family farm in Dartmouth while her husband Charles commanded one whaler after another on Pacific voyages. Despite her years of experience, Caroline did not find raising a family an easy task. Two years after expressing such delight at the birth of her second son, she was evidently having problems handling her first one, then nine years old, and wrote to warn Charles, "I think Norman begins to need the care of a judicious man." She found her two daughters easier to deal with; she especially appreciated the help of her oldest child, Eleanor. Nonetheless, at one point, Caroline wrote in exasperation, "If I have got to work any harder I had rather go to the Alms house." In her next letter, she complained, "I call it a trial to bring up a family mostly without any Father to help manage." [115] For some women, then, extensive community interaction on shore evidently did not always mitigate the stresses of what was widely perceived as single parenting. With an absent father, the Victorian "Empire of the Mother" could be an unhappy realm indeed.[116]

Despite both the range of women's activities and their vital necessity, career whalemen, like so many men of the period, did not consider women's work to be labor in a productive sense, just as they failed to recognize women's substantive contributions to the industry itself.[117] Work, especially heavy manual labor, was something many mariners emphatically did not want their wives to do. First mate Charles Peirce told his wife, "You dont seem to say much about your health. I do hope you do not over work yourself, loocking out for every thing, both out doors & in." He coyly reminded her, "You know Eliza, I have always strickly forbiden you to work to[o] hard, and you know Wifey, thou hast Promised to honor, and *obey* thy Husband." [118] William Ashley, who had left his wife Hannah behind on his parents' farm in Acushnet, wrote: "Han I have bin thinking it is to bad to ceep you thare to Fathers working like a squaw[,] so I want you to hire a good girl to help you[,] and then if you can not get a long[,] moove to New Bedford and write to me and I will send you a way to live if you have not got enough." [119]

Like Charles and William, Henry Beetle worried about his wife performing manual labor. In April 1846 he wrote to Eliza, "You gave me a small description of a days work you done, I fear you will shorten your days. . . . I do not want my wife to work so hard. Is there no one you could get to cut your wood? . . . if I was with you I could help you do a few of the chores, but as I am not, I rather you would hire your wood cut." The following September, Henry wrote again: "I must say to you cut no more wood . . . I hope I shall be able to support you and little sis [their daughter Adeline] without you doing such work." In October: "I want you to be carefull of your health and dont cut any more wood"; and in March 1847: "When I begin to write, my mind is far, far away where I wish to be to cut some wood." In fact, in every single letter Eliza received from him over the next year, Henry insisted that she avoid cutting wood, even though he apologized, "I feel very sorry that I did not leave you better provided for but you must take the will for the deed." [120]

At first glance, Henry Beetle's preoccupation with the woodpile reads a bit comically now, 150 years later. On further consideration, though, his repetitiveness appears significant, laden with a symbolism expressing ideas about gender and class. For centuries a supply of firewood had been a basic necessity of life, one of the essentials granted by New England towns to their indigent and often specified as part of widows' portions.[121] Henry Beetle's inability to provide his wife and child with the means to acquire wood seemed to stand for his failure as his family's sole support and thereby, with the new definitions of masculinity and femininity, challenged his very manhood. The image of Eliza outside, swinging an ax and hewing wood, seems to have upset Henry's notions of female delicacy and dependence.

None of Eliza's letters have survived. Henry's great delight at hearing from her indicates that her correspondence was probably not recriminatory, though his insistent reiteration suggests that she may have gone ahead and did what she needed to do in spite of his protestations. After all, how could she and Adeline stay warm by taking his will for the deed? While Henry worried from afar about the proper form of women's work, Eliza had to supply the substance of her child's needs.

As they had done from the colonial beginnings of the fishery, whalemen and the industry at large continued to rely on family members on land for support, both tangible and intangible. Some of support changed form in the nineteenth-century environment, as the industry, along with the American economy more generally, expanded and restructured; more of it, however—in particular, much of the content of women's work and responsibilities—remained unchanged. Despite the continuities, though, women's relationship to the fishery and to the men at sea was radically reconceptualized in the nineteenth century, showing the influence of the new ideas about sexual difference. Under increasingly trying conditions—men's absences of up to five years at a time—these men and their female relations were persuaded to fill crucial, complementary roles and to perform necessary services by the new cultural forms, which stressed the dependency of the women at home and defined the manhood of career mariners in part by their ability to provide for their families.[122] These notions were built into the social relations of work within the industry as it developed and were incorporated into the occupational identity of the career whalemen. The concepts shaped the mariners' relationships both with their employers, the managing shipowners, and with the men under their command at sea. The rhetoric also had real consequences for the gendered allocation of responsibilities and distribution of cash and other resources—even as it downplayed or failed to acknowledge altogether the substantive support that nineteenth-century women continued to provide both to maritime enterprise directly and to their families and communities on shore.

The linchpin of the whole system was widely understood to be the emotional bonds between the career mariners at sea and the women in their families at home—their mothers, sisters, and, above all, their wives. In particular, the conjugal relationship—idealized as the passionate union of two hearts, "the silken cord wound round us," as Leonard Gifford expressed it—inspired the sense of responsibility that sent men to sea and the longing that brought them home again. A parallel understanding of love and its importance also recruited women to provide a myriad of services to the fishery and the fishermen. Sustaining their families, households, and communities while their men plied the seas and did battle with the leviathan whale was difficult enough for these women. As we shall see in Chapter 5, it was even more problematic to maintain the requisite passion and intimacy during repeated separations stretching over years and thousands of miles. By midcentury, a more restricted pool of career whalemen went away on more difficult voyages of markedly longer duration, repeatedly over more of their lives. The impact of the fishery's expansion and brutalization on maritime women's and men's experience of gender and family life was enormous.

LOVE, MARRIAGE, & FAMILY
IN THE NINETEENTH-CENTURY
WHALING COMMUNITIES

On Sunday, 3 February 1850, 21-year-old Ruth Grinnell took up her pen and began to write a letter, which she addressed on the back:

> James M. Sowle   Ship Harbinger
> Westport   Fisher   Pacific Ocean

Some twenty months earlier, on 15 May 1848, the whale-ship *Harbinger* had left the harbor of Westport, Massa-chusetts (just west of New Bedford), under the command of a Captain Fisher. James Sowle, in his mid-twenties, was the first mate (or second in command) of the *Harbinger*. He was also Ruth's fiancé. By February 1850, the ship and James were somewhere deep in the South Pacific. Back in Westport, on eight or nine different occasions over the next seven weeks (usually on Sundays), Ruth continued her letter to James, filling all four sides of the folded paper with nearly three hundred narrow lines of tight script and small, fanciful doodling. When she finished three pages, she decided to use the back page too and to send the letter in an envelope instead—so she simply wrote (sideways) right over the address. She eventually filled in the margins and every other blank space on all four pages, writing sideways, upside down, across, and between lines already written. She remarked to James, "I think you will have quite a job to read this letter, and when you have done so I think you had better destroy it, it is such a looking thing."[1]

She was right: the letter *is* hard to read, even more so now after a century and a half of fading. But we are fortunate that James did not take up her suggestion to destroy the letter. It is not a particularly unusual or remarkable document, though its careful preservation by the recipient and by succeeding generations indicates its emotional importance, just as with so many of the thousands of similar letters sent between ship and shore that have survived to today. Ruth's letter to James, though, is remarkably revealing of the pervasive influence of the dominant mid-nineteenth-century ideals about love, marriage, womanhood, and manhood—and their contradictions.

"Very unexpectedly I take up my pen to address to you a few lines," Ruth began, in a formal tone and formulaic phrasing, "but Oh! where can I find happiness, except it is in conversation with you: true a few trifling lines scrabbled on a piece of paper and very doubtful whether it will ever meet your view, affords but a small share of pleasure in comparison to what it would be, could I behold you face to face, and enjoy your society forever, in this and the future world." A few lines later, though, she abruptly switched into a less formal, less literary tone: "I said that it was unexpectedly that I took up my pen, but to-day is the sabbath and I am extremely lonesome and sad, I have not written to you before in a very long time, I think not since last spring, thinking then that it would be almost useless to write as it would be but a short time before you would be on your passage home, but I am afraid of being disappointed."

This opening proved characteristic of the whole document. Throughout Ruth's letter, formulaic references to romantic conventions, expressed in elaborate and sometimes stilted sentences, alternate with passages that are less formal, less structured, and less complex in terms of syntax and vocabulary. Significantly, Ruth turned to romantic formula most often when she wrote about her feelings for James. She drew on prescribed ideals, expressed through literary conventions, to work out this new, most intimate, exclusive relationship and her role in it. In contrast, the less formal, anecdotal, and spontaneous passages deal most often with other people—their friends, families, and neighbors, men as well as women—the broad local community in which Ruth lived and experienced every day. The alternating pattern in Ruth's letter does not reflect, as some historians have suggested, a sex-segregated world in which more formal and strained relationships between men and women were differentiated from more familiar and emotionally intense ones between women themselves.[2] Instead, the alternation points to a fundamental tension between prescription and description, between, on the one hand, increasingly inflated cultural expectations of the exclusive and intimate marital relationship (expectations that were deeply implicated in American political and economic life), and, on the other, the competing demands of the whalemen's occupation and community life on shore.

As the fishery expanded in the nineteenth century, whalemen were absent from their homes on longer and longer voyages, over greater distances, and, for many of them, over more of their adult lives. Most men in this group first went to sea in their midteens. James shipped out on his first voyage in 1837 at either age 12 or 14 (the sources disagree). Quite typically, over the next thirteen years before his marriage in 1851, James made at least five voyages, with intervals at home in between ranging from two to six months. It must have been during one of these rather short interludes, probably his last time home before shipping out on the *Harbinger*, that he and Ruth formed an exclusive commitment. James continued to ply the sea until at least 1869, making voyages well into his forties. For men and women like James and Ruth, not only courtship but also the resulting marriages were considerably complicated. Gender role prescription became particularly important to maritime couples as they tried to create and maintain private and emotionally close relationships over extremes of time and space.

James and the *Harbinger* would not return to their home port of Westport until 25 July 1851, over three years out, even though Ruth wrote plaintively, "I hope you will not prolong your voyage to a great length of time for I had rather see you than all the oil a dozen such ships as the Harbinger would hold." Strictly speaking, it wasn't up to James, which Ruth surely knew; the length of a voyage was worked out, over time, between the captain, the shipowners, and fate—or, more precisely, the accidents and natural disasters to which whalers were only too susceptible. James could have chosen to leave the ship midvoyage, but that would have compromised his reputation in the industry as a committed whaleman and thereby jeopardized his chances for promotion to captain. James chose to remain with the ship. Ruth well understood the dynamics in such masculine decisions: she qualified her plea by adding, "Excuse my weakness," referring to the cliché that a woman's judgment might be impaired by the strength of her love. That love, sustained by a whole set of such romantic clichés and gender conventions, survived the 38-month separation: James and Ruth were married just two weeks after his return from sea. For this couple, the script worked. Within a year, James was off to sea again, this time as captain.[3]

It is a simple, even obvious point, but one with profound emotional consequences: men like James derived their identity primarily from their work. They were first and foremost whalemen; they would carry the memories and even the bodily marks of seafaring to the grave. If they made it to the top rank, they would be called "Captain" for the rest of their lives. Women like Ruth derived their identity from their connections to these men, as maritime daughters, sisters, mothers, and especially as sea-wives or, as they were often popularly termed at the time, "Cape Horn widows."[4] As discussed in Chapter 4, marriage mattered to the career whalemen in part because it provided the justification and often the inspiration for their seafaring as well as compensation for some of its more brutal aspects. Anchored by a shared understanding of exclusive conjugal love, marriage was a comforting and stable point of reference for the men while they were tossed about by wind and wave, attempted to exert absolute authority over ship and crew, and risked their lives in mortal combat with the leviathan whale. Most women in the whaling communities also married, despite their personal familiarity with the rhythms, risks, and tragedies of the fishery. The assumptions they shared with the men about the nature of womanhood and manhood, love, and marriage were crucial to sustaining the relationships that formed the core of their identities during the separations mandated by the fishery. But, over the course of women's and men's relationships, from courtship to marriage to becoming parents to being widowed (a trajectory in the maritime context that was punctuated by repeated partings and separations), prescription inextricably mingled with description in ways that validated and heightened certain aspects of women's experience and downplayed or negated others, emphasizing female emotional roles to such an extent that, paradoxically, it made men's absences even harder to survive.

All that remains from Ruth's own hand is the one long letter she wrote to James, yet from its closely written pages a strong impression of her personality and the texture of her life emerge for us, as they did for Ruth herself in the very act of writing. A number of historians have noted that rising literacy rates and improvements in communication technology and transportation enabled nineteenth-century couples, family members, and friends to connect frequently and at length through written correspondence.[5] The difference for Ruth was that, given James's occupation, her writing not only supplemented but had to substitute for more immediate interaction. She insisted—she had to—that her moments with James "are all fresh in my memory as if it were but yesterday, and never will the recollections of them and a hundred other things be erased from my remembrance." Ruth reaffirmed their attachment both by committing her memories and thoughts to paper and by bringing them to James's attention. In so doing, she also developed and practiced the new role she was entering, sailor's sweetheart and future wife, working out the details of her evolving relationship with James and with her family and community.[6]

Ruth drew on pervasive ideas about manhood and womanhood that by then permeated the whaling communities of southeastern New England just as they did most of American society at large. The dominant but rather schizophrenic ideal of manhood called for the public exercise of self-control, strength, courage, competitiveness, and occupational competence and authority, but also expected fidelity, compassion, and tender, loving intimacy within private family relationships.[7] Nantucketer Roland Russell advised his twin sister Jane in 1838 that men were supposed to be "smart, active, industrious, sober [and] virtuous." Given reports of his sister's sailor-suitor, Roland considered him "well worthy of your first & best affections."[8]

Such affection was not only what women could bestow on their loved ones, it was one of the core elements that (ostensibly) defined their very characters. Captain Hiram Coffin implied as much when, in 1823, he reminded his 11-year-old daughter Betsey of her long-deceased mother: "My Dear Love revere your Mothers Memory for she was every thing that was Lovely in Woman. She was an honour to her Sex. Such a Mind . . . was the Seat of all the Superior qualitys—of Modesty, Chacity [chastity], Sincerity, Virtue, piety, friendship, and Love. She caused every body to

Love her that New her."[9] Expressing a similar understanding of female sensibility and sympathy, in 1841 Captain Seth Pinkham described his wife as "one who has been taught to feel by living experience, most sensibly, the vibrations of every pang."[10] From "on board the Bark Stella" in 1864, Captain Seth Blackmer told his "dear *treasure* of a wife" that she was a "trusting Loveing and industrious little Woman the moddle of mothers and who strives to make Home happy."[11] These sorts of idealizations of women as tender, modest, chaste, selfless, sympathetic, emotive, maternal, devoted, and domestic (and also often diminutive) abound in the nineteenth-century ship-to-shore correspondence—just as in contemporaneous literature. Melville himself described Captain Ahab's wife as "a sweet resigned girl," summing up much of the essence of Victorian feminine ideals.[12]

Women were also supposed to be particularly and uniquely pious: religiosity had now become even more firmly a female gender characteristic, closely linked to domesticity. The flood tide of evangelical Protestantism rising in early nineteenth-century America promoted sensibility, surrender to strong feeling, specifically in the immediate experience of God's presence at religious revivals. But by midcentury, mass public revivals had declined and even ministers in their pulpits preached that such religious experiences were most appropriately located in the private "gingerbread cathedrals of home." As the more naturally feeling, sensitive, and loving beings, women were assumed to be more susceptible to spiritual influence and thus more suited to proselytize. Marriage and motherhood were sacred duties, and women's love for husbands and children was infused and reinforced by (rather than competing with) love for God.[13]

Faced with the void of prolonged separation of uncertain length, over vast distance and with severely limited channels of communication, Ruth and other maritime women and men were forced to rely on the prevailing assumptions about the innate nature of womanhood and manhood as they pursued the romantic ideals those ideas supported. These cultural prescriptions proved to be instrumental. Indeed, in constructing her relationship with James and her own identity in that relationship, Ruth invoked virtually every trope in the Victorian sentimental sourcebook.

Ruth portrayed herself in accordance with romantic conventions and ideals of femininity in several ways:

Woman as nurturing, sympathetic supporter: "James do not be discouraged, keep up good sprits and if you do your duty to God and man nothing more is required of you. Do not, my love, hesitate to write me as often as ever on account of your unluckiness, — so much the more I want to hear from you, that I can sympathize with you."

Woman as moral arbiter: "James do you swear at all[?] I hope not, after the promises you made to me . . . I sincerely hope my own dear James does not take Gods name in vain . . . James I do not want you to deceive me by swearing when you are out of my presence . . . or to try to make me think that you do not for you know that I abhor deception."

Woman as religious exhorter: "I was very sorry to hear you had been sick; but I am glad you realize the shortness and uncertainty of time. Oh my dear James, may you wisely consider the subject and throw it not carelessly aside, remember that you are momentarily exposed to danger and that God alone is your protector, and can you expect him to guard you while you continue in sin and disobedience to him? Go now to your Saviour and plead and beseech him to forgive your sins and to make you a new creature, sinless before the world. James if you ever need religion you need it now . . . Let not my entreaties be in vain, I cannot repent for you, would that I could."

Woman as flighty and capricious: "*James* do not think I am crazy when you see this scrabbling for I am nothing more so than I *used to be*" (her emphasis; line followed by doodles of a bird, a flower bud and leaves, diamonds, and cross hatches).

Along with the construction of her own feminine identity, Ruth also characterized her and James's relationship in terms lifted straight from the romantic blueprint:

The love object as the focal point of one's earthly existence: "What should I do if you should die, I should long to die, all I have to hold me here is you."

The loved one, the companion of one's heart, as the only true friend: "I should like to know where you are to-day, whether you are sick or well[,] dead or alive. I wish it was so that you could be here then I should not be so lonesome. You know that I have no dear friend to whom I can pour out my joys and griefs[,] none that will share them with me."

Love conquers all: "It is not because I love you any the less, no, for every day do I love you more devotedly, time and distance does not make me forget, but the longer I am seperated from you the more I miss your society."

Association of romance and love with natural phenomena, and courtship in particular with twilight (an in-between or liminal identity linked with the moment in between day and night): "It is now sunset . . . I wish you could be here that we might have a friendly chat, or take a short walk and contemplate the vast works of nature."

Association of issues of the heart and communion with solitude, again especially at nightfall: "Now is the time that I most miss you, now that the day is over and the shades of night come on and all is still and I am left alone to my own reflections, what but you, at such an hour as this, would occupy my thoughts. James my dear do your thoughts ever roam as far as here[,] do you ever think of me?"

Association of the sabbath and religious observance with human love, its celebration, and its suffering: "To-day is the sabbath and I am extremely lonesome and sad" and "20 months have rolled into eternity since you left your native land, but were I certain that in 20 months more you and I would be here where I now am, I should be far more cheerful than I now am, but my absent one I must bid you adieu for a time, and good night for the present."

Explicit association of love with literary expression, particularly poetry (at least rhyme):

Remember when these lines you see
A friend that often thinks of thee,
When far upon the distant sea
Think of a friend that thinks of thee.

The fear of deceit[14] *(the flip side of total commitment):* "Have I centered my all in a false deceiving man: even should I marry you[,] how easily might you destroy my happiness—" and "James my love[,] will what I have written interest you enough for you to read it, or will you when have read a few words, say, Oh foolish nonsense I do not care any thing about it, she will think that I read it and that will do just as well. James do I judge you wrong if I do excuse me, and if I do'nt I hope I shall find it out before it is too late, can you my dear one blame me for doubting when there is so much deception in the world."

The private, heart-centered home in opposition to the external public realm: "The world seems so cold and thoughtless but if you were here then should I have a friend in whom I could confide, in whom I could . . . trust, shall I say, trust, would that I could say so without doubt." (That is her ellipsis, which underscores the self-consciously literary form of her phrasing here.)

In striking contrast to the sentimental passages directly concerning her relationship with James and also notably at odds with the fears she expresses about the "cold and thoughtless" world filled with "deception," about a third of Ruth's letter consists of chatty, informal segments which describe a closely interconnected world of peer group, family, and neighbors. In one such section, for example, Ruth informed James: "We have had a very morderate winter so far but little very cold weather . . . Isaac Brightman had the misfortune to break his leg. I do not know how it happened. James Hazzard split his Puree pan coasting down hill on the ice . . . Tell Peleg [another local man aboard the *Harbinger* with James] his father is here, they have not moved from the Wilkie house I think they will stay another year." A week later, she added, "Last Thursday I went to the Point, I called to your sister's, I found her quite well, but your mother was there and she is miserable; she is very much stuffed at the lungs and very billious." Ruth included news of other local whaleships as well: "The Catherwood that sailed just before you, is reported with 300 bbls sp [barrels of sperm oil] but they happened to be fortunate. The Mattapoisett is doing very well[.] Samuel Devol is in her." [15] In these less self-conscious passages, Ruth defined herself and James within their local community. By communicating this kind of information to James, she enabled him to maintain at least a vicarious place at home and stressed their shared interest in it, even while he traveled to the other side of the world.

Even in some of these less formal passages, Ruth was overtly flirtatious, sometimes with a coyness that may have been intended to raise his insecurities as hers were raised by his very absence. "Jim I am about to give you up and take Mr. [scrolling line of loops] can you interpret that long name, its no matter if you cant." Some passages later: "You recollect of hearing me speak of Henry Buffington, well he is courting Lydia Ann Case. what do you think of that, I think she would not have you at any rate whatever if she can get a dandy and a gentleman. [tiny doodle of flowers in a basket] I think you had better look out for there as been a great dandy here today, Charley Sisson from Fall River, a merchant tailor, and a single gentleman too. and James he went to the Point rocks with me. where you and I *used* to go. But he did not carry the Point rocks off with him and we will go there again if you ever get home. wont we" (her emphasis).

Ruth's teasing with its undercurrent of threat served as a sort of ritualized test of emotional commitment, which, cultural historian Karen Lystra explains, characterized courtship at this time. Lystra finds that such ritualized exchanges between lovers formed "the central structure" of American courtship and describes how "[c]ourtship spirals of doubt and reassurance intensified the emotions and solidified the identification of couples going into marriage. . . . The courtship testing that preceded marriage was a ceremony that helped to clarify and strengthen the couple's feelings for each other." [16] A few lines after the "Point Rocks" passage, Ruth demanded, "James I should like to know what the reason is you do'nt write nothing about coming home, do'nt you think or care any thing about it." But with James so far distant, Ruth had to supply both call and response of the ritual exchange; perhaps it was too dangerous to leave unanswered until James returned. She immediately answered her own question: "I know you do my own dear love, and I hope you may be permitted to return."

Because of Ruth's late decision to use the fourth page for text rather than the address, there are two endings to the letter. As with the opening passage, both endings abruptly juxtapose romantic literary conventions with everyday commonplaces. Ruth wrote, first: "I have not room for much more, I hope you will get this, and that I shall see you as soon as will be reasonable, do write when you are coming home. bring all the remarkable curiosities you can easily obtain, without much expense, Dearest I am thine and I trust thou are mine forever."

In the second ending, she crammed into a corner on the back page in very small writing a whole list of platitudes, which neatly sums up nearly all of the contradictions in Victorian romanticism and gender ideals. "Now James I am going to send this letter hoping that you may in due time receive it although it is a mess of nonsense, but my love do not get angry for you know we are a weak sex. my prayers are that you may return once more that we may be permitted to meet again. James be a good boy be careful of your health, write often, do not swear, tell Peleg not to swear. I wish you would come home this fall. do not be discouraged, your life and health is all. the last report [of the *Harbinger*] was in December 50 bbls more than when you wrote I have not got any letters of that date but am in hopes to and now my own dearest James Fare well for a Season[.] Yours forever R. A. G."

Ruth's letter did, apparently, reach its destination, for it was carefully saved and returned, probably in July of 1851, with James and the *Harbinger* (but not with Peleg, who had drowned somewhere in the Pacific in August 1850). The letter, preserved in the manuscripts collection of the New Bedford Whaling Museum Library, is all we have of Ruth 150 years later. But the document is, I think, remarkably evocative of the person she was and was trying to be. Ruth's efforts at self-definition come across now as derivative and perhaps even just slightly comical, but they are deeply poignant nonetheless. After all, when she wrote the letter, she hadn't seen James in nearly two years; what else—other than prescription and convention—did she have?

Courtship and marriage—her own and those of her peers—surface again and again in Ruth Grinnell's letter to James. "Oh, Oh, Oh, you cannot guess who is married no less than Christiana Manchester to Mr Joseph Brownell of Little Compton . . . Maria Slocum is not married but expects to soon. almost every one is marrying off, I am afraid you wont get back and I must improve the opportunity while one presents, and as for you, you can take Selina, ha, ha." Poor Selina; Ruth again made her the butt of an arch joke, in the margin: "I saw Selina [Ball?] the other day I expect she is waiting very patiently your return James do you calculate to marry her when you get home. Tell Peleg Rhoda Manchester has lost her beau John but tell him Abbie Albert has got a beau I believe."

Courtship was the process by which individuals paired up—formed that all-important, exclusive, intimate relationship—and separated themselves off from others in constructing a new family unit. As it had in the previous century, the performance of courtship rituals and activities continued to occur within a communal context of peers and community-based activities. But in the nineteenth century parents and other community elders exercised considerably less direct influence over courtship and marriage choice, and young women and men exercised considerably more individual freedom. When Jane Russell of Nantucket wrote her twin brother Roland in 1838 about her indecision over a prospect of marriage, she reported that she had "Friends to Advise me some one thing and some other but after all tell me too suit myself." [17]

Jane was anticipating the return of her whaleman-suitor from the Pacific: "they have been absent 39 months and probably will not stay many more," she thought. She told Roland that she had been "very much tried and perplexed in my own mind" and felt deeply the lack of "a Father's Counsel and a Mother's advice" (both their parents had died several years earlier). Roland agreed with Jane on the "importance of weighing well every argument for or against the single & the Married life" because "upon this depends in a great measure your Happiness or Misery during life." Jane declared, "I am half Inclined to live an Old Maid [but] from the acquaintance I formed with Mr. Thomas S. Andrews I seemed to think that If I were to make a Choice of a Companion it might possibly be him." One of her reservations seemed to be his family, which, she wrote, "is not just what I should like." (It is not clear what about Andrews's family bothered Jane; perhaps it was his oldest sister's bearing of a child out of wedlock some fourteen years before.) Roland advised Jane that "it would be gratifying to be connected with a person of respectable parentage & who are in good standing in society" but added that, given Mr. Andrews's own evident virtues, "friends or fortune" were "of minor consequence." Jane had only asked for her twin brother's "good advice," but Roland concluded somewhat pompously, "if . . . you have well considered the dutys and responsibilities of the married life & the disadvantages and perplexities of a life of celibacy I should cheerfully give my consent to your union with the man of your choice."[18] Jane did so choose; she married Thomas shortly after his return in 1839. Their son, whom they named Roland, was born the following year.

The historian Ellen Rothman, in her history of courtship in America, describes how in the late eighteenth and early nineteenth centuries, "girls and boys met on the lanes and commons of the village and in the houses of their neighbors and kinfolk; they encountered each other in church, schoolroom, and shop. . . . They went berrying, riding, picnicking; they sang and danced together at parties and balls." Well into the antebellum period, as in the previous century, "male-female socializing did not depend on special occasions but was integrated into the routine of everyday life." Furthermore, "young people had the autonomy and privacy to develop relationships that were sexually and emotionally intimate, and they did."[19]

In her letter to James, Ruth Grinnell described in some detail the activities by which she and James courted, which, judging by the research of Rothman and other historians,[20] seem quite typical of their period, region, and socioeconomic setting: "James do you remember our visit to N.B. [New Bedford], and our walk to look up the horse and carraige, . . . our strolls about the meadows after wildflowers, and the time we went to meeting to the schoolhouse, and the numerous walks to the Point rock, and one time I hid your knife in the sand, and you said 'Oh blast you' have you forgotten all these. And oh James the last Sabbath you were here when you came down . . . And the morning you sailed."

A remarkable set of sources allows us to compare the expectations and attitudes of Ruth and James with those of other maritime courting couples

The charming watercolor, "Popping Corn," ca. 1856, by local artist Benjamin Russell, conveys a vivid sense of socializing and especially courtship in New Bedford–area parlors. Courtesy of Old Dartmouth Historical Society–New Bedford Whaling Museum (Neg. 2954)

and to assess their typicality: a mailbag of dead letters dating from the 1840s and 1850s, preserved among the papers of a midcentury postmaster in the New Bedford area. It appears that Ruth and James were not unusual in their courtship, either in their activities or in their reliance on prescription. Constant reference to ideals of romantic love and companionship was the most important means by which many whalemen and their sweethearts pledged themselves to each other, distinguished themselves from their communities as separate couples, and sustained their ties over such extremes of time and distance.

Signing herself his "affectionant girl," Susan Hathaway wrote to George Anderson, then at sea on the bark *Governor Carver*, a letter much shorter and not as neatly written as Ruth's but which hit many of the same romantic notes. Susan told George, "I received your letter . . . and was very much pleased to here from you and here you were well and injoying your self so well try and injoy your self has well as you can untill you get home and then we will bouth injoy our self together in Ma's front room." "Dear George," she confided, "I dream of you every night . . . but when I awake in the morning I find it is but a dream. . . . you wrote that there was never was a homesicker man then you all for me but if you fell worse then I do I pity you for I felt very bad[.] I could not go in the frount room for a long time I miss you so." She promised, "George it is you I love no toung tell and Dear George I will not decive you I will be true to you while you are fare fare away from me[.] do not be afraid of it for I will keep my word there is no one that can take your place for you was the first that I can say that ever I love." She closed with just one ending (but with a bit of doggerel that Ruth might have appreciated): "You must escuse all mistakes and bad writting for my pen is porr[,] my ink is pale[,] my love shall never fale."[21]

New Bedford spinster Lydia Davenport, whose two sisters both married whalemen, noted the exclusivity implied by romantic love and its paradoxical quality in the maritime setting. She recorded (rather pettily or maybe drearily) in her diary, "I rode [in the carriage] under rather peculiar circumstances, I felt that I was the 'third person' of the party; it was my dear Sister, and the *One* she loves best on earth, and who seems to love her with all the fervor of devotion; but," she pointed out, "he is soon to leave her for a long voyage." Lydia ended on a pious and perhaps conciliatory note: "May the rich blessings of Heaven, be shed around their different paths while separated, and may they be reunited and spend many years of happiness, in this world and be prepared, to spend a never ending Eternity in praising God for his goodness toward them."[22]

Shared moments of intimacy might be snatched at the Point rocks, in Ma's front room, during a carriage ride despite a sister's presence—or even on a ship in port, as Jared Gardner reminisced to his wife Harriet, in "that burth where once we wer lock in each others armes." Jared remembered "the libertis that I took be fore we wer married," apparently with guilt-free pleasure, since he added, "I have no doubt but that you will forgive me for that. Men are too much alike in that respect but we will not dwell too long on that. I can truely say that the three months that we wer togather was the hapyest time that ever I spent . . . with the one who is dearer than all."[23]

Jared, who had married Harriet just three weeks before he left Nantucket in the whaleship *Washington* on 14 May 1840, would be gone for three years. Measuring time at home in weeks and the time at sea in years was typical, especially for the men who rounded Cape Horn and whaled the lucrative grounds of the Pacific. Elijah Chase asked his mother to give his sweetheart "Lucritia," "my love in full. . . . Tell her that she must cheer up, for it is only 40 months more before we shall put away for home."[24] Jane Russell sent news about one of her brothers to another in 1837: "Reuben is going out Master of the Ship Susan . . . he has been at home 3 months

now—quite a visit for a Cape horner." [25] With the intermittent and prolonged absences of nineteenth-century whaling voyages, intimate relationships had to develop in short, intense periods of only weeks, interspersed with difficult multiyear separations.

The staccato rhythms of maritime courtship created insecurities on
shore and at sea that only repeated reiteration of prescription could allay.
Sarah Pierce wrote her sweetheart, Captain Elijah Chisole, "I saw by your
first [letter] that you thought I had either forgotten you or forgotten my
promise I felt very sorry to think that you thought so for I have taken great
paines to write you every chance their has been . . . I have written you 13
letters since you sailed." (He had left New Bedford on 29 June 1852; her
letter was dated December 24.) Sarah insisted, "It is almost impossible for
me to forget one that I thinks loves me as you do . . . I think of you both
day and night." In fact, she felt so strongly that she declared, "I want you
dearest before you come home to make your mind up that you will never
leave me again to go to sea for I never could be happy with you at sea and
I at home far from you that I love." [26]

Separation, especially during courtship, raised all sorts of fears as well
as unhappiness. Women like Ruth Grinnell and Sylvia Tucker expressed
concern about deception before their marriages. Ruth worried, "have I
centered my all in a false deceiving man?" Sylvia Tucker, writing in 1852
to accept John Leonard's proposal of marriage, explained, "I think I should
have answered sooner if I had not heard so much and been warned so many
times to beware of deceitfulness (but now I trust in you)" and she signed
her letter, "One not deceitful, Sylvia." [27]

It is not always clear what Ruth, Sylvia, and other women feared when
they referred generally to "deception." Other than the threatening possibility that he had stopped caring for her, the only specific sin that Ruth
warned James against was profanity: "I sincerely hope my own dear James
does not take Gods name in vain . . . James I do not want you to deceive me
by swearing when you are out of my presence." Her appeal echoed those of
other maritime women, such as Joan Waterman, who had written a quarter of a century earlier, in mild suggestion to her husband, "I hope you
will try to keep your temper and not use no profane language." [28] Words
were what comprised their relationships during separation, and words, at
least those words known to be common to the seafaring subculture, were
in part what some women tried to control.

Certainly they had plenty to feel insecure about: they stayed home while
the whalemen roamed the world. Susan Cromwell informed her husband

that "John Enos got married at St. Catharines brought his wife home in the Ship & Cynthia feels verry bad to think he serv'd Eliza such a mean trick . . . I realy pity her she is disappointd & mortified."[29] Perhaps the fears of Ruth, Sylvia, and the others were justified. But the absent men felt insecurities, too. Charles B. Babcock told his brother Henry, who was serving as mate of the bark *LeBaron* out of Newport, Rhode Island, "I called on Sarah at Mr Hammond store where she is clerken and invited her to go a sailing with us but she was so engaged she could not go . . . dear Harry I am affraid that she has proved herself unworth of you and in my opinion the best of girles would not remain true in the absence of 2 years of a lover, mark my word they are faithless things unless you are with them every day."[30]

Apparently a certain Sallee Brown in Westport proved so, as William Davol informed his brother Edward, then somewhere in the Indian Ocean. "In your letter to George you requested him to acknowledge to Sallee Brown When he read it he said he should do no such thing . . . I should consider you as insane indeed if you were to marry a girl that was not virtuous . . . it can be proved to a demonstration that a certain chap in Westport did stay with Sallee the night before he sailed and she having the flowers [i.e., was menstruating[31]] did paint the map of the world on his shirt tail, and when he went a board he gave it to davy Jones [i.e., threw it overboard]. She has turned off her beau and some think that you will marry her yet [but] I consider you as having stood on the verge of an awful precipice and crawled back just in time to save your neck &c."[32]

It may have been Sallee's lack of discrimination rather than the act itself that was at issue. Rothman found that what young women and men actually did when courting in the antebellum period demonstrates that "sexual boundaries between unmarried women and men were still loosely drawn and crossed with relative ease. . . . Coquetry and seduction were condemned, but flirtation and sexual playfulness remained common features of male-female social life." Rothman suggests that in the nineteenth century, as it had been in the eighteenth, such behavior was tolerated (though not necessarily condoned) in the close-knit local communities where other family members could assure marriage if pregnancy resulted.[33] Whaleman Jared Gardner certainly admitted with pleasurable memory but no self-consciousness that he "took liberties" before he and Harriet married, and "D." Allen wrote her seafaring brother matter-of-factly, "Little Edmand goes to see Beck Petty and stays till morning. I expect nothing else but they will be married in a few weeks."[34]

The flexible attitudes about premarital intimacy demonstrate that the modern notion that all aspects of marriage from sex to cohabitation begin with the wedding ceremony itself was not yet firmly in place. Rather, the evidence from the whaling communities indicates the persistence of an older custom by which the multifaceted transition from single to married status occurred over several weeks and culminated not with the wedding but with the new couple independently "setting up housekeeping." [35] The achievement of married status could be even more complicated in the maritime setting, because the transition frequently continued for the first several years *after* marriage. In a very common practice, new wives simply remained in their parents' homes when their husbands shipped out again. Their familiar identity as daughter, evolving over years, sometimes overwhelmed their newly acquired, still uncertain sense of themselves as wife when their husbands were gone.

Just twenty-five days after they were married, Susan Gifford's husband John shipped out on a Pacific whaling voyage. He would be gone for three and a half years, while Susan continued to live with her parents in the small village of Mattapoisett, some miles east of New Bedford. Susan began her diary the day John left, 15 November 1859, with the simple entry: "The Ship Milo Sailed to day my Husband sailed Mate." [36]

For the first few days, Susan's entries addressed John directly; she still felt his presence that immediately. "I felt very bad after you had gone. I did not know what to do with myself[.] I went up stairs and cried till my Head ached and I felt most sick. Mother came up said I must not give way to my feelings so if I did I should be sick so I went down stairs but every thing seemed so lonesome and dreary that I felt as though I did not care whether I did any thing or not. . . . It is dark and cloudy out to night and I expect you feel rather lonesome[.] I judge by myself[.] I have such a sense of loneliness come over me once in a while that I dont know what to do[.] *You* was all the World to me and now you are gone." [37]

But, with her husband absent, Susan's life gradually began to reassume its pre-wedding rhythms in work and relationships. "It is a beautifull day, I think it must be pleasant where you are I wish I was there, I have been sewing for Mother this forenoon and shall sew a little more this afternoon[.] I did think some of going out . . . but have given it up[.] If you was here we would go and make some calls[.] Mother has got the work ready and I must stop for the present." [38]

The entries filled with intense longing continued for just about a month. Then, Susan's emotions began to calm and the sense of her being someone's wife seems to have slipped away: December 31 was the last time she addressed John directly in her diary. In the new year, her entries were considerably abbreviated and generally nonreflective, becoming largely lists of weather conditions and local events. For the entire year of 1860, John was mentioned only twenty-two times, and always in the third person. On May 15, Susan simply recorded, "Went to Uncle George and helped them move and sewed on carpet[.] did not go to Meeting felt two [*sic*] tired[.] six Month since John went away." Their first wedding anniversary passed without remark; Susan was busy anyway, assisting at the birth of her sister-in-law's baby.[39]

As with Ruth Grinnell and her letter, all we have of Susan Gifford is her diary. We do not know the ending of Susan's story. In the back of the volume are a few lists and notations that indicate that John returned, they resumed married life, and she went with him to Brooklyn, where he may have been stationed for a few years. (He appears to have been associated with the Brooklyn Naval Yard during the Civil War.) But we do not know how (or if) her identity as wife survived during their separation, what reunion felt like, or how she negotiated her second transition from daughter to wife when he returned in 1863. The slim volume records that she did write letters to John, nine of them by the time the diary ends in December 1860. Perhaps it was in her correspondence that she expressed the feelings toward and concerns about her husband appropriate to a young wife. They were not in her diary.

In contrast to Susan Gifford, Julia Fisk of Groton, Connecticut, recorded in her diary mention of her husband nearly every day. Julia had already been married nine years and borne two children when her husband, Captain Silas Fisk, set sail for the Pacific on the whaleship *North Star* in 1859. In the brevity forced on her by the size of the tiny ($2\frac{1}{2}'' \times 3\frac{3}{4}''$) pocketbook she used as a diary, Julia's entries acquired a certain mantralike quality. "Spent the eve thinking of Husband, sad"; "just four months since Silas sailed very lonely & sad"; "I feel uncommon sad on account of my dream of Silas last night"; "had Clara [her sister] for company but thought much of Silas"; "Oh where is my dear Husband," ran the litany of longing.[40] Julia did not seem to need to elaborate in writing what she felt, to work out the emotion and behavior appropriate to a wife. Her diary entries served more like making notches in a post, a way of reminding herself that she was indeed married and indeed devoted to her husband, whom she would accompany to sea on at least two voyages.

In terms of the references to their husbands, Susan's and Julia's diaries represent two ends of a continuum. The private journals of other women married to whalemen fall somewhere in between, with intermittent mention of their absent spouses. The diaries share, though, a similar absence of introspective depth or meditative length. In their often terse record of weather, place, and the daily activities of many people, these documents strongly resemble the contemporaneous rural midwestern diaries examined by historian Marilyn Motz. Motz observed that "it is not inward to the self but outward to the world that the rural diarist looks, thus defining himself through his place in society and nature." [41] I located just seven midcentury diaries of onshore wives, kept while their husbands were at sea, disappointingly few compared to the dozens belonging to seagoing captains' wives that have been preserved. In form and content, six of the seven diaries identify the keeper largely in terms of her daily experience and immediate community—as do all six of the additional relevant shoreside women's diaries and about two-thirds of the twenty women's sea journals I examined.[42] The romantic reflections and sentimental effusions—in other words, the effort to construct, through writing, a self in relation to marriage and a husband—are found much more often and consistently in the letters exchanged between lovers and spouses.

Despite the obvious problems raised by seafaring, the majority of professional career whalemen and the women at home did marry, after all. As Chapter 4 describes, the social relations of work of the industry positively encouraged it. In their letters, none of the unmarried women expressed any reluctance to becoming involved with a sailor as opposed to men in other occupations; in fact, the topic simply never came up. Certainly, throughout the midcentury period, whaling remained one of the most important and visible elements in southeastern New England's regional economy, employing thousands of young men. And, certainly, a successful career paced by rapid promotion and the eventual command of a vessel conferred on a man prestige, perhaps even allure, and possibly (though not as certainly) affluence. What is more surprising than their choice of partners is the tenacity with which these women, even with their obvious familiarity with the industry, clung to hopes of romantic love and exclusive, intimate companionship within marriage—expectations characteristic of courtship but which also persisted long after the wedding.

Indeed, the most striking feature of the letters between wives onshore and husbands at sea is the articulation of loneliness and longing—in the sample represented by the midcentury dead letter file as well as in collections of letters preserved intentionally. The intensity of yearning varies from individual to individual, along with the quality of grammar, spelling, and penmanship, which suggests a range in education and class status. Nonetheless, common to most of the letters is expression of an emotional interdependence stemming from the romantic ideal of passionate and companionate marriage. In elaborate calligraphy with scrolling flourishes, "H. B. C" told her spouse, "I did not know till I was deprived of you how much I did love you . . . my heart yearns after you in the most endearing ties. there is not a moment in the day but what my mind is on one that is dearer than life to me." Sarah Coggeshall wrote to her husband in an awkward, barely literate scrawl, but expressed sentiments none the less heartfelt: "i am very Lonsam[,] i Miss your Compney very Much . . . i ned not tel you how i fel[,] you can think Somthin A bout it for thar is no one on this urth that i love but you." [43]

The men wrote back with language couched in the same romantic conventions, expressing very similar feelings.[44] Jared Gardner commented to Harriet, "It has been sead that salt watter and long absence will wash away love but the watter must be salter than brine and absence longer than life to wash away the love of you my dear dear lamb." [45] Samuel Braley wrote for his Mary Ann: "It is the best consolation that I have, to know that there is one heart that beets for me with the purest love[.] Twas not long since that I thought that no one cared much for me; but when I looked into thy bright eyes, and witnessed thy acts of kindness, I no longer doubted." [46] Both halves of many maritime couples turned to prescription as they tried to sustain ardor in spite of the personal stresses and uncertainties inherent in seafaring.

Letters and diaries specifically written to be sent or exchanged with one another were the most important vehicles for women and men both. Historian Steven Stowe has observed, "Letters often were the very substance of relationships otherwise strained by distance, gender differences, or emotion. Such letters existed as a bond and a commentary on the bond." [47] Testifying to their importance, many correspondents sent duplicate letters by different vessels, a wise precaution since so many letters never reached their destination. Ann Burgess began one missive to her husband Paul by explaining, "2 or 3 opportunities to send letters to the Pacific soon induce me to begin a letter to you, but as it is so uncertain about their reaching you I expect there will be a great deal of repetition in them." Captain William Loring Taber simply copied over some of his long and very loving letters

Letter from Susan Hathaway to her whaleman-sweetheart George Anderson, datelined New Bedford, 15 November 1850. Note how she addressed the envelope to "Mr. George A. Anderson, Bark Gov. Carver of Westport, N. Atlantic Ocean." Courtesy of Old Dartmouth Historical Society–New Bedford Whaling Museum (Neg. 16194)

to his wife Susan, word for impassioned word, and sent them by different carriers; she received several of the duplicates and carefully saved them all, precious in spite of their redundancy.[48]

Letters and diaries written for others not only affirmed the socially prescribed expectations, the objects themselves also acquired a powerful symbolic value and were incorporated into the activities by which both maritime women and men sustained their relationships over distance and time. Letters often acquired a positively talismanic quality. On a missive to her husband John, Sylvia Leonard kissed one corner, which spot she labeled "Sylvia kiss" and on the opposite corner, had their infant kiss, labeling it, "Johnnie kiss." [49] The maritime historian Margaret Creighton found that sometimes sailors, unhappy in not receiving letters themselves, sought to purchase them from more fortunate colleagues. For instance, Ezra Goodnough recorded in his diary that he sold a letter from a "young lady" of his hometown for "two heads of tobacco, it being a very scarce article." [50] There seems to have been no parallel to this sort of fantasy life among the women onshore. There is no evidence that any of the several dozen women encountered in this study bought or otherwise tried to acquire love letters intended for someone else: for them, the individual himself rather than the role was the focus.

Letters were perhaps the most important objects by which relationships were sustained. But there were other kinds of objects, too. In her examination of journals, letters, and logbooks of some two hundred New England whalemen, Creighton finds frequent mention of the "Home Cake," a special baked item that signified a special relationship of one at home to one at sea. Susan Hathaway informed her sweetheart George Anderson of their acquaintances: "James Clark has gorn to sea . . . Harriet Slott gave him a cake." When George Bowman, second mate of the *Albion*, received a cake from his wife to commemorate their anniversary, he noted, "It caused my mind to wander back to her." "Your cake how did that taste[?]" Ruth Barker Post inquired of her husband, "Like a chip I suppose." Marshall Keith's cake, made by his betrothed, Sarah Pope, was preserved with alcohol—so well preserved that it exploded. Keith reported that, on opening, it was "nocked higher than a kite" but was still "in good order," and he ate it with appetite.[51]

Pictures, not surprisingly, were treasured. These included painted miniatures, as in the earlier period, but with the introduction of daguerreotypes in 1839 and other technologies shortly thereafter, inexpensive photographic portraits quickly became more readily available and popular.[52] "Your Picture you said was not a good one," Charles Peirce wrote his wife Eliza, "but the more I loock at it the better I like it . . . how I should like to kiss the original. I have to kiss the Picture." [53] Captain Albert Goodwin allowed himself once a week, Saturday evening, to set out the daguerreotypes of his wife and children, each of which he kissed in turn.[54]

Miniature portraits were often cherished mementos of absent family members. This one in a locket, of Captain Thomas Burdett (b. 1814) of Nantucket, was probably painted shortly after his marriage in 1840. Courtesy of Old Dartmouth Historical Society–New Bedford Whaling Museum (Neg. 4807)

Sylvia Leonard was four months pregnant with their first child when her husband of just five months, John, left the port of Fairhaven as captain of the whaleship *Lydia*, his first command, on 14 October 1854. A month later, she wrote him, "How does my miniature look any thing like me now or cant you tell[?]" She continued, "Your [picture] is excellent every one says so," in spite of the fact that "Nat has so much fun about the pants gaping open in front." Later, after the baby was born, Sylvia enclosed for John a miniature of their new son with a letter in which she told him, "I am in a great hurry for you to see your darling little child and see what you think of his mothers doing since his father went away." With another letter she sent along "a little shoe that you may have a little momento of your darling boy." [55]

Correspondence and packages from loved ones were welcomed on shore and at sea both, but the contrasting use of the letters and other objects by women and men provides a clue to the different meanings of romantic love and expectations of marriage held by women and men. Maritime historian Margaret Creighton finds that shipboard culture generally limited the men's invocation of such memories to special times and places: "Letter-writing was restricted to the dogwatch [off-duty hours] or to Sundays, and a ritual that honored loved ones at home was similarly timed. . . . On Saturday nights, particularly in the aftercabin [officers' quarters], mariners set aside time (and alcohol on nontemperance ships) for a toast to 'sweethearts and wives.'" A sea song jotted down by a sailor in 1843 mentions the custom:

A sailor loves a gallant ship
And messmates bold and free
And even welcomes with delight
Saturday night at sea.
One hour each week we'll snatch from care
As through the world we roam
And think of dear ones far away
And all the joys from home.[56]

Interestingly, other than the visual representations, women at home were less likely than the men at sea to refer in their letters or diaries to specific objects as having special symbolic significance in association with the absent lover, spouse, or parent. The neglect is particularly striking considering the thousands of scrimshaw items carved from whales' teeth and bone with which whalemen filled up many of the tedious days or weeks between whale sightings. Domestic articles were among the most popular scrimshaw items, often intended for gifts to women at home, but if women were reminded of men at sea when they were using the whalebone pie crimpers, crochet hooks, swifts, hair pins and corset stays, they did not mention it in their writings.[57]

Perhaps this should not be surprising. Though scrimshaw is now con-

Scrimshaw implements, whale ivory table set, carved by Captain Fred Smith of New Bedford, Mass., for his wife, Sallie. Courtesy of Mystic Seaport Museum, Mystic, Conn. (41.396.3)

sidered folk art and is avidly collected today, specialist Mary Malloy notes that a century ago it was viewed not as art but merely as recreational carving.[58] After all, the men at sea were in a wholly masculinized environment that only rarely included women. They may have needed specific material things to affirm their connections as husbands, fathers, sweethearts, or brothers to those people and places far distant. In contrast, for many of the women, the people with whom they lived, their overall surroundings, and even the very texture of their life served to remind them of who and what was missing. "They all speak of you often and wish you was here," Sylvia Leonard wrote her husband John, while on a lengthy visit with her in-laws; in closing, she noted, "every one joins me sending love to you your mother in a particular manner." [59] Every day was filled with activities and conversations that brought forcibly home their anomalous status as "Cape Horn widows": married, yet single.

For the women, the certainty of marriage and confirmation of their identity as wife began not so much with the wedding (often a few short weeks before the husband shipped out) but rather with the birth of their first child. As the widely popular nineteenth-century poet and author Lydia Sigourney put it, it was motherhood that truly "breaks the bonds to the father's home and attaches them to husband and child." [60] Unlike the scrimshaw or other gifts from seafaring men, the one kind of "object" that did serve as specific reminder to the women of those absent was, in fact, not an inanimate thing at all but something quite animate, sometimes rather too lively for their mothers' tastes: the children. Sylvia Leonard told John, "People ask me some times if I know I have got a husband and I tell them I think I have good proof of it for Johnnie looks very much like you." [61] Harriet Gardner told her husband Jared, then in the Pacific on the Nantucket brig *Lady Washington*, "Alfred [their son] is a *splendid looking fellow*. I have to kiss him every day, he reminds me so much of you." [62] In a letter numbered "32," George Coffin's wife Selina reported to him, "Jethro Frank . . . talks about you often and I cant make him say he is anything but Pa's Boy oh his Pa is all to him." [63] Every time Sylvia, Harriet, and Selina looked at their children, they saw their husbands too.

Many nineteenth-century mothers actively promoted a relationship between young children and their seafaring fathers in an effort to maintain a place in the family for the absent men as well as to reinforce their own conjugal bonds. The contrast between their encouragement and pleasure and the discomfort and sadness expressed by Lydia Almy in 1797 when her small son's prattling reminded her of his father (described in Chapter 2) is striking. Caroline Gifford, for example, wrote to her husband about their son, born after his father had left and now not quite two years old: "I showed him your picture & told him to kiss it which he did," and "I ask Charlie where Pa Pa is[,] he says gone in Ship & in Batter meaning water." [64] Betsey King reported to her husband James, "The children speak often of you especialy Betsey[.] your minature she often wants to see and to kiss it, to please her I have taken the chain of[f] and hung it up over the mantelpiece and every night before she goes to bed she says I want to see my father." Mother Betsey mused, "I think she has some recloctions of you."[65]

If young children on shore had only distant recollections of their fathers, or perhaps none at all, the women also worried that distance and time might fade from the minds of the men at sea memories of older children or acknowledgement of the existence of babies born (as so many were) after their fathers had left. Sylvia Leonard told her husband of the infant son he had yet to see: "I learn [Johnnie] to say papa[.] he begins to speak a good many words very plain," and she added, "Can you realize that you have such a darling boy at home[?]"[66]

From the beginning, Sylvia had been particularly concerned that John share in, or at least remember, his role as parent. When he had left, back in October of 1854, Sylvia had included a surprise in addition to the sweetmeats and cider, the shirts, and the socks she had packed for him. In her letter of November 13, she wrote, "By the way how does your baby come on[?] I suppose you have found this one in your trunk before this[.] we have all wished to be a mouse in the wall when you found that and hear you laugh[.] pretty good joke dont you think so." A week before the baby was due, Sylvia finally heard back from John, and she wrote in reply that "joy came with [your letter] finding you were well and getting along so nicely and found your baby[.] You must while away your lonesome hours with that."[67] Samuel Braley, another absent father, evidently did; he noted in his shipboard journal: "Today I was overhauling my trunk and found something nicely rolled up in Tishue paper with a card accopaning with a Ladies name on one side and on the other 'dear pa please give me a name' Query I wonder if they allways come done up in paper[.] If I was at home tonight somebody would get kissed in pay for their gift."[68]

By combining discussions and rituals on shore with written records and even toy representations of children sent to the men at sea, Sylvia Leonard, Mary Ann Braley, and so many other wives like them attempted to create at least imaginatively a nuclear family of father, mother, and children. For many women, children certainly may have filled the emotional gap left by their husbands' absences and, with the constant demands and immediate needs of infancy, muted the intermittency of maritime marriage. But the insistent attempts by these mothers to share the joys of parenthood with their seafaring husbands underscore the connection they made between familial roles and relationships. Even with the men gone for years at a time, the experience of motherhood reinforced rather than replaced the women's sense of themselves as wives.

For many maritime wives, the transition from single to married life was prolonged well beyond courtship and the wedding itself, lasting until one or more children appeared. Confusingly, but unavoidably, these women also experienced the emotions and circumstances that typically accompanied the end of marriage and the loss of a husband long before death actually occurred. In her reminiscences of mid-nineteenth-century New Bedford, Maud Mendall Nelson recalled that "to have a seaman's chest carried out of the house for its three years' cruise, was a sorrow almost as harrowing as if it had been a coffin." [69] Every time a married whaleman shipped out, he left behind a wife who became a "Cape Horn widow." The traditional and pervasive literary tropes associating the ocean with eternity and leave-taking with death resonated with particular power for the wife watching her husband's ship disappear, slowly, over the horizon.

The heroism of sailors at sea, risking life and limb in the noble pursuit of the leviathan whale, was explicitly associated in popular opinion with the heroic suffering of their loved ones at home. For example, the July 1838 issue of the *Sailor's Magazine and Naval Journal* (an evangelical periodical ostensibly aimed at sailors but more likely read by people onshore, especially women) carried a report lifted from the *Boston Recorder*, titled "Perils of the Sea." The report made clear that the sea's perils were felt as much by women onshore as by the men at sea. It listed some shocking statistics compiled by the Barnstable County (Cape Cod) Seaman's Friend Society: the number of Cape Cod seamen lost during the year 1837 (78) and the number of seamen's widows then living on the Cape (914!). The report went on to speculate on the kinds of deaths men suffered at sea — mainly "violent and terrible" — "thus they are swept away, while hope of the future is high in their hearts, and they indulge in golden dreams of one day returning from their perilous employment, to the unbroken comfort of their domestic circles." But, pathetically, the domestic circles are far from unbroken or comforting. The report went on to meditate at length on the misery of "the mother, the wife, the sister," whose hopes for the lost seamen are "slowly and painfully extinguished as every rattling wheel and footstep passes by" and "disappointment pierces anew the bleeding heart." [70]

Suffering and self-sacrifice were not, of course, unique to mariners' wives but rather were widely considered throughout transatlantic Victorian culture to be an inevitable portion of women's fate in life, even a crucible of female strength, and, as a major source of women's influence over others, a positive social force. Sarah Josepha Hale, the influential editor of *Godey's Ladies' Book* and a major architect of the ideology of domesticity, defined woman's heroism as "the calm endurance of afflictions." She claimed that "[f]emale genius never appears so lovely as when, like the trodden chamomile, it springs, apparently, from the very pressure that threatens to destroy it." Another widely read author, Elizabeth Oakes Smith, asserted that "[s]uffering to a woman occupies the place of labor to a man, giving a breadth, depth, and fullness, not otherwise attained." [71] In fact, as Smith here implies, an important part of women's work was to suffer, particularly for their husbands and children.

Maritime men and women agreed. Captain Samuel Braley wrote tenderly and typically to his wife, who was then in the advanced stages of pregnancy, "I never knew how much I loved thee till now when thou art about to suffer for me." [72] Eliza Brock, wife of one Nantucket whaleman and mother of another, clipped from the newspaper and inserted into her diary a poem by T. B. Read titled "The Brave at Home." She must have found meaning and perhaps comfort in the poem's claims for glory on behalf of "the maid who binds her warrior's sash / With smile that well her pain dissembles," "the mother who conceals her grief / When to her breast her son she presses," and especially "the wife who girds her husband's sword / 'Mid little ones who weep or wonder / And gravely speaks the cheering word / What though her heart be rent asunder" who, the poem argued, "hath shed as sacred blood as e'er / Was poured upon a field of battle." [73]

Another article printed in the July 1838 issue of the *Sailor's Magazine*, attributed to the *New-Hampshire Telegraph* and titled simply "The Mariner's Wife," specifically applied these ideas about the inevitability and intensity of women's suffering to the maritime context. The anonymous author wrote:

We can scarcely conceive a situation more wretched than that of the wife of an active sailor from the time she weds until the scene of life is closed. The anxiety which her husband subjects her to, will prey upon and finally destroy the finest constitution. Every wind that blows is a source of fear; every rain that falls causes sorrow; every cloud that rises is big with the fate of her nearest friend. These feelings, which tug at the heart-strings, are honourable to the nature of women, but noble and generous as they are, they are poisonous to her existence, and sink too deeply into the breast to be eradicated. One parting scene is hardly over before another must be endured—one happy meeting succeeds another only to make the pain of parting more severe. These are not trifles, but facts which many a bosom will acknowledge to be true. . . . In how many instances are their worst fears realized—how many wear the weeds of widowhood at an early age, and how many have children that never knew a father's care. Those who make long voyages pass but a small part of their time with their families; a few months at home, answer for years at sea, and they finally drop away, before they have hardly bestowed a thought upon death; or without, in many instances, leaving a competency for his family; and she who has borne up against trouble in her early life has to struggle with poverty in its decline." [74]

These are hostile words, blaming the irresponsibility of seamen for the burdens on the women at home. The account suggests explicitly that the affective ties that bound maritime women to maritime men did so inevitably at a tremendous cost to the wives—costs that were emotional and physical as well as financial.

Melville, in *Moby-Dick*, described the "sailors' wives and widows" attending services in New Bedford's Whaleman's Chapel. "So plainly did several women present wear the countenance if not the trappings of some unceasing grief," Melville's narrator Ishmael reported, "that I feel sure that here before me were assembled those, in whose unhealing hearts the sight of those bleak tablets [cenotaphs memorializing men lost at sea or abroad] sympathetically caused the old wounds to bleed afresh. Oh! ye whose dead lie buried beneath the green grass; who standing among flowers can say—here, *here* lies my beloved; ye know not the desolation that broods in bosoms like these." [75]

To make sense of their suffering and to structure their feelings about their family members absent at sea, Cape Horn widows turned to religious rituals of mourning and, more generally, to sentimental attitudes toward death. Sylvia Leonard suggested as much when she wrote her husband, "William Crowell sailed two weeks ago and left his beautiful wife here to mourn for him. Ah I can sympathize with her deeply." [76] Susan Cromwell similarly told her husband how she "sufferd in body & mind & while I mourn your absence." [77] Like Queen Victoria herself, Victorian Americans raised mourning to an elaborately practiced art form, a "cult" which the cultural historian Karen Halttunen describes as "a form of sentimental social bonding." Halttunen observes that "mourning over lost loved ones was believed to demonstrate the enduring strength of family ties. Within the sentimental view, death was not powerful enough to sever the bonds of domestic love . . . the bonds of love that stretched across the great divide of death were thus believed stronger than those ties that bound families together in life."[78] The concepts and the cultural scripts associated with death proved useful to Cape Horn widows, providing the solace of familiar practices and a socially esteemed status as they mourned for their sea-faring husbands.

The blurring of the boundary between virtual and real widowhood was perhaps inevitable with the religious affirmation of romantic love and conjugal passion. In the eighteenth century, pious Quaker sea-wife Lydia Almy had achieved at least an uneasy resignation to her husband's absence by restraining her fears and feelings of deprivation, in part by understanding the trials of separation as part of a larger providential design. After the floodgates of Romanticism and evangelical religion opened at the turn of the nineteenth century, this approach no longer worked. Even the most devout mariners' wives found encouragement in church too for the notion that married love consisted of the transcendent, even ecstatic union of two souls. Separation was best explained, as well as endured, through mourning. The frequent references to an afterlife in heaven "where partings are never known" were not as trite as they sound to us today—and they resonated as forcefully for Cape Horn widows as for real ones.[79]

It was all too easy to make the transition from virtual to real widowhood when the need arose, as it so often did. And there seems to have been little incentive to take a second husband. In nineteenth-century America, widowers tended to remarry more often than did widows;[80] it is not surprising that this was the case in the whaling communities as well. I have complete marital histories (including death dates for both spouses) for forty of the ninety couples studied here. Of the forty pairs, seventeen men were widowed, and twelve of them (70 percent) remarried; of the twenty-three women who were widowed, just four of them (17 percent) remarried. This is by no means a large or generalizable sample, and the measure is a crude one that does not take into account age at spouse's death, wealth, or other such factors; however, the pattern is very clear nonetheless, as are the implications. The loss of one's husband, paradoxically, did not necessarily mean the loss of a maritime woman's identity as wife. For so many of these women, becoming a wife required not only taking on a particular role and set of functions to perform, it also seemed to emphasize a focus on a particular individual that lasted beyond his death.

It was different for the men. Susan Cromwell remarked to her whale-man-husband, "Capt Peakes is . . . a verry smart widdower like all the rest that looses there wifes when absent, I presume to say [is] looking for another." [81] The frequency of their remarriage underscores just how crucial it was to a whaleman to have a wife representing his interests, caring for his children, and preserving his place on shore.[82] Interestingly, and tellingly, after Ruth Grinnell Sowle died in 1862, James married her sister, Phebe. So too did Captains Philip Howland, Thomas Andrews, and Seth Blackmer marry their deceased wives' sisters. Even within my limited study group, this is a striking number—a quarter of the remarrying men wed their sisters-in-law—which seems to have gone without remark at the time. The phenomenon of what we might call sororal remarriage dramatizes not only the functional importance of a wife but also how limited the pool of women was from which men more often at sea than on land could draw, and the importance to their remarriage of personal familiarity. Sororal remarriage also hints that (nearly like the love letters they might buy and sell), to the men at sea, the women at home were as individuals in some ways interchangeable.

Even within these second marriages seemingly inspired by convenience rather than the sort of passion that was expected to animate the first marriage, however, conjugal love was deemed important by both partners. Philip Howland exclaimed in a typical letter to his second wife, Patience (his first wife's older sister), "Thee cannot comprehend how dear thee is. I have to guard against making thee my idol . . . thy letters breathe the essence of love on evry line." Though he had thought it "impossible for two to occupy the same place in one bosom," he told Patience, "I no longer doubt feeling assured that the dear one that has gone is rejoiced to see thee by her side not occupying her place but thy own[.] she must look upon you and if such things are allowed[,] her influence is extended to us." [83] Patience, at home with three stepchildren and assorted other relatives with needs and demands (including elderly and infirm parents), responded to Philip in more prim, sometimes even guarded prose. But she too insisted that "in the duties, cares, and pleasures of the present, as well as in plans for the future, I have reference to you, and life would indeed wear a gloomy aspect if I thought it must be spent in separation from each other," and she signed her letter "with much love." [84]

In the summer of 1842, Jane Russell Andrews of Nantucket died of dysentery just a few weeks after she lost her two-year-old son to the same disease, while her husband Thomas was cruising "on the line" in the South Pacific. Jane's sister Ann reported the tragic news to their brother Roland and commented, "No doubt it will be a great blow to Thomas to hear of the death of both of them." Ann herself felt "the loss more sensibly every day" but insisted, "When I compare their happiness with our world of trouble and care I am led to say, Lord thy will be done and not mine." She found solace, and thought Thomas would too, in knowing that Jane had died with "full assurance that all was well and that she had rather depart and be with Crisht [Christ]." Ann also took comfort in preparing Jane's "things" for Thomas, in particular having Jane's miniature altered. "I think it looks better," she told Roland, and "it will be a great satisfaction to Thomas, if he is permitted to return again." Three months after Jane's death, the family received a letter from Thomas—presumably addressed to Jane, though Ann did not specify. She told Roland, "Thomas seemed to write in very good spirits but how little he thinks of what he has got to hear and how little prepared it made me feel very unpleasant . . . at the time he was writing[,] Jane was quite unwell. . . . I am in hopes he will not hear of her death until he gets home if that is for the best . . . I must try to submit to the will of him who ordereth all things." Thomas no doubt did appreciate the miniature of Jane and other efforts on his behalf—and he and Ann also took comfort in each other. Thomas returned in 1843. He and Ann were married the following year, shortly before he left home again, this time as master of the whaleship *Charles Carroll*.[85]

Both women and men were forced to rely on prescribed domestic ideals about manhood and womanhood, love and marriage, to maintain their relationships as husbands' voyages lengthened dramatically. Sociologists and psychologists tell us that relationships are sustained during absence through typified and idealized recollections. Separation necessarily replaces the immediate experiences of a participant with memories that become outdated. Over time, these memories were shaped more by prescription than actual description. Psychologist Edmund Bolles points out that memory is "an act of construction instead of retrieval. . . . a living product of desire, attention, insight, and consciousness."[86] We can see these dynamics at work in Charles Peirce's letters home: in 1862, he wrote his wife Eliza, "I often see you in my dreams, and always the same kind, loveing

Wife I left at home." With such vivid, and outdated, imagery in his head, he was startled when he received her picture a year later: "When I opened your letter and took out your picture, I see at once you had been sick, and had altered so, it started the tears from my eyes at once." He quickly reassured her, "I never loved you more than at that moment, so cheer up my love." [87]

Especially important, as Charles Peirce and Ruth Grinnell insisted, was the faith in the enduring power of love no matter how long or far distant the separation. John Chapman agreed, writing his wife from sea, "those who have been separated know what love is." Sylvia Leonard told John, "[Nat] says [to me] you had better take a copy of the latters you write now and write them over again bye and bye[.] seemed to intimate that love as it grows older grows colder[.] I dont know but what it does in some cases but," she assured him, "I think or indeed I know it will not in our case[.] Seperation from you will never change my affection for you." [88]

This was a matter of some debate among mariners' wives, as Sarah Howland wrote to her husband: "Abner Tucker has returned to his home after an absence of more than 7 years and I suppose his wife is a happy woman[.] Hannah Howland was speaking of him yesterday. she thought if her husband had voluntarily left her so long she never should have received him again[,] but I told her she knew nothing about it[,] for I thought if at times she felt almost estranged from him[,] when he returned her affection would return also without any abatement." [89] Three years after her husband had shipped out, Sylvia Leonard still expressed a similar faith: "When I look around upon other people and see them enjoying the happiness of Matrimony[,] I envy them . . . But ours will be sweet wont it John . . . it will be Honey moon all the time with us." [90]

The same cultural resources that provided maritime women and men with the scripts for surviving separation also taught them how to behave and feel when reunited. "Oh, sweet affection! in thy holy chain / All hearts are captive," even the hearts of the "hardy sailor" and his "gentle wife and children dear," proclaimed the poem "Homeward Bound," printed in *Godey's Ladies' Book* in 1838. "The hardy seaman now . . . Strains his rough eye to catch the distant shore . . . And from his manly cheek wipes off a tear . . . / Strain every nerve bold mariner—for one / Thou dearly lov'st, with sweetly smiling brow, / Waits to embrace thee when thy duty's done. / And thou, fair Maiden, never heed that tear . . . fear not, a faithful heart is near / With open arms to greet his lovely one. / Fond Father! . . . Soon shalt thou kiss thy fair and blooming boy." [91] Focusing on the triumphant moment itself, the poem described in detail the appropriate behavior for each player in the sentimental drama of reunion—a script well understood by Captain Thomas Dallman, who wrote his wife in April 1849, "hitherto I have counted the months since we parted and the years before we meet but it is now reversed and I begin to count the months to come till the arrival (as I anticipate) of the happiest day of my life."[92]

The poem failed, however, to describe what to do and how to feel in the days that followed that first embrace (nor did Captain Dallman speculate on them in his letter). Prescription can structure and thereby help maintain connection over time and distance, but the costs could come due at the time of reunion. The theories about female domesticity and male breadwinning were ambiguous, even contradictory, in determining who was supposed to hold what sort of power within households and marriages. According to law and custom, the husband were ostensibly the head and master, but according to the newer concepts, mothers and wives were both responsible for the home and idealized as the emotional center and source of moral authority for their families. For the career whalemen, who held absolute command and exacted total obedience on board ship, and for their wives grown used to a measure of autonomous decision-making at home during the men's absences, reunion held the potential for confusion and struggles over authority. One whaleman described in his sea journal the plight of a captain named Stetson. Stetson was reputedly worth $100,000 "in cold cash" and could certainly afford to give up whaling altogether. When he returned home from a voyage, he "would take his seat in the chimney corner and smoke his pipe." But, eventually, his fellow whaleman recounted, "his return got to be an old story in the house" and "women began to shove him from one corner to another, and he could not stand it, so he was obliged to come away."[93] The situation might be exacerbated further in cases where wives, like Caroline Gifford of Dartmouth and Harriet Allen of New Bedford, looked for their husbands' return to resolve problems they had encountered during the men's absences but found instead that the men viewed time ashore as vacation and failed to take the problems seriously.[94]

There is evidence that these were not uncommon tensions. During his second voyage after his marriage to Patience, his deceased first wife's sister, Philip reiterated firmly, "There is no woman on Gods footstool that I could or would take to my bosom in preference to the one whom I now have . . . I love thee for thyself, I love thee for the sake of thy Sister whom I have evry reason to believe wished this union and there is no other woman that I could receive as a joint tenant in my heart."[95] Perhaps he was responding to Patience's letter, sent shortly after he had shipped out, in which she had written, "From the moment you left us, I have felt more inclined to think of whatever tends to bind our hearts together in the bonds of a strong affection, paramount to, and overcoming those trifling unpleasant occurrences, which for the time being, interrupt the flow of kindly feeling but change not our love. Oh no, that is a thing too deeply rooted in our hearts, to be permanently affected by trivial circumstances."[96] Protestations of abiding affection aside, what had those "trifling unpleasant occurrences" been? The realities of togetherness sometimes, perhaps inevitably, ran counter to expectations developed over long separation, in which memory blurred so easily into fantasy.

Captain Samuel Braley, for one, clearly confused his memories of his real wife, Mary Ann, with his vision of the ideal Victorian wife. The journal he kept during his first voyage after their marriage, which he addressed to her, overflows with his love, expressed in the familiar romantic conventions. Samuel's conflation of imagination and memory, though, created problems when he and Mary Ann were reunited. The journal of his second voyage contains ample evidence that home and Mary Ann were not precisely what and who he had remembered. He wrote bitterly, "Folks little know . . . on shore the weary hours we Sailors have to pass," and he complained that at home he could not be an honest man "without being scholded [sic] at." A few days later, he observed darkly, "As for the joys of domestic life, I do not pine for them as I once did, for I find that they to[o] have their bitter draughts to be swallowed."[97] No account exists of Mary Ann's side of the story, but it is clear that in this marriage the gap between the real and the ideal was experienced with unhappiness and discord.

Caroline Gifford clearly felt oppressed by the responsibilities she was forced to shoulder during her husband Charles's repeated absences. Her letters are filled with complaints and the often repeated wish that her husband would stay at home to help out, as she wrote in 1866, "I hope you get along nicely & will make enough so that you will never have to go to sea again." Charles, who spent the first twenty-four years of their marriage most often at sea, finally retired from whaling sometime in the late 1870s. Having him home must not have lived up to Caroline's expectations — she filed a petition for formal separation and support in 1885. The record does not indicate where she lived after that, but Charles drew up an agreement with his unmarried daughter, Mary, to keep house for him for $3 per week, an arrangement that apparently lasted until his death in 1900.[98]

As Caroline, Charles, and undoubtedly many more maritime couples like them discovered, domestic prescription did not provide a clear script on power relations within the household. And the lengthy, repeated separations mandated by a career in the whalefishery prevented them from working out, as nonmaritime couples could, an acceptable division of authority in daily face-to-face interaction.

Surprisingly, sexual fidelity did not seem to be the source of conflict in these maritime marriages. None of the wives whose papers I examined expressed a concern about their husbands' sexual faithfulness. It is possible that accusatory letters between antagonists were simply not saved as often or with the same care as were loving missives between committed partners, though I did come across a few fairly bitter passages. Sexual fidelity, however, was not the issue of contention. In the midcentury mailbag of dead letters described above, there are no overt accusations of this type either. Thus, despite the well-deserved reputation of seamen for philandering in foreign ports, in this respect too maritime women acted like their landlocked sisters, among whom "explicit discussions of sexual faithfulness were unusual."[99] Domesticity—in this case, the demand that women be faithful, chaste, and also blind to men's transgressions—seems to have trumped the customary indiscretions of maritime men.

While maritime wives and sweethearts evidently preferred to let the issue of sexual fidelity lie buried, it apparently troubled many of the men at sea. Charles Babcock had told his brother at sea, "In my opinion the best of girls would not remain true in the absence of 2 years of a lover, mark my word they are faithless things unless you are with them everyday." Charles Peirce assured his wife Eliza in 1861, "I shal return to you, as fresh and chaste as when I left you. I never for one moment have forgotten our Marriage vow." Yet such references were unusual in letters to wives; more often, the worry surfaced in the men's journals. Samuel Braley recorded how he had dreamt that Mary Ann had been unfaithful to him and, though he was relieved to awake, he observed glumly, "How many poor Sailors have . . . had unfaithfull wives and they none the wiser for their slips, but it is only tit for tat; not one man in ten that is true to his wife."[100]

But it was not really "tit for tat," as Samuel's own remarkably frank journal makes clear. His record offers us a candid look at the pervasive midcentury double standard of sexual propriety when, at the island of Mahe in the Indian Ocean in 1850, he wrote, "Had [my hair] cut, cleaned my teeth, so that I can make a conquest of some of the black-eyed-brunitts at Mahe. Old fool! pritty thoughts for Sunday." Such activities were not the sole perquisite of the captain: a few weeks later, Samuel recorded several cases of "Ladys feaver" among the crew which he, as captain, had to treat. Yet Samuel did not appear to consider his extramarital activities in the Indian Ocean as conflicting with his obligations to Mary Ann, at least not in his waking hours. Drawing on racially and geographically specific ideals of womanhood, he put the women of Mahe in a different category from his wife. He explained to Mary Ann in 1851, "Whenever I speak of women in general, you are never included . . . you are my *wife* [his emphasis], the best half of myself." [101] (Ezra Goodnough, still unmarried, had a somewhat more cynical assessment of the relative virtues of hometown women compared to those on Mahe: he noted in his shipboard diary, "We can hire the girls in Mahe to remember us[—]that is more than the girls at home will do.") [102]

A survey of court records for Bristol County, which included New Bedford and many of the surrounding coastal towns, suggests that divorces may not have been any more common for mariners than for their land-based peers. The court records list eighteen completed suits for divorces during the five years from 1830 to 1835. Just five were brought by men, three mariners and two nonmariners, all of whom sued their wives on the grounds of adultery (one on adultery *and* desertion). Unfortunately, in the thirteen suits brought by wives, more than half of the men have no occupational designation. None of the six who do were mariners. The seven without designation are charged with various combinations of cruelty (which implies the man's presence), adultery, desertion, and nonsupport. [103]

In the period from 1845 to 1849, there were forty-one divorces in Bristol County, an increase that reflects the rapidly growing population of the region, due largely to the expansion in the whalefishery. Of the suits that specified the husband's occupation, nearly half were seafarers: seven men were listed as mariners and eight were not. (Unfortunately, since the records do not indicate the husband's occupation in well over half the cases, we still cannot conclude that mariners were disproportionately represented here, though it seems possible.) Three of the seven seamen brought suits against their wives, two for adultery and desertion and one for adultery alone; all the charges were upheld. The other four seamen were charged by their wives, two for desertion, one for desertion and adultery, and one just for adultery. Here too all the suits were proven and divorces granted. [104]

Still, despite the apparent equity in granting divorce to seamen and to seamen's wives, the sexual double standard informally encoded in maritime culture appears to have been enforced judicially as well. In one unusual but particularly revealing case, Mrs. Almira Read of New Bedford petitioned for divorce from her captain-husband on the grounds that he had committed adultery "at Maui one of the Sandwich [Hawaiian] Islands" with "a certain lewd Kanaka [native Hawaiian] woman." Mrs. Read asked for separation—and also for a rather considerable alimony settlement. Though Captain Read appeared in court and contested them, the charges were upheld and Mrs. Read granted her divorce. But, her husband's affluence notwithstanding, the judge awarded her alimony of only $1 a year.[105] This must have been a punitive decision, suggesting that the judge in effect recognized the husband's wrongdoing but also blamed the wife for making it an issue at all. "The sailor is true to his Sal or his Sue, as long as he's able to keep them in view," sang the men at the capstan; "men are too much alike in that respect," Jared Gardner commented, adding "but we will not dwell too long on that." [106] What happened several thousand miles—and years— away was evidently not appropriate for the women at home to judge.

What women could—and did—judge were the emotional costs of separation. Sarah Pierce wrote Captain Elijah Chisole, "I want you dearest before you come home to make your mind up that you will never leave me again to go to sea. for I never could be happy with you at sea and I at home far from you that I love." [107] Nancy Childs wrote her husband John, who had been gone for nearly two years, a classic reiteration of objections: "I recieved your letter last tuesday and was glad to hear from you but wish you had written when you thought you should come home but I hope it will be soon but I hope you will olter your mind about going to cape horn for I can never think of being seperated from you so long as that." Developing on this theme, she continued, "I hope you will be able to do something ashore for what comfort can we take if we have to live so fare apart"— though she backed down from her challenge by immediately adding, "but you will want to hear something else[—]we are all in good health." [108]

Women involved in longer relationships with whalemen, it seems, learned from experience of the peripatetic nature of sailors. Libby Spooner wrote to her husband Caleb, "I try to be reconcil'd to my lot and be thankful when I see so many whose trials are greater than mine." A page later, though, she observed sardonically, "Nehemiah talks of moveing back to the farm I think he best wait till spring but he is a *sailor* and consequently very *uneasy*. I know something about it, they never stay set down in one place till they get so stiff and old they cannot get out of it." Sylvia Leonard similarly told her husband that his brother George was "determined upon not going to sea again but he will get tired of this common life and long for a more changeable one." She reflected knowledgeably, "I guess sailors are rather of that disposition." [109]

Sarah Howland did not criticize her own husband Philip directly. She nonetheless pointed out the clear conflict between a sailor's preference for a "changeable" life and his commitment to his wife when she told Philip, "Oliver Seabury . . . has spun me several yarns about himself and wife that was quite amusing. he thinks he never could leave home long enough to make a whaleing voyage but I doubt whether his attachment to his wife is much stronger than many that follow the seas for a livelihood." Rachel Putnam did not find her situation amusing at all. Three weeks after her husband shipped out, she wrote bitterly in her diary, "I think sometimes such a married life as mine, hardly deserves the name. And how feels my Husband, about these continual separations? I presume he would *rather* stay on shore, but still he continues to go, and *leave me behind.* . . . I have no pleasure in the past, present, or future!!" [110]

Caroline Gifford wrote to her husband Charles, "I am in hopes . . . that you will not have to go to sea again unless," she added pointedly, "you can enjoy yourself better on land." On one of Caroline's later letters, their daughter Eleanor penned a mixed message by way of postscript: "It seems a long time for a man to be away from his folks three or four years at a time. I send my love to you and hope you will prosper . . . for it seems as though you ought to stay at home a while and not be on the water all your days." (Eleanor, for all her ambivalence, proved to be her father's daughter too: she herself married a whaleman—another Gifford from Dartmouth, David L., probably a cousin. But she, unlike her mother, accompanied her husband to sea.) [111]

Ruth Barker Post was more direct. She reported to her husband at sea, "the girl who has lived with us so long left us verry suddenly the first of summer, I do not know [why], it may be a prospect of marriage, if so I do not blame her if she can get a *man to stay with her.*" Lizzie Howes was perhaps the most forthright of all, declaring to her seafaring husband, "I think a seafaring man should *never* marry[—]such is my opinion." [112]

It is difficult to tell just how much of an impact the women's complaints had on the industry itself. Some wives tried to persuade their husbands to give up whaling altogether. Myra Weeks told her husband, "I hope you will be blest with a short and prosperous voyage and then make up your mind to stay at home the remainder of your days for if ever you go to sea again I think you will have more than just yourself to fit out . . . I think that there must be some way to get a liveing without your always being away from your family and friends." [113]

Captain William Loring Taber was stung when his wife Susan doubted his intention to leave off whaling: "You wrote you wish you could think that this was the last time we should be seperated, you know that many have said so before, [but] that Agents give successful captains such inducements that they cannot resist them, and you will not insure one of my ambition against their temptation." He protested, "My greatest ambition is to gain enough of this world's lucre to maintain my family through life, without ever having through necessity to deny them any necessary want." Three years and another voyage later, William reported to Susan, "I do not think any one can offer me inducements enough to leave my family again, unless I meet with misfortunes that would bring them to want, . . . if this voyage is well ended, I feel that I can stay at home . . . I think a married man's place is at home with his family, and if he can stay, he ought to." [114] This time, he held to his word, returning a year later to give up commanding ships and manage them from shore instead.

Captain John Deblois felt tortured by the conflict between his loyalties to his career and to his wife, as one of his seafaring friends described in a letter to Mrs. Deblois. The friend wrote to Henrietta, "I must tell you he is very home sick[.] he said to me Thom I should be willing to give two thousand dollars if I could leave the Ship and go home to my dear wife. for I know . . . she loves me as well as I do her. He read your letters to me with tears in his eyes and [said] Thom never mind if the Lord is willing I shall be with her in less than one year oil or no oil. . . . If I was at liberty as you are to go home to my wife I would fly to her the first opportunity. I told him to give the Ship to [first mate] Mr. Baker and then we would go home together. But he said no I do not like to leave the Ship untill the voyage is up and the Ship Safe in New Bedford harboar and then he whould fly to his dear wife never more to be seperated in this world untill death." (Captain Deblois was able to resolve the contradiction between career and marriage by taking Henrietta to sea with him on his next voyage—an option for some captains in the midcentury period that, as discussed in Chapter 6, raised its own set of problems.) [115]

William Ashley told his wife Hannah, "I think some times if I ever get home again alive and well I never will leave you again. Oh what is the use to talk all I want is to see you awfully and I cant help it." He wrote wist-

William Ashley (1833–1909) of Acushnet, Mass. William made just three whaling voyages between 1852 and 1862. The first one ended after a year in shipwreck; the second lasted almost five years. William married Hannah Crapo a year before he shipped out on his third voyage in December 1862, as first mate under the command of his older brother. William wrote home, "It does very well for single men to be goin . . . but I do not think it is healthy for the married ones." He left halfway through the voyage and returned home for good in 1864. Privately owned, reproduced by permission

Hannah Crapo Ashley (1835–1933), wife of William, of Acushnet, Mass. Hannah lived with her husband's parents on their rural farmstead while William whaled in the Pacific and Arctic in 1863 and 1864. Privately owned, reproduced by permission

fully of Hannah and the baby he had never seen: "I think more about you than any thing elce how you are geting along . . . with a Baby and all those scalawag things to loock out for." "If I was at home," he promised, "I would make that old salt meadow ring." After an absence of nearly two years, William concluded, "It does very well for single men to be goin [whaling] a life time but I do not think it is healthy for the maried ones."[116] Shortly thereafter, he requested his discharge and left the voyage halfway through it, returning to Hannah and the farm in Acushnet, where he settled down permanently.

Other mariners took the less drastic measure of switching into other maritime industries that required shorter and more predictable absences from home. "John goes with John Cornell smaking [i.e., fishing]," Sally Wood told her brother Horatio, explaining, "I suppose you have heard he was married last fall & hase givin up whaling." Philip Howland and Leonard Gifford attempted to move into the transatlantic carrying trade, and David Allen also briefly tried out Great Lakes shipping as an alternative to whaling. For all three, though, the occupational moves were not successful. By the mid-nineteenth century, specialization in the maritime trades seemed to make switching careers midstream more difficult than earlier generations had found it: both Howland and Allen returned to whaling in short order. Poor Gifford fared the worst of the three; on his first merchant voyage, he fell ill and died of a brain inflammation in Capetown, South Africa.[117]

Most career whalemen continued to ply the sea—leaving their wives behind them—as long as they were physically able, despite their often fervent protestations during each voyage that *this* one would be their last. "I am determined that the ocion shall never seperate us again not as long as we can live in love & harmony with each other & no grate loss of property befalls us," Charles Weeks stated firmly. "Perhaps you will say that I roat you so before but would go again," he admitted, but he swore (how many times?) that "you may be assured my dear if you ar ever blessed with the cite of your affectioned husband once more that he is determined never to be seperated from you untill death."[118] Captain Edward R. Ashley (William's older brother) wrote home to his parents from the Pacific, "I do not think I shall ever gow a whaleing again Caty says she will not let me." Caty, who joined Edward aboard his ship for much of the voyage, jotted in her sea diary a year later, "Such is the life of Sailors and their wives they are made up of meetings and partings." She foretold her own future: Edward made at least two more whaling voyages—and left her behind.[119] Captain

William Jackson wrote to a friend about his "dear wife . . . saying lay aside your Charts and stay at home with me. . . . My Caroline's health is not of the very best, & she does not wish for me to leave her again and my little Daughter is a bright loving little thing . . . their united persuasions are enough almost to persuade the brooks from running toward old Ocean, and I don't see how I ever can go again." Nonetheless, within six months Jackson had shipped out again. A confirmed sailor's seaward impulse was apparently a force as irresistible as natural law itself.[120]

On 21 May 1853, Eliza Brock set sail from Nantucket on the ship *Lexington*, bound round Cape Horn on a Pacific whaling voyage. She was the captain's wife and the only woman on board. We will meet more such "sister sailors" in the next chapter; here I would like to draw our attention to one of the poems Mrs. Brock carefully copied into the back of her sea journal:

> The Sailor's Wife
>
> Thou o'er the world, and I at home —
> But one may linger, the other may roam,
> Yet our hearts will flee o'er the bounding sea
> Mine to thy bosom, and thine to me.
>
> Thy lot is the toll of a roving life,
> Chances and changes, sorrow and strife,
> Yet is mine more drear to linger here
> In a ceaseless, changeless war with tear.
>
> I watch the sky by the stars' pale light,
> Till the day dawn breaketh on gloomy night,
> And the wind's low tone hath a dreary moan
> That comes to my heart as I weep alone.[121]

It is not clear from where Eliza Brock took the poem, but the verses were evidently popular; they were reprinted in the March 1861 issue of the *Sailor's Magazine* with an additional stanza: "With the morning light. Oh! would I could see, / Thy white sail far on the breaking sea, / And welcome thee home o'er the wild wave's foam, / And bid thee no more from my side to roam." [122]

Captain Edward Ashley (1824–1900), William's brother, of Acushnet, Mass., capped a long and successful career at sea with three highly profitable voyages as master in the 1850s and 1860s. Privately owned, reproduced by permission

Adra Catherine Braley Ashley (1834–1906), wife of Edward, of Acushnet, Mass. She sailed with Edward on the first two of his three voyages as captain, between 1853 and 1860. Privately owned, reproduced by permission

The poem explains in some measure why Brock chose to join her husband at sea. Its appearance in Brock's journal, along with many other bits of poetry and prose that she added to her own record (including the poem by T. B. Read quoted earlier in this chapter), documents the extent to which new ideas about love and marriage profoundly affected the way whalemen's wives, those few at sea and the many more on land, understood themselves and their lives. Here in Eliza Brock's diary, the manly sailor's occupation takes him roving and roaming around the world in an active life full of chances, changes, and strife. In explicit contrast is the setting and role of the wife: she is at home, fearful and alone, passively waiting, watching, and weeping. While the anonymous poet associates sorrow with the sailor's experience, his wife's life is yet "more drear," empty without his presence. The set of oppositions is mitigated only slightly by the brief and ineffectual mention of romantic union: their hearts, fleeing over the bounding sea. That exclusive romantic relationship between the sailor and his wife somehow survives prolonged and repeated separations, yet it mostly serves as the cause of risk to the man and misery to the woman.

Real sailors, too, were identified by their occupation, their lives organized around the time they spent and the activities they performed at sea. Sailors' wives were defined by their marriage to maritime men; female lives on shore were also structured by the time men spent at sea and the demands of maritime employment. Both men and women tried to bridge the gap between sea and shore through reference to exclusive romantic love and companionate marriage. Both sexes used similar language, professed similar goals, and expressed a similar sense of loss in their separation from their spouses—but the uniform terminology masked the ubiquitous sexual and emotional double standards and the centrality of men to women's experience.

The diaries and letters reveal clearly that, even with the prolonged and repeated absences of their lovers and husbands, women still relied on romantic ideals of love and marriage. In fact—*because* of the men's absences—the women had to. Prescription was both instrumental and pervasive. But the ideal of a transcendent, religiously affirmed love did not make the men's absences any easier for the women to survive emotionally. In fact, the women's tenacious adherence to the scripted romantic ideals only allowed them to experience more deeply an unhappiness with the terms of their own individual lives.

In the poem, "the sailor's wife" is shown as isolated, abstracted from her community; the love between sailor and wife exists without reference to broader social or economic circumstance. However, most maritime women did not, could not, simply wait and weep alone. Despite the intensified focus on the conjugal relationship, the lives of whalemen's wives continued, as they had in the previous century, to be characterized by extensive community interaction and flexible household arrangements. Both elements were crucial to enabling women to survive the seamen's absences and to sustain family and community ashore. Yet, as we will see in the next chapter, the way in which female experience was conceptualized either did not recognize these elements or reassessed them in a negative rather than positive light. The surviving evidence testifies to maritime women's struggle to accommodate the tense interplay between their ideals and their aspirations, the responsibilities they felt for others, and the demands of their men's seafaring careers.

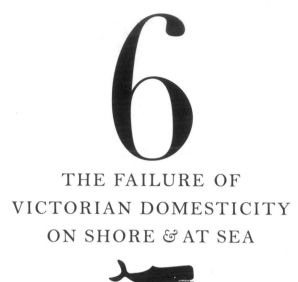

6

THE FAILURE OF
VICTORIAN DOMESTICITY
ON SHORE & AT SEA

This chapter begins with a tragic love story, a true one, but one that nonetheless replicates many of the typical conventions of Victorian domestic fiction. It is the story of Philip Howland and his first and second wives, sisters Sarah and Patience Potter Howland, whom I introduced briefly in Chapter 5. In 1852, eleven years and three children into their marriage, Sarah confided to Philip, "What would my life be if deprived of thee is a question I often ask myself but I can give it no answer and may I never experience the wretchedness it would occasion, for thy love is the one bright spot in my life." But deprivation is a relative thing; in the thirteen years of their marriage, Sarah and Philip spent a cumulative total of just two years in the same place. In 1851, two years after one of Philip's departures, Sarah exclaimed, "Can it be that we are so widely sepperated for I [think] I can hear thy step and thy well known voice falls on mine ear as in days gone by." She dreamed of a time when they would remain together: "In all my pictures of domestic happiness which imagination often portrays, [I see] the husband and father returning after the toils of the day are over to take his accustomed seat."[1] But Sarah's fantasy of domestic bliss, so clearly patterned on Victorian sentimental iconography, was doomed to disappointment. Sarah was then living on her father's farm in rural Dartmouth, outside of New Bedford, caring for her enfeebled mother, her invalid brother, and her own small children. Philip was commanding the whaling bark *Susan* somewhere in the Pacific Ocean, half a world away. He did not return until July 1853, a full four years after he had left.[2]

Over the course of his voyage, Philip repeatedly urged Sarah to join him at sea, as many whaling masters' wives were doing by midcentury. But her sense of her family commitments complicated Sarah's decision-making. "Oh Philip," she wrote, "I try hard to reconcile myself to leaving all our little ones at home and go with thee if thee should go again but as yet I cannot satisfy my own mind what is right to do." The conflict between her responsibilities as wife and mother even haunted her sleep, as she described in 1852: "I dreamed thee was at home making preparation for another four years voyage and it was a long time before I could decide whether it was best to stay at home or go with thee . . . when the day of thy departure arrived I felt all the bitterness of another separation and began to reproach myself for staying—I thought I followed thee to the door and stood while thee was harnessing thy horse but befor thee had started I heard Lycurgus [their son] calling tis time to get up ma and I awoke."[3]

Sarah never did join her husband on board ship, nor did she find domestic fulfillment on shore. She died the following year, less than four months after Philip's return.[4] She was just 36 years old and left behind three children under the age of 11.[5] In an undated letter, some time close to the end of her life, she had written poignantly to Philip: "I had hoped that we might have enjoyed many years together and seen our children grow up around us . . . and that we might have been partakers of that domestic happiness for which my heart has longed . . . I have always had a good home but I have ever felt homeless."[6]

A year after losing Sarah, Philip married her older sister Patience. Even as he continued to ply the sea for a living, and even after Patience and the children moved out of the parental farmstead and into rented lodgings in New Bedford, Philip wrote to Patience of "our own dear circle" and a "home where all study to make each other truly happy," a place where "affliction is robbed of its sting" and "it matters not if the world is cold." He became more determined than ever to take his reconstituted family with him, promising Patience (in a rather self-centered but typical turn of phrase) "when I leave home again the endearing objects of domestick happiness will be in personal attendance." After some initial reluctance, Patience seemed willing to go. But Philip and Patience, too, never achieved the ultimate goal of nuclear family reunion, either at sea or on shore. Having convinced his wife, Philip could not convince the ship-owners. While arguing with his employers about permitting Patience and the children to join him midway, Philip died at sea in 1866. The aptly named Patience outlived him by twenty-seven years.[7]

Like most other Americans of their time, Sarah, Philip, and Patience Howland idealized and glorified "the home," associating it with refuge and rejuvenation, personal authenticity, an unconditional faith both in their God and in other family members, and the daily performance of conjugal love and self-sacrificing maternal nurture. In the midcentury complex of ideas and values that made up the pervasive culture of domesticity, the private, compassionate, domestic "female sphere" of the home was understood to be the polar opposite of the rough-and-tumble, cutthroat, amoral public "male sphere" of work and politics.[8] In fact, the elemental divide between land and sea appeared to correspond precisely to the prevailing conceptual division between female and male spheres, and so for maritime Americans it reinforced the geographic logic of the dominant Victorian understanding of gender. Career whalemen and their Cape Horn widows (even Quaker ones like the Howlands) reiterated the same sentimental phrases about "domestick happiness" that landsmen and women did, perhaps even more fervently because of their typically frequent separations and all too often broken family "circles." Absence, they agreed, generally "made the heart grow fonder."[9] Absence also emphasized the desirability of "home sweet home" at the same time that it highlighted the instability of maritime family life.

Sarah Howland's touching declaration, "I have always had a good home but I have ever felt homeless," suggests both the extent to which she subscribed to the domestic ideal of an intact nuclear family in its own private dwelling and the measure by which she felt her life fell short. As this chapter illustrates, Victorian maritime women were caught in a painful bind that their eighteenth-century foremothers had not faced. If they tried to maintain a household based on a nuclear family, they then felt acutely the lack of an element they considered essential: the husband and father. If, driven by loneliness, financial or material necessity, family responsibility, or a combination of such factors, the women merged households with other kin or neighbors, they then felt keenly the lack of a private, marriage-based home. By the mid-nineteenth century, some captains' wives sought to resolve their dilemma by actually accompanying their husbands to sea. But these women too only ended up facing a new set of hardships that also, perhaps most dramatically of all, demonstrated both the tenacious hold of domesticity and its ultimate failure in the maritime context.

In August 1855, Hepsabeth Russell Bunker of Nantucket marked the wedding of her friends "Charles Brown & Wife" by copying into her diary the "lines from the printer on their marriage & plate of Cake." The verses read:

> Across the threshold led
> And every tear kissed off as soon as shed
> His house she enters, there to be a light
> Shining within when all without is night
> A Guardian angel, o'er his life presiding
> Doubling his pleasures and his cares dividing
> May they live a thousand years.[10]

This diary entry presents an interpretive problem, particularly since Hepsabeth did not include any additional commentary or personal reflection beyond the poem itself. Hepsabeth Russell Bunker was the daughter, niece, sister, and widow of whalemen and the acquaintance of many more; her journal is filled with concise listings of Nantucket ships departing and arriving, reports of local whalemen and their catches, successes and failures. After her husband's death and perhaps before as well, while he was absent at sea, she supported herself with her needle. She was intimately familiar with the fishery's dangers for those at sea and its demands on those on land, excruciatingly familiar with conjugal separation and loss. Nonetheless, Hepsabeth seems to have been able to imagine a bride as a delicate, emotional creature, a wife as a guardian angel, and marital love as composed of mingled tears and kisses.

The poem (or at least the part that Hepsabeth recorded) neglects the husband and focuses all attention on the wife, outlining her role in some detail. She is to serve as a light shining within her husband's house in contrast to the threatening darkness outside; to preside over his life from within that sanctuary by devoting herself to augmenting his pleasures and mitigating cares; and thereby to offer the millennial possibility of salvation, human perfection, and a thousand years of happiness here on earth. With its Christian references, the opposing of the light of the home to the darkness of the external world, and especially the foregrounding of the wife, who is both self-sacrificing and authoritative, this is a classic description of marriage according to the midcentury culture of domesticity.[11] It is also a rendering of marriage that seems conspicuously inappropriate to the experiences of sea-wives and widows like Hepsabeth Bunker.

Many of the beliefs and practices associated with domesticity were clearly incongruent with maritime life, but that does not mean that they were irrelevant. Hepsabeth Bunker's, Sarah Howland's, and so many other sea-wives' adherence to domesticity makes more sense when we understand how its tenets were in part embraced by and in part imposed upon maritime culture. The domestic analysis that linked social and personal problems to corruption or lack of proper home life and which identified women's influence as the solution was directly applied to maritime experience in a range of virtually inescapable ways.

Two of the most influential literary women in nineteenth-century America, Lydia Hunt Sigourney and Sarah Josepha Hale, were both major architects of the culture of domesticity and active in the direct application of domestic ideals to the New England maritime context. The prolific Sigourney, known as the "Sweet Singer of Hartford," was the most popular female poet in Victorian America. She wrote so many sentimental "effusions" (as she herself termed her poems) on maritime themes that they were collected into a volume titled *Poetry for Seamen* in 1845, which was enlarged and reissued in 1850 as *Poems for the Sea* and expanded and republished again in 1857 as *The Sea and the Sailor.* In her autobiography, Sigourney referred to the collection as "a little book of poetry which might go with [sailors] in their chests, a prompter of salutary thought when they should leave the charities of home."[12] Sigourney, who claimed "some personal acquaintance with the Ocean," wrote several of the poems from the perspective of the sailor himself, including the final one in the 1857 volume. Titled "The Happy Home," the concluding poem begins,

> Thoughts of my happy home
> Are pleasant on the Sea,
> For there, my best beloved one
> I know, remembers me,

And teaches with a glowing cheek
Our babe, his father's name to speak.

By the end of the poem (and the book), the sailor describes his wife's and child's love for him as "a diamond shield . . . o'er my bosom thrown" and the "little window" of his "humble home" as "the light-house of my brightest dreams." [13] His home, wife, and child provide more than just pleasant memories, then; they are implicitly the source of the sailor's physical and spiritual salvation.

One of the founders and long-time activist president of the Boston Seamen's Aid Society was the famous author and editor Sarah Josepha Hale, who had herself suffered the loss of her brother at sea. [14] In an 1853 publication, Hale proclaimed that "WOMAN is God's appointed agent of *morality*, the teacher and inspirer of those feelings and sentiments which are termed the virtues of humanity." She reinterpreted Adam and Eve, arguing that "the wife was of finer mould, destined to the most spiritual offices, — the heart of humanity, as her husband was the head" because "she was the *last work* of creation . . . the link which pressed nearest towards the angelic." [15] Hale developed certain maritime variations on these themes in her 1848 epic poem, *Harry Guy, the Widow's Son: A Story of the Sea.* Although a pious old salt and a pure young boy intervene on Harry Guy's behalf at crucial moments in the epic, what fundamentally makes possible the redemption of the wild and reckless seafaring title character was that he felt for his widowed mother "a worshiping, / A reverential love." Even as Harry ran off to sea, "one feeling pure remained, / And, like the angel in the den. . . . His mother!—at the thought, his heart / Was softened and subdued." When Harry finally returns in glory after many tragic trials and tribulations, Hale wrote, "You never will conceive / The triumph of that mother's heart,— . . . / Unless like her you've watched, worked, prayed, / And wept for those you love." [16]

In 1826, the Reverend John Truair, working out of New York City under the joint aegis of two new evangelical reform groups aimed at sailors, the New York Bethel Union and the Marine Bible Society, issued an appeal for the formation of a national society dedicated to seamen in an address titled "A Call from the Ocean, or an Appeal to the Patriot and the Christian, on Behalf of Seamen." His efforts bore fruit with the formation of the national American Seamen's Friend Society in 1828, which served as a sort of umbrella organization for the already more than seventy "port societies" existing up and down the eastern seaboard of the United States.[17] Truair began his call to action with explicit reference to domesticity's assumptions about the importance of family and home life, pleading, "O think on the mariner toss'd on the billow / Afar from the home of his childhood and youth: / No mother to watch o'er his sleep-broken pillow, / No father to counsel, no sister to soothe."[18]

Truair particularly emphasized the victimization of sailors on land, where they were "prey to the most villains, prostitutes and publicans." He and other reformers denounced the waterfront boardinghouses, which doubled as grogshops, gambling dens, and brothels, the dangers of which were now judged to outweigh by far the risks of life at sea. Those traditional vices to which seamen were famously prone—profanity, profligacy, promiscuity, intemperance, general unsteadiness, and hostility to organized religion—stemmed not from their innate depravity nor from their exposure to the ocean's dangers, the reformers thought. Instead, as summarized in the New Bedford Port Society's 1831 annual report, these flaws and fatal habits derived from sailors' missing the benefits of the "mutual guardianship and instruction" of church membership and attendance, "the restraint of public opinion," and especially the "sweet charities of the domestic circle."[19]

In 1842, the Reverend Francis Wayland delivered the annual address to the New Bedford Port Society. He too insisted that the high mortality rate of seamen was due not to the "peculiar dangers" at sea but rather "almost entirely" to their life of vice on shore, to which they were irresistibly impelled because they were "cut off by necessity from all the endearments of the domestic society. . . . [The sailor] feels but too commonly that he is an outcast."[20] The Reverend John Weiss, addressing a group of New Bedford whaleship owners in 1849, also stressed the "intimate relation between goodness and external condition" and also characterized the waterfront as more threatening than whaling itself. Weiss dramatically described how whalemen, "these heroes of a three years campaign . . . come home to fall into the hands of harpies, to be stripped in grog-shops . . . they land, and are adrift."[21]

"Your homes," Weiss told the shipowners, "repair the deficiency in your love of virtue, and atone for the weakness of your wills. You cannot calculate your moral conditions if you were rendered homeless . . . [if you were deprived of] the genial atmosphere, the irresistible, conservative influence of home." He continued, "imagine yourself a member of that floating population in every city, who look from afar at your peace and comfort, who look in at the windows of your homes . . . longing to be seated within the charmed circle of that firelight, where affection, refinement, decency, honor, expand like grain in the sun . . . and the four walls seem to repel the infections which you are forced to breathe daily." Therefore, he argued, "the first prerequisite for the moral improvement of seamen, for their improvement as a class, is a Seamen's Home."[22]

Of all the activities undertaken by the midcentury maritime reformers, the movement to build Sailor's Homes was one of the most enduring and popular. The first such home may have been the Mariners' House in Boston, established about 1835 by the Seamen's Aid Society then under the leadership of Sarah Josepha Hale. (Hale later worked into her epic poem *Harry Guy, the Widow's Son* a specific plug for Sailor's Homes: in describing a ship's return to home port, she added, "Are there not some, ay, many found, / Who have no home or friends? . . . Oh! Christians of America, / Go, haste with purpose kind, / And greet these men, and teach their feet / The 'Seamen's Home' to find.") Other cities up and down the eastern seaboard and on the Great Lakes followed Boston's lead. In New York, the American Seamen's Friend Society sponsored a temperance Sailor's Home in 1837, which was replaced by a more "commodious" structure they built for the purpose in 1841; another, for "colored sailors," was established in 1855. In 1851, the New Bedford Port Society opened its Mariner's Home, appropriately enough in the stately, eighteenth-century mansion of whaling magnate William Rotch Jr., donated for that purpose by his daughter, Sarah Rotch Arnold, after William's death in 1850.[23]

The establishments probably never provided housing for more than a few hundred seamen a year each, an insignificant number in ports like Boston, New York, and New Bedford, where tens of thousands of sailors came and went each year. The reformers appear to have met with general disinterest on the part of seamen themselves and active resistance from boardinghouse keepers and other waterfront retailers and suppliers.[24] Yet the attempt was significant, for the preoccupation with the Homes against such formidable odds demonstrated the reformers' attribution of maritime vice to the lack of home influence and especially their faith in the power of domesticity to relieve the corruption of even the most hardened seamen and forestall their victimization by "harpies" and other species of "landsharks."[25]

Not surprisingly, reform-minded women appear to have taken the lead in the Sailor's Home movement. An anonymous piece in the January 1842 issue of *Sailor's Magazine* directly addressed "the Female Associations, organized for the benefit of Seamen, and to the Ladies generally," exhorting them: "Ye who taste the sweets of home, and enjoy the comforts of the domestic fireside—sheltered from the storm, with your loved ones around you, think of the wandering, homeless sailor; think of his perils and dangers at sea, and the snares and temptations that beset him on shore. Does he not need, does he not deserve at our hands an asylum—a *Home*; where he may enjoy some of the comforts from which he has been so long estranged!" [26] Many evidently answered the calls to action, including the "young ladies" of the Brooklyn Female Bethel Society, the "female friend to seamen", in Hartford, and the "Old Mill Sewing Society" of Bridgeport, Connecticut.[27]

The ladies of the Newburyport Female Bethel Society contributed some household articles to the New York Sailor's Home built in 1841, explaining, "We have always regarded such Homes as of superlative importance, and as an indispensable auxiliary in improving [seamen's] condition." They concluded their report with a short verse, proclaiming, "So may humble hands, With labour and care, / For the sons of the sea a Home prepare." [28] While men's organizations usually held title to the real estate, in many cities (including New Bedford) the women's auxiliaries furnished and managed the Sailor's Homes—properly so, both women and men thought, because of women's presumed innate ability and responsibility for creating a suitably restorative and uplifting domestic environment.

Lots of historians have identified nineteenth-century domesticity's preoccupation with the long-suffering yet powerful figures of mother and wife. Many have persuasively argued that this understanding of female influence propelled thousands of women into a panoply of social reform movements, ranging from the relatively modest Sailor's Home efforts to the much broader and more visible campaigns for abolition, temperance, and women's rights.[29] But the bifurcated focus on the female center of the domesticated home and the homelessness of sailors by nineteenth-century activists and twentieth-century historians alike ends up obscuring maritime women's own experience of home and family life. It also obscures the extent to which maritime home life was structured not by women's influence but rather by the dynamics of seafaring.[30] In the end, it did not matter how hard or successfully maritime women tried to be properly angelic and domestic, or even if they tried at all. Rather the personal, social, and financial consequences of whalemen's absences continued to locate their wives and mothers in constantly reconfiguring households and to launch them into peripatetic travels. These patterns of community interaction were nothing new—they had originated with the whaling industry itself a century before—but now they rarely approximated the stable home life and nuclear family that nineteenth-century maritime women so idealized.

According to widespread assumption and prescriptive confirmation throughout much of the United States in the mid-nineteenth century, three principles dictated appropriate household formation. "each conjugal family of husband, wife, and children should live in its own household; . . . each household should have an adult male at its head; . . . [and] people without conjugal families of their own should be included in the households of their kin."[31] Like their fellow Americans, maritime women and men also practiced these principles as far as they could. They adhered to the emerging definition of the family as private, nuclear, and founded in marriage, and they similarly loaded the conjugal relationship with expectations of intensive, romantic, exclusive love. But while men went to sea, women remained on land, enmeshed in broad and diffuse networks of extended kinship, friends, and neighborhoods.

Where and with whom a maritime woman resided was largely determined by the related factors of age, family status, and access to resources. Young couples rarely "set up housekeeping" after marriage, since the new husband often shipped out on his next voyage soon after the wedding. The new wife seems to have most often remained in her parents' household, where her absent husband was now considered resident by Massachusetts law.[32] Hannah Burgess, five months pregnant with her first child, continued to live with her widowed mother when her husband left in 1828. Elisabeth Taber did the same, as she reported to her husband John: "I am with Mother and Father yet . . . & getting along very good father has bought Gilbert Tabers place we are living hear at the present."[33] Susan Snow Gifford, daughter of a ship's carpenter, also continued to live with her parents when her husband set sail, just twenty-five days after their wedding in October 1859. Susan told her husband how she particularly welcomed her sister's return to relieve her loneliness: "Abby . . . says she is coming to stay tomorrow night, *only think* I have stayed alone [i.e., had her own bedroom within her parents' household] ever since you left now she will stay home all the time and I shall not be quite so lonesome."[34]

Others returned to their own or their husband's parents' homes when their husbands left. Mary T. Smith told her husband Parker in 1827 that she "had concluded to continue boarding at father's this winter at least and more than probable I shall continue at home while you are absent as I do not like to keep house alone."[35] Married just over a year, Hannah Ashley lived with her husband's parents on their farm in Acushnet after he shipped out in December 1862. Moses Snell wrote to his son, then at sea, that the son's wife "came home with me and your Mother yesterday she is going to stay here awhile."[36]

Susan Snow may have stayed with her parents after her marriage to John Gifford, but her sisters-in-law did not. John's brothers Charles and Robinson had married a pair of sisters, Sarah and Lucinda Hudson, in a form of extreme endogamy not uncommon to the whaling communities. It appears from the 1860 federal census household enumeration for Mattapoisett that, while her husband Charles went whaling, Sarah Hudson Gifford and her toddler son lived with her younger brother, a sailmaker, and his wife—all four boarding with a farmer with the surname of Bolles. Meanwhile, Susan noted in her diary that Lucinda was "keeping house for Aunt Eliza" while Lucinda's husband was at sea and Aunt Eliza out of town.[37]

The Spooner family of New Bedford illustrates just how flexible maritime kinship and household formation could be. Caleb Spooner Sr. was a moderately prosperous cooper, but all three of his sons who survived to adulthood—Gideon, Shubael, and Caleb Jr.—went whaling. Gideon began seafaring in 1825 at age 19 and made captain, on his sixth voyage, when he was 33. Gideon's seafaring career lasted twenty-two years, of which he spent perhaps a cumulative total of three years at home between voyages. Shubael and Caleb Jr. each first shipped out when they were 15, in 1832 and 1834 respectively. Shubael was also promoted to captain at age 33; all in all, he made eleven voyages spanning twenty-six years, of which about four were spent on shore. Caleb Jr.'s whaling career lasted a full thirty years, of which roughly four and a half were spent on shore; he made captain at age 31 and completed a total of nine voyages, four of which he commanded.[38]

The first Spooner sibling to marry was Charlotte; she married Henry Clark in 1831 and left her parents' household. Her brother Gideon married in 1835 and seems to have brought his wife Elizabeth into his parents' home at 40 North Street: at least, that remained his legal residence, and so her primary residence as well. In 1839, their sister Sophia married another whaling captain, George Clark, who also—in the legal sense, since most of the time he was actually at sea—moved into the Spooner household.[39] Elizabeth, Sophia, and the two Spooner sisters who did not marry evidently all lived together, caring for their children as well as the aging Spooner parents, while their men went whaling. Sophia died in 1845, during one of her husband's voyages. The evidence suggests that the other Spooner women raised her child until George Clark came home, remarried, and moved into his new wife's parents' home, taking his son with him.[40]

Caleb Sr. also died in 1845, while all three sons were at sea. Gideon, the oldest, retired from sea when he returned from his four-year voyage in 1847, settling down as the new head of the household in the Spooner home at 40 North Street, but the generational transition in property ownership did not immediately alter the siblings' residential patterns. Caleb Jr. married Elizabeth Hathaway in 1853, but he and now presumably Libby (as she was known) remained officially if not actually in residence at 40 North Street too; at least, that is the way Caleb Jr. was listed in the New Bedford City Directory for 1855. By 1865, Caleb Jr., Libby, and their two young daughters had apparently moved out of the ancestral home, since Caleb was then listed as owning a house on West Willis Street.[41]

In 1852, seven years after his father's death, Shubael's address was also still 40 North Street. He was not listed in the 1855 directory, but in the 1859 directory he was credited with owning a house at 107 Hillman Street. We do not know if Shubael's removal from his father's home coincided with his marriage to Elizabeth (Lizzie) Francis, since we do not know the actual dates of either event; maybe the precipitating factor was the birth of his and Lizzie's daughter Ella on 26 March 1858. The marriage and perhaps the move to Hillman Street must have taken place during one of Shubael's last two stints on land, either the four months he was at home from July to November 1853 or during the year and a half between May 1857 and October 1858, when he left on what was to be his final voyage. The *Whaleman's Shipping List* provided the grim report: the New Bedford bark *Montezuma*, "Shubael S. Spooner, Master," was last seen later that year "in a terrible gale of wind. . . . [T]here is no doubt but she was lost, and all on board perished."[42]

The Spooner family thus expanded and contracted with the demographic rhythms of the whalefishery as well as the more common rhythms of birth, marriage, and death. Though whalemen typically married when they had access to income they thought sufficient to begin a family, it appears that their wives rarely maintained an independent household until they had reached midlife, until they had several children, or until they achieved the financial capability to support a separate establishment during the husband's absence.

Age, proximity, and ability of parents or siblings to offer support undoubtedly factored into the decisions. While young brides generally stayed with relatives, older women like Harriet Allen and Patience Howland rented lodgings for themselves and their children. During their husbands' absences, Caroline Gifford and Mary Ann Braley each managed growing families and kept the family farms going with the intermittent help of siblings, in-laws, and hired hands. Julia Fisk ran a seaside boardinghouse during summers, assisted by her own parents and sister as well as her husband's parents and siblings, both families living not with Julia but very nearby.[43]

The relationships that Cape Horn widows experienced on a daily basis emerged from their work of sustaining their households, communities, and the people therein.[44] As in the previous century, which couple actually formed the core of a household and who was added to the household continued to be highly variable, depending on stage in life course, availability of resources, and individual preference. Kinship continued to be reckoned flexibly. The women's understanding of family was malleable and contextually defined, assumed to confer emotional closeness, social interaction, and material support if needed. The actual intensity of the emotional bond and the amount, form, and timing of sociability and support depended on circumstance. Furthermore, family networks were reinforced and extended by connections between households, links that continued to demonstrate both a tendency toward endogamous marriages and a now secular "tribalism" based on overlapping identifications with place and occupation.[45]

Identifying where a woman was considered to "live" is one thing; determining when and where she came and went is another. The censuses and city directories indicate legal residences and whom officials identified as the heads of the households. But these sources present a static image, representing just one frozen moment, and normative rather than actual family relationships.[46] The picture that emerges from letters and diaries demonstrates instead that maritime women were almost as constantly in motion as their seafaring men were out on the vast oceans.[47] (They were probably busier, too, given the long stretches of inactivity between whales that the men experienced at sea.) Like household formation and residence, female mobility seems to have followed rhythms determined by age and access or accessibility to family, friends and neighbors.

Ann Russell of Nantucket, daughter and sister of several whalemen, reported to her brother Roland that she had been staying at "Aunt Eunice's a few days I intended to have got here a number of weeks ago but Maria wanted I should stay there a few weeks. . . . I ben going down to Elizas this week to stay a few days as I have not ben there at all." She remarked, "I have not been to half the places that I have been invited to but I begin to be tired a visiting . . . Maria wanted I should stay there a week longer but . . . I told her I wanted to be settled somewhere." [48] Not yet married herself, Ann was available to help out Maria, the wife of her whaling-captain brother, with the couple's several young children. Ann also helped nurse her sister Jane's year-old son in the weeks before he died and then nursed Jane through what turned out to be the young mother's own final illness.

New bride Susan Snow Gifford, of the small, busy village of Mattapoisett, remained a member of her parents' household after her husband shipped out. This did not mean that she stayed there, however. During the first month John was gone, Susan spent only five days at home, a pattern that remained stable throughout the year. Her diary is filled with references to church services and Sabbath School concerts; sewing circles, literary meetings, and lectures at the Temperance Hall; picnics and parties, skating and sailing; weddings, confinements, and funerals; short trips to local shops and longer excursions to stores in New Bedford. [49] Susan recorded innumerable calls on neighbors and relatives, sometimes involving labor (e.g., "Went to Uncle George and helped them move and sewed on carpet") and sometimes just pure sociability (e.g., "Went to Lizzie Winstons to a Candy party, a good many there"). [50] Her network was large, too: in that first month she mentioned by name thirty-eight individuals, twenty-seven women and eleven men. Susan wrote wistfully, "I have such a sense of loneliness come over me once in a while that I dont know what to do." She was lonely—but she was virtually never alone. [51]

Women with children of their own or with greater responsibilities for the care of property remained home more often than did new wives like Susan. But this did not necessarily mean they had less interaction or a more constricted social circle. Hannah Ashley lived with her husband's parents on their farm in rural Acushnet, though Hannah made an overnight visit to her widowed mother in New Bedford about every six weeks or so. According to the brief but almost daily entries in her tiny "pocket-book" diary for 1864, she stayed at home about half the time: ten days out of twenty in January, thirteen days out of twenty-five in June. Still, it was a rare day, only three or four a month, in which she saw only her parents-in-law: a regular stream of visitors flowed in and out of the farmhouse. Over a three-month period, Hannah mentioned forty-eight different individuals, ten men and thirty-eight women.[52]

The one exception to Hannah's social routine was the month of March, when she bore her first child: she stayed in twenty-eight days and went out only rarely. (Four days after giving birth, Hannah went "a sleighing" — a mistake, since she was laid low for the next two weeks!) But being confined to the house around the time of her "confinement" actually seemed to increase her interaction with others. First a close female neighbor and then Hannah's sister-in-law came in to help care for the new mother and baby; Hannah had no sister of her own, and her mother may have been infirm. Hannah also recorded that she "had a number of callers to see the baby" almost every day for about two weeks after the child was born.[53]

Childbirth and care for the young, the sick, and the elderly seem to have resisted being drawn into the market economy and instead remained occasions for cooperative female endeavor, as women's labor shifted from household to household in response to need. In January 1863, Harriet Allen paid a doctor $30 for a number of his visits to treat her and her two children over a period of time. She called in the doctor again when her 2-year-old daughter Nellie fell seriously ill later that spring. It was not the doctor, however, but rather a series of female friends, relatives, and neighbors who came in — without pay — and watched Nellie around the clock for several days.[54]

The opportunities for sociability — whether purely times for entertainment or occasions for shared work, shared belongings, and collaborative care for others — brought women in and out of each other's homes on a daily basis. In fact, for many sea-wives, the visits lasted not hours but days or weeks. A sense of the dynamic flow, interaction, and cooperative effort characterizing maritime community life is conveyed in Nancy Childs's chatty letter to her husband John: "Oliver and his folks are as well as comon[.] I have ben over there and staid 4 weeks and worked for them[.] I left bub [their young son] with Mother and he was contented enough . . . if nothing happens you will see your portrate in him for he looks so much like you that every one speaks of it. we have moved down into the shop where we used to live and Stephen lives where we did when you left and John B. Colman has taken there roomes."[55]

The shoreside community of maritime women does not much resemble what historian Carroll Smith-Rosenberg identified as the sex-segregated "female world of love and ritual" in which "men made but a shadowy appearance." [56] Lots of men—fathers, brothers, in-laws, friends, neighbors—were certainly present too, and not as the distant and alien figures Smith-Rosenberg proposed.[57] Nevertheless, in the sea-wives' letters and diaries that I examined references to other women were both more numerous and, except for the conjugal relationship itself, often qualitatively more important than references to men. Smith-Rosenberg's famous essay introduced us to the "intense and sometimes sensual female love" that was "both a possible and an acceptable emotional option" for nineteenth-century women, and even compatible with marriage. Given the loneliness that so many of them expressed, it is surprising how few of the whalemen's wives appear to have engaged in the kind of intensely romantic relationships with other women described by Smith-Rosenberg. Of course, this reflects the evidence that has survived rather than actual incidence, but concrete documentation of romantic friendship surfaced for just two of the several dozen women examined in this study.

On 13 February 1860, Susan Colt Norton of Edgartown (Martha's Vineyard), was on her second voyage at sea with her whaling-captain husband when she wrote a letter to "My dear little Sallie." [58] "O how very much, I want to see you tonight, to have one of the dear good old talks, such as we used to enjoy," Susan exclaimed. "Darling, I need not ask if you miss me, but I hope you have found some true, good, loving friend to supply my place; not that I would be forgotten, or loved the less, but it would make me unhappy to think that you are alone, with no sympathizing friend in whom to confide." She continued cozily, "And now sit down by my side and tell me all about yourself, all that has occured . . . since our separation on that sad October day."

As expressed in this one surviving letter, Susan's friendship with "Sallie" (probably a school chum named Sarah Linton) exhibited many of the features of the relationships between sea-wives and husbands described in Chapter 5, in its references to exclusive passion, mutuality, and fidelity. Susan referred to Sallie as "Darling" and the "dear friend of my heart," and she requested many letters with private, personal content. She also coped with separation in part by setting it into a religious framework: "Dearest friend, we may never meet again on earth, even while I write, you may be passing from this to the eternal world—let us each strive to live a Godly life in Christ, then we shall have the blessed assurance of a happy reunion above." She signed off with "a wealth of love, and shower of kisses from your ever true Susie." Nonetheless, at the same time Susan described how she was less lonely on this voyage than on a previous one and declared that with her husband she was "happy and contented in his love and society." Neither Susan nor her husband evidently viewed the two relationships as competing; "Shubael speaks of you often, says I must give his love to you," Susan reported.

Harriet Allen of New Bedford also enjoyed a close relationship with another woman (also a school friend) that may have been romantic—at least it certainly was from the friend's point of view. Harriet herself did not describe her feelings either for her husband, David Allen, or for her friend, Satira Connor, with any specificity in the surviving family papers. In her diary for 1863, though, Harriet did record the daily activities of "S." with nearly as much detail as she did her own during the period that Satira lived with her and her two young children (both while David was at sea and after he returned). Evidence of the nature of their relationship surfaces in Satira's diary for 1854 through 1859, in which references to her passion for Harriet (and, actually, for a few other young women too) abound. When Harriet (who had married in 1850) set sail with her whaling-captain husband in June of 1857, Satira was miserable: "The 'Platina' sailed this morning. . . . What I suffered words cannot tell . . . my spirit has gone with her. my present life has become cheerless & inanimate. . . . My idol, my darling—where on the wide waters shall I seek you tonight?" A month later: "Oh! what a life I am living. . . . the best part of myself is gone from me. . . . When Harriet returns I shall be myself again—but never till then. Oh, a letter from her would be more to me than aught else except seeing her, my own, my only treasure, none other like her." [59] Satira does not mention David, Harriet's husband, at all, not even to blame him for taking Harriet away.

Harriet and David returned from sea in April 1860 with a new son. Four months later, David shipped out again, leaving behind the boy and Harriet, now pregnant with their second child. At some point during this voyage, Satira moved in with the chronically ill Harriet, helping manage the household and care for the children. David returned in 1863 and Satira continued to live with them—until she married David's brother Fred, another sailor. On 2 January 1865, Harriet recorded in her diary, "Washed this afternoon. S. went to the dentist's & I went for my bonnet. . . .

Fred here this evening. S. at work upon her bonnet. I have been knitting & shivering with cold. My throat is very sore. After D. & Mary [a relative boarding with them] retired—S. told me of her plans. She will leave me this week—& will marry Fred—I cannot believe it. though I have seen it so long." On 5 January, Harriet wrote, "this evening she has gone out & I feel sure that she will be married tonight. I let her have $5.00 & those stockings. . . . D. was determined to sit up as long as I—but I got him to go up stairs & then S. told me she was going tomorrow & bid me 'good bye.' She has not told me in words but I know they are *married*." The next day, Harriet claimed, "It was like S. to elope in that [secret] style. I do not care, if it pleases her. I do not feel slighted or injured in the least. I shall miss her very much—but expect to see her often—She is Cousin now." At the end of the entry (which continued with mundane details of daily activities), Harriet mused, "Every thing seems strange—& unnatural."

The intensely loving relationships between Susan and Sallie, Harriet and Satira, were not atypical in Victorian America, especially not among young women who went to boarding school together as these two pairs did. In fact, their school experience may have been key in forming romantic bonds before they married. For the other maritime wives I studied, it seems that husbands' absences and the frustration of the conjugal bond did not promote the substitution of a similar kind of romantic relationship with anyone else on shore, female or male. Laurel Thatcher Ulrich has usefully pointed out the difference between a "new, more sentimental [form of] intense personal relationships" and an older form of relationship "originating in a traditional world that organized work by gender and encouraged communal rather than individual identity." [60] The former characterized the romantic bond that the majority of sea-wives focused primarily on their husbands. The latter typified the bonds most maritime women had with each other: often intimate and affectionate, but not necessarily exclusive or romantic.

For example, sisterly solace in physical closeness within a communal environment—the more traditional sort of female friendship—is implied in "Melintha's" jocular letter to one William Albert. (It is not evident exactly who this Melintha was, but she was clearly a close friend, perhaps also a relative, living next door in William's father-in-law's household.) "Now William," Melintha wrote, "I gess you will laugh when you come to no how ruth slept the first week after you went away." William had left in early August of 1844, shipping out on the Westport bark *President*. His wife Ruth gave birth to their second child just a little over a week later.

Melintha thought William would be amused by Ruth's behavior in the final days of her pregnancy: "She and prissillah [Ruth's sister] would go to bed and she would Lay untill the clock struck 10 and then she would come and get into bed with Melintha [either Ruth's small daughter or the author of the letter] and Lay then untill it was Light and then she would go home [next door] and get into bed and Lay untill breakfast time and that is the way she did." [61] (Below Melintha's note, on the same piece of paper, Ruth's father, who signed himself "Abm Borden the Cobler of Tiverton," told his whaleman son-in-law that he had cleaned William's gun for him and also reported his plans to go up to Providence for a "Grate Demicrat Mass Meeting.")

Despite what appears to have been bed-hopping in two different households, Ruth wrote to William, "You have been gone 3 weeks this morning and it seems to me that you have been gone 3 months for time never did seem so long to me before as it does now." She reported that their "little Ann Moriah . . . is 2 weeks old to day . . . she is a nice great fat baby has black hair and black eyes, and is pretty quiet . . . I am better than I have been before in a great while and I think if nothing happens and I keep still 2 or 3 weeks more I shall be as well as I ever was." But, she added on the bottom of the page, a week later, "You do not know how lonely I feel I miss you so much." [62]

Many such Cape Horn widows found particular relief for their loneliness in a traditional maritime sisterhood with other sea-wives who shared their experience of conjugal separation.[63] In the small village of Mattapoisett, Susan Snow Gifford spent much time visiting with her husband's brother's wife Lucinda while the two brothers were both at sea. On one occasion, Susan recorded in a diary entry addressed to her husband John, "Lucinda and I have talked of you and Robinson all the afternoon[.] havent your ears burned[?] I should have thought they would." [64] Just down the street and around the corner, Mrs. Arunak Crossman stayed over with "Cousin Eliza Merrihew" whose "husband is at sea in the Ship Sarah," as Mrs. Crossman explained to her own husband, then in the whaling bark *Stafford.*[65]

Captain Stephen Bailey acknowledged both the distress and the comforts of maritime sisterhood when he appended a postscript to a letter being written by his first mate Jared Gardner to Harriet Gardner, back on Nantucket. In a ponderous attempt at humor, Bailey asked Harriet to "please go and see my Eliza as often as possible[,] for misery likes company[,] you know." In 1864, Captain Seth Blackmer similarly urged his wife Hannah, "you must get Jennie Howland to spend the winter with you[.] I venture to say there would be some noise and you would have some fun."[66] Such ties could be established by mail, too. Elisabeth Ann Worth requested that her captain-husband "remember me to Mr Slocome[.] I have received three letters from his wife." Mrs. Worth added, "Her letters is very good and I was glad to find she was a Child of God as well as her Companion[.] I understand he takes Comfort with you[—]I was glad to hear you lived in unity with each other" (i.e., shared a common evangelical Protestant orientation).[67]

In 1858, Libby Spooner told her husband Caleb, who was then at sea, "Lizzie write me a long letter full of troble down spirited enough she feel Shube's departure deeply . . . Cornelia Winslow is with her now [two] lonely ones togather."[68] Libby's sister-in-law Lizzie Spooner and her friend Cornelia Winslow spent much time together while their husbands went whaling. (The friendship between Lizzie Spooner and Cornelia Winslow was evidently long-lasting; five years later, Harriet Allen noted in her diary that she had received a social call from the pair.)[69] Libby's phrase aptly summarized one of the central paradoxes for maritime women: they were "lonely ones togather," women whose relationships were based in part on the shared experience of conjugal deprivation. For these sea-wives, such sisterhood was simply not a satisfactory substitute for family life, a domestic "circle," or a "home" founded in a private, intact marital relationship. Libby Spooner concluded, "but tis our lot God help us."[70]

First mate Ambrose Bates was tormented by his restlessness. "In vain I have sought a place upon the globe that I might settle down in quiet contentment," he confessed to his diary in 1867. "Although I have been blessed with all the heart could ask[,] still as it seems almost against my will I find myself volunteerly flying from all I love on earth." He wrote with painful self-scrutiny:

> It was morning and I longed for evening
> It was evening and I longed for home
> I was at home and I longed for the sea

Now whire shall I fly to amuse myself
but alas [I] know of no place excepting
I could combind Land and sea together.[71]

Ambrose's versifying vividly captures the contrapuntal rhythms on which the whalefishery was based. Career mariners felt pulled between two worlds — the one of work, which conferred on them an occupational identity, and the other of home, from which they gained a sense of self that loosely referred to a nuclear family, kinfolk, local community, a building or place, and geographic place of origin. Their understanding of home itself was vague and expansive, conflating some or all of these elements.

Half a year after leaving Nantucket on the ship *Washington* in 1840, Jared Gardner told his new wife Harriet: "Ask [brother] George if he is aware of the comfort he takes while he is hard to work wher he can look up to the house from the corn field or [illegible] and sea his dear companion about the house feading her chickens or some such thing . . . tel him not to turn fool and leave house home farm wife and cum round [Cape Horn]." Jared's homesickness permeated the numerous letters he wrote over the three-year voyage. By 1843, Jared's misery had deepened to such an extent that he proclaimed, "Oh dear wife[,] should I be blessed to return once more to my dear bosom wife I feal that I would never leave her again" and "Oh Nantucket Nantucket let me plank my foot there and Ill bid cape horn adieu." His longings for person and for place — for "house home farm wife" — were overlapping and mutually reinforcing. But not strong enough to overcome the pull of the sea: Jared "planked his foot" on Nantucket on 24 September 1843 and a year and a half later shipped out again.[72]

John Chapman was similarly unhappy, and in his homesickness similarly conflated person and place. After a year's absence, he wrote his wife: "Laura dear i have not had a chance to write to you before and darling i did not dare to say good bye for fear of breaking down . . . Laura i must have been crazy to have shipped in this vessel but now that i am here i am going to make the best of it . . . when i do get home darling look out for i will give my clothes away so that i will have to stay in the house." He ended the letter by musing, "how sweet that word sounds[,] HOME," and jotted in a final postscript: "P.S. . . . you can bet a pair of split drawers that when i get home with you again I will stay there." [73]

Libby Spooner wrote in December 1858 to her husband, who was by then over a year out on the New Bedford bark *Cornelia*, "Dear Caleb, I have just received a letter from Gideon asking for more letters & I thought the most of the ships had gone but it appears there are some 3 or 4 more chances." [74] Libby welcomed the news from her husband's brother Gideon; she hadn't been aware of the additional opportunities to send letters to the men at sea, being out of town herself. In fact, while Caleb cruised the Indian Ocean on the hunt for whales, Libby spent months on end in extended visits to various relatives and connections throughout the New Bedford area. She outlined her busy schedule for Caleb: "I was down to Grandfathers last sunday they are all well. . . . I have been away near four weeks[.] Lydia [their young daughter] did not get any better on the flat and so I came up here on the hill with her, I am staying with Uncle Gamaliel['s] widow[—]she is alone keeping house for her father[.] I shall stay two or three weeks longer when I shall go back to Grandmothers[,] stop a short time then go out and stay a few weeks with Cynthia then to [George's?] and back and get ready to start for home by the last of May." [75]

"I have got to roveing so much are you not afraid you will not be able to keep me at home when you wish?" Libby teased Caleb. "Well you need not fear," she assured him, "for the more I knock about the more anxious I am to settle down quietly somewhere in fact sometimes I feel I shall never want to leave its shadow should I be so fortunate as to ever gain its shelter and be able to say 'At Home,' the very words sound dear to me." [76] Libby used nearly the same domestic reference to "Home" as John Chapman had, and she also described her movement around the region as "roveing," a term often applied to sailors. But here too, as with the understanding of romantic love explored in Chapter 5, men and women might use the same words but they often meant (and experienced) quite different things.

Harriet Allen shared both Libby Spooner's ideals and her keen sense that her own life fell short. During her husband David's whaling voyage to the Indian Ocean from August 1860 to December 1863, Harriet lived in a rented dwelling in New Bedford with her two small children, her friend Satira Connor, and sometimes a hired "girl." On 13 May 1863, Harriet wrote in her diary with dismay that the landlord had informed her they would have to move: "Mr. Cook called just after dinner, & stated that he had sold his house & wanted to move into *this*. He wants me vacate early in *June*. I am sorry. There are many reasons why I would rather remain here until D. comes." [77]

During Harriet's search for new lodgings, she expressed a great deal of anxiety; it seems as though she associated the disruptions of moving with a more fundamental instability. "We looked at two 'tenements,' one on

Allen St & one on Grinnell St . . . I am sick of both I am sick of every place but this," she wrote on 16 May 1863. The following day brought the statement: "I would rather remain *here* than move any where." With the help of relatives, in-laws, and friends, Harriet finally located a "very fine place" on County Street which she decided to take even though it was too large and expensive; she determined to meet the rent by subletting the upstairs chambers. Four days later, though, she recorded, "I am wretched about it," and on moving day, June 10, she wrote, "I am sick mind & body." [78]

The next day, she observed, "Last Evening when I came to my new home for the first time, I was quite impressed with its cheerful aspects. Satira & Fred [Harriet's live-in friend and Harriet's brother-in-law] had arranged the sleeping & setting rooms very nicely. A cheerful fire was blazing upon the hearth. . . . The Ivy looks very beautiful against this [wall]paper." But despite the place's evident conformation to Victorian aesthetics, she felt compelled to add, "This morning I see some things that annoy me." And when she visited her former residence, she noted, "I am homesick when I go there." [79]

A year later, their dwelling was again sold out from under them. Harriet lamented, "The house is *gone!* . . . I am sorry D[aniel] did not buy it when he first came home [in December 1863]. I did not quite like it & did not care to buy it . . . but I fear now that [I] shall never have one as good . . . I shall always remember that I *might have had it.*" They moved to another rental property in early August, this time with David there to help, but Harriet was still unhappy. "Have brought the last thing from the house & given up the key. I am *home-sick!*" she declared.[80]

Poor Harriet seems to have suffered from chronic and frequently incapacitating illness, a perpetual cash flow problem, sometimes intrusive in-laws, the hired girl's addiction to opium, anxiety over the progress of the Civil War, and an understandably fretful disposition. Harriet idealized the past, felt oppressed by the present, and worried about the future.[81] For example, she mused, when she visited her mother's grave, "The days that I passed with her are green in my memory, are dearer than any I hope to see in the future." [82] Her unhappy attitude was clearly projected onto her current abode—wherever it happened to be—while she felt nostalgic attachment to her previous residences.

The major source of her homesickness and her sense of instability, though, seems really to have been David's regular absences. Harriet's diary, the earliest surviving volume of which begins on 1 January 1863, a year and a half after David's departure on the bark *Platina*, mentions

David only occasionally and seldom with reference to Harriet's feelings. Interestingly, the undercurrent of irritability continues in the diary after David's return in December of 1863, perhaps partially in response to his peripatetic behavior even when at home. The one exception: after David left in early April 1864 to try his hand at Great Lakes shipping, Harriet noted, "miss D. very much."[83]

David returned at the end of May to report that "he had quite an experience of Lake life—& did not like it." Harriet then burst forth in a bitter and unusually assertive passage, "I see how it will be. D. will go to *sea;* very likely this *Fall.* He thinks *now* that he will not go without his *family,* but he *will.* He will not find ship owners willing to allow us all to go & he will go for three years & probably *longer*—& I shall remain at home *just* as I *did* this last voyage."[84] She was right, except that he did not actually leave until May of 1865, a full year later, as master of the bark *Sea Fox.* And he was gone only two years, not three: David returned to New Bedford in May of 1867.

Harriet was also right about the consequences of David's departure on the form of their family life. By 1865 they were finally "housekeeping," living in a house of their own, though with various kinfolk boarding or staying with them. But Harriet's chronic health problems apparently meant that she would not be able to maintain the place on her own without hiring help during David's voyage. So "D & I had a talk about the expediency of boarding for a while. . . . For the sake of the children I prefer housekeeping but I *must* have my family by *itself.* If I get better I can take care of them. . . . It would be very pleasant if we could afford it."[85] Evidently they could not. They appear to have rented out their house, and Harriet and the children seem to have moved into smaller and less expensive rented lodgings.

It was on the subsequent voyage, this time for a different managing owner, that David did take Harriet and their two children with him.[86] The bark *Merlin* left New Bedford on 23 June 1868, bound for the Indian Ocean. And at last, Harriet apparently felt at home. Her sea journal is markedly happier in tone, despite seasickness and other various illnesses, injuries, and misfortunes typical to whaling. In her last entry of the four-year voyage, Harriet wrote, "Have been very busy getting our things packed. Every body anxious to get home—excepting myself. I am, only for David's sake [he was quite ill] & to get the children in school. . . . My little cabin never looked better to me than *now* . . . This is my *home.* I have *no other.* I want to see my friends but I do not feel that I am *going home.* . . . there have been many things annoying yet I have enjoyed being here with my family." [87] Even through her characteristic irritability and nostalgia, we can see that for Harriet, the essence of "home" was not a place but rather a sense of stability derived from an intact marriage relationship and nuclear family life, in which, as Sarah Howland had put it, "the husband and father return[s] after the toils of the day are over to take his accustomed seat." [88]

Harriet Allen and her daughter Nellie were the only women aboard the *Merlin,* but they were not the only ones at sea in 1868. In a practice that became more common in the 1840s and peaked in the late nineteenth century, hundreds of wives of captains in the New England whalefishery accompanied their husbands to sea. Given the pervasive assumptions about the rigid gender division between land and sea, their numbers are surprising (though, of course, still trivial compared to the hundreds of thousands of seafaring men). Mainstream maritime historians have generally considered the "sister sailors" (as whaling wife Mary Brewster termed herself and the other such women she met abroad) [89] to be both anomalous and irrelevant to the work at hand, which indeed they were. But their stories are fascinating, and important to this discussion because the women's experiences at sea dramatically expose the power, the forms, and the contradictions of domesticity in the maritime context.

The whaling wives were undeniably unusual among their contemporaries: they traveled thousands of miles on voyages that lasted years at a time, deep into the Pacific, the Indian, and even the Arctic Oceans. [90] In deciding to join their husbands, these women made excruciating choices between conjugal love and duty on the one hand, and family and community expectations on the other. Once at sea, they found themselves isolated and confined as the only women, far distant from the networks of kin and female connections, in all-male workplaces on what were essentially floating slaughterhouses. Many valiantly tried to gain control over their lives by attempting to carve out a small feminized space on board the male-dominated workplace of the ship and to extend a small measure of female influence. They tried to recreate domestic routines at sea and familiar patterns of female interaction in port. Their experiences were not, in general, pleasant: most were (at one time or another, if not continuously) seasick, uncomfortable, lonely, bored, or alienated. [91]

Love pulled some wives to sea, duty pushed others. Most of the seagoing wives expressed their sense that their most important function was to be at their husbands' side. Susan Norton, daughter of one whaling captain and wife of another, drew on the notion that home was not a place but rather the marital relationship itself, declaring to her stepmother from shipboard in 1859, "this now is my home & duty is here." To her romantic friend "Sallie," Susan explained gently, "I have a good, true, kind, affectionate husband . . . and it is a comfort to know that my presence here makes it a home for him, when without me I can realize what an anxious dreary life his would be." To her sister, Susan joked about wives' marital responsibilities, "Shubael [her husband] says if I wasn't here, he should fret and be cross all the time, so you see I am good for something." [92] Conjugal love and domestic duty were the two most common and the only clearly acceptable justifications for women's going to sea and thereby breaching the rigid boundaries between home and work, land and sea. Both rationales implicitly or explicitly made the husband the central reference point for the wife's life—underscoring how important to these women's sense of self was not only their married status but also the daily practice of conjugal companionship.

Mary Brewster felt both imperatives. On board the ship *Tiger* in December of 1845, she wrote, "Well do I recollect the feelings which a year ago pervaded my mind, that of my Husbands desired return. . . . spring came and with it brought his return, then did I say we will part no more but if the sea must be your home it shall be mine." She declared, "Here I am happy in the society of one who loves me for myself alone." And she insisted, "I am with my Husband and by him will remain. No seas can now divide us. He can have no trouble, no sorrow, but what I can know and share. When perplexed with the duties of the ship . . . I can sooth his ruffled feelings . . . If sick no hand like mine can sooth the sad heart and administer to his wishes. I am . . . cheered with my dear Companions society also with the conviction in coming I did perfectly right." [93]

Mary Brewster, one of the earlier wives to accompany a seafaring husband, invoked her love and her duty to her husband apparently to counter criticism. At the beginning of her sea journal, she recorded with palpable defiance: "I have chosen my own place of residence not from the impulse of the moment but after much calm and sober thought[.] In coming my own conscience tells me I was doing right and what do I care for the opinion of the world . . . with much opposition I left my native land[,] few had to say one encouraging word . . . [and] She who has extended a mothers love and watchfulness over me said her consent should never be given[,] in no way would she assist me. and if I left her she thought me very un-grateful. . . . Well thank Heaven it is all past and I am on board of the good ship Tiger and with my dear Husband." [94] For Mary, who did not yet have any children, the tension between sea and shore was between her role as wife and her role as dutiful daughter. To her, the choice was clear and the conflict externally imposed. Several months later she again observed, "Of the two my husband or friends I must be separated from[,] leave me him and all the rest I gladly joyfully resign[,] preferring his society far more than to those who can be found at home or abroad." [95]

Though the captain's privilege of carrying a wife to sea became more common by the 1850s, the practice remained controversial throughout the midcentury period. If at first the wives had to overcome the objec-tions of their families and communities on land, later the main obstacle to their going came from within the industry itself, particularly the ship-owners. On the flyleaf of her diary, Mary Brewster had pasted a news-paper clipping, which reads, in part: "Of late years a very sensible custom has arisen among the masters of vessels visiting the Pacific, that of being accompanied by their wives. We have heard of some close-fisted and nig-gardly owners who object to the custom, but every body knows that their objections are founded upon the lowest principle of selfishness. . . . The system . . . works so well, that we predict it will become more and more fashionable. You, reader, may not think so, well, wait and see!" And at the bottom, Mary had penciled, "good Mr Damon."

In 1842, three years before Mary set off, the American Seamen's Friend Society had sent the Reverend Samuel Damon to Honolulu, where he served as the pastor of the Seamen's Chapel for forty-two years. During that time, with his wife and other missionaries throughout the Pacific, Damon stood as a staunch advocate for seagoing captain's wives, serving as host and resource to literally hundreds of whaling captains, officers, and their families. In 1858, Damon published a proud note in his mission news-paper, *The Friend:* "A few years ago it was exceedingly rare for a Whaling Captain to be accompanied by his wife and children, but now it is very com-mon. . . . The happy influence of this goodly number of ladies is apparent to the most careless observer." [96]

The *Sailor's Magazine*, the American Seamen's Friend Society periodi-cal, even advocated that the practice be extended to all married seamen: "Most of those among seamen who have families, do not see them oftener than once in two, three or four years. . . . The evils and sad effects of such a course [which the editorial did not specify] are many and great. . . .

We hope the time may come when every married man in this part of the world will be accompanied by his wife. 'What, therefore, God hath joined together, let not man put asunder.' " [97]

A few shipowners, most notably Charles W. Morgan of New Bedford, agreed that women might bring a positive, temperate influence to the sea-faring environment: Morgan noted in his diary on 25 July 1849, "There is more decency on board when there is a woman." [98] It is more likely, though, that the reverse was true: there was more chance of there being a wife on board when the captain was already committed to values like temperance. Historian of American whaling Elmo Hohman claims that after 1840, the majority of U.S. whalers were temperance ships, sailing without alcohol on board.[99]

In the end, though, the privilege of bringing a wife along was gener-ally restricted to just the most favored, the most successful, or perhaps the most persuasive captains. The majority of managing agents tolerated wives at sea with considerable reluctance, and then only as the price to pay to retain a good captain.[100] For example, Thomas Knowles & Com-pany agreed to allow Philip Howland's second wife, Patience, to join him aboard their bark *Mary & Susan* only "at the end of two years if the Ship has one thousand Barrels of Sperm Oil in that time." [101]

New Bedford agents Swift & Allen turned down one of their captains outright. "We have no recollection of ever refusing to grant any favor asked by you," they wrote to Captain Josiah Chase, "and are now very sorry to feel the necessity of declining your proposition to send out your wife. The owners of our ships have suffered to the extent of 20,000$ by having the Capts wife on board." The men in the counting rooms back in New Bedford were particularly concerned about the disruptive female tendency to bear children. They wrote to Captain Chase, "Your wife like all *females* is much more likely to get sick at sea than any *man*, under ordinary circum-stances[,] and extraordinary ones [i.e., pregnancy] are about sure to arise soon after she meets you." (One wonders if that remark was intended to flatter the captain.) They continued, " — the like of which in two instances caused our ships to leave good whale ground in the midst of a season." The agents concluded, "After such a famine as our ships have threaten[ed] us with, we must appeal to your *sympathy, gratitude*, and sense of *right*." [102] Human birth was not supposed to interfere with the profitable pursuit of cetacean death.

Nor was human death. Shipowner Matthew Howland's letter to a cap-tain whose wife had joined him at sea and subsequently died suggests

Mary L. Burtch Brewster (1822–1878), of Stonington, Connecticut, one of the earliest of the American whaling captains' wives who sailed with their husbands. Mary made at least two voyages with her husband William, between 1845 and 1851. Daguerreotype by J. Gurnsey, ca. 1854. Courtesy of Mystic Seaport Museum, Mystic, Conn. (48.1146); photograph by Mary Anne Stets

Captain William Brewster (1813–1893), Mary's husband. By permission of the Old Lighthouse Museum, Stonington Historical Society, Stonington, Conn. Courtesy of Mystic Seaport Museum, Mystic, Conn. (92–6–60A); photograph by Claire White-Peterson

that the owner's sympathy for the captain, while sincere, was unequal to his concern for the effect of the unhappy event on the voyage: "Respected Friend. . . . the death of Mrs. Green was sad news indeed . . . but we hope that thee will look on the bright side and believe that this sore bereavement . . . was the ordering of Divine Providence. . . . we are in hopes after arriving in Port and becoming somewhat reconciled to thy great loss, thee will take a calm and dispassionate view of thy situation and responsibility in having a large amount of Property confided to thy charge, and decide at once to pursue the voyage without any unnecessary delay and bring it to a favorable termination . . . believing this course will be most satisfactory to thy friends and relatives of thy Wife and all concerned." Howland had confided earlier to his contact in Paita, Peru, from whom he had received the news of Mrs. Green's death, "we hope [Captain Green] will have no idea, and we can hardly imagine he will, of abandoning the voyage or delaying the ship in Port longer than is really necessary . . . as considerable time & money have already been expended (perhaps necessarily) on account of his wife's illness." [103] The appropriate separation of family and work, implicit in the midcentury mindset, and even more the tension between the demands of a husband's love and his occupation were here rendered tragically explicit.

Eliza Williams reflected, shortly after setting sail, "Now I am in the place that is to be my home, possibly for 3 or 4 years . . . it all seems so strange, so many Men and not one Woman besides myself." [104] Ironically, the captains' wives' isolated and confined situation as the lone woman on a vessel that usually carried some thirty or more sailors, more closely resembled the "hermetic world" the female sphere was supposed to be than did their lives back in their home communities onshore. A whaleship is not a big space on which to live and work for months at a stretch, and to the only female on board, it seemed even smaller, restricted as she was to a "private" place carved out within the floating factory.

In 1856, Henrietta Deblois described in minute detail, in letters home, the vessel on which she sailed. The *Merlin* was a fairly typical whaler, rigged as a bark, displacing 348 tons and just 108½ feet long. "She carries four boats," Henrietta wrote (note how she adopted the custom of referring to the ship as "she" in describing the whaleboats that were hung along the sides of the ship, held ready in position to lower and chase after any

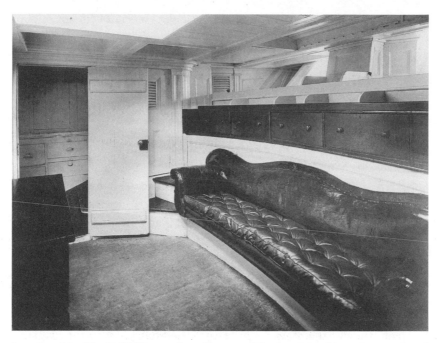

Interior of the *Charles W. Morgan* aftercabin, 1925. The captain's cabin at the stern (rear) of the whaleship, this is where his wife spent most of her time while at sea. The open door leads to the stateroom (bedroom) and head (toilet) for the captain and his wife. Five different wives sailed on this particular vessel between 1864 and 1913. Courtesy of Mystic Seaport Museum, Mystic, Conn. (51.4414)

whales sighted).[105] Henrietta observed that "on board Ship, every inch of room is of importance." The captain's stateroom on the *Merlin* was six by ten feet and contained a bed for Henrietta and her husband, mounted on gimbals, plus several built-in lockers. A tiny but private toilet and wash-stand, the captain's "head," was tucked into a triangular corner off their stateroom.

The captain's stateroom adjoined the captain's cabin, also called the aftercabin or transom cabin. This compartment measured something like six by eight feet and contained a remarkable profusion of stuff. Henrietta's description of the furnishings in theirs included this catalog of items: "a green Brussels carpet with a tiny red flower sprinkled all over it . . . a blk walnut sofa, one chair, a small mirror with a gilt frame—over this is the Barometer—at the side of this hangs the thermometer. Under the mirror is a beautiful carved shelf . . . a beautiful little landscape done by our cousin Kate hangs over the Sofa. A Melodeon[,] Music[,] books[,] work baskets and bags, give this room quite a home look." Henrietta did not say, but many such aftercabins also contained the captain's chart table and chair and a stove in cold weather, as well as potted plants, caged birds, other ornaments, curios and photographs, sewing machines, and any other domestic items for which the seagoing wives found a place.

Besides the door to the stateroom, other doors led off the aftercabin to the narrow stairway up to the deck and to the "main" or "forward" cabin, the dining room which, on the *Merlin*, extended eight by ten feet and was dominated by a large table with two benches bolted to the floor on either side. Here the captain and his wife, and the officers as well, took their meals and relaxed. "Out of this room," Henrietta added, "are two staterooms on one side where the mates sleep . . . at the end is an entry one side of which is a stateroom where sleeps the fourth mate Steward & Cabin boy—on the other side a nice large pantry—further along is the steerage where the Boatsteerers[,] Shipkeeper[,] and Cooper live. For'ard is the Forecastle where the seamen live, I cannot take you there as I have not been there myself but am told it is very nicely fitted up."

Henrietta and the other such wives settled quickly into the captain's quarters. Eliza Williams recorded that "the little Cabin that is to be all my own is quite pretty; as well as I can wish, or expect on board of a ship." [106] The women claimed ownership of the small space allotted to them, arranging and decorating it to suit their tastes. Mary Brewster, though suffering intense seasickness, resolutely set to the task: "I have been regulating my rooms," she wrote in her diary, "making curtains packing away and unpacking[.] I work a little then vomit[,] rest at intervals[,] and so have accomplished considerable." [107] Julia Fisk wrote home, "I have taken down my window curtains to wash, and covered my settee over. (I . . . had a partition [built] across my room from the door to the stern) and that small room makes a nice place to put our trunks and chests in . . . and from that partition to the rudder Silas has made a very nice settee, as the other was so high and uncomfortable. . . . now I have it covered with blue [calico] and a nicer looking one I never saw." [108] In a letter written from the Arctic ocean to their young son in Connecticut, Julia's husband Silas described the cozy domestic scene: "We have . . . plenty to eat and live quite comfortable We had a gale of wind near the land and mother got a little fritened I tell hur she has got the seasick all scared out of hur for she was not so seasick as I was. . . . You cannot think how much mother and I talk about you and Birty [their daughter] we set down eavenings and tak about you[.] would you not like to look into our cabbin and se how we look[?] wall if you had looked in last night you se a little table two settes a little stove and Mother and I singing." [109]

On some ships, the captain might also have the ships carpenter build a small room ("roundhouse") on deck for his wife's use. Martha Brown, while in Honolulu, noted that another whaling captain and wife of her acquaintance "have been having a room made on deck," and added hopefully, "Perhaps my husband will be willing to indulge me with one if posible. I think it must be much pleasenter sometimes, and with a child, very convienient. Mrs. Gray had a nice cabin on deck furnished very prettily." [110] Mary Brewster was delighted with hers: as she remarked, now she had "no occasion to go below and am entirely separate from the officers." Further, she and her husband could "take our meals at our own table and when seated imagine we are keeping house; here I am with my husband alone, and we are both making great calculations upon our enjoyment." [111]

The remarkable isolation from crew that is evident in Julia Fisk's and Mary Brewster's accounts—having no contact beyond the three or four officers, the steward, cook, and cabin boy—characterized the experience of many seagoing wives. Mary Brewster did not even meet the officers on board her husband's ship—the men with whom she would be sharing most of her meals, in the main cabin—until the voyage had been underway more than three weeks. (Until then, she had been laid up in her berth, trying to overcome a particularly severe encounter with seasickness.) Azubah Cash, in her sea journal, never even mentions crew members at all.

Other wives, certainly, were friendlier and more sociable—even, at times, overbearing. According to maritime historian Margaret Creighton, the wives' "associations with the crew ranged from dispensing gifts to softening ship discipline" and could even lead to praise by some crew members. One George Coffin observed that his captain's wife was "liked very much by all." But other women suffered the antagonism of crewmen who resented female intrusiveness or even just female presence. According to first mate Marshall Keith, his captain's wife was "a source of trouble." [112] And the fourth mate on the *Eliza Adams*, Abram Briggs, found it especially irksome that the captain had added a window "in the forward part of the [deck]house, so Mrs. Hamblin can set down & look whats going on on deck, who goes over the bows [i.e., to relieve himself], or to the Urine barrell." [113]

Claiming additional space from the already tight quarters of the ship for the exclusive use of the captain's wife and children could exacerbate the sailors' resentment. Briggs complained when Captain Hamblin enlarged the cabin and deckhouse and took up more of the ship's space to accommodate his growing family, and griped that the presence of the captain's wife and children turned their ship into "hell afloat." The distinction in the industry between the career mariners and the men under their command was sharpened still further by the class-based and, no doubt, sometimes sexual tensions created by the particularly blatant exercise of privilege that the wife on board represented. Only the captain could enjoy female companionship and intimacy during the long, tedious months between reprovisioning calls in port, and only the captain could enjoy even this meager semblance of marriage and family life during the years of separation from home.

Yet, despite the grumbling of Briggs and other such sailors, all but the captain's stateroom, aftercabin, main cabin, and parts of the deck were understood to be strictly male territory. While in passage or when there were no whales in sight, the captain's wife might walk the full extent of the deck, though on some vessels she was restricted from going farther forward than the main mast. But when the weather was stormy and the seas too rough, the best place for the captain's wife was below in her cabin, perhaps even in her berth. On 6 July 1864, Clara Kingman Whelden, in the middle of the North Atlantic on the ship *John Howland*, bound for Cape Horn and the Pacific, found the wind kicking up. Clara recorded bravely in her diary, "I have found it somewhat difficult to walk the deck some part of the time, but I got along as well as could be expected until finally forced to go to bed, where I have been a greater part of the time. Tuesday we had, what Captain called a 'moderate gale,' and things tossed about lively . . . I am slightly sea-sick whenever we have a heavy sea, but I soon find relief by taking the bed which is always right side up. . . . [it] is unaffected by any motion of the ship, and I find it a great convenience during a gale." [114]

And when a whale was caught, killed, cut in, and boiled—the decks awash with gore, dirt, and slime; the tryworks billowing greasy smoke; intense activity engaging all of the men above and below deck—the women stayed out of way. Despite the concerns of the shipowners, in general the presence of a lone woman on board ship did not appear to disrupt the work process much. On whaleships, they were absolutely excluded from the work at hand, from anything that was absolutely essential or even just related to whaling.[115] These women, their presence, their activities, and the space they occupied represented a radical division between male and female spheres—between men's work (production) and women's work (reproduction, and also consumption). (One junior officer described the captain's wife on his ship as "the most hoggish and greediest female that ever existed," and a sailor on Mary Brewster's voyage complained that the captain was stingy with the food supplied to the crew because "he has his wife aboard & therefore wishes not to get out of potatoes, mollasses, sugar, butter &c.")[116]

On the ship, the captains' wives found themselves isolated, perhaps resented, and, most significantly, irrelevant to the main activity, whaling. A year into her voyage, Mary Lawrence remarked that she and her 6-year-old daughter were "supernumaries; nothing for us to do but look on." Sarah Smith wrote in her diary that it was "Blowing a Gale[,] [men] trying to boil but hard work. nothing for me as usual." Mary Brewster insisted that she was "perfectly willing to be alone when whaling is the business," but she was nonetheless forlorn when her husband was too preoccupied with the local whale population to spend the evening chatting or reading aloud with her.[117]

Several of the wives demonstrated their marginalization to the work of whaling by a marked lack of interest in the process. Susan McKenzie, who at the time had spent at least two years and probably longer in the Pacific, described her first view of the cutting process: "After supper I went up and sat in a boat to see them cut the whale in. I was there an hour and a half sitting perfectly still watching them for the first time[.] in all my being at sea I have only seen the whale come in, without seeing how it was done." [118]

But other women showed great interest from the outset in the whale (they marveled at its size and strange appearance) and in the work of whaling. Like Mary Brewster and Eliza Brock, Eliza Williams provided in her diary a detailed description of the work process. The mate even took her down into the blubber room, an area usually off-limits to the wives, to see the men cutting up the pieces of the whale. Her account, though accurate, was clearly written from the perspective of an outsider. She found many aspects of whaling repellent. "The smell of the oil is quite offensive to me," she reported, and observed later that "the constant noice of heavy chains on deck, the driving of the hoops, the turning over of the casks of oil til it seemed as if the ship shook, and the loud orders of the Officers—all together, would make a nervous person go distracted I think, but it cannot be avoided on board a whale ship." [119]

After the novelty of the first whale or two, Mary Brewster preferred to stay in her compartments during the processing: "Dirt and grease is all the go. I keep below nearly all the time and in my room as the decks are getting rather soiled and the try smoke very disagreeable to my olfactory nerves." Annie Ricketson slipped on an oil-covered step and sprained her ankle; she had to wear her husband's slipper on her swollen foot. (The next day, her captain husband set both the steward and the cabin boy to scrubbing the stairs with soap and sand.) [120] Julia Fisk wrote in some dismay, "Dear me[,] it makes a dreadful dirty ship getting oil. especially the cabin stairs[.] I found that the bottoms of my skirts got so dirty & such a job to wash dresses I concluded to take my old dark calico dress and made me a bloomer which I find to be a grand thing." [121]

Whether they altered their clothing, suffered minor injury, or not, Eliza Brock and many other wives carefully noted the date and amount of oil and bone of each whale caught, thereby reflecting their relationship to the work at hand, but, not surprisingly, emphasizing how it affected them — in the profitability and the length of the voyage as well as the captain's mood. Mary Brewster wrote, "Whales in sight all day for which the boats have been lowered in vain. I have been a looker on and begin to feel quite anxious to catch a whale as I am so much taken up with this new business I do but very little [else]." [122] By the end of her voyage on the *Addison*, Mary Lawrence was nearly obsessed, like the men on the ship, with getting whales.

Whaling was dangerous business, the risks of which were all too clear. Severe injuries and deaths at sea were common — and commented upon at length in many women's diaries, often with sorrow and even horror. For some, watching their husbands set off in the small whaleboat and actually participate in the battle with the whale was exciting, if nerve-racking. For others it was simply too excruciating to bear, and they had to retire below deck for the duration of the hunt. Mary Hayden Russell, after witnessing the difficulties her husband and son had out in the boats chasing down a whale in a rough sea, wrote in the letter-journal she kept to send to her daughter: " 'This,' thought I, 'is the way that these 'Sons of Ocean' earn their money that is so thoughtlessly spent at home.' Could some of the ladies whose husbands are occupied in this dangerous business have been here this few hours past, I think it would be a lesson they would not forget. It would teach them prudence and economy more powerfully than all the books ever written on the subject since the invention of printing." [123] Russell's tart reminder clearly expressed her perception that men were the providers and women the dependent consumers; it also conveyed the association of men with daring deeds and women with thoughtlessness.

Many of the very tasks that defined women's sphere on land were at sea taken out of the woman's province. In fact, the presence of a woman aboard ship did not even disrupt the way in which the "female" work performed by the cook and the steward was customarily assigned to particular men or boys within the crew by virtue of their age, race, or inexperience.[124] The wives at sea rarely cooked, except to make something special like gingerbread, cake, or pie or the traditional donuts fried in the trypots to celebrate the achievement of 1,000 barrels of oil. Indeed, some of them were not even allowed in the ship's kitchen or galley. Mary Lawrence assembled a chicken pie to celebrate April Fool's Day in 1857 but had to send it in to the galley to be cooked. She noted ruefully, "It was not baked well; the crust was not done. I should have more courage to make knickknacks if I could attend to the baking of them, but of course it would not do for me to go into the galley."[125] Instead, Mary and the other wives spent much time sewing and mending their own clothing and that of their husband and children; occasionally, perhaps, they might sew or knit something for the cabin boy or other favored men on board. They did wash and iron their own laundry, generally —an arduous task made considerably more difficult on shipboard—and sometimes their husband's or children's, but as a rule they did not wash for anyone else.

Sometimes a wife at sea might nurse the sick among the crew. Likewise, she might help keep the official logbook (though that was more often the first mate's duty). She might learn navigation and take the ship's position, knowledge and skills that were the prerogative of just the career mariners; if she was good at it, she might in turn teach navigation to the junior officers. Some sketched, practiced music, observed exotic flora and fauna and collected exotic curios, or tried their hand at Victorian fancywork if they had the materials. But mostly the women sewed and trimmed, knit and crocheted. They wrote letters and diaries, even poems, puzzles, and songs. They walked on the deck in the good weather (or perhaps, as Martha Brown did, jumped rope using one of the lines on deck) for exercise and fresh air.

They prayed and observed the Sabbath to the extent they were inclined to and could at sea, though regular church attendance and participation in a congregation were things that most seaborne women particularly missed. And they read voraciously, devouring nearly anything they could get their hands on, from year-old newspapers to the Bible, from Byron to Harriet Beecher Stowe, from edifying tracts like *Woman's Mission* to the collection of racy seafaring yarns titled *Tales of the Ocean and Essays for the Forecastle*.[126] Elizabeth Stetson took with her over a hundred books and acquired more during the voyage.[127]

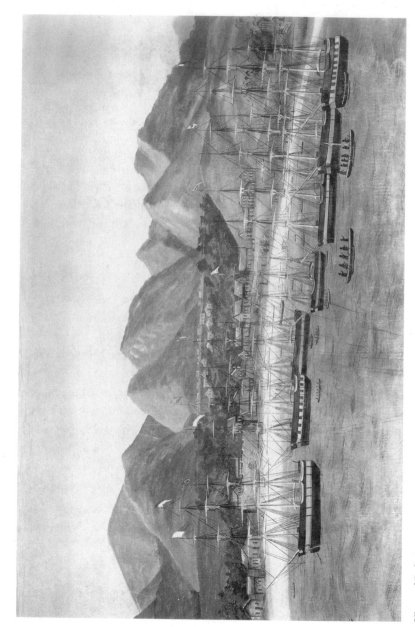

View of Lahaina, an important reprovisioning port for the American whale fleet in the Pacific and also temporary home for many captains' wives, including Mary Brewster. Detail of Russell-Purrington Panorama, "A Whaling Voyage Round the World," ca. 1848. Courtesy of Old Dartmouth Historical Society–New Bedford Whaling Museum (Neg. 3053)

Mrs. M. C. Fisher reported, "I spend a great many hours in this little cabin alone during the whaling season, and if I were not fond of reading and sewing, I should be very lonely." Mary Brewster (who appears to have produced entire wardrobes for herself, her husband, the cabin boy, and even a jacket for the steward) claimed, "Work has been my amusement to keep me from being lonesome." But Sarah Smith wrote wearily, "Nothing to be seen & nothing to be done," and she admitted, "I do not mutch[—] knit lace and read[.] it is getting tedious."[128] Eliza Brock simply marked too many of her days "dreary dreary dull." Captain Shubael Norton described his wife's activities: "Sue plays, sings, sews, reads &c"[129] — and in that terse "&c" we can glimpse the marginalization, isolation, and boredom that commonly characterized the day-to-day experience of wives at sea. Many of the women relished the occasional "gams" or visits with other whaleships at sea, especially if there were another captain's wife to visit with. And many of them looked forward with great anticipation to meeting other "sister sailors" in port.

As the practice of captains' bringing wives to sea expanded over the middle decades of the century, small communities of Yankee maritime women developed in some of the more usual ports of call: Fayal in the Azores; Paita, Tombes, and Talcahuano on the western coast of South America; Russell in the Bay of Islands, New Zealand; Vasse on the south-western coast of Australia; and, perhaps most famously, Honolulu, Lahaina, and Hilo in the Hawaiian Islands. The wives might be left behind because they were ill or found shipboard life particularly uncomfortable, or their husbands might decide not to take them up to the more treacherous Okhotsk or Arctic seas. Their separations from their husbands were considerably shorter, lasting only the few months of a whaling season, but the whaling wives left ashore still missed their families and friends back home and, as only temporary (and sometimes reluctant) residents of the foreign ports, they still found little to occupy themselves.

Underscoring the religious element in Victorian domesticity's understanding of womanhood, the whaling wives in port generally spent much of their time and sometimes boarded with the American and English Protestant missionaries who were stationed locally. Many of the "sister sailors" particularly enjoyed attending regular church services and prayer meetings (and at times may well have made up the majority of the congregation, despite the missionaries' efforts in the field). They also spent much time together, occasionally combining households and resources while their men were at sea just as they were accustomed to doing at home.

Some appreciated the beautiful scenery, flora, and fauna, which they found exotic, but virtually none expressed much understanding or interest in the local inhabitants: the Yankee women considered them dirty, ignorant, sometimes offensive. These women's exposure to such radically different cultures thoroughly reinforced their allegiance to their own set of norms—including, notably, domesticity—and only served to strengthen their sense of its (and their own) superiority.[130]

In 1871, the New Bedford whaleship *Merlin* visited an island off the east coast of Africa. The captain, David Allen, and his wife Harriet had dinner with the local leader. Harriet noted in her diary, "I should have enjoyed the dinner very much if the ladies could have sat with us at table. The Prince says their [Muslim] religion will not allow it. Being a woman I felt insulted and degraded for their sakes. How I long for the power to take them away, to give them their birth right—freedom. And not only them but all miserable women slaves the world over." [131] Harriet could recognize women's subordination in other cultures, but not in her own.

One of the reasons the Yankee "sister sailors" might put into port and why the lonely women expressed such a desire for female companionship was the eventuality—indeed, the likelihood—of childbirth. In their home communities like Nantucket and New Bedford, whalemen's children tended to be born at intervals several years apart, intervals corresponding more to the length of whaling voyages than to women's reproductive cycles, in a testament to marital fidelity.[132] The information in their sea diaries suggests, not surprisingly, that the rate of pregnancy increased markedly for the women who accompanied their husbands to sea. The unappreciative shipowners quoted above had a valid point: captains' wives on board did indeed get pregnant, and often. Fourth mate Abram Briggs was equally unappreciative; he was disturbed that his ship, the *Eliza Adams*, put into port four times in a six-month period so, as he put it, "the cow [could] calf" and to meet the needs of the new mother and infant. He added sarcastically, "By the time our voyage is at an end [the captain] will have a crew enough to mann a boat of his own." [133]

The actual circumstances of bearing children either on board ship or in foreign ports was rarely described in any detail in the women's diaries. Most often there is simply a gap in the record keeping or only brief reference that invokes typical euphemisms of the period: Lucy Crapo was "taken sick," Martha Brown "confined." Whatever the description, it could not have been easy. At sea, the constant motion of the ship, cramped quarters, limited supplies, and only a husband in attendance must have rendered the experience difficult and even dangerous, to state the obvious. Most of the pregnant women were instead left ashore in a convenient port and there might be able to draw upon the assistance of other women: other "sister sailors," missionaries, perhaps a sympathetic boardinghouse keeper, and, if funds permitted, hired local help.

Martha Brown was left in Honolulu four months before she was due. After her second child, a son, was born, her husband returned to Honolulu and took the two of them off for a summer season of whaling in the Sea of Okhotsk, off Siberia. Martha noted, "I of course, after a stay of 8 months on shore, was obliged to go through the regular process of initiating, namely sea sickness. . . . then it was that Edwin turned nurse and performed all the little duties for the babe— except one. And it was really amusing to see that whaleman bathe, powder and dress that little one of four months." [134]

But Martha, who delighted in the son she bore in Honolulu, had left her 2-year-old daughter with her mother back in Orient, New York (at the eastern end of Long Island), in order to accompany her husband to sea. It was not an easy decision. "O dear O dear I do not want to go to sea, no that's what I don't," she wrote, early in the voyage, "I am not sorry I came, however, if Edwin must, but Oh I want my dear baby, my darling Ella." "Why did I leave her at home?" she asked herself. "Had I known I should have [been] as well as I have been, I think I should never [have] been persuaded it was best." In May of 1848, on the occasion of her daughter's birthday, Martha had not seen Ella for more than a year and a half. Martha found it "a homesick day" and admitted in a letter that "I could think of nothing else . . . but that precious little one; she has if alive . . . commenced the fourth year of her earthly existence. . . . Oh that I may have wisdom from on high to enable me to discharge my duty as a Christian Mother." [135]

But women like Martha Brown, in going to sea, chose conjugal over maternal responsibilities. Discharging their conjugal duty by nurturing and influencing their husbands was perceived by nearly all the seagoing wives as their single most important responsibility, cited by many as the reason they shipped out with their husbands at all. As Mary Brewster put it, "[I] hope I may be a useful companion, a soother of woes, a calmer of troubles and a friend in need, a sharer of his sorrows as well as of his joys." [136] The charge was not an easy one. Martha Brown admitted to her diary that "I have tried to encourage Edwin untill I am nearly out—I know not what to say to him next." [137] Susan Norton may have been more successful: her husband Shubael told his father-in-law, "I am wicked but not so bad as I should be without Sue." [138]

Total immersion in the male sphere at sea, however, could and often did dramatically reveal the fundamental limitations of women's influence. The lines of authority might be ambiguous at home, but they were very clear on board ship. Many wives, watching their captain-husbands command the work process and the ship with skill and utter authority, were impressed with the men's importance in a way they never saw from land. Mary Lawrence observed, "We are, as it were . . . in a little kingdom of our own of which Samuel is prime ruler. I never should have known what a great man he was if I had not accompanied him. I might never have found it out at home." [139] Some captains seem to have found it difficult to juggle their two very different roles—the distant and authoritative taskmaster and the affectionate, kind, and companionable spouse—which now alternated many times a day rather than between the more clear-cut shift from voyage to shore leave. No matter how easily their husbands moved between deck and aftercabin, though, the basic structure of shipboard life severely tested the belief that wives were supposed to exert moral influence from their subordinate position.

One Sunday Mary Brewster recorded in her diary, "I have been reading the book entitled Woman's Mission, found much that was good and well worth treasuring up. One sentence in particular—All woman had a mission to perform and in all circumstances in life it should be their aim to establish peace and love and unselfishness, to be achieved by any means and at any cost to themselves, in the cultivation first of themselves then in all over whom they have any influence, of an unselfish and unworldly spirit.—In any way in every way in which God and man can be served it is theres [sic] to serve, gracefully, peacefully, unostentatiously." [140]

Mary Lawrence wrote, "I exert all my powers to keep up the spirits of the captain and officers, and I really believe that they are in far better spirits than though Minnie [her young daughter] and myself were not here." While isolation from the crew characterized the experience of most of the seagoing wives, a few tried to extend their moral and religious influence beyond the captain's quarters. This Mary was one of the more energetic wives, at least early in the voyage; she recorded in her diary, "Last Sabbath I gave Minnie some Bibles and Testaments . . . to carry forward to the men if they like to have them. So she filled her little carriage and went. . . . She came back very quick with an empty carriage, had it reloaded, and went again until she gave away every one that we had. She said they all wanted one, even the Portuguese, that could read. I could but think they were taken far more readily from her than they would have been from anyone else. It may be we can do some good through her," she mused.[141]

But Mary was to be disappointed. Early in the voyage, she heard the sailors singing "Home Sweet Home" and "Do They Miss Me at Home?" and wrote hopefully, "I have yet to find out that sailors belong to another class than that of human beings. . . . I shall not think they are entirely depraved as long as I hear them singing their Psalms tunes." But her optimism proved misplaced, and her efforts and Minnie's proved ineffective against the drunkenness and rowdiness for which sailors were notorious. A few short weeks after Minnie distributed the Bibles, the ship made port in Lahaina, and Mary recorded in her diary, "Saw several of our sailors . . . who told me that one of our number had been taken to the fort for drinking and being unruly in the street. It made me feel badly; I had hoped there would be no such doings among our crew. I thought better things of them, but my husband has always told me that sailors would be sailors, and that after we had been in port, my eyes would be opened. I am fearful that it is so." Five days later her impressions were confirmed: she noted, "We went on board. . . . Found a state of affairs on board which made my heart ache: four men were in irons [for drinking, fighting, and attempted desertion]. . . . This is the beginning of trouble to me." [142]

While she lamented the need, Mary did not question the form of shipboard discipline of shackling the men in irons. Many more of the wives took exception to flogging, which was by midcentury still used but under attack. An active anti-flogging campaign succeeded in having the practice declared illegal in 1850, but flogging on shipboard persisted for some decades after (all forms of corporal punishment at sea were finally outlawed in 1898).[143] In 1861, Elizabeth Stetson recorded in her diary that, while her captain-husband was temporarily off the ship, the mate flogged one of the sailors. "I do not think it was right," she wrote—and underscored the entry for emphasis—but she was powerless to stop it.[144] Local legend has it that the owners of Captain John Oliver Norton's ships encouraged his wife Charity to go along on his voyages, to help prevent her "bucko" husband from meting out the unusually harsh discipline for which he was notorious. According to the story, she successfully interceded on several occasions.[145]

Martha Brown, though, seemed to think flogging was justified. Like Mary Brewster, Martha lamented instead the necessity of the discipline rather than its form. Noting that a sailor had been guilty of three different infractions (gambling, fighting, and swearing), Martha described her husband's response in her diary, addressed to her mother: "The Capt.'s patience was clear gone—he went on deck and gave him 5 or 6 lashes with the end of the topgalent bowlin. Then for the first time I learned he had floged a man several weeks before. . . . You who live on land do not know half the trials a sea Capt. is subject to. . . . Of course there must be some rules and regulation on board ship. . . . [the man must] abide the conciquences if he does not abide by the rules. So Mother, you see I have very little influence so far," she concluded.[146]

Regarding temperance and sexual fidelity—two areas in which sailors were notoriously lax—the influence of captains' wives did not, as a rule, extend further than the aftercabin, as Mary Lawrence had noted with distress. While mention of drinking was not uncommon in the women's diaries, discussion of sexuality, licit or illicit, was rare, despite the widespread and well-documented interaction between whalemen and local women in many ports. It was, indeed, a spectacular silence, not unlike the denial demonstrated by their contemporaries, the white plantation women in the antebellum South, despite the scores of light-skinned slave children whose existence testified so patently to white men's infidelities.[147] There are a few documented instances in Pacific ports when a whaling captain allowed women to board the ship and provide sexual services to the crew while the captain's wife was still on board.[148] This, though, appears to have been rare—the ships carrying wives did indeed, as Charles Morgan claimed, seem to be more "decent," at least while the women were actually on board.

Ships without wives were another matter. Early in 1847, Mary Brewster recorded indignantly in her diary, "I see I am not the only female in the bay. [R]eport has told of three which were kept on board. . . . I saw a female in a boat passing our ship bound to a neighboring one with the skipper by her side. Oh shame shame is not felt here, if actions which are so public is what we must judge from, and they speak louder than words. Such individuals I look upon in a different view and wish to have no connection with their actions I abhor." A few days later, she returned to the topic, "Some indeed act here as though their *wives* and children were not in the least regarded by them, and when out of their sight was truly out of mind. Such are not worthy of the appellation of *Husband* nor as friend . . . they [should not] be countenanced by those who profess good *morals* and principles, neither should they associate with them." [149]

But explicit reference to sexuality in the writings of the captains' wives was quite unusual. Rather than address the absolutely pervasive sexual double standard in foreign ports, more of the seagoing wives explicitly took on the problem of Sabbath whaling. Here, too, however, they ultimately had little influence. Mary Brewster confided to her diary in 1846, "Capt Wilbur is the first man that I have seen who observes the sabbath at sea—he allows no whaling done on that day. I can see no reason why an individual can be justified in not keeping one day in seven at sea as well as on shore." [150] Eventually, as the voyage lengthened, many of the women seemed to come around to the view held by the majority of their husbands and vividly expressed by Melville's fictional Captain Bildad: "Don't whale it too much a' Lord's days, men, but don't miss a fair chance either, that's rejecting Heaven's good gifts." [151] Overall, the influence of the women over their husbands or anyone else at sea seems relatively minimal, their efforts notwithstanding. "It is whaling times now," Eliza Williams wrote, "and the ladies must submit." [152]

Remember (from Chapter 5) how Julia Fisk of Groton, Connecticut, recorded in her 1859 diary mention of her husband, Captain Silas Fisk, nearly every day during his absence. In her tiny pocketbook, she wrote in one entry, "Just four months since Silas sailed very lonely & sad," and in others, "Oh where is my dear Husband"; "Thought much of Silas now[.] I am lonely up stairs. If I could kiss him"; and "Oh My Dear Dear Husband how I long to be with you." [153] By October 1859, a year after Silas had left, Julia's loneliness overcame her. She left her children with her parents and unmarried sister and traveled to San Francisco to join Silas aboard his ship.

This was not the first time Julia had accompanied Silas at sea. The famous Lydia Hunt Sigourney had apparently met Julia Fisk during an earlier visit at the Connecticut seashore. When she learned that Julia intended to join Captain Fisk aboard the ship *North Star* in 1855, Sigourney wrote with evident approval: "My dear Mrs Fisk, I have just received your letter saying you have decided to sail with your husband, and hasten to send you both some books,—to which I add a few pamphlets and periodicals,—thinking that light reading might be agreeable on so long a voyage, and that you might like some to distribute to the sailors.—I also send a package of peppermints made with very pure sugar,—one of which, occasionally put in your mouth, when you begin to feel seasick, may be useful." At the end of the letter, Sigourney added a postscript: "P.S. Tell the Captain that . . . I should prize the gift of a gallon of oil, from a whale of the 'North Star's' catching." [154] To Sigourney, even a whaling voyage could be domesticated by bringing along some reading and some peppermints, and its hard-won product, measured in thousands of barrels and sold in a highly competitive international market, could be reduced to the gift of a souvenir gallon. (Melville would have been horrified.) Sigourney suggested that Mrs. Fisk might distribute appropriately improving reading to the sailors, thereby extending a Christian woman's moral influence not only over her husband but also over the crew.[155]

According to both her and his accounts, Julia's and Silas's reunion in 1859 was ecstatic. But Julia's longing for those from whom she was separated, now especially her children, continued unabated, despite her previous experience (or Mrs. Sigourney's peppermints). Julia's diary closed the year with such entries as "have thought of home & dear little children"; "thought of home and Church"; "feel rather lonely when I think of home"; "to day is Christmas have thought and talked much of home think children hung up stockings"; and "Oh now I am on board ship I wish I had Bertie [her daughter] with me she would be so much company . . . I dreamed of home last night." [156] On shore or at sea, Julia could not resolve the fundamental tension between, on the one hand, her desires for an exclusive, passionate, conjugal relationship practiced daily, and on the other, her maternal love, sense of family responsibility, and longing for the rituals of community life on shore. In April 1855, somewhere in the South Pacific aboard the Nantucket ship *Lexington*, Eliza Brock provided a concise analysis of sea-wives' domestic frustrations in a short, unhappy verse: "While on the seas, my days are spent / In anxious fears, oft discontent. / No social circle here is found / Few friends, to virtue here abound. / I long for home, sweet home denied, / with those I love neer, by my side." [157]

Julia and Silas Fisk, Eliza Brock, and so many other maritime women and men were powerfully influenced by the mid-nineteenth-century idealization of what the historian Mary Ryan has called "the hermetic world of marriage, love, and home." [158] Yet, for the women onshore, that world simply did not exist on a practical level. Persistent, fluid patterns of interaction between kinfolk, friends, and neighbors continued to link households and wove together communities, enabling women to meet their assigned responsibilities of sustaining and renewing families under the extreme stresses of the whalefishery. High levels of female mobility were marked by continuous rounds of visits, ranging from half-hour calls to weeks at a time, involving shared work as well as sociability during men's absences. Just as their foremothers had done, midcentury mariners' wives appreciated the necessity and appropriated these forms of social inter-action. Yet, many of them also were troubled by what they perceived as a discrepancy between their experiences and their ideals. They longed for domesticity within a separate sphere just as prescribed: a stable, private home, a nuclear family, and a husband in residence to love and nurture. They were faced with often excruciating choices between their roles as wife, as mother, as daughter, as friend.

A surprising number of captain's wives made the more daring but ultimately more conservative—decision to join their husbands on board ship, essentially opting for sensibility over sense. Their choice represented a striking attempt to live up to what the dominant culture of domesticity preached, in particular the value of affectionate and companionate mar-riage and the ameliorating female influence of home life. In practice, a cap-tain's wife's going to sea meant the intrusion of a lone adult female into an aggressively (and sometimes hostile) male workplace and masculine ship-board culture. The personal costs, they found, were extraordinarily high. Paradoxically, the emphasis on marriage often broke up nuclear families, as many children were left behind. Also left behind were networks of ex-tended kin and friends and community institutions, which the women at sea sorely missed. At the same time, the "sister sailors" had very little last-ing impact on the whaling industry or on society at large; their presence and efforts did not alter either the layout of the ship, the social relations of work in the industry, or gender roles and relations in maritime communi-ties. Wives at sea proved to be, in the end, a failed experiment in combining maritime work and home life.[159]

CONCLUSION

The Nantucket Girls Song

THE NANTUCKET GIRLS SONG

I have made up my mind now to be a Sailors wife,
To have a purse full of money and a very easy life,
For a clever sailor Husband, is so seldom at his home,
That his Wife can spend the dollars, with a will thats all her own,
Then I'll haste to wed a Sailor, and send him off to sea,
For a life of independence, is the pleasant life for me.
But every now and then I shall like to see his face,
For it always seemes to me to beam with manly grace,
With his brow so nobly open, and his dark and kindly eye,
Oh my heart beats fondly towards him whenever he is nigh,
But when he says; Good bye my love, I'm off across the sea
First I cry for his departure; Then laugh because I'm free,
Yet I'll welcome him most gladly, whenever he returnes
And share with him so cheerfully all the money that he earns
For he's a loveing Husband, though he leads a roving life
And well I know how good it is, to be a Sailors Wife.
    February 1855   Martha Ford
    Bay of Islands, Reefside[1]

"The Nantucket Girls Song" is found on a page toward the end of the diary
kept by a Nantucket captain's wife, Eliza Brock, during her sojourn at sea

aboard the whaleship *Lexington* from May 1853 to June 1856. In the middle of February 1855, the *Lexington* was at anchor with four other American ships off the small village of Russell in New Zealand's Bay of Islands, a minor provisioning stopover for whalers. Eliza Brock went ashore and found two other Nantucket whaling captains' wives there, both staying with a resident American doctor and his wife, Martha Ford. The Fords made a practice of entertaining American captains and their wives. Eliza Williams stayed with them for ten days in February 1860 and noted in her diary, "The Doctor and his Wife are very kind and social and take a great deal of pains to make it all pleasant for the captains and their wives stopping with them. . . . The house was full of Ship Masters when we got there."[2] In 1855, Eliza Brock stayed in Russell for a week and, though she did not much like her boardinghouse, she clearly enjoyed her several visits at the Fords' and with the other white women. On February 28, just after her stay on shore concluded, Brock wrote, "I always feel sad and lonely when leaving Port, always leave some dear friends behind who have been kind to me and mine & found many friends at the Bay of Islands; I never expect to see them again, but shall ever cherish their love to me in my memory."[3]

On the face of it, "The Nantucket Girls Song" seems to validate what I expected when I began this project so many years ago. Martha Ford's ditty provides a high-spirited and funny (if conflicted) vision of women's autonomy onshore in the absence of their seafaring men. We can imagine Eliza Brock and the other Nantucket "sister sailors" laughing together in Martha Ford's parlor, perhaps even composing the lyrics of "The Nantucket Girls Song" together there in the Bay of Islands, so many thousands of miles away from home—and so far away from the very life of which they sang in celebration. When set in the context of Martha Ford's parlor, the witty insouciance of "The Nantucket Girls Song" seems ironic—and it is even more stunningly so in the context of Brock's sea diary, where it contributes a jarring note of bravado in her record of unhappiness on shipboard. More characteristic of the volume as a whole are Brock's entries on the diary page facing the song: a four-line, untitled stanza about "good news" received "from friends that I have left in tears / From friends that I've not seen for years"; a short prose excerpt by Lydia Hunt Sigourney titled "The Sailor's Funeral"; and an unattributed meditation in verse about death titled "Beyond the River."

The confusion and strain reflected in Eliza Brock's diary are symptomatic of the contradictions within the dominant nineteenth-century gender system more generally and were shared by many of Eliza's contemporaries, maritime and nonmaritime alike. Of course, we have already learned of these contradictions from the impressive body of women's history scholarship published in the last twenty-five years or so. But juxtaposing Eliza's text and context reveals and illuminates with unusual clarity a fundamental discrepancy at the heart of Victorian domesticity. The "Nantucket Girls Song" notwithstanding, Eliza Brock did not remain at home on Nantucket to enjoy the independence of a whaleman's wife or the community of her friends, neighbors, and kinfolk. Instead, she was pulled to sea to join her captain-husband by the very tenets of domesticity that, paradoxically, then rendered her experience on board ship so alienating. In a painful sort of cognitive dissonance that made her miserable whether at sea or onshore, Eliza's understanding of herself and her world in part shaped her experience yet remained profoundly at odds with her life.

This particular dissonance was new. It had been different for Eliza's grandmothers, for whom the rhetoric more closely and consistently approximated reality. On colonial Nantucket, congruent social practice and gender role definition facilitated and shaped the development of the American whaling industry. Local notions of Quaker truth and duty reinforced both the subordination of individual selves to family and community and a clear hierarchy of patriarchal authority that withstood men's repeated absences at sea. Women's energy and strength were recognized and even encouraged but were carefully channeled into community sustenance, organized by fluid interactions between flexible households. The fishery's expansion depended in part upon the willingness and ability of those on shore to do whatever was necessary to support extended families during the repeated and prolonged absences of the whalemen. The sexual division of seafaring work from home was already total, the work of whaling was arduous and risky, but the social relations of work at sea were not yet so brutal nor so different from relationships on land. Spousal separation was difficult, but it was shorter then — a matter of months rather than years — and it was made more bearable by religious faith and community practice.

By the end of the century, though, Nantucket's particular accommodation to seafaring broke down under the pressures of religious reform, revolution, and romanticism. The inward turn and reduced authority of Quaker discipline, exacerbated by the distresses of the Revolution, altered local understandings of gender and family roles, in particular eroding the subordination of individual interests to community needs. As a consequence, well before they felt the impact of structural change in the whale-fishery itself, maritime women and men became increasingly susceptible to new ideas about sexual difference—ideas that emphasized women's presumed delicacy, sensibility, and dependency in contrast to men's assumed strength, rationality, and autonomy. The Romantic inflation of feeling, part of the widespread "revolt against patriarchal authority" and bolstered by resonance in contemporary political debate, emphasized love and companionship within marriage and began to render less tolerable the separations demanded by seafaring careers.

Rapid expansion and reorganization in the whalefishery and the region in which it was based formed a part of the sweeping economic and social transformations of the early nineteenth century. These transformations were interpreted locally (as elsewhere) in light of the new concepts of sexual difference, evolving into a geographic understanding of gender that divided the world into complementary but distinct male and female spheres. In the whaling communities, then centered on New Bedford, the obvious, complete, and strikingly gendered division between land and sea appeared to correspond perfectly and thereby reinforced the emergence of domestic ideas and ideals. Produced by the interplay of cultural and structural developments, local and national (even transnational) trends, these contingent and contradictory notions became common sense and defined the limits of what women and men could envision.[4]

As the whalefishery continued to expand and restructure over the course of the nineteenth century, the new ideas about manhood and womanhood became embedded in its social relations of work. Gender concepts provided a necessary, unifying force within the industry, helping to counteract the anarchic effects of expansion and the corrosive impact of increased diversity and stepped-up levels of violence on board ship. The career whalemen who formed the stable core of the far-flung pursuit shared with their employers a common understanding of manly authority, occupational commitment, family responsibility, and female dependence and domesticity—conflicting ideas that both sent the mariners to sea and brought them home again in a contrapuntal rhythm that was essential to the industry's functioning.

At the same time, women were recruited to sustain household and community by complementary ideas of love, marriage, motherhood, and family. Women's roles and responsibilities as wives and mothers were required by the demands of the men's occupation and reinforced by the social relations of work within the industry. The rigid division of labor in the whalefishery,

A gathering of New Bedford whaling captains in 1861, commemorating their contribution to the Union cause by sailing two dozen obsolete whalers, loaded with stone, to
Charleston, S.C., where they were sunk in an unsuccessful effort to blockade the Con-
federate port. "Captains of the Stone Fleet," 1861, copy of Beirstadt Bros. photograph.
Courtesy of Old Dartmouth Historical Society–New Bedford Whaling Museum (Neg.
2175)

where only men were involved directly in the shipboard processes, meant
that family life, household organization, and women's work on shore had to
remain as they had been: flexible and responsive to need and circumstance.
Much of the substance of women's work, however, was newly masked by its
redefinition as a labor (and suffering) for love only, a symbolism that only
raised the emotional stakes in marriage even higher. The texture of the
women's daily life rarely compensated for the perceived gap left by marital separation; rather, paradoxically, it most often served to remind them
of their anomalous status as "Cape Horn widows"—married, yet single.

In maritime communities, as elsewhere in nineteenth-century America,
women and men both—from the barely literate to the highly educated—
identified the marital relationship as something distinctive and loaded it
with expectations of intensely romantic and exclusive love. This loving
and companionable relationship was supposed to anchor a close, nurtur-

"Captain's Wives," ca. 1865, unknown photographer. Courtesy of Old Dartmouth Historical Society–New Bedford Whaling Museum (Neg. 2943)

ing, and private family comprised only of mother, father, and children, described in complementary opposition to a heartless public world. But the longer and longer voyages forced women and men to rely on prescribed gender roles to construct their identities within courtship and marriage, maintain their relationships with their absent sweethearts and spouses, and sustain family life over separations that now lasted years. Ironically, the reliance on prescription sharpened further the differences between sea and shore and ended up reinforcing the very ideas and ideals that the fishery made impossible to achieve.

The high price of contradiction was felt both on shore and at sea, at home and abroad. Back in New Bedford in 1858, Libby Spooner confided with poignant simplicity to her seafaring husband, Caleb, "O the life of a sailor and sailor's wife[—]how frought with sorrow & heartpangs." Motivated by the prospect of just such heartpangs, Susan McKenzie accompanied her captain-husband to the Pacific, where she was dropped off in Honolulu in 1869 while he cruised the icy Okhotsk Sea for a season. She too reflected disconsolately, "How much of patience and other Christian graces are necessary to prepare one to endure the trials and anxieties (to say nothing of the hours of loneliness and heart aches) incident upon a life of the sailor's family." [5] Immersed in the grime, toil, and brutality of the industry on board ship, Libby Spooner's brother-in-law, Shubael Spooner, expressed his longings by carefully engraving a tender, idealized vision he labeled "domestic happiness" right onto a whale's tooth itself.

Both the virtual widows onshore enmeshed in widespread and flexible community networks *and* the men isolated at sea in all-male vessels were as powerfully affected by the changing ideas about womanhood and manhood as were their landed peers. This most masculine enterprise, the hunt of the leviathan whale, as well as the practice of maritime family and community life ashore were both shaped by and in turn themselves reinforced prevailing concepts about sexual difference, conjugal responsibility, affection and companionship, male breadwinning and female domesticity. But, though neither the realities of life at sea or on shore matched expectations and ideals, the discrepancy was felt differently by men and women. Seafaring men were subjected to a sort of bipolar alternation between "male" and "female" worlds that was often difficult to negotiate but which nonetheless approximated conceptual consistency. In contrast, maritime women lived in a world that was neither organized nor operated according

Inscribed "Domestic Happiness," this scrimshawed whale tooth, ca. 1835, is attributed to Captain Shubael S. Spooner of New Bedford, Mass. Spooner, whose brothers Gideon and Caleb were also whalemen, first went to sea at age 15 and made at least ten whaling voyages over a twenty-seven-year career, during which he spent a cumulative total of only a little more than four years on land. This carefully detailed image, engraved on a whale tooth, suggests that Spooner, while at sea, sought to reconcile the two contradictory elements of his life by combining a highly idealized vision of family life with the ships viewed through the window and set above the interior scene. Spooner married Elizabeth Francis either in 1853 or in 1857; in 1859, on his third voyage as captain, he was lost in the Indian Ocean with all hands. Courtesy of the Kendall Whaling Museum, Sharon, Mass., U.S.A. (S-749-B; Neg. 754) to the terms of the rhetoric. Examining the gender dynamics in this particular location dramatically illustrates the necessity, pervasiveness, and thus the power of ideas and the language with which they are expressed, even when those ideas are painfully contradictory or implausible.

Melville used the story of Captain Ahab and the metaphor of the whaling voyage to explore questions of self, soul, and humanity; of individual and community; of man's ability to control his own destiny. The monomaniacal Ahab was of course tragically wrong: he could not triumph over the seas nor could he "bring the infinite to an accounting," [6] and he destroyed himself and the *Pequod* in the trying. Our voyage has been the reverse of the *Pequod*'s in *Moby-Dick*, taking us from eighteenth-century Nantucket to nineteenth-century New Bedford, from the sea and shore to the mainland and the mainstream. Indeed, it is the story writ bold of the new, incredibly tenacious gender order then emerging in American society more generally. The American whalefishery no longer exists, but we are still living with the legacy of Victorian domesticity. In tracing the course of the New England whaling community over a century and a half, this study has sounded the complex and evolving interaction between cultural prescription, individual perception, and material structure that shapes human experience. The interlocking stories of Ahab and of Ahab's wife are compelling, not only for their romantic evocation of the Age of Sail or the inherent poignancy of a past that is gone but also for their lasting human resonance.

APPENDIX

Annotated List of Major Informants by Family

Much of the material for this book was drawn from the experiences of sixty-six families, many of them extended, encompassing 200 individuals and ninety marriages. The
earliest marriage took place in 1740, the latest in 1872. At least sixteen of the men can
be confirmed to have died at sea or in foreign ports. (Refer to Notes section for key to
abbreviations used in entries below.)

ALBERT, Tiverton, R.I.
William C. Albert (1816–1893) and Ruth Borden Albert (1820–1886), m. 1839. Letters:
    Ruth to William, 1844; "Melintha" (probably a relative) and Ruth's father Abraham
    to William, no date [ca. 1844]. Other reference: mentioned in letter from Mary Ann
    Booth to brother John C. Borden. All references in CC.

ALLEN, New Bedford, Mass.
David Allen (b. 1823) and Harriet Butler Allen (b. 1829), m. 1850, New Bedford. Diaries:
    Harriet on land, 1863–67 (KWM Log 401-A, v. 1–2) and at sea, 1868–72 (KWM
    Log 401). Misc. papers.
Frederick S. Allen (b. 1830) and Satira Conner Allen (of Dartmouth, Mass.; b. 1833),
    m. 1865. Diary: Satira on land, 1854–1859 (KWM Log 401-B).

ALMY, Portsmouth, R.I.
Christopher Almy (1771–1855) and Lydia Hill Almy (of Smithfield, R.I.; 1769–1837),
    m. 1794. Diary: Lydia, 1797–99 (Lydia Hill Almy diary typescript, 1797–99, Phillips
    Library, PEM).

ASHBEY, Mystic, Conn.
Henry Ashbey and Jane Ashbey. Letters: from Henry, ca. 1848–50, merchant mariner
    (Coll. 39, MSM).

ASHLEY, Acushnet, Mass.

Williams Ashley (1787–1870) and Delana Allen Ashley (1789–1867), m. 1819. Williams was a merchant captain; their sons, William and Edward, were both whalemen. Letters: between Williams and Delana and other family members, ca. 1817–20 (private collection).

William Allen Ashley (1833–1909) and Hannah Howland Crapo Ashley (1835–1933), m. 1861. Letters: from William to Hannah, 1863–64; between Hannah and her brother Philip Crapo during the Civil War (in which he served) and after. Diary: Hannah on shore, 1864 (private collection).

Edward R. Ashley (1824–1900) and Adra Catherine Braley Ashley (1834[?]–1906), m. 1853. Letters: from Edward to parents and other family members (private collection). Diary: Catherine's sea journals, 1857–60 (Baker Library, Harvard Business School, Boston, Mass.).

BARLOW, Rochester, Mass., and Providence, R.I.

Seth Barlow (ca. 1768–1810; possibly died abroad or at sea). Commonplace book. Letters: copies of letters to wife and other family members written during merchant voyage to northern Europe, 1810 (Mss. 64, Series B, Subseries 16, ODHS).

BEETLE, Holmes Hole, Martha's Vineyard, Mass.

Henry William Beetle (1815–1899[?]) and Eliza Ann Beetle (b. 1819, Farmington, Maine), m. 1840. Letters: from Henry to Eliza, 1844–56; a few from misc. family members (Henry Beetle Hough papers, PPL).

BLACKMER, Acushnet, Mass.

Seth Blackmer (1819–1903) and first wife Catherine Mendell (1833–1853), m. 1851; and second wife Hannah Mendell, Catherine's sister (1840–1913), m. 1857. Both wives were his cousins. Letters: Seth to Hannah, 1864, private collection; Hannah to Seth, 1864, published.

BRALEY, Rochester, Mass.

Samuel Tripp Braley (1817–1870, d. in foreign port) and Mary Ann King Braley (1824–1907), m. 1845. Mary probably lived in Fairhaven while Samuel was at sea, but when he was on land (1857–63), they lived on the small Rochester farm she had inherited. Journals: Samuel's at-sea journals kept on board the *Arab*, 1845–49 (Logbook 255, KWM); the *Arab*, 1849–53 (Logbook 258, KWM); and the *Harrison*, 1854–57 (Logbook 261, KWM).

BREWSTER, Stonington, Conn.

William E. Brewster (1813–1893) and Mary Burtch Brewster (1822–1878), m. 1841. Diary: Mary's sea journal, 1845–48 (Logbook 38, MSM).

BRIGGS, Dartmouth, Mass.

Walter Briggs Jr. (b. 1813) and Cynthia Gary (or Garey) Briggs (b. 1817), m. 1840 or 1842. Letters: two from Cynthia to Walter, 1848 and 1850, CC.

BROCK, Nantucket, Mass.

Peter C. Brock (1805–1878) and Eliza Spencer Brock (1810–1899), m. 1833. Diary: Eliza's sea journal on board the *Lexington*, 1853–56 (Logbook 136, NHA).

BROWN, Orient (Long Island), N.Y.

Edwin Peter Brown (1813–1892) and Martha Smith Brewer Brown (1821–1911), m. 1843. Diary: Martha's sea journal, 1847–49; Martha's biographical reminiscences told to her daughter in 1900 (published).

BURGESS, Fairhaven, Mass.

Paul Cooke Burgess (1802–1831, d. at sea) and Ann Hathaway Burgess (1808–1881), m. 1827. Letters: Ann to Paul, 1828–29 (Mss. 94, Subgroup 1, Series A and Subgroup 2, Series A, ODHS).

BURGESS, Sandwich (Cape Cod), Mass.

Hannah Rebecca Crowell Burgess (1834–1917) and William H. Burgess (1829–1856, d. at sea), m. 1852. William was a merchant captain and involved at least part of the time in transshipment of whale oil from Hawaii. Hannah went to sea with him, was on board when he died, and navigated the ship into port. Diary: Hannah at sea and on land, some entries by husband (Hannah Rebecca Burgess collection, Sandwich Historical Society, Sandwich, Mass.).

CASH, Nantucket, Mass.

William Cash (1816–1882) and Azubah Handy Cash (of Barnstable, Mass.; 1820–1894), m. 1839. Diary: Azubah's sea journal, 1850–53 (Logbook 312, NHA).

COFFIN/MACY, Nantucket, Mass.

John Coffin (1708–1788) and Kezia Folger Coffin (1723–1798), m. 1740. Misc. papers from misc. collections (NHA).

Kezia Coffin Fanning, daughter (1760–1820), and Phineas Fanning (1750–1798), m. 1777. Diary: extracts and notes made from Kezia's. Other: Misc. papers and typed notes (primarily Mss. 2 Folder 4, NHA; also misc. papers from other collections, NHA).

Caleb Macy (1719–1798) and Judith Folger Gardner Macy (Kezia Folger Coffin's sister; 1729–1819), m. 1749 (her second marriage). Daybook: Judith's, 1783–1805 (Mss. 10, AB 37, NHA); copy of *No Cross, No Crown* (Rare Books 289.6 Pen, NHA); misc. papers (Mss. 96, Folder 12; Mss. 17, Vol. 1, NHA). Account book: Caleb's, 1740–65 (Mss. 10, AB 99, NHA); misc. papers (Mss. 96, folder 3¾, NHA).

Obed Macy, Caleb and Judith's son (1762–1844). Books/Diaries: "Obed Macy's book: Family Mirror" (Mss. 119, Folder 3, NHA); journals, Vols. 1–3, 1799–1822 (Mss. 96, NHA).

Silvanus Macy, Caleb and Judith's son (1756–1833). Account of in Obed Macy's "Family Mirror" (Mss. 119, Folder 3, NHA); other papers in misc. collections.

Ruth Macy Chase, Caleb and Judith's daughter (1771–1818) and Job Chase (1772–1818), m. 1796. Account of in Obed Macy's "Family Mirror" (Mss. 119, Folder 3, NHA); also misc. papers in other collections, NHA.

COLEMAN/FOLGER, Nantucket, Mass.

Samuel Coleman (1773–1825) and Phebe Folger Coleman (1771–1857), m. 1798. Samuel was a merchant mariner. Letters: from Phebe to Samuel, 1800 and 1808; from Phebe to her brother Walter, 1820 and 1829 (Mss. 107, Folder 17, NHA); from Phebe to her parents, 1810 (Mss. 118, Folder 49, NHA); Phebe's commonplace book, 1797–

1806 (fMS Typ 245, Department of Printing and Graphic Arts, Houghton Library, Harvard University, Cambridge, Mass.).

COLT/NORTON, Edgartown and Holmes Hole, Martha's Vineyard, Mass.

Henry Colt (b. 1803) and first wife Nancy Baylies Colt (1804–1842), m. 1825. Letters: to and from Henry, Nancy, and other relatives, ca. 1839–56 (Capt. Henry Colt papers, Box 115B, unnumbered envelope, MVHS).

Susan Maria Colt Norton, Henry and Nancy's daughter (1836–1863), first wife of Shubael Hawes Norton (1828–1901), m. ca. 1858. Letters: mainly from Susan and Shubael to others while they were at sea together, 1858–62 (Capt. Shubael Norton and Susan Maria Colt Norton papers, Box 125B, Envelope 22, MVHS).

CRAPO, Westport, Mass.

Reuben Williams Crapo (1829–1907) and Lucy Ann Hix Crapo (1833–1910), m. 1853. Diary: Lucy's sea journal, 1866–1867, written on board the New Bedford bark *Louisa* (Typescript, Logbook 899, MSM). Letters: from Lucy to her sister Ruth Ellen Hix Mosher (also seagoing, wife of Captain Andrew J. Mosher), written on board the bark *Linda Stewart*, 1878–80 (Mss. 56, Series M, Subseries 32, ODHS).

CROMWELL, Holmes Hole, Martha's Vineyard, Mass.

Peter Cromwell (1814–1857, d. at sea) and Susan Cleveland Cromwell (b. 1814), m. 1844. Letters: from Susan to Peter, 1851–55; from daughter Susan, 1854; scattered letters from other family members (Box 96B, MVHS).

DALLMAN, New Bedford, Mass.

Thomas Dallman (ca. 1814–1859) and Selina V. Hurl Dallman (b. 1819). Letters: from Thomas at sea to Selina, 1849 (Mss. 56 Series D, Subseries 1, ODHS).

DAVENPORT, New Bedford, Mass.

Lydia G. Davenport (of Little Compton, R.I.[?]; 1823–ca. 1902), spinster (sister-in-law of whalemen). Diary, 1853–68 (Mss. 64, Series D, Subseries 4, v. 1–2, ODHS).

DEBLOIS, Newport, R.I.

John S. Deblois (d. 1885) and Henrietta Tew Deblois (she predeceased him by several years, according to his obituary), m. 1845. Letters: from Henrietta to John, 1846; letter-journal of Henrietta on board the bark *Merlin*, 1856; from John to family, 1843–44; from John to Henrietta, 1861; Other: selected entries from the original longer journal of her voyage, 1856–59, and after her return to 1860 (Newport Historical Society, Newport, R.I.).

DIMAN, Bristol, R.I.

Martha J. Diman (b. 1816) and her father John Gardner (b. 1788). Martha's father was a sailor during at least part of her early life (he "went packeting"). Diary: Martha, brief entries, 1841–55, with some autobiographical information at beginning (privately owned).

DREW, Nantucket, Mass.

Gershom Drew (1774–1826[?], d. in foreign port) and Abigail Gardner Drew (1777–1868), m. 1795. Diary: Abigail Gardner Drew Diary and Reminiscences, 1799–1818

(Octavo vols. "D", AAS). Letter: from Abigail to her aunt, 1801; misc. family correspondence (Pinkham-Gardner Family Correspondence 1794–1826, Misc. Mss. Boxes "P," AAS).

FARNSWORTH, New London, Conn.

Mary Emma Weaver Farnsworth (1830–1910) and E. Seymour Farnsworth (of Brattleboro, Vt.; d. 1883), m. 1853. Seymour was a merchant mariner, employed by Pacific Mail Steamship Company. They moved to San Francisco permanently ca. 1855. Mary's "Life Story 1830–1875" as told to descendant, ca. 1901; includes reminiscences of her childhood in New London, Conn., and Groton, Conn. (Misc. Vol. 155, 156, MSM).

FISK, Groton, Conn.

Silas W. Fisk (b. 1824) and Julia Edgecomb Fisk (b. 1826), m. 1850. Diary: Julia's 1859 pocket-book diary. Letters: from Julia or Silas to family members (Silas W. Fisk papers, VFM 1007, MSM).

FOLGER/WYER, Nantucket, Mass.

Simeon Folger (1762–1847) and Phebe Wyer Folger (1766–1839), m. 1787. Letters: from Simeon to Phebe, 1787–94 (Mss. 118, Folder 40, NHA); from misc. connections to Simeon, 1790s (Mss. 118, Folder 14, NHA); to Simeon and Phebe from their son, Shubael Folger (b. 1792), 1810–11 (Mss. 118, Folder 39, NHA).

Joseph Wyer, Phebe's brother (1754–1811, lost at sea) and Margaret "Peggy" Pinkham Tupper Coffin Wyer (d. 1804), m. 1791. Joseph was Margaret's third husband. Her first was Benjamin Tupper Jr. Her second, Bartlett Coffin, was killed by a whale in 1786. Letters: to Joseph from Simeon, 1792 (Mss. 145, Folder 5, NHA); from Joseph to Margaret, 1803 (Mss. 145, Folder 5, NHA); other letters from him to her at Nantucket Atheneum, 1797–1804 (NA).

FOLGER, Nantucket, Mass.

William C. Folger (1806–1891). Though not himself a sailor, William's writing is very descriptive of the local society and economy, including women's work and social relations. Diary: William, 1835–43 (Mss. 118, Folders 85, 86, NHA).

GARDNER, Nantucket, Mass.

Elizabeth Chase Gardner (1766–1840) and Captain Asa Gardner (1765–1795), m. 1784. Letters: to and from Elizabeth's adult children (Mss. 87, Folders 33, 35, 55, 72, NHA).

Susan Gardner (1789–1872[?]), wife of Benjamin Gardner (1784–1824), m. 1807. Susan relocated to Havre with her husband. He went whaling from London and Havre and died in Havre.

George Gorham Gardner (1786–1846) and Lydia Barnard Gardner (1786–1867), m. 1807.

GARDNER, Nantucket, Mass.

Jared Gardner (1818–1896) and Harriet Morey Gardner (n.d.), m. 1840. (Also of Nantucket but only distantly related to the other Gardners listed just above.) Letters: many from each to the other, ca. 1840–54 (Gardner Family Papers, AAS).

GATES, Mystic, Conn.

George Washington Gates (1825–1897) and Julia Ann Fish Gates (1831–1884), m. 1853. Letters: several from Julia to George, 1864–77; a few from George, a merchant mariner, to Julia, 1876–77 (Coll. 153, MSM).

GIFFORD, Dartmouth, Mass.

Charles Henry Gifford (of Westport, Mass.; 1824–1899) and Caroline Wing Gifford (of Dartmouth, Mass.; 1827–1909), m. 1849. Letters: from Caroline to Charles and from their daughter, Eleanor, to Charles, 1865–1870 (Mss. 56, Series G, Subseries 7, ODHS). Other: Separation petition (1885) and other probate records, Bristol County Courthouse, Taunton, Mass.

Eleanor Gifford (1850–1931), daughter of Charles and Caroline, and her cousin, David Gifford (1844–1904), m. 1872. Eleanor went to sea with David in the mid-1870s. David's papers (Mss. 56, Series G, Subseries 8, ODHS).

GIFFORD, Falmouth (Cape Cod), Mass.

Captain Henry Foster Gifford (1818–1904) and Harriet Butler Gifford (1825–1894[?]), m. 1849. Diary: Undated, handwritten notes labeled "notes taken from Mrs. Harriet Gifford's Diary or Journal [on land] and Capt. Henry Gifford's Voyage as Master"; sporadic and brief notations, ca. 1853–54. Book: Large volume titled "Henry F. Gifford Recollections of voyages on whaling ships 1831–1849" which appears to have been written long afterward from his journals and memories (Papers of Henry F. Gifford ca. 1846–1866, Gifford Family Collection, Falmouth Historical Society, Falmouth, Mass.).

GIFFORD, Mattapoisett, Mass.

John Lincoln Gifford (of Falmouth[?]; b. 1829) and Susan Snow Gifford (1832–1873), m. 1859 in Mattapoisett. Diary: Susan, 1859–64, with major entries for 1859–60 only; brief record-keeping notations for later years (privately owned, on deposit at ODHS).

GIFFORD, New Bedford, Mass.

Leonard Sanford Gifford (1821–1868; b. Tiverton, R.I.; d. in foreign port) and Lucy Roberts Gifford (of New Bedford, 1832–1873), m. 1857. Letters: from Leonard to Lucy, 1851–57; from Leonard and Lucy to her aunt while Lucy was at sea with Leonard, 1857–63 (Mss. 98, Subgroup 1, Series A, and Subgroup 2, Series A, ODHS); from Leonard to agents Wilcox & Richmond (Papers of the ship *Hope* of New Bedford, 1851–57, VFM 1066, MSM).

HAWES, New Bedford and Fairhaven, Mass.

John Hawes (1768–1824) and first wife, Mercy Taber Hawes (1766–1803), m. 1792; and second wife, Mary Tallman Willis Hawes (1769–1858), m. 1804. John was a merchant mariner. Misc. papers, including one letter from Mercy to John, 1798 (Mss. 11, Subgroups 1 and 2, ODHS).

HOWES, Dennis (Cape Cod), Mass.

Abner Howes and Lizzie Howes. Abner was a merchant mariner. Letters: from Lizzie to Abner, 1854; to and from Abner and misc. relatives, ca. 1853–58 (Hamer Family

Papers, Schlesinger Library, Radcliffe Institute, Harvard University, Cambridge, Mass.).

HOWLAND, Dartmouth, Mass.

Philip Howland (1819–1866, d. at sea) and his first wife, Sarah Potter Howland (1817–1853), m. 1841; and second wife, Patience Potter Howland (1815–1893), m. 1854. Letters: Between Sarah and Philip, 1840s to 1852; between Philip and Patience, 1850s to 1860s; misc. letters from children and other family members and connections; also legal and other documents (Philip Howland Family papers, KWM). Correspondence and business papers of Philip (Mss. 55, Subgroup 2, Series K, Subseries 2 and 3, ODHS).

LAWRENCE, Falmouth (Cape Cod), Mass.

Samuel Lawrence (1818–1892) and Mary Chipman Lawrence (of Sandwich, Mass.; 1827–1906), m. 1847. Diary: Mary's sea journal, 1856–1860 (published).

LEONARD, Dartmouth/New Bedford, Mass.

John Wood Leonard (of Rochester, Mass., 1828–1866) and Sylvia Tucker Leonard (of Dartmouth, n.d.), m. 1854, in Dartmouth and/or New Bedford. Letters: extensive correspondence primarily from Sylvia to John, 1854–57 (privately owned).

McKENZIE, Dartmouth, Mass.

James H. McKenzie (1830–1888) and Susan Stimson McKenzie (1834–1927). Diary: Susan, fragment of her sea journal in Honolulu and on board the *Europa*, 1869–72. Letters: one from James to Susan from sea, 1873; some to Susan from "cousin Charlie," 1852; some to James and Susan at sea from misc. relatives, 1874 (Susan Stimson McKenzie file, Whaling Mss., NBFPL).

NORTON, Edgartown/Tisbury, Martha's Vineyard, Mass.

Richard E. Norton (of Edgartown, b. 1819) and Jane Ann Cottle Norton (of East Tisbury, b. 1830), m. 1847. Letters: written transcriptions (by descendant), between Richard and Jane, 1848–56 (Richard E. Norton Correspondence, Box 50B, Envelope 2, MVHS).

PEIRCE, Fairhaven, Mass.

Charles H. Peirce (1830[?]–1876; fell ill abroad, d. shortly after arriving home) and Eliza B. Tobey Peirce (n.d.), m. 1859. Letters: Charles to Eliza, 1859–1874 (Mss. B85-41.1, ODHS).

PICKENS, Fairhaven, Mass.

Thaddeus Pickens (1774–1811, d. at sea) and Peace Bennett Pickens (1775–1812), m. 1797. Thaddeus was a merchant mariner. Letters: between Thaddeus, Peace, and others, 1800–1811 (Mss. 24, Subgroups 1–3, Series A, ODHS).

PINKHAM/GARDNER, Nantucket, Mass., and Kennebunk, Maine

Letters: of various family members, 1794–1826, including Paul Pinkham (1736–1799); his brother-in-law. Silas Gardner (1753–1826); his son, Paul Pinkham Jr. (1763–1807), and his wife, Mercy Cobb Pinkham ([?]–1835); Silas Gardner's nieces, Hannah Gardner (1772–1848) and Abigail Gardner Drew (1777–1868; see above under

Drew family entry) (Pinkham-Gardner family correspondence, Misc. Mss. Boxes "P," AAS).

PINKHAM/MARSHALL, Nantucket, Mass.

Seth Pinkham (b. 1786) and Mary Brown Pinkham (b. 1791), m. 1809. Letters: from Seth to Mary, 1841; from Mary to unidentified daughter, 1859; from daughters Elizabeth Pinkham Crosby and Rebecca Pinkham Mitchell to their seagoing sister, Malvina Pinkham Marshall, 1859–60; from Marshall family members to Malvina and husband Joseph Marshall, 1858–59 (Mss. 302, Folders 1, 3, 3, 4, 13, 14, NHA).

PUTNAM, Manchester, N.H.

Rachel Hurd Putnam, wife of New England merchant captain Horace B. Putnam. Although not part of the whaling industry or the immediately local region, Rachel writes with remarkably clear expression of the conflict between domestic ideals and seafaring. Diary, 1855–56 (Phillips Library, PEM).

RICKETSON, New Bedford, Mass.

Daniel L. Ricketson (1837–1886, d. at sea; grew up in Long Plain, Acushnet) and Annie E. Holmes Ricketson (b. 1841), m. 1857. She went with him on at least three voyages. After he died on the final one, she returned home and married twice more. Diaries: Annie, shore diary, 1865–66 (Logbook 943, ODHS); sea journal, 1871–74 (published).

RUSSELL/ANDREWS/BUNKER, Nantucket, Mass.

Letters: of various Russell siblings and other family members, including Alexander Russell (1790–1834, d. at sea) and wife Maria Coffin Russell (1796–1861), m. 1817; Reuben Russell (b. 1799); twins Roland Russell (b. 1816) and Jane Russell Andrews (1816–1842); Ann M. Russell Andrews (b. 1820); Thomas Andrews (1813–1878, d. at sea, first wife Jane Russell m. 1839, second wife Ann Russell m. 1844); Eliza Morris Russell (1808–1881) (Mss. 172, Folders 2, 4, 8, 10, 14, NHA).

Hepsabeth Russell Bunker, daughter of Alexander (1820–1896), and first husband, whaling captain David P. Bunker (1816–1855), m. 1842; and second husband William Clisby. Diary: Hepsabeth, 1855–58; with sewing accounts, 1849–51 (Mss. 159, Folder 1, NHA).

RUSSELL/MOUNT, Nantucket, Mass.

Mary Hayden Russell (1784–1855), wife of Captain Laban Russell (b. 1780), m. 1802. Laban Russell was part of the Nantucket removal to Nova Scotia, and then to Milford Haven, Wales; the ship on which he took his wife and sons was the *Emily* of London. Diary: Mary's sea journal, 1823–24, addressed to her married daughter Mary; two sons also were on board (Mss. 83, Folder 1, NHA); letter-journal (no date) of Captain Forman Marshall Mount (of England; d. 1827) addressed to his wife, Mary Ann Russell Mount, daughter of Mary and Laban (b. 1803) (Mss. 83, Folder 2, NHA).

SMITH, New London, Conn.

Capt. Parker Hempstead Smith (1795–1851). Letters: to and from first wife, Mary T.

Smith, beginning 1827 (privately owned, but substantial excerpts published in the New London newspaper *The Day* on 8 February 1936; clipping in Coll. 102, MSM).

SOWLE, Westport, Mass.
James M. Sowle (or Soule; b. 1825) and Ruth Grinnell Sowle (1829–1862), m. 1851. Letter: One long, detailed letter from her to him (Mss. 56, Series S, Subseries 24, ODHS).

SPOONER, New Bedford, Mass.
Three brothers and a sister, and their spouses:
Caleb Spooner (b. 1819) and Libby (Elizabeth) Hathaway Spooner (b. 1833), m. 1853.
Shubael Spooner (1817–1859, d. at sea) and Elizabeth Francis Spooner (n.d.), m. [?].
Gideon B. Spooner (1806–1872) and Elizabeth Gibbs Spooner (1813–1872), m. 1835.
Sophia Spooner Clark (1808–1845), first wife of George H. Clark (n.d.), m. 1839. Letters: from various family members (CC). Other misc. papers (Mss. 64, Series S, Subseries 63, ODHS).

STARK, Mystic, Conn.
Mary Rathbun Stark. Mary's husband was a merchant mariner involved in transshipping whale oil from San Francisco and Honolulu. Mary went on a voyage with her husband while their children stayed behind with grandparents. Letters: from Mary to daughter and mother, 1855–56 (VFM 196, MSM).

STICKNEY, Dartmouth, Mass.
Mary J. Stickney, wife of Almon L. Stickney. Diary: Mary, the first part of her sea journal was kept on board the *Cicero*, 1879–80 (Mss. 95, Subgroup 2, Series A, ODHS).

SWAIN, Nantucket, Mass.
Eunice Swain (1765–1852) and James Hussey (1759–1825), m. 1786. Journal/Poetry, 1776–1788 (NA).

TABER, Mattapoisett, Mass.
William Loring Taber (of Rochester, Mass.; b. 1826) and Susan Goodspeed Taber (b. 1828), m. 1851. Letters: many from him to her, 1850s (William Loring Taber Papers, Mattapoisett Historical Society, Mattapoisett, Mass.).

WATERMAN, Duxbury, Mass.
Martin Waterman (1793–1860) and first wife, Joan Cushing Waterman (1795–1845), m. 1819. Martin was a merchant mariner. Letters: between Martin and Joan; also from Martin to his children, 1815–46 (Coll. 141, MSM).

WEEKS, Mattapoisett, Mass.
Ansel Weeks and first wife, Betsy Hiller Weeks (Charles's parents). Letters: between Ansel and Betsy (Mattapoisett Historical Society, Mattapoisett, Mass.).
Eliza Cushman Weeks (b. 1844) and her brother Charles W. Weeks (b. 1832). Diary: Eliza, 1861–62, kept in Charles's logbook (LB88-10, vol. 15, ODHS).

WEST/BUNKER, Nantucket, Mass.
Phebe Hussey West (1783–1846), wife of Capt. Paul West. Letters: Phebe, papers and correspondence (Mss. 13, Folder 14, NHA).

Sarah West Bunker (1817–1858), Phebe and Paul's daughter and wife of James Madison Bunker Esq. Diaries: Sarah, pocket-book diaries, 1850 and 1858 (Mss. 13, Folder 17, NHA).

WHELDEN, New Bedford, Mass.

Clara Kingman Whelden. "[E]xtracts from a few of many preserved letters written to relative and friends . . . when at sea and port, on voyages with her husband Captain Alexander Whelden," 1864–68. Typescript volume (whereabouts of originals unknown) dedicated to "Mrs. Susan A. McKenzie in Grateful Remembrance of Friendship." (Mss. 56, Series W, Subseries 12, ODHS).

WILLIAMS, Wethersfield, Conn.

Thomas William Williams (1820–1880) and Eliza Azelia Griswold Williams (1826–1885), m. 1851. Diary: Eliza's sea journal, 1858–61 (published).

WINSLOW, Nantucket, Mass.

Perry Winslow (1815–1892 or 1816–1890) and Mary Ann Morrow Winslow (1820–1900), m. 1843. Letters from Perry to Mary Ann, ca. 1847–63 (Mss. 166, NHA).

WINSOR, Duxbury and Fairhaven, Mass.

Zenas Winsor Jr. (of Duxbury; 1816–1860) and Lucia Russell Allen Winsor (of Fairhaven). Zenas sailed out of New Bedford as master of merchant ships to China and Antwerp. Letters: from him to her, 1851–57; from her to him, 1852 (Mss. 56, Series W, Subseries 40 and Mss. 80, Series K, Subseries 4, ODHS).

NOTES

ABBREVIATIONS

AAS
  American Antiquarian Society, Worcester, Mass.
CC
  Alexander Cory Dead Letter Collection, Old Dartmouth Historical Society–New Bedford Whaling Museum, New Bedford, Mass.
KWM
  Kendall Whaling Museum, Sharon, Mass.
MMM
  Men's Monthly Meeting Minutes, Nantucket Society of Friends (Quakers), Nantucket Historical Association, Nantucket, Mass.
MSM
  Mystic Seaport Museum, G. W. Blunt White Library, Mystic, Conn.
MVHS
  Martha's Vineyard Historical Society, Edgartown, Mass.
NA
  Nantucket Atheneum, Manuscript Collections, Nantucket, Mass.
NBFPL
  New Bedford Free Public Library, Special Collections, New Bedford, Mass.
NHA
  Nantucket Historical Association, Edouard A. Stackpole Research Center, Nantucket, Mass.
ODHS
  Old Dartmouth Historical Society–New Bedford Whaling Museum Library, New Bedford, Mass.

PEM

Peabody Essex Museum, Salem, Mass.

PPL

Providence Public Library, Nicholson Whaling Collection, Providence, R.I.

WMM

Women's Monthly Meeting Minutes, Nantucket Society of Friends (Quakers), Nantucket Historical Association, Nantucket, Mass.

INTRODUCTION

1. The literature on Melville and *Moby-Dick* is oceanic in scope. I have found the following especially useful: Sten, *Sounding the Whale*; Springer and Robillard, "Herman Melville"; Brodhead, *New Essays on Moby-Dick*; Duban, *Melville's Major Fiction*; Dimock, *Empire for Liberty*.

2. See Sager, *Seafaring Labour*, 238.

3. See Stein, *Seascape and the American Imagination*; Moseley, "Images of Young Women"; Baker, *Folklore of the Sea*; several essays in Nadel-Klein and Davis, *To Work and To Weep*; and the introduction and several essays in Creighton and Norling, *Iron Men, Wooden Women*.

4. I borrow this evocative metaphor from literary critic Annette Kolodny's enlightening article "Turning the Lens on 'The Panther Captivity.'" The lens I am suggesting here is, of course, a gender analysis. For useful overviews on the construction of gender and its utility as a category of historical analysis, see Scott, "Gender: A Useful Category of Historical Analysis"; Rapp, Ross, and Bridenthal, "Examining Family History"; and Laslett and Brenner, "Gender and Social Reproduction."

5. See, e.g., Rediker, *Between the Devil and the Deep Blue Sea*; Vickers, *Farmers and Fishermen*; Creighton, *Rites and Passages*; Dening, *Mr. Bligh's Bad Language*; Bolster, *Black Jacks*.

6. The class was Professor Mary Beth Norton's at Cornell University, and we had just read Barbara Welter's pioneering article "The Cult of True Womanhood, 1820–1860."

7. Ibid.

8. The literature on the "cult," "ideology," "cultural politics," or "discourse" of domesticity is vast. See Cott, *Bonds of Womanhood*, esp. chap. 2 and the new preface in the second edition; Ryan, *Empire of the Mother* and *Cradle of the Middle Class*; Smith-Rosenberg, *Disorderly Conduct*; van de Wetering, "Popular Concept of 'Home'"; McDannell, *The Christian Home*; Nylander, *Our Own Snug Fireside*; Coontz, *Social Origins of Private Life*; Mintz, *Prison of Expectations*; Boydston, *Home and Work*; Stanley, *From Bondage to Contract*; Theriot, *Mothers and Daughters in Nineteenth-Century America*. The work of literary critics and historians is also important, including the scholarship of Baym and of M. Kelley, and the new work by Romero, *Home Fronts*. On the closely related English version, see Davidoff and Hall, *Family Fortunes*; see also the useful introduction and many of the essays in Helly and Reverby, *Gendered Domains*.

9. See Gleason, "Identifying Identity"; Heller, Sosna, and Wellbery, *Reconstructing Individualism* (especially the essays by Natalie Davis, Nancy Chodorow, Ian Hacking, Carol Gilligan, and Martha Nussbaum); Taylor, *Sources of the Self*; LeVine, *Culture, Behavior, and Personality*; D'Andrade, "Cultural Meaning Systems"; Geertz, *Interpretation of Cultures*; Goffman, *Presentation of Self*; Marsh, "Identity"; Rosaldo, "Toward an Anthropology of Self and Feeling"; Bourdieu, *Outline of a Theory of Practice*; J. P. Butler, *Gender Trouble*.

10. Laqueur, *Making Sex*, chaps. 2–3; K. Brown, *Good Wives, Nasty Wenches*, 42–72; Alpern, *Amazons of Black Sparta*, 26–35.

11. For a concise review of these interpretations, see Kerber, "Separate Spheres, Female Worlds, Woman's Place"; quotations from Cott, "Domesticity," 181.

12. Cott, "Domesticity," 181.

13. The brief outline of the history of American whaling in this paragraph and the next two is compiled from the following sources: Byers, *Nation of Nantucket*, 79–85, 145–50; Vickers, "Nantucket Whalemen," 281; Hohman, *American Whaleman*; Starbuck, *History of the American Whale Fishery* and *History of Nantucket* (hereafter *American Whale Fishery* and *Nantucket*); Albion, Baker, and Labaree, *New England and the Sea*, 114–18; O. Macy, *History of Nantucket*; Labaree et al., *America and the Sea*; Davis, Gallman, and Gleiter, *In Pursuit of Leviathan*; L. B. Ellis, *History of New Bedford*.

14. I find Thomas Bender's definition of community most useful: "A community involves a limited number of people in a somewhat restricted social space or network held together by shared understandings and a sense of obligation. Relationships are close, often intimate, and usually face to face. Individuals are bound together by affective or emotional ties rather than by a perception of individual self-interest." See his *Community and Social Change in America*, 7.

15. Vickers, "Maritime Labor," 284–93; Hohman, *American Whaleman*; Starbuck, *American Whale Fishery*.

16. At least within the whaling industry, if not other maritime trades, Samuel Eliot Morison's portrayal of Massachusetts farm boys making good at sea seems to have been accurate. On classes in nineteenth-century American society, see Ryan, *Cradle of the Middle Class*; Blumin, *Emergence of the Middle Class*; Montgomery, "Working Classes of Pre-Industrial America"; Bridges, "Becoming American"; Wilentz, *Chants Democratic*; and Roediger, *Wages of Whiteness*.

17. These letters are found in the Alexander Cory Dead Letter Collection, CC.

18. Melville, *Moby-Dick*, 26.

CHAPTER ONE

1. Melville, *Moby-Dick*, 86, 77.

2. Robertson-Lorant, *Melville*, 321–23. For Melville's sources of information about Nantucket, see Bercaw, *Melville's Sources*.

3. Crevecoeur, *Letters*, 107, 109, 125–26. Most historians take Crevecoeur's description at fairly close to face value. Recently, literary scholars have reexamined Crevecoeur's achievement. According to Everett and Katherine Emerson, the

Nantucket portion was evidently composed first around 1772 and then rewritten after 1777; thus, Nathaniel Philbrick argues, the work operates "on two different historical levels, interweaving the island's prosperous past with the chaotic darkness of its Revolutionary present." In this more multidimensional depiction, Philbrick suggests, Crevecoeur actually "remains remarkably faithful to the historical record." Philbrick, "House Upon the Sand," 96, 106, 107, 111; Emerson and Emerson cited in Philbrick, "House Upon the Sand," 115. See also Philbrick, "Nantucket Sequence in Crevecoeur's *Letters.*"

4. Crevecoeur, *Letters*, 157.

5. In 1807, the Reverend James Freeman objected to Crevecoeur's account in part because "his pictures, though striking likenesses, are always flattering likenesses: every face glows with the blush of sensibility, and is irradiated with the beams of happiness." Freeman, "Notes on Nantucket," 37.

6. Two hundred years later, historian Edward Byers concurs, suggesting that Crevecoeur had recognized an essential truth about the relationship between Nantucket and mainland America. "Nantucket," Byers writes, "for all its peculiarities and isolated quaintness, belongs to the American mainstream. Its development has paced that of the larger nation, coming to embody enduring features of liberal American society." Byers, *Nation of Nantucket*, xi.

7. Ibid., 145.

8. Crevecoeur, *Letters*, 130.

9. For general information on the colonial whalefishery, see O. Macy, *History of Nantucket*; Starbuck, *American Whale Fishery*; Vickers, "Nantucket Whalemen"; Hohman, *American Whaleman*, 23–33; Byers, *Nation of Nantucket*, 77–101, 139–70; R. Ellis, *Men and Whales*, 97–101.

10. Quoted without attribution from the English Annual Register, 1775, p. 85, in Starbuck, *American Whale Fishery*, 60.

11. Crevecoeur, *Letters*, 109; largely substantiated by Byers, *Nation of Nantucket*, 77–101, 139–70. See also Vickers, "First Whalemen of Nantucket" and "Nantucket Whalemen."

12. Byers, *Nation of Nantucket*, 140; quotations from Crevecoeur, *Letters*, 110–13; Josiah Quincy, "Account of a Journey of Josiah Quincy—1801," in Crosby, *Nantucket in Print*, 116–17; Melville, *Moby-Dick*, 76. Reverend James Freeman, who visited Nantucket in 1807, also thought that "there is not much elegance" in the town's appearance (Freeman, "Notes on Nantucket," 127). For other descriptions of eighteenth-century Nantucket's landscape, see Walter Folger's 1791 "Topographical Description," 96–98; the 1811 account by Joseph Sansom, "Description of Nantucket," 137–48; Zaccheus Macy's 1792 account, 101–2; and Henry Barnard Worth, "Nantucket Lands and Land Owners," 53–82, 183–283.

13. Crevecoeur, *Letters*, 112; 1751 Nantucket petition to the Massachusetts General Court, quoted in Byers, *Nation of Nantucket*, 145; Crevecoeur, *Letters*, 111.

14. R. Ellis, *Men and Whales*, 99.

15. The story, which is repeated in several sources, appears to have originated in O. Macy, *History of Nantucket*, 48.

16. Peleg Folger journal, sloop *Seaflower*, entry dated 25 July 1752, Peleg Folger Journal, 1751–54, NA; Crevecoeur, *Letters*, 139, 134. (Crevecoeur's general description of whaling appears on 133–40.)

17. Vickers, "Nantucket Whalemen," 279.

18. Ibid., 281; Byers, *Nation of Nantucket*, 139–45; Starbuck, *American Whale Fishery*, 19–77; Hohman, *American Whaleman*, 23–33.

19. Vickers, "Nantucket Whalemen," 281.

20. *Boston News-Letter*, quoted in Starbuck, *American Whale Fishery*, 32fn.; Crevecoeur, *Letters*, 157.

21. See Vickers, "Maritime Labor"; also Dye, "Early American Merchant Seafarers"; Rediker, *Between the Devil and the Deep Blue Sea*, esp. 10–14, 155–58; Morison, *Maritime History of Massachusetts*, 105–18; Lemisch, "Jack Tar in the Streets."

22. Vickers, "Nantucket Whalemen," 296. For a discussion of young women's labor as part of family economy, see Dublin, *Transforming Women's Work*, chaps. 2, 3; Cott, *Bonds of Womanhood*, chap. 1; Ulrich, *Midwife's Tale*, chaps. 2, 4.

23. Vickers, "Nantucket Whalemen," 290–95.

24. Crevecoeur, *Letters*, 128–29. As Vickers puts it: "Nantucket parents sent their sons to sea at an early age. After several years of schooling and possibly a short apprenticeship in a landsman's trade, most boys were assigned their first whaling berth about the age of fifteen. . . . Though study and practice the most forward of them graduated to the higher ranks in remarkably short order. By their late teens a good proportion were earning a steersman's lay, and before the age of twenty-five, the best had secured posts as mates and captains." Vickers, "Nantucket Whalemen," 285.

25. Worth and Gardner quoted in O. Macy, *History of Nantucket*, 214.

26. Vickers, "Nantucket Whalemen," 285 and passim. See also Vickers, "Maritime Labor," 284–93.

27. Obed Macy, "A Short Biography of the Life and Character of Caleb Macy," in "Obed Macy's Book: Family Mirror," Mss. 119, Folder 3, NHA.

28. Vickers, "Maritime Labor," chap. 6; Byers, *Nation of Nantucket*, 194–95; Peleg Folger, Journal, 1751–57, NA. Compare to the labor relations in the eighteenth-century Anglo-American merchant fleet as described in Rediker, *Between the Devil and the Deep Blue Sea*, chap. 5.

29. Byers, *Nation of Nantucket*, 93, 165–70 (quotation on 170); see also Vickers, "Maritime Labor," 292–304; Starbuck, *Nantucket*, 143–44.

30. Christopher Starbuck and Co. to Nicholas Brown and Co., 4 October 1774, quoted in Byers, *Nation of Nantucket*, 170; see also 258.

31. Orders of the Ship *Edward* to Capt. Micajah Gardner, 1793, Mss. Box 4, NA.

32. At least some of the shipowners appear to have adopted what labor historian Philip Scranton terms a "double father" role, part of the "customary duties and status of community leaders." Scranton, "Varieties of Paternalism," 238, 239.

33. Walter Folger Account Book, 1764–1810, Mss. 10, AB 150, NHA.

34. From 1764 to 1770, a Reuben Swain was charged four times for "half a ship's boat," twice for mending a boat, and once for a plank trough. Similarly, from 1765 to 1768,

a John Coffin was charged for two half ship's boats, a new "5 handed boat" and, later, for mending it, and eight "bent timbers" (important in ship and boat construction) along with a few other sundries; in exchange, Coffin supplied seventy barrels and a thousand cedar boards. Ibid.

35. Dinah and Mary Clark appear to have been sisters, daughters of John and Mary (Challenge) Clark. This Dinah Clark was born in 1716, never married, and died in 1797. Her sister Mary was born in 1730 and "died single," though her date of death has not been determined. It is possible, though less likely, that the Dinah Clark listed in Folger's account book, with transactions dating from 1778 to 1784, is instead the daughter of James and Rachel (Trott) Clark, born in 1757 and married to Paul Dillingham in 1788. See the *Nantucket Vital Records* and the Barney Genealogical Records, Mss. 186, vol. 1, 275, NHA. Unfortunately, Anna Flood and Mary Folger cannot be identified with any certainty from these sources.

36. See accounts with Mary Clark (1768–78), Anna Flood (1777–78), Mary Folger (1771), and Dinah Clark (1778–84) in Walter Folger's Account Book, Mss. 10, AB 150, NHA.

37. See the accounts with Seneca Boston (1772), John Cathcart (1774), and Barzillai Folger Jr. (1767–77), in ibid.

38. Ibid.; Barney Genealogical Records, Mss. 186, vol. 3, 148, NHA; Starbuck, *American Whale Fishery*, 186–87.

39. "Daniel Killey" account for 1792, Walter Folger Account Book, Mss. 10, AB 150, NHA; Barney Genealogical Records, Mss. 186, Vol. 5, 60, NHA; Starbuck, *American Whale Fishery*, 188–89.

40. Micajah Coffin Waste Book, 1789–1793, entries for January and February 1789, Mss. 36, Folder 2, NHA.

41. See the arrival dates listed for the Nantucket vessels in the early 1790s in Starbuck, *American Whale Fishery*, 186–89.

42. Micajah Coffin to Moses Rogers of New York, 19 June 1788, Micajah Coffin Letter Book, 1785–1788; Coffin to James Parsons & Sons of New York, 7 July 1790, Micajah Coffin Letter Book, 1790–1795; both in Mss. 36, Folder 4, NHA.

43. Quotation from Blackstone, *Commentaries*, 1:430. For a comprehensive description of coverture in colonial British America, see Salmon, *Women and the Law of Property*, and Shammas, "Anglo-American Household Government." But see also Erickson, *Women and Property*, for an important distinction between the letter of the law and actual practice.

44. Morison, *Maritime History of Massachusetts*, 8–186; Albion, Baker, and Labaree, *New England and the Sea*, 3–96; Vickers, "Maritime Labor."

45. In addition to the evidence I provide later in the chapter, see Ulrich, "Housewife and Gadder"; 21–34; Ulrich, *Midwife's Tale*, 75–101; and Ulrich, *Good Wives*, 40–43. For examples of seamen's families turning to shipowners for assistance in Newport, R.I., see Crane, *Dependent People*, 45, 72–74, 91–92.

46. Lydia Almy, Diary, 1797–1799, entry dated 20 June 1799, PEM. (As a devout Quaker, Almy numbered rather than named the days and months in her diary. I have modernized the references here to make the rhythms and patterns of her life more accessible.)

47. Ibid., entries dated 21 September 1798, 22 September and November 1798, 8 July and 24 April 1798.

48. Mary Newbegin request, 22 12th month 1741; awarded £3, 29 1st month 1742; in MMM, Mss. 52, Book 2, NHA; Eunice Guinn award, 30 11th month 1761, in the WMM Mss. 52, Book 10, NHA (dates as in original). The division of responsibilities between the Men's and the Women's meetings for indigent or temporarily needy Friends is not clear from the surviving records. While the Women's meeting appears to have given assistance exclusively to women, the Men's meeting helped both men and women. Also see Byers, *Nation of Nantucket*, 125–26.

49. For a detailed description of the ways in which New England towns assumed responsibility for and offered assistance to seamen's families in distress, see Herndon, "Domestic Cost of Seafaring."

50. Byers, *Nation of Nantucket*, 255–58. See also O. Macy, *History of Nantucket*, 88–90, 167–71, 178–79.

51. Many thanks to Rus Menard for pointing this out to me. See the reference to "the credit crises and commercial slumps that troubled the Atlantic economy in the early 1760s" in McCusker and Menard, *Economy of British America*, 352.

52. See entries in the Record Book for the [Nantucket] Inferior Court of Common Pleas, 1721–1785, for the sessions 4 October 1763, 6 March 1764, and 26 March 1765, Office of the Superior Court; and Registry of Deeds, Book 7, p. 118, Registry of Deeds Office; both offices in the Nantucket Town and County Building, Nantucket, Mass.

53. *Nantucket Vital Records* and the Barney Genealogical Records, Mss. 186, Vol. 5, 309, NHA. Only one of their children's birthdates is listed: their first child, Anna, born in August 1743. By the time Zephaniah encountered all his financial woes, it is possible that three or more of his children were in their teens and presumably able to contribute to the family finances.

54. Ulrich, *Midwife's Tale*, chap. 2.

55. Crevecoeur, *Letters*, 157. Historian Laurel Thatcher Ulrich's evocative characterization of colonial New England women's work seems particularly apt here: "Economic and social differences might divide a community; the unseen acts of women wove it together" (Ulrich, *Midwife's Tale*, 96).

56. Ulrich first elaborated on the concept of "deputy husbands" as identified by Cotton Mather in 1692; see Ulrich, *Good Wives*, 35–50.

57. Simeon Folger to Phebe Folger, 2 February 1788, 7 March 1791, Mss. 118, Folder 40, NHA.

58. Albion, Baker, and Labaree, *New England and the Sea*, 54–85.

59. Simeon Folger to Phebe Folger, 8 November 1798, Mss. 118, Folder 40, NHA.

60. Judith Folger to Peter Folger, 6 June 1768, NA.

61. On the private and public schools on Nantucket, see Byers, *Nation of Nantucket*, 126–27, 304–6.

62. Phebe Coleman to Samuel Coleman, 9 February 1800, Mss. 107, Folder 17, NHA.

63. Lydia Almy diary, August 1797–June 1799, entry dated 21 December 1797, PEM. See also entries for 24 January, 28 February, 7 March 1798 and passim for examples of cash-producing activities.

64. For just a sample of her range of activities, see Almy Diary, entries December 1797 (butchering a pig), 28 February 1798 (tanning leather), 14 May 1798 (weaving), 6 June 1798 (whitewashing), 10 July 1798 (haying), 12 May 1799 (bottling cider), PEM.

65. Ibid., entries dated 30 August and 8 May 1798.

66. For women's work on the mainland, see Cott, *Bonds of Womanhood*; Norton, *Liberty's Daughters*; Dexter, *Colonial Women of Affairs*; Ulrich, *Good Wives* and "Housewife and Gadder"; Jensen, *Loosening the Bonds*; and Boydston, *Home and Work*.

67. In their extensive study of occupational listings and household inventories in colonial Nantucket, Carpenter and Carpenter found that all fifty-two weavers they could identify in the seventeenth and eighteenth centuries were male, who were supplied with yarn by all-female spinners. They suggest that the number of identified spinners is distorted by lack of data before 1750 but found that between 1751 and 1776 there were ninety-eight women (some married) termed "spinster" compared to twenty-six male weavers, a typical ratio of about four spinsters per weaver. Carpenter and Carpenter also suggest that all of the women listed in official records as spinsters were "those who practiced spinning as a regular operation . . . for money or [barter]." Carpenter and Carpenter, *Decorative Arts and Crafts of Nantucket*, 88. However, Judith Macy's daybook (1783–1807) lists at least one female weaver, Rebeccah Coffin (Judith Macy daybook, Mss. 10, AB 37, NHA); and Walter Folger's account book also seems to imply the existence of women weavers (Mss. 10, AB 150, NHA). Ulrich has identified a transition from men to women in the weaving trade over the course of the eighteenth century; see Ulrich, "Wheels, Looms, and the Gender Division of Labor."

68. The Record Book of the Court of General Sessions, 1721–1785, records for the pre-Revolutionary period those licensed to keep inns and sell liquors, tea, coffee, and chinaware. A small number of women were among the licensees. The records of the Inferior Court of Common Pleas (kept in the same bound volume, 1721–1785) provide examples of women suing to recover debts. For example, on 6 March 1764 Ann Gardner, Spinster, sued to recover £15 10s, loaned two years earlier to mariner Zephaniah Pinkham. After the Revolution, licensing was recorded in the Selectmen's Journal, 1784–95. For example, on 5 October 1790 the clerk noted the people granted licenses to keep inns (one woman and three men) and retail "spirituous liquors" (thirteen people, three of whom were women). The volume also lists the people "assisted and supported by the Town," some of whom were boarded at the town's expense in private households, some headed by women. See, for example, the entry dated 22 March 1790 recording that the "Widow Brooks" was to be boarded at "Margaret Coffins" for "6/" per week, in Record Book of the Court of General Sessions and the Inferior Court of Common Pleas, 1721–1785; and Selectmen's Journal, 1784–1795, both held in the vault at the Superior Court Office, Nantucket Town and County Building, Nantucket, Mass. Walter Folger's account book provides examples of women's spinning, weaving, sewing, selling dairy products (milk), making wine, and doing laundry. See also John Coffin Account Book, 1786–1820, Mss. 10, AB 518, NHA; Judith Macy Day Book,

1783–1807, Mss. 10, AB 37, NHA; Caleb Macy Account Book, 1740–1765, Mss. 10, AB 99, NHA; Betsey Carey Account Book (recording guests and charges for commercial boarding house), 1816–1829, Mss. 10, AB 536, NHA; Eliza Mitchell Reminiscences, 1894–1896, Mss. 23, NHA.

69. Ulrich, "Housewife and Gadder," 24–25, 28.

70. Crevecoeur, *Letters*, 157.

71. O. Macy, *History of Nantucket*, 53.

72. Kezia Coffin Fanning diary, 7 April 1779, 30 November 1781, and 20 October 1785, Mss. 2, Folder 4, NHA. For a discussion of traditional social childbirth, see Ulrich, *Midwife's Tale*, 12, 61–66.

73. Abigail Gardner Drew diary, 3, 15, 16, 20, and 25 January 1799; see also entries dated 2, 4, 5, 13, 19, 22, 23, and 26 January 1799; "Drew Abigail Gardner Diary and Reminiscences," Octavo vols. "D," AAS.

74. Almy Diary, December 1797, January 1798, 22 May 1798, 24 March 1799, November 1797, and 25 December 1797, PEM.

75. Judith Folger to Peter Folger, 6 June 1768, NA.

76. Joseph Wyer to Margaret Wyer, dated "Lisbon Agust [*sic*] 18th 1797," NA.

77. On her children's spiritual state, see Lydia Almy diary, 3 June 1798, PEM. She left her children with Isaac Lapham on 11 March 1798, with "neighbor Baker" on 14 January 1799, and with Salley Pearce in January 1798.

78. Logue, "Case for Birth Control before 1850." For the other side of the argument, see Byers, *Nation of Nantucket*, 182–85.

79. Bloch, "American Feminine Ideals in Transition," 126; Cott, *Bonds of Womanhood*, 46–47, 84–92.

80. Dexter, *Career Women of America*; Byers, *Nation of Nantucket*, 178.

81. W. F. Macy, *Nantucket Scrap Basket*, 93–94.

82. Retail licenses granted, 4 March 1760, Record Book of the Court of General Sessions and the Inferior Court of Common Pleas, Vol. 1 (1721–1785); Retail licenses granted, 5 October 1790, Selectmen's Journal, Vol. 2 (1784–1795). Eliza Barney quoted in Dall, *The College, the Market and the Court*, 197–98.

83. Mary Pinkham to "Capt Brown," Nantucket, 17 February 1764, Nicholas Brown & Company Records, John Carter Brown Library, Brown University, Providence, R.I.

84. See, for example, charge vs. Mercy Coffin, 1732, in "Records of the Courts from 1721," Mss. 35, Folder 1, NHA; charge vs. Eunice Garlow and Betsy Currington, 3 October 1797, in the Record Book of the Court of General Sessions of the Peace, Vol. 2 (1786–1802), Nantucket Town and County Building, Nantucket, Mass. The warning out of off-island women Elizabeth Hutchinson (widow) and her three daughters, all of Martha's Vineyard; single woman Mary Gibson of Boston; and single woman Zubia Nickerson of Chatham, 2 October 1760, in the Record Book of the Inferior Court of Common Pleas, Vol. 1 (1721–1785), Nantucket Town and County Building, Nantucket, Mass., may indicate indigence, illicit activities, or both.

85. Crevecoeur, *Letters*, 159.

86. Cleary, "'She Merchants' of Colonial America"; Crane, *Ebb Tide in New England*, chap. 3; Wilson, *Life After Death*, chap. 4; Norton, *Liberty's Daughters*, 138–51.

87. Ulrich, *Midwife's Tale*, 80, 84, 96.

88. Eliza Ann M'Cleave, Ruth Macy Chase's daughter, noted, "Grandfather wanted Grandmother before she married James Gardner, but she was engaged to Gardner." See Mary F. Allen, "A copy of Eliza Ann M'Cleave's letter about my great grandmother Judith Macy's picture," 11 April 1879, Mss. 96, Folder 12, NHA.

89. All her children predeceased her except her daughter Ruth and three sons, Caleb Jr. and the well-known and prosperous merchants Silvanus and Obed. Three daughters died in infancy, including two named Keziah, perhaps named after her sister. Judith's first son, Elisha, did not enjoy good health nor a capacity for hard labor; he died in midlife in 1806. Caleb Jr., the fifth son, seems to have been feeble both of mind and body and required care his entire life. Another son, Barzillai, died of consumption at age 30 in 1789, and Judith's 22-year-old daughter, her namesake, died just a few months later that same year. In 1818, Judith, by then a widow for the second time, also saw her daughter Ruth lose a husband.

90. Obed Macy, biographical account of his mother, Judith Macy, in "Obed Macy's Book: Family Mirror," 16 April 1825, in Mss. 119, Folder 3, NHA.

91. Ibid.

92. Ibid.; also S. J. Macy, *Genealogy*, 111.

93. Caleb Macy will (dated 3 April 1793), inventory of estate (23 July 1798), and division of estate (dated 14 October 1799 and recorded 16 May 1814?), Mss. 96, Folder 3¾, NHA.

94. Caleb Macy account book, 1740–65, account with Richard Macy, 14, 15, 60, 87; account with Shubail Pinkham Jr., 33; Mss. 10, AB 99, NHA.

95. Judith Macy daybook, 1783–1807, Mss. 10, AB 37, NHA.

96. In the 1740s through the 1760s, Caleb's account book lists many transactions in which he obtains foodstuffs like molasses, corn, pork, flour, cheese, codfish, butter, apples, onions, turnips, sugar, chocolate, rum, coffee, and wine. He also acquires some cloth and items of clothing, although the amounts seem quite insufficient to supply the growing Macy family with even the most basic clothing. The transactions recorded in Judith's daybook, many of which also deal with trading foodstuffs and cloth, imply that by the 1780s she is now taking charge of supplying the household with food and clothing. For a detailed discussion of clothing and cloth needs in eighteenth-century Anglo-America (and a review of the relevant scholarship), see Hood, "Material World of Cloth."

97. Judith Macy daybook, 1783–1807, Mss. 10, AB 37, NHA.

98. Judith Macy appears frequently in the records of the Quaker women's meeting as appointed to several positions of respect; see, for example, appointments made 28 5th month 1787, 28 1st month 1788, 13 3d month 1788, 25 1st month 1790, 28 3d month 1791, WMM, Mss. 52, Book 10, NHA.

99. Obed Macy's biographical accounts of his brothers Silvanus, Barzillai, and Caleb Jr., in "Obed Macy's Book: Family Mirror," Mss. 119, Folder 3, NHA; see also S. J. Macy, *Genealogy*, 158.

100. Judith Macy daybook, April 1792, 1 December 1791, Mss. 10, AB 37, NHA.

101. See Byers, *Nation of Nantucket*, 42–43, 78–79, 145–46, 279; Crevecoeur, *Letters*, 116; Worth, "Nantucket Lands and Land Owners," chap. 9.

102. Judith Macy, estate inventory, 3 September 1819, Mss. 96 Folder 12, NHA.

103. O. Macy, *History of Nantucket*, 34–36, 115; Carpenter and Carpenter, *Decorative Arts and Crafts of Nantucket*, 87; Byers, *Nation of Nantucket*, 43; Crevecoeur, *Letters* 116; Josiah Quincy, "Account of a Journey of Josiah Quincy—1801," in Crosby, *Nantucket in Print*, 116–17.

104. Crevecoeur, *Letters*, 116.

105. Byers, *Nation of Nantucket*, 279.

106. Quote from W. F. Macy, *Nantucket Scrap Basket*, 26; on Nantucket girls' marriage preference for successful whalers, see 20. See also Hart, *Miriam Coffin*, 1:93–95.

107. Elizabeth Chase Gardner to Susan Gardner, fragment, 23 October ca. 1826, Mss. 87, Folder 33, NHA.

108. Sansom, "Description of Nantucket," quotation from 143, italics in the original.

109. Anonymous diary, undated, ca. 1821–32, Mss. 28, Folder 7, NHA.

110. The literature supporting these characterizations of colonial New England is voluminous. Coontz has usefully summarized the key points relating to family life and the connections between families, households, and communities in "Households and Communities in Colonial America," chap. 3 of her study *The Social Origins of Private Life*. See also Folbre, "Patriarchy in Colonial New England"; and Norton, *Founding Mothers and Fathers*.

111. Ulrich, *Good Wives*, 39.

112. W. Folger, "A Topographical Description," 97.

113. Ulrich has concluded that "ambitious men in early America were often involved in many things at once—farming and running a gristmill, for example, or cutting timber and fishing." This sort of male "occupational pluralism," she suggests, mirrored the complexity and diversity of women's work in sustaining households (Ulrich, *Good Wives*, 39). See also Vickers, "Competency and Competition"; and Boydston, *Home and Work*, esp. chap. 1.

114. For a particularly elegant explication of the gendered nature of the preindustrial economy in rural New England, see Ulrich, *Midwife's Tale*, 75–90 and passim.

115. Ulrich, in her book *Good Wives*, has provided the most sensitive and detailed account of women's roles in colonial New England, including "goodwife," "help-meet," and "deputy husband." In addition to the Coontz study cited in note 109, see also Norton, *Liberty's Daughters* and "Evolution of White Women's Experience in Early America"; and Cott, *Bonds of Womanhood*.

116. Judith Macy, estate inventory, 3 September 1819, Mss. 96, Folder 12, NHA; addendum to will, 21 October 1813, Mss. 17, Vol. 1, NHA.

117. For the typicality of Macy's attitudes, see Ditz, *Property and Kinship*; and Shammas, Salmon, and Dahlin, *Inheritance in America*.

118. Obed Macy, biographical account of his mother, Judith Macy, in "Obed Macy's Book: Family Mirror," 16 April 1825, in Mss. 119, Folder 3, NHA.

119. Crevecoeur, *Letters*, 158–59. See also O. Macy, *History of Nantucket*, 52–53.

CHAPTER TWO

1. Crevecoeur, *Letters*, 141.
2. Ibid., 144–45.
3. Ibid., 128.
4. Byers, *Nation of Nantucket*, 108 n. 14.
5. Hohman, *American Whaleman*, 10.
6. Dunn, "Women of Light"; Bacon, *Mothers of Feminism*, quote on 45–46. See also Frost, *The Quaker Family in Colonial America*, 10–29; Tolles, *Quakers and the Atlantic Culture*, 36–72; and Worrall, *Quakers in the Colonial Northeast*, 99–165.
7. Crevecoeur, *Letters*, 158–59.
8. Thomas Story quoted in Starbuck, *Nantucket*, 529–30.
9. Byers, *Nation of Nantucket*, 28–36, 52–55, 84, 122; see also O. Macy, *History of Nantucket*, 51; Starbuck, *Nantucket*, 516–18, 546–48; Dell, "Quakerism on Nantucket," 3–5, 7–8; Leach and Gow, *Quaker Nantucket*, 5–30. Leach and Gow use the term "Nothingarians," 9.
10. Story quoted in Starbuck, *Nantucket*, 525.
11. Byers, *Nation of Nantucket*, 105–7, 114–15, Samuel Fothergill's 1755 remark quoted on 106; Philbrick, *Away Off Shore*, 34–35.
12. Quoted in Starbuck, *Nantucket*, 518.
13. On Sarah Starbuck Austin and Hephzibah Starbuck Hathaway, see Leach and Gow, *Quaker Nantucket*, 11–12.
14. Starbuck, *Nantucket*, 697–99; Philbrick, *Away Off Shore*, 34. Both refer to Tristram Coffin as the "patriarch" of Nantucket in part because of his powerful influence and in part because of the sheer number of his descendants. According to Philbrick, at Coffin's death in 1681, he had seven children, sixty grandchildren, and several great-grandchildren; in 1728, 1,128 of his 1,582 descendants were still alive and living in New England. In 1792, Zaccheus Macy described Coffin as "the old grandfather to almost all of us" (quoted in Crosby, *Nantucket in Print*, 99).
15. Quoted in Starbuck, *Nantucket*, 520. Philbrick also notes that Nathaniel Starbuck could not sign his own name: extant legal documents carry his mark only, and a surviving Starbuck family account book is attributed to Mary and their son Nathaniel Jr. (Philbrick, *Away Off Shore*, 78).
16. Richardson quoted in Starbuck, *Nantucket*, 521; see also Jensen, *Loosening the Bonds*, 155–56, on the popularity of the Deborah reference among eighteenth-century Pennsylvania Quaker women.
17. Quoted in Starbuck, *Nantucket*, 525.
18. Extensive extracts from Richardson's journal, including the entire account of his 1702 visit, are reprinted in Starbuck, *Nantucket*, 520–24. A description of "Parliament House" can be found in Byers, *Nation of Nantucket*, 103, among other sources.
19. Quoted in Starbuck, *Nantucket*, 521–22.
20. Stuard, "Women's Witnessing," quotation on 12; Dunn, "Latest Light on Women of Light"; Mack, *Visionary Women*, esp. 236–61.
21. Carroll, "Early Quakers and 'Going Naked as a Sign'"; Mack, *Visionary Women*, esp. 165–211.

22. Stuard, "Women's Witnessing"; Dunn, "Latest Light on Women of Light"; Mack, *Visionary Women* and "Gender and Spirituality." According to Mack, the first Quaker missionaries to America were Mary Fisher and Anne Austin, who traveled to Barbados to preach in 1655 and made it to Boston in 1656 (Mack, "Gender and Spirituality," 33). Robert Leach identifies the first visiting minister to Nantucket as Jane Stokes in 1664 (Leach and Gow, *Quaker Nantucket*, 11), though Edward Byers notes that this visit is rumored but not substantiated (Byers, *Nation of Nantucket*, 104).

23. There are a great many descriptions of early Quaker belief and practice. For one concise account, see Frost, *The Quaker Family*, 10–29.

24. Quotation from Mack, *Visionary Women*, 226.

25. Quoted in Dunn, "Latest Light on Women of Light," 72–73.

26. Byers, *Nation of Nantucket*, 179.

27. Quoted in Forbes, "Quaker Tribalism," 146.

28. Nathan Prince to Thomas Prince, Nantucket, 4 September 1722, letter reprinted in full with modernized spelling and punctuation in Cadbury, "Nantucket and Its Quakers in 1722."

29. Byers, *Nation of Nantucket*, 104; Leach and Gow, *Quaker Nantucket*, 29.

30. Leach and Gow, *Quaker Nantucket*, 104, 28.

31. In one of his justifications for a separate meeting for women, Fox argued: "Women cannot for civility sake and modesty sake speak amongst men of women's matters, neither can modest men desire it, and none but ranters will desire to look into women's matters" (quoted in Levy, "Birth of the 'Modern Family,'" 38–39). On the establishment of separate women's meetings and what happened to them in England and North America, see Stuard, "Women's Witnessing"; and Dunn, "Latest Light on Women of Light."

32. Dunn was among the first to suggest the consequences of female self-governance in her article "Women of Light." For more recent considerations, see Stuard, "Women's Witnessing"; Dunn, "Latest Light on Women of Light"; and Soderlund, "Women's Authority."

33. Byers, *Nation of Nantucket*, 108–10; Leach and Gow, *Quaker Nantucket*, 18–19; see also Worrall, *Quakers in the Colonial Northeast*, chap. 4; Frost, *The Quaker Family*, 3–4; Soderlund, "Women's Authority."

34. Byers, *Nation of Nantucket*, 173; and Leach and Gow, *Quaker Nantucket*, 46, 81–82. These are estimates; exact membership figures do not exist.

35. Interpretation is based on analysis of the Nantucket women's monthly meeting records, 1708–40 and 1753–66. Dorcas Gayer Starbuck (1675–1747) married Mary's son Jethro in 1694; she served both as clerk and treasurer of the meeting, holding thirty-eight appointments from 1708 to 1734. Dinah Coffin Starbuck (1674?–1750) married Mary's son Nathaniel Jr. in 1690; she also served as meeting clerk and held seventeen appointments from 1714 to 1740. Mehitable Gardner (d. 1777) was the daughter of Mary Starbuck's daughter Mary Starbuck Gardner; she married Philip Pollard in 1724 and was active in the women's meeting from 1737 to 1765. Hephzibah Starbuck (1700–1764), Dinah and Nathaniel's daughter, married Sylvanus Hussey in 1723 and was active in the meeting from

1726 to 1762. Priscilla Coleman (1713–1797), daughter of Mary Starbuck's daughter Priscilla and John Coleman, married Samuel Bunker in 1731; she received her first appointment in 1758 and became treasurer in 1764. Rachel Norton (d. 1767) married Priscilla Coleman's husband's cousin Joseph Coleman (no marriage date found); she became active in the meeting in 1759 and was appointed clerk in 1764.

36. Byers, *Nation of Nantucket*, 111–13.

37. Ibid., 109.

38. Soderlund, "Women's Authority," 727; see also 745 and passim.

39. The New England Yearly Meeting was given institutional authority over all the local meetings in the region when George Fox visited North America in 1672. See Worrall, *Quakers in the Colonial Northeast*, chap. 4; Leach and Gow, *Quaker Nantucket*, 17–23. According to Byers, "the Quaker regional structure allowed Nantucket Friends the local autonomy they had cherished in their religious affairs since leaving the mainland." Byers's examination of the minutes and other records of the yearly and quarterly meetings indicates that "only a few" Nantucket representatives attended and those did so on an irregular basis to boot; see Byers, *Nation of Nantucket*, 108–9.

40. Frost, *The Quaker Family*, 210–11.

41. Worrall, *Quakers in the Colonial Northeast*, chap. 4; Frost, *The Quaker Family*, chap. 3.

42. WMM, 29 4th month 1713; see also, e.g., 4th month 1714, 7th month 1714, 1st month 1720, 1st month 1734, and passim, Mss. 52, NHA (dates as in original).

43. Leach and Gow, *Quaker Nantucket*, 56.

44. Byers, *Nation of Nantucket*; Leach and Gow, *Quaker Nantucket*; Starbuck, *Nantucket*; O. Macy, *History of Nantucket*.

45. Leach and Gow, *Quaker Nantucket*, 46, 81–82.

46. See esp. Byers, *Nation of Nantucket*, chap. 8.

47. Crevecoeur, *Letters*, 139–40.

48. Woolman's 1760 visit is mentioned in Byers, *Nation of Nantucket*, 175. Byers cites Amelia Gummere's 1922 edition of the *Journal and Essays of John Woolman*; she mentions Woolman's admiration of Nantucket plainness but does not provide a direct quote. I have been unable to find the original reference itself in any of the several more recently published editions of Woolman's journals or other writings.

49. Lancaster, *Architecture of Historic Nantucket*; Carpenter and Carpenter, *Decorative Arts and Crafts of Nantucket*, 7–8 and passim.

50. Crevecoeur, *Letters*, 139–40 (emphasis in original).

51. Ibid., 158–59. See also O. Macy, *History of Nantucket*, 52–53.

52. Soderlund, "Women's Authority," 745, 727.

53. 1800 Nantucket census, Mss. 122, Book 1, Folder 2, NHA. Singulate mean age at marriage was calculated according to the procedure described by John Hajnal in "European Marriage Patterns in Perspective." I am deeply indebted to research assistants Andrea Foroughi and David Ryden and especially to colleague and premier historical demographer Steven Ruggles for their coding and analysis, respectively, of this rare census.

54. Wells, "Quaker Marriage Patterns" and *Population of the British Colonies*, esp. 83–88; Jensen, *Loosening the Bonds*, 11–13, 171.

55. Crevecoeur, *Letters*, 141, 144; Byers, "Fertility Transition in a New England Commercial Center" and *Nation of Nantucket*, 90–92, 181–82; see also Vickers, "Nantucket Whalemen," 285.

56. Frost, *The Quaker Family*, 150–83; Levy, *Quakers and the American Family*, 133–35.

57. Crevecoeur, *Letters*, 158.

58. For a usefully concise account of Puritan love and sexuality, see Seidman, *Romantic Longings*, esp. 13–16. Puritan minister Benjamin Wadsworth is quoted on 15. Seidman draws mainly on Edmund Morgan's landmark study of New England Puritan family life, *The Puritan Family*.

59. Phillips, "Life of Catharine Phillips," 11:220.

60. Leach and Gow, *Quaker Nantucket*, 41; Byers, *Nation of Nantucket*, 105, 173.

61. Judith Folger to Peter Folger, 6 June 1768, NA.

62. WMM, 7 and 25 10th month 1738, Mss. 52, NHA (dates as in original).

63. Crevecoeur, *Letters*, 158; O. Macy, *History of Nantucket*, 52, 213.

64. Mack, *Visionary Women*, 222–25.

65. Peleg Folger journal, 28 March 1752, 10 August 1754, NA.

66. Peleg Folger's poem appears in O. Macy, *History of Nantucket*, 279–81. For more information on Folger, see Philbrick, *Away Off Shore*, 111–21.

67. Mack, "Gender and Spirituality," 57.

68. Quoted in Starbuck, *Nantucket*, 522.

69. Mack, *Visionary Women*, 226; Dunn, "Women of Light" and "Latest Light on Women of Light"; Soderlund, "Women's Authority"; Levy, *Quakers and the American Family*, chap. 6.

70. Woolman, *Journal and Major Essays*, 113–15.

71. Frost, *The Quaker Family*, 64.

72. Quoted in Levy, *Quakers and the American Family*, 13.

73. Byers, *Nation of Nantucket*, 176–85; see also Forbes, "Quaker Tribalism," 145–73.

74. Crevecoeur, *Letters*, 160.

75. Folger, quoted in Crosby, *Nantucket in Print*, 97. Obed Macy also observed of colonial Nantucketers: "they were so closely connected by birth, similarity of pursuits, and habits of intimacy, that in some respects they appeared and conducted as one family" (*History of Nantucket*, 66).

76. Abigail Gardner Drew's age and marital and maternal status were reconstructed from the published Nantucket vital records; from the Barney Genealogical Records, Mss. 186, NHA; and from the collection notes for "Drew, Abigail Gardner Diary and Reminiscences," Octavo Vols. "D," AAS.

77. Abigail Gardner Drew diary, entries dated 3, 15, 16, 20, and 25 January 1799; see also entries for 2, 4, 5, 13, 19, 22, 23, and 26 January 1799; "Drew, Abigail Gardner Diary and Reminiscences," Octavo Vols. "D," AAS.

78. See also the Nantucketer Francis Joy's will, probated 11 September 1823, which specifies in great detail (down to the closets) which areas of his house were to be used by his surviving widow Elizabeth and which were to be used by his wid-

owed daughter-in-law Judith and her four children. Joy's will and house division is described in Carpenter and Carpenter, *Decorative Arts and Crafts of Nantucket*, 37–39. Carpenter and Carpenter, who have extensively studied Nantucket probate records and household inventories, suggest that this kind of division was common.

79. Nylander, *Our Own Snug Fireside*; Ryan, *Cradle of the Middle Class*, 145–55.

80. Information and quotation from Abigail Gardner Drew to Marcy Pinkham, 10 December 1801, Pinkham-Gardner Family Correspondence, 1794–1826, Misc. Mss. Boxes "P," AAS; and Starbuck, *American Whale Fishery*.

81. An eighteenth- and nineteenth-century "female world of love and ritual" was first identified and described by historian Smith-Rosenberg in her important article of that title (see Smith-Rosenberg, *Disorderly Conduct*, 53–76). Other historians have built upon Smith-Rosenberg's insights; see esp. Ryan, *Cradle of the Middle Class*, and Kerber, "Separate Spheres, Female Worlds, Woman's Place."

82. Abigail Gardner Drew to Marcy Pinkham, 10 December 1801, Pinkham-Gardner Family Correspondence, 1794–1826, Misc. Mss. Boxes "P," AAS; and Starbuck, *American Whale Fishery*.

83. Kezia Coffin Fanning diary, 21 December 1790, Mss. 2, Folder 4, NHA; Crevecoeur, *Letters*, 142; Edmund Gardner to Charles Gardner, 14 August 1807, Mss. 87, Folder 28, NHA.

84. The exact proportions from the 1800 census are as follows: 43.5 percent of married women and 19.2 percent of married men aged 20 to 24 years are listed as living with their parents; 30.8 percent of married men aged 20 to 24 years are listed as residing in their wives' parents' households. Among all households, 16.4 percent contain married children of any age; 29.04 percent are extended, and 16.04 percent include non-kin. 1800 Nantucket Census, Mss. 122, Book 1, Folder 2, NHA. For the definitive discussion of comparable census information from England and elsewhere in colonial America, see Ruggles, *Prolonged Connections*, 5 (Figure 1.1), chap. 1, and passim. Wells provides further corroboration in his study of the population in colonial British America: he found that on Nantucket in 1764 there were 1.46 families per household, a number exceeded by only one other Massachusetts county (Cumberland, at 1.82). In most of the counties, the number of families per household ranged from 1.11 to 1.38. See Wells, *Population of the British Colonies*, 86–96.

85. A number of early New England community studies have documented these concepts and demographic patterns. See, most recently, Ulrich's *Midwife's Tale* and Vickers's *Farmers and Fishermen*.

86. Crevecoeur famously described an unusual habit on Nantucket, possibly another adaptation to men's absences: "A singular custom prevails here among the women, at which I was greatly surprised and am really at a loss how to account for. . . . They have adopted these many years the Asiatic custom of taking a dose of opium every morning, and so deeply rooted is it that they would be at a loss how to live without this indulgence" (*Letters*, 160). Literary scholar Nathaniel Philbrick suggests that if Crevecoeur's observations were indeed true, Nantucket women's dependence on opium can be interpreted as a consequence of the whalefishery's stressful impact on home life (Philbrick, "Nantucket Sequence in Crevecoeur's

Letters"). Opium was certainly available in colonial Anglo-America and was not infrequently prescribed by physicians in a number of commonplace pharmaceutical preparations, such as paregoric elixir (also known as Camphorated Tincture of Opium), anodyne balsam, and newer forms of laudanum. Nantucket did not yet have its own newspaper, but advertisements in newspapers elsewhere in the colonies also offered opium mixtures in the form of patent medicines like Bateman's Drops, Daffy's Elixir, and Godfrey's Cordial. According to Trudy Eden, medicinal and recreational opium use may well have increased in America during the eighteenth century, provoking resistance from some types of healers and condemnation of "opium eaters" by advocates of temperance and moderation (Eden, "Turks and the American Woman"). Many thanks to Dr. Eden for supplying me with a copy of her paper. One of the healers critical of the medicinal use of opium (along with other innovative and intrusive medical practices by local physicians) was the Maine midwife Martha Ballard, as documented by Ulrich in *Midwife's Tale*, 254–61. Unfortunately, no evidence has yet been uncovered that can conclusively document Crevecoeur's observations on Nantucket. It seems unlikely that the sober Quaker matrons would have turned to opium (or any drug) for other than strictly medical reasons, but we cannot completely rule out a local idiosyncrasy. For now, we just don't know.

87. Almy diary, October 1797, PEM.

88. Compare to the diaries described by Motz, "Folk Expression of Time and Place," and discussed in Culley, *American Women's Autobiography*, esp. the essays by Culley, Taves, and Smith; and S. Smith, *Poetics of Women's Autobiography*.

89. Almy diary, 19 May, 16 September 1798, October 1797, 22 May 1798, PEM.

90. Ibid., 9 September 1798, 9 May 1799, 20 May 1798.

91. Ibid., 12 December 1797, 5 April 1798, 18 March 1799, 5, 23, 14 January 1798, 6 September 1798, 19 May 1798.

92. Ibid., 24 January 1798.

93. Quotation taken from Titus 2 in the 1795 edition of *The Holy Bible*, published in Trenton, N.J., by Isaac Collins. A copy of this edition was originally owned by the Greenwich (R.I.) Monthly Meeting and is now held at the Rhode Island Historical Society. It may well be the same edition read by Lydia Almy.

94. Almy diary, 31 January, November, 1 April, 5 August, 9 May 1798, PEM.

95. Ibid., ca. November 1797, 24 January 1798.

96. Ibid., 31 January, November, 1 April, 5 August, 9 May 1798.

97. Melville, *Moby-Dick*, 86, 87.

98. Ibid., 107.

CHAPTER THREE

1. Phebe Folger, Commonplace Book, Nantucket 1797, fMS Typ 245, Department of Printing and Graphic Arts, Houghton Library, Harvard University. For a brief description and discussion of the manuscript, see Seeler, "Phebe Folger's Watercolors," 13–18.

2. On commonplace books and American women's reading and writing in this period, see Blecki and Wulf, *Milcah Martha Moore's Book*, esp. the two introductory essays, and Thornton, *Handwriting in America*, chap. 1. On the typicality of these sorts of themes and this sort of literature in the reading of educated young ladies of the period, see also Bushman, *Refinement of America*; Shields, *Civil Tongues and Polite Letters*; Armstrong, *Desire and Domestic Fiction*; Davidson, *Revolution and the Word*.

3. Starbuck, *Nantucket*, 535.

4. W. F. Macy, "Hon. Walter Folger Jr.," 47–55; Crosby, *Nantucket in Print*, 95.

5. Bushman, *Refinement of America*; Shields, *Civil Tongues and Polite Letters*; Breen, "Narratives of Commercial Life" and "Empire of Goods"; Carson, Hoffman, and Albert, *Of Consuming Interests*.

6. Byers, *Nation of Nantucket*, 260.

7. Worrall, *Quakers in the Colonial Northeast*; Marietta, *Reformation of American Quakerism*; Pestana, *Quakers and Baptists in Colonial Massachusetts*.

8. Phillips, "Life of Catharine Phillips," 11:220.

9. Sarah Barney to Mary Pemberton, 19 3d month 1763, cited in Byers, *Nation of Nantucket*, 185.

10. WMM, 26 11th month 1759, Mss. 52, NHA.

11. Ibid., 27 8th month 1764.

12. Leach and Gow, *Quaker Nantucket*, 92, 102.

13. The case of Abigail Myrick is recorded in WMM, 29 8th month 1763; that of Eunice Guinn in WMM, 12th month 1765, 27 1st month, 26 5th month 1766, Mss. 52, NHA.

14. MMM, 21 12th month 1770, Mss. 52, NHA; Rhode Island Quarterly Meeting, 4 11th month 1771, New England Yearly Meeting collection, Rhode Island Historical Society, Providence, R.I. See also Byers, *Nation of Nantucket*, 180. At this time, the Nantucket Monthly Meeting was attached to the regional Rhode Island Quarterly Meeting in the Society of Friends' pyramidal organization.

15. Byers, *Nation of Nantucket*, 193.

16. Leach and Gow, *Quaker Nantucket*, 105, 107.

17. Byers, *Nation of Nantucket*, 186–88; Leach and Gow, *Quaker Nantucket*, 85–92.

18. Phillips, "Life of Catharine Phillips," 11:220 (emphasis added).

19. George Churchman, Journal, entry dated 24th day, 6th month, 1781, 4:57, Quaker Collection, Haverford College, Haverford, Pa.

20. Dell, "Quakerism on Nantucket," 21.

21. Byers, *Nation of Nantucket*, 185.

22. Numbers computed by Byers, *Nation of Nantucket*, 260–66; see also Marietta, *Reformation of American Quakerism*, esp. chaps. 11 and 12; Pestana, *Quakers and Baptists in Colonial Massachusetts*, 176–86; Worrall, *Quakers in the Colonial Northeast*, 88–91.

23. Numbers compiled from the Nantucket Quaker records, MMM and WMM, Mss. 52, Vols. 2 and 8, respectively, NHA.

24. Quoted in Byers, *Nation of Nantucket*, 265; Leach and Gow, *Quaker Nantucket*, 97–108.

25. Byers, *Nation of Nantucket*, 266.

26. In his thorough study of the Quaker reform movement in Pennsylvania from 1748 to 1783, Marietta argues that the Revolutionary War actually benefited the re- formers, since in peacetime "Friends prospered, became proud of their ability to regulate or control their lives, and forgot that there had ever been a time of adver- sity in their collective past. . . . It seemed that God did not speak loudly enough in peacetime to awaken them. War was better. The din of it broke through even their impaired faculties and caused them to question their presumptions. . . . The war was also as effective a form of discipline as any Friends could have devised. Without an innovation in Quaker codes or administration, the wheat was resifted and the chaff removed" (*Reformation of American Quakerism*, 252).

27. My account of Nantucket's Revolution is primarily indebted to Byers, *Nation of Nantucket*, esp. 201–28. I also draw upon Stackpole, *Nantucket in the American Revo- lution;* Starbuck, *Nantucket*, 176–260; O. Macy, *History of Nantucket*, 81–122; Rotch, *Memorandum;* and the Kezia Coffin Fanning diary, 1775–1800, Mss. 2, Folder 4, NHA.

28. Quoted in Leach and Gow, *Quaker Nantucket*, 119.

29. Described in and quoted from Byers, *Nation of Nantucket*, 208–9.

30. Memorial from the Selectmen of the Town of Sherburn . . . to the Massachusetts General Court, 14 July 1775, quoted in Starbuck, *Nantucket*, 184–85.

31. Kezia Coffin Fanning diary, entries dated 23 and 24 May 1775, Mss. 2, Folder 4, NHA.

32. Ibid., entry dated 1 December 1775; see also, e.g., entries dated 10 March, 23 April 1776.

33. Quoted in Byers, *Nation of Nantucket*, 217.

34. Quotation from O. Macy, *History of Nantucket*, 112.

35. Ibid., 99, 122–24, 89, 113–15.

36. Byers, *Nation of Nantucket*, 229–33; Stephen Higginson to John Adams, 1785, quoted in ibid., 230; Bjork, quoted in ibid., 233.

37. Crevecoeur, *Letters*, 145–47, quotation on 145.

38. Byers, *Nation of Nantucket*, 231–45; McDevitt, *House of Rotch*, chaps. 7–9; Philbrick, *Away Off Shore*, 135–42; Stackpole, *Whales and Destiny*, esp. chaps. 3, 4, 16. The term "peripheral suppliers" is from Philbrick, 136.

39. Labaree et al., *America and the Sea*, chaps. 5 and 6; see also Byers, *Nation of Nan- tucket*, 248; and Jehle, *From Brant Point to the Boca Tigris*.

40. O. Macy, *History of Nantucket*, 140.

41. Byers, *Nation of Nantucket*, 265, 298; Leach and Gow, *Quaker Nantucket*, 147–60.

42. Byers, *Nation of Nantucket*, 253–56.

43. O. Macy, *History of Nantucket*, 140.

44. Byers, *Nation of Nantucket*, esp. 102–21, 153–58, 171–88, 192–99. Woolman's 1760 visit is mentioned in Byers on 175.

45. Leach and Gow, *Quaker Nantucket*, 124–26, quotation on 126.

46. George Churchman, Journal, entry dated 22nd day, 6th month, 1781, 4:51, Quaker Collection, Haverford College, Haverford, Penn. I am indebted to Lucy Simler for supplying this quotation.

47. Described but not quoted directly in Leach and Gow, *Quaker Nantucket*, 101.

48. Kezia Coffin Fanning diary, entry dated 19 January 1777, Mss. 2, Folder 4, NHA.

49. Brock and Clark's inventories are listed and described in Carpenter and Carpenter, *Decorative Arts and Crafts of Nantucket*, 27–32.

50. Ibid., 8.

51. Franklin, "Letter to Kezia Coffin."

52. WMM, 18 9th month 1773; MMM, 29 10th month 1774, Mss. 52, NHA.

53. MMM, 29 3d month 1773, 27 10th month 1777, Mss. 52, NHA.

54. Marietta, *Reformation of American Quakerism*, 22–23.

55. For examples, see MMM, 26 11th month 1770, 25 3d month 1771, and every monthly meeting in 1773 except February; and WMM, 26 7th month, 30 8th month, 25 11th month 1773, 28 2d month, 30 5th month 1774; all in Mss. 52, NHA.

56. Kezia Coffin Fanning diary, entry dated 19 January 1776, Mss. 2, Folder 4, NHA.

57. For examples, see MMM, 29 3d month 1773, 28 3d month, 25 4th month, 30 5th month 1774, 2 8th month, 25 9th month 1775; and WMM, 30 8th month 1773, 30 5th month, 26 12th month 1774, 25 3d month, 27 5th month 1776; all in Mss. 52, NHA.

58. Quoted in Levenduski, *Peculiar Power*, 46–47.

59. James Barker, "Account of the thoughts and religious meditations of his wife, Sarah [Coffin] Barker, during her confinement," 30 November 1804–14 December 1804, Nantucket, Mass., in Barker Journal, Mss. 64, Series B, Subseries 12, ODHS.

60. Ibid.

61. Marietta found a parallel pattern of gender differentiation in charges and discipline among Pennsylvania Quakers; see Marietta, *Reformation of American Quakerism*, esp. 27–31.

62. Assessment is based on analysis of the Nantucket Men's and Women's Monthly Meeting minutes for the 1770s: MMM Book 2 (1708–72) and WMM Book 10 (1708–87), Mss. 52, NHA.

63. George Churchman, Journal, entry dated 27th day, 6th month, 1781, 4:59–60, Quaker Collection, Haverford College, Haverford, Penn.

64. See Laqueur, *Making Sex*, esp. chaps. 5 and 6; Poovey, *The Proper Lady and the Woman Writer*, chap. 1; Bloch, "Untangling the Roots of Modern Sex Roles" and "American Feminine Ideals in Transition."

65. WMM, Mss. 52, Vol. 8, NHA. This paralleled the Pennsylvania situation; see Marietta, *Reformation of American Quakerism*, for analysis of types of infractions and disciplines.

66. Kezia Coffin Fanning diary, entry dated 13 January 1777, Mss. 2, Folder 4, NHA; record of her disownment for marrying out in the WMM, 28 April 1777, Mss. 52, Vol. 8, NHA.

67. Byers, *Nation of Nantucket*, 264.

68. Routh, "Memoir of Martha Routh," 12:463.

69. Fliegelman, *Prodigals and Pilgrims.* See also Smith, "Parental Power and Marriage Patterns"; Norton, *Liberty's Daughters*, 228–38.

70. Starbuck, *Nantucket*, 628–29.

71. R. D. Brown, *Knowledge Is Power*, esp. chap. 5. See also Gilmore, *Reading Becomes a Necessity of Life*, 18–27, 114–34, and passim.

72. My understanding of the multiple American revolutions of the Age of Revolution, especially the cultural and gender implications, is particularly (but not exclusively) indebted to the scholarship of Ruth Bloch, T. H. Breen, Richard Bushman, Cathy Davidson, Jay Fliegelman, Rhys Isaac, Linda Kerber, Jan Lewis, Mary Beth Norton, David Shields, Carroll Smith-Rosenberg, and Gordon Wood.

73. Davidson, *Revolution and the Word*; see also Shields, *Civil Tongues and Polite Letters*; Armstrong, *Desire and Domestic Fiction*.

74. Bloch, in her essay "Religion, Literary Sentimentalism, and Popular Revolutionary Ideology" (319–20), describes the widespread criticisms of sentimental fiction by clergy, which parallel Sarah Barker's exhortations.

75. The other possible author was born Eunice Barnard; she was disowned by the Nantucket women's meeting in February of 1774 for "keeping company with a man not under the care of Friends." Her intentions to marry William Swain were recorded on 30 December 1773. They had four children by 1777. Given the earliest date in the journal of 1776 and the last of 1788, it would make her a young married mother in her twenties and early thirties when she wrote the journal, if she were the author. Internal evidence suggests she was not, though: some of the poetry and the letters imply that the author is not married, and one page contains the signature of George Hussey (possibly the uncle of Eunice Swain Hussey's husband James, whom she married in 1786, and possibly the George Hussey who owned the brig *Lark* mentioned in the manuscript). Also, according to the notes in the Eliza Barney Genealogical Records, Eunice Barnard Swain moved with her family of origin to New Garden, N.C., in 1774, though the record for her husband, William Swain, states that he took his family to Easton, N.Y., sometime later—in either event, it seems as though she probably left the island.

76. Bloch, "Religion, Literary Sentimentalism, and Popular Revolutionary Ideology" 315–17.

77. Eunice Swain, Journal/Poetry, 1776–1788, NA.

78. Karen Lystra found that this sort of exclusive passion shared by two lovers was the standard ideal of white, middle-class love in Victorian America, though she does not trace its roots to eighteenth-century Romanticism or revolutionary politics. See Lystra, *Searching the Heart*.

79. The critical literature on Romanticism is vast and contested. I found accessible entry points in Ward, *Romantic Literature from 1790 to 1830*, and Mellor, *Romanticism and Gender*.

80. Some historians call this the beginnings of "secularization," sometimes identified as part of "modernization"; see, for instance, R. D. Brown, *Modernization*, and Saum, *Popular Mood of Pre-Civil War America*.

81. Abigail Gardner Drew, Diary and Reminiscences, Octavo vols. "D"; and letter from Abigail Gardner Drew to Marcy Pinkham, 10 December 1801, in the Pinkham-Gardner Family Correspondence, 1794–1826, Misc. Mss. Boxes "P," AAS.

82. The Index to Crew Lists in the Melville Room of the NBFPL contains entries for Alexander, Ebenezer, George, Gershom, and James Drew on New Bedford and Fairhaven vessels from 1808 to 1824.

83. Vital and genealogical records consulted: *Vital Records of Nantucket*; Barney Gene-

alogical Records, Mss. 186, NHA; William C. Folger's genealogical notes, Mss. 118, Book 8, NHA. Also consulted were Nantucket probate records, Book 5 (1804–15), for inventory of estate of Gershom Drew Sr. His son, Nabby's husband, is appointed one of two administrators of his father's estate and is identified as a mariner. There is no probate record for Gershom Jr.

84. On the new concept of home and on the emergence of the culture of domesticity in the late-eighteenth- and early-nineteenth-century Atlantic world more generally, see Davidoff and Hall, *Family Fortunes*. For an earlier description of the American version, see Cott, *Bonds of Womanhood*. The literature on domesticity in the nineteenth century (with which it is usually associated) is voluminous and is discussed in Chapter 6.

85. Lewis, "Republican Wife," 693.

86. Bloch, "Religion, Literary Sentimentalism, and Popular Revolutionary Ideology," 315–317 (quotations), 329.

87. My understanding of this has been influenced by, among other works, Brownstein, *Becoming a Heroine*; Radway, *Reading the Romance*; and Sicherman, "Sense and Sensibility."

88. Fliegelman, *Prodigals and Pilgrims*, 129. See also Bloch, "Gendered Meanings of Virtue in Revolutionary America" and "Religion, Literary Sentimentalism, and Popular Revolutionary Ideology."

89. Phebe Coleman to Samuel Coleman, 9 February 1800, Mss. 107, Folder 17, NHA.

90. According to the *Nantucket Vital Records* and the Barney Genealogical Records (Mss. 186, 2:152, NHA), Phebe and Samuel Coleman had three daughters born on Nantucket: Eliza, born in 1800; Lydia, born in 1802; and Phebe, born in 1805. They appear to have had two additional daughters after moving to Hudson in New York state, Laura and Matilda, though the records do not give the birthdates.

91. Phebe Coleman to Samuel Coleman, 19 September 1808, Mss. 107, Folder 17, NHA.

92. See the Records of WMM, 1787–1813, Mss. 52, Book 11, NHA, under the date 3 August 1809, for Samuel Coleman's request.

93. Phebe Folger Coleman to "Honoured Parents," 22 July 1810, Mss. 118, Folder 49, NHA. Samuel died in 1825, leaving behind Phebe and, in the final count, five daughters. After his death, Phebe continued, with characteristic energy and enterprise, operating a grist mill. In 1829, she wrote from the New York countryside to her famous Nantucket brother Walter Jr., "I have made a little improvement here this spring. I have got another run of stones in the mill . . . we have been so crowded with custom all winter that we have not been able to grind our own as fast as we could have sold the flour while it commanded a good price." Phebe Coleman to Walter Folger, Esq., 5 July 1829, Mss. 107, Folder 17, NHA. At least two of her daughters returned to the whaling region of southeastern Massachusetts, though not to Nantucket itself: one married a man from New Bedford, the other a man from Fairhaven, right across the Acushnet River. Phebe too returned in the end; she seems to have spent the end of her long life with her Fairhaven daughter, at whose home she died in 1857. Information about Phebe Folger Coleman's later life is drawn from a 1946 letter from great-granddaughter Laura H. D. Saun-

derson to Mr. Philip Hofer, a collector who bought the commonplace book from Saunderson in 1946 and then donated it (and the letter) to Harvard University's Houghton Library.

94. Crevecoeur, *Letters*, 145–47, quotation on 145.

CHAPTER FOUR

1. Hart, *Miriam Coffin*, title page.
2. Ibid., 3 (emphasis in original).
3. Ibid., 173–74, 317.
4. The vast literature on this topic has been powerfully synthesized and summarized in Sellers, *Market Revolution*. In terms of its gender dimensions, I have been most influenced by Ryan, *Cradle of the Middle Class*; Smith-Rosenberg, *Disorderly Conduct*; Sklar, *Catharine Beecher*; Lebsock, *Free Women of Petersburg*; Davidoff and Hall, *Family Fortunes*; Boydston, *Home and Work*; Stanley, *From Bondage to Contract*.
5. L. B. Ellis, *History of New Bedford*, 59, 64; Crapo, *Centennial in New Bedford*; McDevitt, *House of Rotch*, 136–56; D. Ricketson, *History of New Bedford*.
6. Morison, *Maritime History of Massachusetts*, 30–32; Labaree et al., *America and the Sea*, 110–59; L. B. Ellis, *History of New Bedford*, 98–117.
7. Morison, *Maritime History of Massachusetts*, 184, 96; Labaree et al., *America and the Sea*, 179–81.
8. D. Ricketson, *History of New Bedford*, 71–80; L. B. Ellis, *History of New Bedford*, 150, 160–61, 227, 243, 509–31, 609, 717; J. F. Kelley, *History of the Churches of New Bedford*, 11–123; Hurd, *History of Bristol County*, 267. Just across the Acushnet River, the rival town of Fairhaven also grew but did not surpass New Bedford. Quakers dominated New Bedford, but Congregationalists held sway in Fairhaven; political differences between the two centers resulted in an acrimonious separation in 1812, when Fairhaven residents petitioned the state and were awarded independent township status.
9. L. B. Ellis, *History of New Bedford*, 227.
10. Davis, Gallman, and Gleiter, *In Pursuit of Leviathan*, 37–46 and passim; Morison, *Maritime History of Massachusetts*, 317; Labaree et al., *America and the Sea*, 289–92.
11. Denison, *Illustrated New Bedford*, 24.
12. Melville, *Moby-Dick*, 50–51.
13. Llewellyn Howland, *The Middle Road* (1963), quoted in Weinraub and Frank, "Nineteenth-Century New Bedford," 56–58.
14. Melville, *Moby-Dick*, 49. My estimate of 10 percent of men at sea at any one time is based on an analysis of occupational listings in the 1836 and 1852 New Bedford city directories: H. H. Crapo, *New-Bedford Directory and Town Register*, 1836 and 1852.
15. Denison, *Illustrated New Bedford*, 26.
16. Stan Hugill, *Sailortown*, quoted in Weinraub and Frank, "Nineteenth-Century New Bedford," 53.
17. Zephaniah W. Pease, "Historical Address."

18. Labaree et al., *America and the Sea*, chaps. 2 and 3; Chandler, *Visible Hand*, 15, 36–38; Hall, "Family Structure and Economic Organization," 44; Arnold, "Merchants in the Forecastle"; McDevitt, *House of Rotch*.

19. James Manchester's account with Isaac Cory, and letter from Nancy Manchester to Isaac Cory, Westport, 10 March 1823, both in Papers Relating to the Schooner *Polly & Eliza*, Mss. 80, Subgroup 1, Series I, Subseries 26, Folder 5; M. Corey to Isaac Cory, ca. 1800, Mss. 80, Subgroup 1, Series A, ODHS.

20. In addition to serving as agent for the shipowners, Thaddeus speculated heavily in private adventures for himself, his brother, and his in-laws. He also owned a share of a commercial wharf and a store in Fairhaven. See Mss. 24, ODHS; and Pickens Documents, ca. 1811–12, Bristol County Probate Records, Probate Office, Taunton, Mass.

21. Peace Bennett Pickens to Thaddeus Pickens, 26 December 1804, in Mss. 24, ODHS; Administratrix appointment, 1 October 1811, Pickens Documents, Bristol County Probate Office.

22. Chandler, *Visible Hand*, 27, 41; Morison, *Maritime History of Massachusetts*, 231–35, 314, 346–47; Labaree et al., *America and the Sea*, 237–57, 277–320.

23. Hohman, *American Whaleman*, 48–83; Davis, Gallman, and Gleiter, *In Pursuit of Leviathan*, 150–213; Creighton, *Rites and Passages*, 21–23, 28–30, 92; Busch, *Whaling Will Never Do For Me*, 5–13.

24. Hohman, *American Whaleman*, 217–71; Moment, "Business of Whaling"; quotation from Davis, Gallman, and Hutchins, "Risk Sharing, Crew Quality," 23.

25. For more detailed descriptions of the process of whaling, see Hohman, *American Whaleman*; Creighton, *Rites and Passages*; Davis, Gallman, and Gleiter, *In Pursuit of Leviathan*.

26. Hohman, *American Whaleman*, chap. 5; Creighton, *Rites and Passages*, 96–111; Busch, *Whaling Will Never Do for Me*, chap. 2; Glenn, "Naval Reform Campaign."

27. Hohman, *American Whaleman*, 89–105; Creighton, *Rites and Passages*, 41–46; Davis, Gallman, and Gleiter, *In Pursuit of Leviathan*, 190–200.

28. Hohman, *American Whaleman*, 217–71; Moment, "Business of Whaling"; Davis, Gallman, and Gleiter, *In Pursuit of Leviathan*, 297–307.

29. Another agreement guaranteed that both parents "give our free Consent for Nathan H Boomer to Sign the Artecles and go in the Ship [Oscar]," further stipulating that "Wee want him to go to his sisters to board . . . if you and he agrees i Want a few lines as Soon as posseable so that i Can Come and See to his things." Agreement with Jonathan Kenney dated Mattapoisett, 18 November 1854; agreement with Abel and Louisa Boomer dated Fall River, 15 November 1854; Josiah Holmes Papers, Coll. 46, MSM.

30. For a detailed enumeration of the deceits and coercions practiced by the recruiting agents, especially in the midcentury period, see Hohman, *American Whaleman*, 89–105.

31. Jon. W. Ketcham to Swift & Allen, 12 June 1849, Swift & Allen Records, Mss. 5, Subgroup 3, ODHS.

32. See, for example, the correspondence between New York attorneys Beebe & Dona-

hue and agents Charles G. & Henry Coffin regarding the claims of a seaman's father to his son's estate, July 1850 (ship *Columbia* 1846–50 papers); and the letters of Moses Denico of East Wassalboro, Maine, to the Coffins, June–September 1853 (ship *Zenas Coffin* 1848–53 papers); both in Charles G. & Henry Coffin Papers, Mss. 152, NHA. See also, e.g., the correspondence between New Bedford public administrator William W. Crapo and Uriah Miller, June–August 1856; Crapo and Horace Webster, December 1858 and March 1859; and Crapo and J. E. Parker, January and June 1861; all in the records of Swift & Allen, Mss. 5, Subgroup 3, Series F, Subseries 1, Folders 49, 56, 57, 60, ODHS. Also in the Swift & Allen records are powers of attorney certified by the U.S. Vice Consul for Fayal, John P. Dabney, enabling the heirs of deceased Azorean whalemen to settle their accounts with New Bedford agents (Mss. 5, Subgroup 3, Series E, Subseries 9, Folder 1, ODHS). See also the records of the New Bedford Port Society regarding Moses How, pastor of the Seamen's Bethel, on deposit at ODHS. Finally, see the copies of the letters of John F. Tucker, Vice Consul of Portugal in New Bedford, to the Acting Consul of Portugal in New York, April and May 1867, in the back of the logbook for the ship *Hibernia* (ca. 1865–69), NBFPL.

33. Charles Wallich to Thomas Knowles & Co., Hoboken N.J., n.d., Knowles Family Business Records, Mss. 55, Subgroup 2, Series Q, Subseries 7, Folder 1, ODHS. Although the evidence is not clear, it is probable that his son, Andrew Wallich, had died on the voyage and that Charles Wallich was trying to recover what was due Andrew at the time of the latter's death.

34. John J. Van Hagen to Charles G. & Henry Coffin, Matteawan, [N.Y.], 1 March 1845, Charles G. & Henry Coffin Papers, Mss. 152, Folder 187, NHA.

35. Creighton, "American Mariners"; and *Rites and Passages*, 49–54, 73–84.

36. Alonzo Taber to William Loring Taber, 13 January 1852, William Loring Taber papers, Mattapoisett Historical Society, Mattapoisett, Mass.; Goodnough quoted in Creighton, *Rites and Passages*, 48.

37. Henry Beetle to Eliza Beetle, 22 August 1845, Beetle Family Papers, Henry Beetle Hough Collection, PPL; George Bowman to Elizabeth Marble, 7 November 1870, Marble Family Papers, KWM.

38. Melville, *Moby-Dick*, 51.

39. Leonard S. Gifford to Lucy Roberts, 30 November 1851, Mss. 98, Subgroup 1, Series A, Folder 1, ODHS.

40. Davis, Gallman, and Hutchins, "Risk Sharing, Crew Quality," 26.

41. Leonard S. Gifford to Lucy Roberts, 15 November 1853, Mss. 98, Subgroup 1, Series A, Folder 2, ODHS.

42. Rotundo, "Body and Soul." See also Stanley, *From Bondage to Contract*, for an insightful discussion of how nineteenth-century men linked their own freedom and the perquisites of manhood to their ability to marry and control their wives' labor.

43. Samuel Braley, "Journal Kept on Board Ship *Arab*," 29 November 1851, 25 May, 27 October 1850, Logbook 258, KWM (emphasis in original).

44. Charles Peirce to Eliza T. Peirce, 27 May 1870, December 1871, 29 March 1874, Charles Peirce Papers, Mss. B85-41.1. ODHS (emphasis in original).

45. Cf. Rubin, "Traffic in Women."

46. Matthew Howland to Philip Howland, 18 March 1856, Philip Howland Family Papers, KWM (emphasis in original).

47. Philip Howland to Thomas Knowles, 29 September 1866, Knowles Family Business Records, Mss. 55, ODHS.

48. George Richmond to Leonard S. Gifford, 19 June 1854, Mss. 98, Subgroup 1, Series A, Folder 2, ODHS; and Leonard S. Gifford to George Richmond, 14 October 1854, VFM 1066, MSM.

49. George Richmond to Leonard Gifford, 19 June 1854, Mss. 98, Subgroup 1, Series A, Folder 2, ODHS (emphasis in original).

50. Leonard S. Gifford to George Richmond, 19 October 1854, VFM 1066, MSM.

51. Eliza Ann Codd to Charles G. & Henry Coffin, October 1846, November 1847, Mss. 152, Folder 174, NHA. Information on birth of child from *Vital Records of Nantucket:* Mary Eliza Codd born to Eliza Ann and John, 10 March 1847.

52. Sophia Brown to Charles G. and Henry Coffin, Nantucket, ca. 1854; Sophia Brown to James Macy [clerk to Charles G. & Henry Coffin], Nantucket, 21 November 1854; both in Mss. 152, Folder 178, NHA.

53. Sarah E. Church to Thomas Knowles & Co., 8 July 1868, Mss. 55, Subgroup 2, Series Q, Subseries 7, Folder 1, ODHS.

54. The Oakman draw bill is quoted in Israel Hatch to Mrs. Rebecca R. Oakman, 10 April 1853, Thomas R. Oakman Correspondence, Mss. 56, Series O, Subseries 2, ODHS. In the early Navy, seamen who were married could leave with the Navy agent draw bills that allotted one-half their pay to their wives. See McKee, "Fantasies of Mutiny and Murder."

55. Hannah Ashley diary, 3 February, 2 June, 3 August, 5 October 1864, and list of payments in back, private collection, Acushnet, Mass.

56. William Troy account with Swift & Allen and the bark *Harvest*, 1847–50, Mss. 5, Subgroup 3, Series C, Subseries 1, Vol. 1, ODHS; "Your affectionate wife" to Orlando H. Houston, 21 October 1855, CC.

57. The weighing of these kinds of concerns against the employers' dependence on their crews was reflected in Captain Smalley's assessment of his second mate, when Smalley wrote the owners: "I think it is a safe thing to advance his due ... Mr Freeman is a good man & whaleman and I hope will continue the voyage ... he has some 60 or 80 dollars due him which I hope you will advance should his parents need it." Orrick Smalley to Thomas Knowles, 30 April 1862, Mss. 55, Subgroup 2, Series C, Subseries 5, Folder 1, ODHS.

58. For a fuller analysis, see Norling, "Ahab's Wife."

59. Mary T. Barnard to Charles G. & Henry Coffin, Nantucket December 1849; Phebe B. Cottle to Charles G. & Henry Coffin, Nantucket, 9 April 1844; Mss. 152, Folders 7 and 15, NHA.

60. Emeline Parsons to William C. Parsons, 8 May 1848, CC; Sylvia Leonard to John Leonard, undated [ca. 1857], private collection, New Bedford, Mass.; see also Harriet Allen diary, 1 January, 24 March, 20 July, 13 August, 14 September 1863, Logbook 401-A, vol. 1, KWM.

61. In her feminist revision of Levi-Strauss's notion of the exchange of women as the

basis of kinship relations, the anthropologist Gayle Rubin argues that "as long as the relations specify that men exchange women, it is men who are the beneficiaries of the product of such exchanges—social organization." Rubin, "Traffic in Women," 174.

62. Henry Beetle to Eliza Beetle, 2 October 1851, 10 September 1854, Beetle Family Papers, Henry Beetle Hough Collection, PPL.

63. Caroline Gifford to Charles Gifford, 19 January 1870, 21 August 1867, Mss. 56, Series G, Subseries 7, Folder 2, ODHS.

64. Power of attorney granted to Charles Tucker by Philip Howland, to "act, transact, and do any and all business during my absence as fully and perfectly as I could do," dated 16 June 1855, power to "cease and be void on the return of the ship Golconda for her proposed voyage," Philip Howland Family Papers, KWM.

65. Harriet Allen diary, 31 March 1863, Logbook 401-A, vol. 1, KWM.

66. Sylvia Leonard to John Leonard, 13 November 1854, private collection, New Bedford, Mass.

67. Henry H. Crapo, "Memorandum Book of Tax Delinquents," ca. 1838–40, NBFPL.

68. Moment, "Business of Whaling."

69. Mrs. Eliza Lewis to Wilcox & Richmond, Nantucket, n.d. [ca. 1854], VFM 1066, MSM.

70. Morison, *Maritime History of Massachusetts*, 158; Hohman, *American Whaleman*, 87–88.

71. For a general description of the development of the U.S. postal system, see Fuller, *American Mail*; and John, "Managing the Mails."

72. William Loring Taber to Susan Taber, 9 December 1852, 25 February 1853, William Loring Taber Correspondence, Mattapoisett Historical Society, Mattapoisett, Mass.

73. Mrs. Charles G. Clarke to Charles G. & Henry Coffin, Pawtucket, 30 May 1849, Mss. 152, Folder 15, NHA.

74. Mrs. J. E. Chase to Swift & Allen, East Limington, 12 June 1862, Mss. 5, Subgroup 3, Series F, Subseries 1, Folder 65, ODHS.

75. "Lady Whalers," *Whaleman's Shipping List and Merchant's Transcript* [New Bedford], 1 February 1853, 2.

76. Robert Greaves to Mrs. Cornelius Marchant, 2 May 1857, MV F. No. 225, DCHS.

77. Philip Howland to Patience Howland, 17 August 1860, 13 February 1862, Philip Howland Family Papers, KWM.

78. Charles H. Peirce to Eliza Peirce, 24 October 1859, 17 February 1862, Mss. B85-41.1, ODHS.

79. William Ashley to Hannah Ashley, 23 September 1863?; Hannah Ashley diary, 28 June 1864; both in private collection, Acushnet, Mass.; Amelia Keen to William Keen, 30 October 1862, Misc. whaling mss., NBFPL.

80. William Loring Taber to Susan Taber, 7 January, 6 February 1853, William Loring Taber correspondence, Mattapoisett Historical Society, Mattapoisett, Mass.

81. William Loring Taber to Susan Taber, 6 February, 15, 13 July 1853, ibid.

82. Phebe C. Sisson to Daniel H. Sisson, 29 July 1848, CC.

83. As Steven Stowe has observed, "letters often were the very substance of relation-

ships otherwise strained by distance, gender differences, or emotion. Such letters existed as a bond and a commentary on the bond." Stowe, *Intimacy and Power*, 4.

84. Harriet Allen diary, 15–24 May 1865, Logbook 401-A, Vol. 2, KWM.

85. Ruth Barker Post to Captain Francis Post, 26 January 1851, quoted in Darden, *My Dear Husband*, 49.

86. Samuel Braley, "Journal Kept on Board Ship *Arab*, 21 December 1850, 12 August 1851, 8 November 1850, Logbook 258, KWM.

87. Norling, "Ahab's Wife," 87.

88. Charles Peirce to Eliza Peirce, 16 March 1863, 17 February 1862, Charles Peirce papers, Mss. B85-41.1, ODHS.

89. Quoted in Creighton, "American Mariners," 9.

90. Samuel Braley, "Journal Kept on Board Ship *Arab*, 21 December 1850 and 23–24 November 1851, Logbook 258, KWM. See discussion of the disciplinary episode in Creighton, *Rites and Passages*, 105.

91. Boydston, *Home and Work*, 142–63.

92. Thompson, "Time, Work-Discipline, and Industrial Capitalism"; Gutman, "Work, Culture, and Society."

93. Jared Gardner to Harriet Gardner, 3 June 1840, Gardner Family Papers, AAS.

94. Dublin, *Transforming Women's Work*.

95. Ruth Grinnell to James Sowle, 3 February 1850, Mss. 56, Series S, Subseries 24, ODHS.

96. "Sister Sally" to Horatio Wood, 9 April (no year but ca. 1861, according to information on the bark *Mattapoisett* in Starbuck, *American Whale Fishery*, 578–79); Perry Lawton to George J. A. Allen, 30 July 1844; both in CC.

97. Harriet Allen diary, 11 March 1863, Logbook 401-A, Vol. 1, KWM.

98. For examples of women's businesses, see occasional advertisements in the local newspapers such as that for Mrs. Cottu's Confectionery at No. 43 Purchase St., New Bedford, on the front page of the *New Bedford Daily Mercury*, 1 April 1837; the 1852 *New Bedford City Directory*, which identifies the occupations of employed women, including five female milliners, three nurses, five dressmakers, three seamstresses and one "tailoress," six boardinghouse keepers, three laundresses, one "fancy box maker," a matron of the Mariner's Home, and a matron of the Orphan's Home (NBFPL). See also the records of R. G. Dun & Company reporting on the creditworthiness of New Bedford and Nantucket proprietors and business people, both male and female, in Baker Library, Harvard University, Boston, and Maloney, "Women in Maritime America."

99. Dexter, *Career Women of America*; Weeks, "Women of Nantucket."

100. For examples of women being charged with prostitution, theft, and illegally purveying liquor, see the New-Bedford City Watch, Daily Record Book, 1 June 1848–24 March 1850, NBFPL; and descriptions of the "Ark" riots, when mobs twice torched a notorious brothel, in L. B. Ellis, *History of New Bedford*, 246–54; Rodman, *Diary*, 37–40; Pease, "Historical Address," ca. 1930, NBFPL. See also the reference to the cases reported in Sanger, *History of Prostitution*, quoted in Maloney, "Doxies at Dockside."

101. Eliza Stanton account in Cook & Snow Ledger Book 1855–70, NBFPL; New Bed-

ford Port Society annual reports for years 1837 and 1838, on deposit at ODHS; Sarah A. Cory to George G. Cory, 14 August 1853, CC. See also Hannah Ashley diary, Ashley Family Papers, private collection, Acushnet, Mass.

102. Sylvia Sowle to Robert P. Sowle, 8 November 1854, CC. Julia Fisk's diary makes note of many preparations for summer boarders on 27 April, and 3, 6, 13–21, 25, 27 May 1859. On 30 May she wrote, "we are now all ready," though she did not receive her first boarder until 29 June 1859. After a slow start, the summer season picked up; by 30 July they had 66 guests. Sigourney's stay at Fisk's is mentioned in L. H. Sigourney to Captain Silas Fisk, 29 August 1855, Silas W. Fisk papers, VFM 1007, MSM.

103. Hannah Blackmer to Seth Blackmer, 18 November 1864, quoted in Darden, *My Dear Husband*, 16–18; for Mary Ann Braley of Rochester, Mass., see Pamela A. Miller, untitled, unpublished biography of Samuel Braley, ca. 1982, chap. 3, p. 3, typescript on deposit at KWM; Caroline Gifford to Charles Gifford, 30 June, 29 September 1865, 23 January, 5 July, 30 September 1866, 21 August 1867, 4 January 1868, Mss. 56, Subgroup G, Subseries 7, ODHS; Caroline Omey to Philip H. Omey, 5 April 1861, CC; Hannah Ashley diary entries, e.g., 21–22, 24, 26–29 January 1864, Ashley Family Papers, private collection, Acushnet, Mass.

104. Abby Grinnell to Stephen Grinnell, 6 September 1845, CC.

105. Sarah Wilkey to Alden Wilkey, 7 September 1845, CC.

106. Harriet Allen diary, 6 and 15 June, 10 and 14 February 1863, Logbook 401-A, KWM.

107. Susan Snow Gifford diary, 15 November 1859, privately owned, on deposit at ODHS.

108. Logue, "Whaling Industry and Fertility Decline" and "Case for Birth Control before 1850."

109. Alexander Hathaway to Henry Brightman, 27 May 1843, CC; Starbuck, *American Whale Fishery*, 390. On this voyage, the whaling brig *Solon* sailed out of the port of Sippican, to the east of New Bedford.

110. Ryan, *Empire of the Mother*; Bloch, "American Feminine Ideals"; Theriot, *Mothers and Daughters*, 17–39.

111. [Selina?] J. Coffin to George Coffin, 2 November 1858, CC.

112. Caroline Gifford to Charles Gifford, 30 September 1866, 27 January, 1 September 1867, Mss. 56, Series G, Subseries 7, ODHS.

113. Betsey King to James King Jr., 10 February 1850, CC.

114. Myra Weeks to William Weeks, 10 July 1842, CC.

115. Caroline Gifford to Charles Gifford, 30 September 1866, 4 January 1868, 16 May, 7 June 1866, Mss. 56, Series G, Subseries 7, ODHS.

116. Term borrowed from Ryan, *Empire of the Mother*.

117. Boydston, *Home and Work*, 142–63; Folbre and Abel, "Women's Work and Women's Households"; Bennholdt-Thomsen, "Towards a Theory."

118. Charles Peirce to Eliza Peirce, 16 March 1863, Charles Peirce Papers, Mss. B85-41.1, ODHS (emphasis in original).

119. William A. Ashley to Hannah Crapo Ashley, 23 September ca. 1863, Ashley Family Papers, private collection, Acushnet, Mass.

120. Henry Beetle to Eliza Beetle, 25 and 29 April, 18 September, 1 October 1846, 5 March 1847, Beetle Family Papers, Henry Beetle Hough Collection, PPL.

121. I am indebted to Paul Clemens for pointing this out. See Keyssar, "Widowhood."

122. As the anthropologist Rayna Rapp argues, "It is through their concept of family that people are recruited to the material relations of households. Because people accept the meaningfulness of family, they enter into relations of production, reproduction, and consumption with one another." Rapp, Ross, and Bridenthal, "Examining Family History," 234.

CHAPTER FIVE

1. Ruth A. Grinnell to James M. Sowle, 3 February 1850, Mss. 56, Series S, Subseries 24, ODHS. Dates and details of the *Harbinger's* voyage are taken from Starbuck, *American Whale Fishery*, 456–57.

2. This still influential and important interpretation was, of course, most famously proposed by the pioneering American women's historian Carroll Smith-Rosenberg in her paradigm-shifting article, "The Female World of Love and Ritual," in *Disorderly Conduct*, 53–76. It was further developed by Mary Ryan in *Cradle of the Middle Class.*

3. Information on voyages and Sowle's whaling career was derived from Starbuck, *American Whale Fishery;* Index to Crew Lists, NBFPL; *Vital Records of Westport, Mass.;* and Sowle-Grinnell wedding certificate, dated 9 August 1851, Mss. 56, Series S, Subseries 24, ODHS.

4. This was a common term for the wives left behind by whalemen who rounded Cape Horn and went into the Pacific; see, e.g., Captain Leonard Gifford's use of the term "Cape Horn widoes" in his letter to his fiancée, Lucy Ann Roberts, 4 December 1855, Mss. 98, Subgroup 1, Series A, Folder 3, ODHS.

5. E. K. Rothman, *Hands and Hearts;* Lystra, *Searching the Heart;* Stowe, *Intimacy and Power.*

6. My understanding of how people craft their identities is influenced by Erving Goffman's dramaturgical model, in which, he suggests, identity is constructed continuously through interactions with others in publicly performed "presentations of self." Goffman, *Presentation of Self.* See also Gleason, "Identifying Identity"; Heller, Sosna, and Wellbery, *Reconstructing Individualism* (especially the essays by Davis, Chodorow, Hacking, Gilligan, and Nussbaum); Taylor, *Sources of the Self;* LeVine, *Culture, Behavior, and Personality;* D'Andrade, "Cultural Meaning Systems"; Geertz, *Interpretation of Cultures;* Marsh, "Identity"; J. P. Butler, *Gender Trouble;* Rosaldo, "Toward an Anthropology of Self and Feeling"; and several of the essays in Hoffman, Sobel, and Teute, *Through a Glass Darkly.*

7. Ryan, *Cradle of the Middle Class,* chap. 4; Rotundo, *American Manhood;* Lystra, *Searching the Heart,* chap. 5.

8. Lines penciled, in a different hand, on the back of the 21 October 1838 letter Jane Russell sent to Roland Russell, Mss. 172, Folder 5, NHA. I am assuming these

were Roland's notes or a draft of the letter in which he responded to Jane's request for advice.

9. Hiram Coffin to Betsey M. Coffin, 5 May 1823, Mss. 150, Folder 33, NHA.

10. Seth Pinkham to Mary Pinkham, 14 April 1841, Mss. 302, Folder 1, NHA.

11. Seth Blackmer to Hannah Blackmer, 10 October 1864, private collection.

12. Melville, *Moby-Dick*, 93.

13. Bratt, "Reorientation of American Protestantism," 78. On the shift from revivalism to domesticity, see also Ryan, *Cradle of the Middle Class;* McDannell, *The Christian Home;* Halttunen, *Confidence Men and Painted Women;* Rabinowitz, *Spiritual Self.* According to historian Karen Lystra, in Victorian America, romantic love did not challenge Christianity but rather "absorbed its basic functions, used its basic language, and retained its basic structure and world view. The 'Romantic Self' became a most powerful God and romantic love became the new salvation alongside Judeo-Christian concepts of God and theology." Lystra, *Searching the Heart,* 257.

14. On the fear of deception that pervaded antebellum sentimental culture, see Halttunen, *Confidence Men and Painted Women.*

15. Oil from the sperm whale was the most valuable type. Vessels would stay out until they had filled their holds with barrels of oil at least once. The number of barrels is significant, then, not only as a measure of success but also as a marker of how soon a vessel might be returning home.

16. Lystra, *Searching the Heart,* 190–91.

17. Jane Russell to Roland Russell, Nantucket, 21 October 1838, Mss. 172, Folder 5, NHA.

18. Ibid.; Roland Russell's notes on verso. See note 8 above.

19. E. K. Rothman, *Hands and Hearts;* quotations on 23, 122. Note that Rothman uses the term "sexual" to connote all physical expressions of intimacy, including those not involving intercourse. See also D'Emilio and Freedman, *Intimate Matters,* 42–84.

20. In addition to E. K. Rothman, *Hands and Hearts,* and D'Emilio and Freedman, *Intimate Matters,* see also Lystra, *Searching the Heart,* and Hansen, *A Very Social Time.*

21. Susan H. Hathaway to George A. Anderson, 15 November 1850, CC.

22. Lydia G. Davenport Diary, 17 October 1855, Mss. 64, Series D, Subseries 4, ODHS. It is not clear to which sister she is referring here.

23. Jared M. Gardner to Harriet M. Gardner, 3 June 1840, Gardner Family Papers, AAS.

24. Elijah Chase to "mother," 10 December 1842, quoted in the Kendall Whaling Museum *KWM Newsletter* 8, no. 1 (Spring 1990): 8.

25. Jane Russell to Roland Russell, Nantucket, 29 July 1837, Mss. 172, Folder 5, NHA.

26. Sarah A. C. Pierce to Elijah H. Chisole, 24 December 1852, CC.

27. Ruth Grinnell to James Sowle, 3 February 1850, Mss. 56, Series S, Subseries 24, ODHS; Sylvia Tucker to John Leonard, 12 July 1852, Leonard Family Papers, private collection, New Bedford, Mass.

28. Ruth Grinnell to James Sowle, 3 February 1850, Mss. 56, Series S, Subseries 24, ODHS; Joan Waterman to Martin Waterman, 13 April 1828, Coll. 141, MSM.

29. Susan Cromwell to Peter Cromwell, 26 July 1854, Peter Cromwell Papers, Box 96B, MVHS.

30. Charles B. Babcock to Henry Babcock, 28 September 1845, CC.

31. According to Partridge (*Penguin Dictionary of Historical Slang*, 332), in early-nineteenth-century slang, "monthly flowers" meant a woman's menstrual flow.

32. William Davol to Edward Davol, 14 May 1847, CC.

33. E. K. Rothman, *Hands and Hearts*, 49, 51.

34. "D. A." to [brother] George G. A. Allen, 31 July 1844, CC.

35. See Ulrich, *Midwife's Tale*; also Nylander, *Our Own Snug Fireside*.

36. Susan Snow Gifford diary, 15 November 1859, private collection, on deposit at ODHS.

37. Ibid.

38. Ibid., 17 November 1859.

39. Ibid., 15 May, 20 September 1860.

40. Julia Fisk diary, 2, 5, 7, 18 February, 6 March 1859, VFM 1007, MSM.

41. Motz, "Folk Expression," 146.

42. Of diaries kept by mariners' wives in the whaling region during their husbands' absences, two that I located are early, dating from the turn of the nineteenth century: those of Lydia Hill Almy and Abigail Gardner Drew. Seven more are from the mid-nineteenth century: those of Harriet Allen, Hannah Ashley, Hannah Burgess, Julia Fisk, Harriet Gifford, Susan Gifford, and Annie Ricketson. I also examined five additional midcentury women's diaries from the local region (those of Sarah West Bunker, Lydia Davenport, Satira Connor Allen, Martha J. Dimon, and Eliza Cushman Weeks) as well as the diary of Rachel Hurd Putnam of Manchester, N.H., kept while her merchant captain husband was at sea. See the Appendix for archival locations and dates. See Chapter 6 for a discussion of the twenty women I studied who went to sea with their captain husbands.

43. H. B. Crossman to Arunak Crossman, 3 October 1858; Sarah Coggeshall to Bradford Coggeshall, 3 May 1858; both in CC.

44. In *Searching the Heart*, her study of Victorian love letters, Karen Lystra argues that men and women expressed reciprocal notions of romantic love and intimacy. She claims that midcentury women and men shared a commitment to an ideal of private romantic love between two individuals "that encouraged them to seek reciprocal understanding" and actually required that they "cross gender boundaries by disclosing and sharing what, from the romantic view, was their essence" (9). While acknowledging that "sex-role divisions" were based generally on prescribed, separate spheres, she argues that the "bridge of romantic love" often allowed men and women to develop "intimate understandings of each other" (9). She plays down the point that such interactions occurred in a larger structural context of unequal power relations. Making the implicit assumption that the spheres were complementary mirror images, she argues that the resulting tensions were roughly equivalent, explaining that women and men "were tugging on the same rope but pulling at opposite ends." Expanding on that image, she notes, "What

might be characterized as men's domain by gender right was defined as money, economic success, and worldly achievement, but men were also expected to identify with love, home, and family *in relation to women*. While woman's domain by gender right was defined as love, home, and family, women were also supposed to identify with money, economic success, and achievement *in relation to men*" (138, emphasis in original).

45. Jared Gardner to Harriet Gardner, 3 June 1840, Gardner Family Papers, AAS.

46. Samuel Braley, "Journal kept on Board Ship *Arab*," 30 January 1850, Logbook 258, KWM.

47. Stowe, *Intimacy and Power*, 4. See also Thornton, *Handwriting in America*, chap. 2.

48. Ann Burgess to Paul Burgess, 8 April 1829, Mss. 94, Subgroup 2, Series A, Folder 1, ODHS. For examples of duplicate letters, see William Loring Taber to Susan Taber, 15 April and 15 July 1853, William Loring Taber papers, Mattapoisett Historical Society, Mattapoisett, Mass.

49. Sylvia Leonard to John Leonard, 22 July 1855, Leonard Family Papers, private collection, New Bedford, Mass.

50. Ezra Goodnough diary, 23 March 1847, quoted in Creighton, "American Mariners," 25.

51. Susan H. Hathaway to George A. Anderson, 15 November 1850, CC; George Bowman and Marshall Keith quoted in Creighton, "American Mariners," 28; Ruth Barker Post to Francis Post, 26 January 1851, quoted in Darden, *My Dear Husband*, 49. See also Creighton, *Rites and Passages*, 200.

52. Newhall, *History of Photography*, 11–49; Darrah, *Cartes de Visite*, 1–25.

53. Charles Peirce to Eliza Peirce, 17 February 1862, Charles Peirce Papers, Mss. B85-41.1, ODHS.

54. Described by Creighton in "American Mariners," based on the diary of Albert Goodwin, ship *Tuscaloosa*, 28 December 1845.

55. Sylvia Leonard to John Leonard, 13 November 1854, 22 July 1855, 30 September 1855, private collection, New Bedford, Mass.

56. Creighton, "American Mariners," 155, song lyrics quoted on 156.

57. On scrimshaw, see Flayderman, *Scrimshaw and Scrimshanders*.

58. Conversation with folklorist and whaling expert Dr. Mary Malloy of the Kendall Whaling Museum and the Sea Education Institute of Woods Hole, Mass., 20 October 1991, Sharon, Mass.

59. Sylvia Leonard to John Leonard, 13 November 1854, Leonard Family Papers, private collection, New Bedford, Mass.

60. Sigourney quoted in Theriot, *Mothers and Daughters*, 26.

61. Sylvia Leonard to John Leonard, 17 May 1857, Leonard Family Papers, private collection, New Bedford, Mass.

62. Harriet Gardner to Jared Gardner, 27 September 1854, Gardner Family Papers, AAS.

63. Selina J. Coffin to George Coffin, 2 November 1858, CC.

64. Caroline Gifford to Charles Gifford, 30 September 1866, 27 January, 1 September 1867, Mss. 56, Series G, Subseries 7, Folder 1, ODHS.

65. Betsey King to James King Jr., 10 February 1850, CC.

66. Sylvia Leonard to John Leonard, 3 July 1856, Leonard Family Papers, private collection, New Bedford, Mass.

67. Sylvia Tucker Leonard to John Leonard, 13 November 1854, 21 February 1855, Leonard Family Papers, private collection, New Bedford, Mass.

68. Samuel Braley, "Journal Kept on Board Ship *Arab*, 22 March 1850, Logbook 258, KWM.

69. Nelson, *New Bedford Fifty Years Ago*, 23.

70. "Perils of the Sea," *Sailor's Magazine* 10, no. 11 (July 1838).

71. On cultural themes defining suffering as part of women's character and fate, see, among others, M. Kelley, *Private Woman, Public Stage* and *Power of Her Sympathy;* the work of Nina Baym, esp. *Novels, Readers, and Reviewers;* Ryan, *Cradle of the Middle Class* and *Empire of the Mother;* and Theriot, *Mothers and Daughters.* Hale and Smith quoted in Theriot, *Mothers and Daughters*, 27. For the British side of things, see Vicinus, *Suffer and Be Still;* and the introduction to Nadel-Klein and Davis, *To Work and To Weep*, esp. the quotation from English poet Charles Kingsley: "Men must work and women must weep" (7).

72. Samuel Braley, "Journal Kept on Board Ship *Arab*, 2 March 1850, Logbook 258, KWM.

73. Eliza Brock's sea journal, loose, undated newspaper clipping inserted close to end of volume; Logbook 126, NHA.

74. "The Mariner's Wife," *Sailor's Magazine* 10, no. 11 (July 1838).

75. Melville, *Moby-Dick*, 52–53.

76. Sylvia Leonard to John Leonard, 29 July 1856, Leonard Family Papers, private collection, New Bedford, Mass.

77. Susan Cromwell to Peter Cromwell, 20 June 1854, Peter Cromwell Papers, Box 96b, MVHS.

78. Halttunen, *Confidence Men and Painted Women*, 126, 130.

79. See, for example, usage by Ann Russell to Roland Russell, 26 July 1842, Mss. 172, Folder 2, NHA. For a discussion of popular attitudes toward death in antebellum America, see Saum, "Death in the Popular Mind," 30–48; and Farrell, *Inventing the American Way of Death.*

80. Keyssar, in "Widowhood in Eighteenth-Century Massachusetts: A Problem in the History of the Family," and Grigg, in "Toward a Theory of Remarriage: A Case Study of Newburyport at the Beginning of the Nineteenth Century," both conclude that eighteenth- and early-nineteenth-century Massachusetts women were much less likely to remarry after being widowed than were men. Grigg found in the port community of Newburyport that half the widowers eventually remarried but only a fifth of the widows did. Farber, in *Guardians of Virtue: Salem Families in 1800*, 138, found a dramatically different pattern in maritime Salem: he argues that captains and captains' wives were almost equally likely to remarry, but that laborers, sailors, and fishermen were less than a third as likely to do so as their wives (9 percent vs. 31 percent).

81. Susan Cromwell to Peter Cromwell, 26 July 54, Peter Cromwell Papers, Box 96B, MVHS.

82. Grigg makes the same argument for widowed mariners in Newburyport; see "Toward a Theory of Remarriage," 204.

83. Philip Howland to Patience Howland, 31 July 1857, Philip Howland Family Papers, KWM.

84. Patience Howland to Philip Howland, 28 June 1854, Philip Howland Family Papers, KWM.

85. Quotations from letters, Ann Russell to Roland Russell, Nantucket, 26 July, 12 September, 3 October, 13 November 1842, Mss. 172, Folder 2, NHA. Other information about Ann and Jane Russell and Thomas Andrews was pieced together from *Nantucket Vital Records;* Barney Genealogical Records, Mss. 186, NHA; and Starbuck, *American Whale Fishery.*

86. Bolles, *Remembering and Forgetting*, xii, xiv. See also Ross and Conway, "Remembering"; and Schuetz, "Homecomer."

87. Charles Peirce to Eliza Peirce, 11 July 1862, 25 December 1863, Charles Peirce Papers, B85-41.1, ODHS.

88. John Chapman to Laura Chapman, 3 October 1888, Mss. 56, Series C, Subseries 8, ODHS; Sylvia Leonard to John Leonard, 21 February 1855, Leonard Family Papers, private collection, New Bedford, Mass.

89. Sarah Howland to Philip Howland, undated fragment ca. 1852, Philip Howland Family Papers, KWM.

90. Sylvia Leonard to John Leonard, 30 August 1857, Leonard Family Papers, private collection, New Bedford, Mass.

91. "Homeward Bound."

92. Thomas Dallman to Selina Hurl Dallman, 23 April 1849, Mss. 56, Series D, Subseries 1, ODHS.

93. William Allen diary, 9 October 1844, described and quoted in Creighton, *Rites and Passages*, 203.

94. For example, see Caroline Gifford's distress at the arrangements about sharing farm tools and barn space made by her husband, (letter, 30 September 1866, Mss. 56, Series G, Subseries 7, ODHS) and Harriet Allen's irritation with her husband's lighthearted and peripatetic behavior during his shoreside visit (diary entries in April and May 1864, Logbook 401-A, KWM).

95. Philip Howland to Patience Howland, 20 November 1861, Philip Howland Family Papers, KWM.

96. Patience Howland to Philip Howland, 18 August 1860, Philip Howland Family Papers, KWM.

97. Samuel Braley, "Journal Kept on Board the Ship *Harrison*," 19 and 25 September 1854, Logbook 261, KWM.

98. Caroline Gifford to Charles Gifford, 23 January 1866; Charles Gifford to Mary A. Gifford, 28 July 1885, Mss. 56, Series G, Subseries 7, ODHS; Bristol County Probate Records, No. 2888, Taunton, Mass.

99. E. K. Rothman, *Hands and Hearts*, 109.

100. Charles Babcock to Henry Babcock, 28 September 1845, CC; Charles Peirce to Eliza Peirce, 13 October 1861, Charles Peirce Papers, Mss. B85-41.1, ODHS;

Samuel Braley, "Journal Kept on Board the Ship *Harrison*," ca. 1854, Logbook 261, KWM. See Creighton's discussion of the mariners' worries in *Rites and Passages*, 179–83.

101. Samuel Braley, "Journal Kept on Board Ship *Arab*," 7 July 1850, 23 June 1853, Logbook 258, KWM.

102. Ezra Goodnough diary, 8 July 1847, quoted in Creighton, "American Mariners," 26.

103. Divorces listed in the Bristol County, Mass., Supreme Judicial Court, Record Book, Vol. 5 (1829–37), Massachusetts State Archives, Boston, Mass.

104. Divorces listed in the Bristol County, Mass., Supreme Judicial Court, Record Book, Vol. 7 (1844–50), Massachusetts State Archives, Boston, Mass.

105. Case of Almira F. Read vs. Daniel H. Read, Supreme Judicial Court of Massachusetts, Bristol Co., Docket Book, Vol. 7 (1844–50), Case No. 123, p. 134 (November 1848).

106. Capstan chantey quoted in Creighton, "American Mariners," 24; Jared Gardner to Harriet Gardner, 3 June 1840, Gardner Family Papers, AAS.

107. Sarah Pierce to Captain Elijah Chisole, 24 December 1852, CC.

108. Nancy A. Childs to John Childs, 6 May 1848, CC.

109. Libby Spooner to Caleb Spooner, 3 December 1858, CC; Sylvia Leonard to John Leonard, 16 May 1856, Leonard Family Papers, private collection, New Bedford, Mass.

110. Sarah Howland to Philip Howland, 26 October 1845, Philip Howland Family Papers, KWM; Rachel Hurd Putnam diary, 24 November 1855, PEM.

111. Caroline Gifford to Charles Gifford, 7 June 1866, and Eleanor Gifford postscript on letter from Caroline Gifford to Charles Gifford, 1 September 1867, both in Mss. 56, Series G, Subseries 7, ODHS; information on David Lewis Gifford was drawn from the David Lewis Gifford Papers, Mss. 56, Series G, Subseries 8, ODHS.

112. Ruth Barker Post to Captain Francis Post, 12 September 1851, quoted in Darden, *My Dear Husband*, 51 (emphasis in original); Lizzie Howes to Abner Howes Jr., 2 October 1854, Hamer Family Papers, Schlesinger Library, Radcliffe Institute, Harvard University, Cambridge, Mass.

113. Myra Weeks to William Weeks, 10 July 1842, CC.

114. William Loring Taber to Susan Taber, 15 July 1853, 20 November 1856, William Loring Taber Papers, Mattapoisett Historical Society, Mattapoisett, Mass.

115. Thomas J. Lee to Henrietta Deblois, Paita, 20 September 1862, Mss. Box 113, John and Henrietta Deblois Papers, Newport Historical Society, Newport, R.I.

116. William A. Ashley to Hannah Ashley, 15 June 1864, 2 September 1864, 23 September [1864?], private collection, Acushnet, Mass.

117. "Sister Sally" to Horatio Wood, 9 April [no year but ca. 1861], CC. For information about captains' attempting to switch maritime trades, see Philip Howland Family Papers, correspondence and papers relating to the bark *Snap Dragon*, ca. 1854, KWM; Leonard Sanford Gifford papers, Mss. 98, Subgroup 1, Series A, Folder 5, and Series B, Subseries 2, Folders 1–2, ODHS. On David Allen's career, see Harriet Allen diary, 7 and 19 April, 28 May 1864, Logbook 401-A, Vol. 1, KWM.

118. Charles Weeks to his (unnamed) wife, 24 November 1829, Mss. coll., KWM.

119. Edward R. Ashley to parents, 1 December 1855, Ashley Family Papers, private collection, Acushnet, Mass.; Adra Catherine Ashley diary, 1857–58, 7 March 1857, Baker Library, Harvard Business School, Cambridge, Mass.

120. Quoted in Creighton, *Rites and Passages*, 203.

121. Eliza Brock sea journal, 1853–56, no page numbering or date, Logbook 136, NHA.

122. "The Sailor's Wife," *Sailor's Magazine* 33, no. 7 (March 1861).

CHAPTER SIX

1. Sarah Howland to Philip Howland, 9 June 1852, 16 August 1851, 7 August 1849, Philip Howland Family Papers, KWM. Time spent together was computed from marriage and death dates in the Vital Records for Dartmouth, Mass., and the Index to Crew Lists, NBFPL.

2. Information about Philip's voyage on the New Bedford whaling bark *Susan*, his first command, was obtained from Starbuck, *American Whale Fishery*, 462–63.

3. Sarah Howland to Philip Howland, 16 August 1851, 25 July 1852, Philip Howland Family Papers, KWM.

4. Vital records show that Sarah died on 10 November 1853. Philip's vessel had returned to New Bedford on 26 July 1853.

5. Dartmouth, Mass., vital records.

6. Sarah Howland to Philip Howland, n.d. (ca. 1852), Philip Howland Family Papers, KWM.

7. Philip Howland to Patience Howland, 13 December 1854, Philip Howland Family Papers, KWM. For information regarding Patience's residential choices, see Patience Howland to Philip Howland, 28 June 1854; also Matthew Howland to Philip Howland, 18 March 1856, Philip Howland Family Papers, KWM. On the arguments between Philip and his employers about allowing Patience to join him at sea, see the correspondence between Philip and the agent Thomas Knowles in Knowles Family Business Records, Mss. 55, Subgroup 2, Series K, Subseries 2 and 3, ODHS.

8. The literature on the "cult," "ideology," "cultural politics," or "discourse" of domesticity and its implications for marriage and family life is legion. See Cott, *Bonds of Womanhood*, esp. chap. 2 and the new preface in the second edition; Ryan, *Empire of the Mother* and *Cradle of the Middle Class;* van de Wetering, "Popular Concept of 'Home'"; McDannell, *The Christian Home;* Nylander, *Our Own Snug Fireside;* Coontz, *Social Origins of Private Life;* Mintz, *Prison of Expectations;* Gillis, *World of Their Own Making.* On the closely related English version of domesticity, see Davidoff and Hall, *Family Fortunes;* see also the useful introduction and many of the essays in Helly and Reverby, *Gendered Domains.*

9. Several of my informants cited this particular aphorism. See, for example, Eliza Brock diary, 28 February 1855, Logbook 136, NHA.

10. Hepsabeth (Russell) Bunker diary, 18 August 1855, Mss. 159, Folder 1, NHA.

11. See the references in note 8 above.

12. Sigourney information was drawn from Bowles, "Lydia H. Sigourney"; quotation from Sigourney's autobiography cited therein on 272.

13. Sigourney, *The Sea and the Sailor*, 151–52.

14. Boston Port Society Board of Managers, *Twentieth Annual Report*, 4–5. On Hale's involvement with this organization, see Finley, *The Lady of Godey's*, 73–80; and Rogers, *Sarah Josepha Hale*, 53–58.

15. See Sewell, "Sarah Josepha Hale," 159–67. Quotation from Hale, *Woman's Record*, 166.

16. Hale, *Harry Guy*.

17. Some of the reform energy unleashed in the Second Great Awakening was aimed at the still notoriously irreligious seamen, whose disruptive presence in the water-front districts of the burgeoning seaports was all the more apparent and intrusive due to expansion in the early national navy and maritime industries. Patterned on British example, the first group specifically aimed at sailors' souls was apparently the Boston Society for the Religious and Moral Improvement of Seamen, founded in 1812. The initial aims were to distribute bibles, hymnbooks, and tracts in waterfront districts and on outgoing ships; advocate Sabbath observance at sea; hire pastors to proselytize to seamen; and provide places for sailors to worship, such as the Mariners' Church in New York, dedicated in 1820. Quickly, though, the reformers began to see a link between sailors' moral and physical well-being, and broadened their efforts accordingly. So, in a number of cities they also began to establish seamen's savings banks and reading rooms, some of which are still in operation today. With considerably less success, they tried to set up employment registry offices and to encourage maritime boardinghouse keepers to run orderly, temperate, and morally sound facilities. See Kverndal, *Seamen's Missions*, 407–536; also Langley, *Social Reform*, 47–67.

18. Truair, *A Call From the Ocean*. This was reprinted widely and included in many of the publications of local port and seamen's friend societies, including the New-Bedford Port Society in its 1832 report.

19. Ibid.; and New-Bedford Port Society, *First Annual Report*, 1831.

20. Wayland, *Claims of Whalemen*.

21. Weiss, "Claims of Seamen."

22. Ibid.

23. For the Boston Mariners' House, see "Benevolence of Females," *Sailor's Magazine* 13, no. 9 (May 1841): 267–69. On New York, see Campbell, "The Sailor's Home," and the American Seamen's Friend Society records, Sailor's Home annual reports, 1838–62, Coll. 158, MSM. For Portsmouth, see the synopsis of the second annual report of the Ladies' Seamen's Friend Society of Portsmouth in *Sailor's Magazine* 9, no. 10 (June 1837): 306–7. For New Bedford, see New-Bedford Port Society for the Moral Improvement of Seamen, *Twenty-second Annual Report* (1852), which describes the generous donation on 17 September 1850 of William Rotch Jr.'s mansion by his daughter, Mrs. Sarah R. Arnold, along with land and sufficient funds to renovate. As described in Chapter 3, William Rotch Jr. (1759–1850) had followed his father and the family enterprise in moving from Nantucket to New Bedford in 1787.

24. Capt. R. Gelston, superintendent of the first and second New York Sailor's Homes, described two mob demonstrations in opposition to the homes in an article in the *Sailor's Magazine* of April 1858. See Gelston, "Reminiscences of Sailors: Early Opposition to the Home," *Sailor's Magazine* 30, no. 8 (April 1858): 232–33. See also the handwritten Sailor's Home Reports, 1838–62, in the records of the American Seamen's Friend Society, Coll. 158, MSM. In his address commemorating the 100th anniversary of the New Bedford Port Society, Zephaniah Pease similarly describes the "vicious" waterfront elements in New Bedford and refers to a retaliatory torching of a church after a brothel was shut down in the late 1820s; see Pease, "Historical Address," NBFPL.

25. On the sanctification, power, and psychological function of the privatized home, see in particular van de Wetering, "The Popular Concept of 'Home.'" For a comparison of the treatment of other problem groups in the same period, see D. J. Rothman, *Discovery of the Asylum.*

26. *Sailor's Magazine* 14, no. 5 (January 1842): 161.

27. See the *Sailor's Magazine* 9, no. 6 (February 1837) and 3, no. 3 (November 1830) for these three examples. Historian Myra Glenn argues that by midcentury, "didactic literature on childrearing used the sailor's life to dramatize the spread of immorality among transient young men." She claims that sailors had special symbolic significance for reformers due to "Jack Tar's transient way of life, as well as his exposure to vice [which] symbolized the moral dangers faced by young men in an increasingly commercial, urban and mobile society." So too, I would suggest, did the representations of sailors' wives and mothers carry symbolic weight, particularly for a female audience. Parallel to the fascination of middle-class, evangelically oriented women with the state of heathen women, expressed through the foreign mission movement, there seems to be a quality of vicarious thrill demonstrated in the dozens of stories, reports, and poems with titles like "Homeward Bound!" "Have You a Mother?" "To My Sailor Boy," "A Sister's Consolation," "The Sailor's Mother," "The Sailor's Wife," and "Baptism of the Sailor's Child." The characters of maritime mothers and wives, especially, embodied in an inherently pathetic way themes of domestic separation, feminine suffering, and the contradictions more generally within domesticity and the concept of separate male and female spheres. See Glenn, "Naval Reform Campaign Against Flogging"; Brumberg, "Zenanas and Girlless Villages." On the themes of domestic suffering and female loss in sentimental literature, see Douglas, *Feminization of American Culture;* Ryan, *Empire of the Mother,* 30–32; and M. Kelley, *Private Woman, Public Stage,* 217–49.

28. [Report of the] Newburyport Female Bethel Society, *Sailor's Magazine* 15, no. 4 (December 1842): 107–8.

29. For an overview of women's reform efforts, see, among others, Ginsberg, *Women and the Work of Benevolence.*

30. A number of historians have suggested that the "women's sphere" was really shaped primarily by men. See, for example, Lebsock, *Free Women of Petersburg;* Boydston, *Home and Work.*

31. Osterud, *Bonds of Community,* 56–57; see 55–85 for general discussion.

32. According to Thomas, *The Town Officer*, 36: "The place where a married man's family resides is generally to be deemed his place of domicil." Both the federal census (after individual enumeration began in 1850) and the New Bedford city directories usually listed the address of a whaleman then at sea as that of his father if he were unmarried and that of his wife if he were married.

33. Elisabeth Taber to John Taber, 2 May 1842, CC.

34. Susan Snow Gifford diary, 2 December 1859, private collection, on deposit at ODHS. It seems clear that Susan was referring to now sharing with her sister Abby the bedroom she once occupied with her husband John. (Since the room was in Susan's parents' house, she probably had originally shared it with Abby before marriage.) In entries addressed to John after his departure, Susan wrote: "*Our room* looked *so* lonesome" (16 November 1859); "Oh John you dont know how I miss you, when I go up in *our* room" (19 November 1859); "Abby came down and staid all night with me last night" (20 November 1859); and "Abby is coming home next week to stay this Winter, and I am *so* glad then I shall not be quite so lonesome" (24 November 1859); emphases in original.

35. Mary T. Smith to Parker Smith, 31 October 1827, quoted in Colby, *For Oil and Buggy Whips*, 39.

36. Hannah Ashley diary, 1863, Ashley Family Papers, private collection, Acushnet, Mass.; Moses Snell to Moses L. Snell, 3 May 1858, CC.

37. Susan Gifford diary, 15 November 1859, private collection, on deposit at ODHS, New Bedford. For information on Lucinda, see Gifford diary entries dated 29 November and 5 December 1859; information on Susan's sister-in-law Sarah is drawn from 1860 federal census, household enumeration for Mattapoisett, Mass.

38. Information on the whaling careers of Gideon, Shubael, and Caleb Spooner was pieced together from the Index to Crew Lists, NBFPL; New Bedford city directories for 1836, 1841, 1845, 1849, 1856, and 1865; and Starbuck, *American Whale Fishery*.

39. I have not yet been able to establish whether any relationship existed between George Clark and Henry Clark, the husband of Sophia's sister Charlotte. The extreme form of endogamy known as "sibling exchange" marriage seem to have been fairly common in the whaling communities, similar to what John Mack Faragher found in the frontier community of Sugar Creek, Illinois. See his *Sugar Creek*, 144–45.

40. Information on Spooner marriages, deaths, and residential patterns was compiled from New Bedford vital records, probate records, and city directories; Index to Crew Lists, NBFPL; 1850 federal census, household enumeration for New Bedford; and the letters from Libby Spooner to Caleb Spooner, 3 December 1858, and from Gideon Spooner to Shubael and Caleb Spooner, 7 December 1858, both in CC. There was probably an additional Spooner sibling, though the record of births does not mention her: New Bedford records show that a Lydia Spooner, "daughter of Caleb," married an Ebenezer Wright in New Bedford in 1842; Gideon mentions "Lydia" in his letter; and Caleb Jr. and Libby named their first daughter, born in 1856, Lydia.

41. See the New Bedford vital records, and New Bedford city directories for 1855 and 1865. Caleb Jr. does not appear in the 1859 city directory.

42. "Missing Vessel," *Whaleman's Shipping List and Merchant's Transcript* [New Bedford], 31 July 1860, 2.

43. Harriet Allen diary, Logbook 401-A, Vol. 1, KWM, Philip Howland Family Papers, KWM; Caroline Gifford letters to her husband Charles, 1865–70, Mss. 56, Series G, Subseries 7, Folders 1–3, ODHS; references to Mary Ann Braley in Samuel Tripp Braley journals, Logbooks 255, 258, 261, KWM; Julia Fisk diary, 1859, VFM 1007, MSM.

44. Laurel Ulrich elegantly describes these relationships as "the fragile threads of ordinary need that bound families together" (*Midwife's Tale*, 100). See also Osterud, *Bonds of Community*, 85.

45. On "tribalism" in colonial and early national New England, see E. Morgan, *The Puritan Family*, 161–86; Forbes, "Quaker Tribalism."

46. Nancy Folbre and Marjorie Abel have described the confusion between normative standards and lived practices in the U.S. census in their article "Women's Work and Women's Households."

47. Cf. Ulrich on female "gadding" in her essay "Housewife and Gadder."

48. Ann Russell to Roland Russell, Nantucket, 3 October 1842, Mss. 172, Folder 2, NHA.

49. For examples of each activity, see Susan S. Gifford diary, 4 December 1859; 15 April, 26 January, 28 May 1860; 19 December 1859; 7 August, 9 April, 20 January, 25 July 1860; 24 November 1859; 13 October, 22 February, 16 June, 19 October 1860; private collection, on deposit at ODHS.

50. Ibid., 15 May, 6 January 1860.

51. Susan's year-long diary begins on the day John left, 15 November 1859. During the first month, 15 November–15 December, Susan recorded entries for all but four days. According to her record of her activities (she may, of course, have omitted some), she went out at least once on twenty-three days. She remained at home for an entire day five times, though on two of those days visitors came in, so Susan interacted just with other members of her household only three days of the entire month. Most of the individuals listed in her diary are by first name only, so it is very difficult to assess how many were related to her by blood or marriage. While I was able to identify six of the women and five of the men as kin, many others were probably related also, given the "tribal" characteristics of the small village of Mattapoisett (including what seems to have been a typically high rate of endogamous marriage). Quotation from diary entries: 15 May 1860 and, addressed directly to John, 15 November 1859.

52. Hannah Ashley diary, 1864, Ashley Family Papers, private collection, Acushnet, Mass. Social interaction patterns were analyzed for the months of January, March, and June.

53. Hannah bore her first and only child, Williams Crapo Ashley, on 8 March 1864. She remained at her in-laws before, during, and after the birth.

54. Harriet Allen diary, 2 January and 17 April–1 May, 1863, Logbook 401-A, Vol. 1, KWM.

55. Nancy A. Childs to John D. Childs, 8 January 1847, CC.

56. Smith-Rosenberg, "Female World of Love and Ritual," in *Disorderly Conduct*, 53–76.

57. See Hansen's study, *A Very Social Time*, for a view that in a number of important respects corroborates mine for many of the same kind of people (even a few of the same individuals) in the same time and place. See also Osterud, *Bonds of Community*.

58. Susan Colt Norton to "Sallie," 13 February 1860, Shubael Hawes Norton and Susan Maria Colt Norton papers, Box 125B, Envelope 22, DCHS.

59. Satira Conner diary, 9 June, 5 July 1857, Logbook 401-B, KWM.

60. Ulrich, "Housewife and Gadder," 31. On nineteenth-century female friendships, see also Cott, *Bonds of Womanhood*; Lasser, " 'Let Us Be Sisters Forever' "; Motz, *True Sisterhood*; and Boylan, "Women in Groups."

61. "Melintha" and Abraham Borden to William C. Albert, ca. August 1844, CC. I am greatly indebted to Dr. Ruth Herndon for doing much of the background research on the Albert and Borden families of Tiverton.

62. Ruth Albert to William C. Albert, 22 and 28 August 1844, CC.

63. On forms and consciousness of sisterhood, see Lasser, " 'Let Us Be Sisters Forever.' "

64. Susan S. Gifford diary, 29 November 1859, private collection, on deposit at ODHS.

65. "H. B. C." to Arunak Crossman, 3 October 1858, CC.

66. Stephen Bailey postscript on letter from Jared Gardner to Harriet Gardner, 2 April 1841, Gardner Family Papers, AAS; Seth Blackmer to Hannah Blackmer, 10 October 1864, private collection.

67. Elisabeth Ann Worth to Gideon Worth, 28 June 1848, CC.

68. Libby Spooner to Caleb Spooner, 3 December 1858, CC.

69. Harriet Allen diary, 15 May 1863, Logbook 401-A, KWM.

70. Libby Spooner to Caleb Spooner, 3 December 1858, CC.

71. Ambrose Bates diary, June and August 1867, quoted in Creighton, "American Mariners," 162–63.

72. Jared Gardner to Harriet Gardner, 3 November 1840, 28 January 1843, Gardner Family Papers, AAS.

73. John A. Chapman to Laura Chapman, 3 October 1888, Mss. 56, Series C, Subseries 8, ODHS.

74. Libby Spooner to Caleb Spooner, 3 December 1858, CC.

75. Ibid.

76. Ibid.

77. Harriet Allen diary, 13 May 1863, Logbook 401-A, Vol. 1, KWM (emphasis in original).

78. Ibid., 16, 17, 21, 24 May, 10 June 1863 (emphasis in original).

79. Ibid., 11, 12 June 1863.

80. Ibid., 8 July, 12 August 1864 (emphasis in original).

81. For a concise definition and description of Victorian sentimentalism, see Douglas, *Feminization of American Culture*, 12, 254–55.

82. Harriet Allen diary, 12 May 1863, Logbook 401-A, Vol. 1, KWM.

83. Ibid., 8 April 1864.

84. Ibid., 28 May 1864 (emphasis in original).

85. Ibid., 2 May 1865 (emphasis in original).

86. The managing owner of both the *Platina* and the *Sea Fox* during David's voyages was the whaling agent Andrew Hicks; the agent of the *Merlin* on her 1868–72 voyage was William Watkins. Starbuck, *American Whale Fishery*, 578, 606, 624.

87. Harriet Allen sea journal, 12 May 1872, Logbook 401, KWM (emphasis in original).

88. Many women's historians have found corroboration in the past for the claim by feminist psychologists that women have a distinctively relational sense of self and understanding of family and community, based on ties with people rather than geographic locations, physical space, or institutions; see, e.g., Theriot, *Mothers and Daughters*. In nineteenth-century domestic fiction written by women, Nina Baym found the widespread portrayal of "home" as "not a space but a system of human relations" (Baym, *Woman's Fiction*, 49). Howland quotation, see note 1.

89. See, e.g., Brewster's reference to a Mrs. Grey met in Lahaina, Mary Brewster diary, 9 October 1846, Logbook 38, MSM.

90. My analysis of the women at sea draws primarily on the shipboard journals of twenty wives: Harriet Allen (1868–72, KWM), Adra C. Ashley (1857–60, Baker Library, Harvard), Mary Brewster (1845–51, MSM; also available in published form), Eliza Brock (1853–56, NHA), Martha Brown (1847–49, published), Azubah Cash (1850–54, NHA), Lucy Crapo (1866–67, ODHS), Julia Fisk (1855–56, 1859–61, MSM), Lucy Gifford (1857–60, ODHS), Mary Lawrence (1856–60, published), Susan McKenzie (1869–72, NBFPL), Elizabeth Morey (1853–55, NHA), Susan Norton (1858–62, MVHS), Annie Ricketson (1871–74, published), Mary Russell (1823–24, NHA), Mary Stark (1855–56, MSM), Mary Stickney (1880, ODHS), Harriet Swain (1852–55, NHA), Clara Whelden (1864–68, ODHS), Eliza Williams (1858–61, published). Published diaries include Mary Brewster, *"She Was a Sister Sailor"*; Martha Brown, *She Went A-Whaling*; Mary Chipman Lawrence, *The Captain's Best Mate*; Annie Holmes Ricketson, *Journal*; and Eliza Williams, "Journal." I also rely on the work (though not necessarily the analysis) of other scholars, especially that of the independent writer and maritime history enthusiast Joan Druett, who has examined every extant diary of a nineteenth-century whaling wife she could locate in both public and private collections from New Zealand to New Bedford—well over a hundred. See Druett, *Petticoat Whalers*, and Brewster, *"She Was a Sister Sailor"* (edited by Druett), as well as several articles cited below. Other scholarship I have drawn upon includes Bonham, "Feminist and Victorian"; Busch, *Whaling Will Never Do For Me*; Creighton, *Rites and Passages*; Springer, "Captain's Wife at Sea."

91. My impressions concur with Joan Druett's; she has concluded that most, though not all, of the Yankee wives were unhappy at sea. See Druett, "Those Female Journals."

92. Susan Norton to "Dear Mother," 6 August 1859; to "Sallie," 13 February 1860;

to "Nannie," 24 July 1859, Shubael Hawes Norton and Susan Maria Colt Norton Papers, Box 125-B, Envelope 22, MVHS.

93. Mary Brewster diary, 31 December 1845, 22 May 1846, 26 December 1845, Logbook 38, MSM.

94. Ibid., 14 December 1845.

95. Ibid., 4 June 1846.

96. *The Friend*, Honolulu, 8 November 1858.

97. "Wives at Sea," *Sailor's Magazine* 30, no. 7 (March 1858): 210. See also Druett, "More Decency and Order."

98. Charles W. Morgan diary, 25 July 1849, Coll. 27, Vol. 3, MSM.

99. Hohman cited in Creighton, *Rites and Passages*, 102.

100. Bonham, "Feminist and Victorian"; Creighton, "American Mariners" and "Fraternity in the American Forecastle."

101. Thomas Knowles & Co. agreement with Philip Howland to command the bark *Mary & Susan*, August 1864, Mss. 55, ODHS.

102. Swift & Allen to Captain Chase, 30 September 1861, Mss. 5, Subgroup 3, Series F, Subseries 2, Vol. 4, ODHS (emphasis in original).

103. Matthew Howland to Captain Joseph Green, New Bedford, 8 August 1860; and Matthew Howland to Grafton Hillman, New Bedford, 7 August 1860; Matthew Howland Collection, 1858–79, Baker Library, Harvard University, Cambridge, Mass.

104. Eliza Williams, "Journal," 7 September 1858.

105. Henrietta Deblois letter-journal, 20 November 1856, Mss. 113, Newport Historical Society, Newport, R.I.

106. Eliza Williams, "Journal," 7 September 1858.

107. Mary Brewster diary, 5 December 1845, Logbook 38, MSM.

108. Julia Fisk diary, 20 April 1856, VFM 1007, MSM.

109. Silas Fisk to Elmer Fisk, 15 October [no year, but probably 1860], VFM 1007, MSM.

110. Martha Brown diary, 27 October 1848, in M. Brown, *She Went A-Whaling*.

111. Mary Brewster diary, 1 October 1847, Logbook 38, MSM.

112. Both quoted in Creighton, *Rites and Passages*, 163.

113. Summarized and quoted in both Creighton, *Rites and Passages*, 166; and Busch, *Whaling Will Never Do for Me*, 153. The mate of the *Nautilus* on its 1870 voyage similarly objected to the captain's wife's observations. He swore at her as she watched the men at work: "Damn you . . . look if you want to" (quoted in Creighton, *Rites and Passages*, 167).

114. Clara Kingman Whelden diary, 6 July 1864, Mss. 56, Series W, Subseries 12, ODHS. She also reported: "Being refreshed from much sleep I felt inclined . . . to laugh when the tin pans moved about, and the cups and saucers took a slide."

115. In this regard, the whalefishery appears to have differed somewhat from merchant shipping. In small coasting vessels, wives or daughters might serve on short local trips as cook or steward to their husbands, fathers, or brothers in a maritime family economy. In the larger, passenger-carrying lines, especially later in

the century and into the twentieth, a few women were employed as stewardesses and paid wages. See Druett and Wallace, *Sailing Circle*; Druett, *Hen Frigates*; and Greenhill and Giffard, *Women Under Sail*.

116. Both quoted in Druett, *Petticoat Whalers*, 41.

117. Mary Lawrence diary, 14 March 1857, in Lawrence, *Captain's Best Mate*; Sarah Smith diary, 21 February 1883, quoted in Busch, *Whaling Will Never Do For Me*, 150; Mary Brewster diary, 1 July 1846, Logbook 38, MSM.

118. Susan McKenzie diary, ca. 1870, in Susan Stimson McKenzie File, NBFPL.

119. Eliza Williams, "Journal," 11 November, 26 December 1858.

120. Mary Brewster diary, 30 June 1846, Logbook 38, MSM; Annie Ricketson diary, 22 and 23 May 1871, in Ricketson, *Journal*.

121. Julia Fisk diary, 30 March 1856, VFM 1007, MSM.

122. Mary Brewster diary, 26 May 1846, Logbook 38, MSM.

123. Mary Hayden Russell letter-journal, 18 November 1823, Mss. 83, NHA.

124. On African American sailors and a racial division of labor in antebellum American maritime industries, see Bolster, *Black Jacks* and " 'To Feel Like a Man.' " On stewards, cooks, cabin boys, and the gendering of labor within whaling, see Creighton, *Rites and Passages*, chap. 7.

125. Mary Lawrence diary, 19 February 1857, in Lawrence, *Captain's Best Mate*.

126. Both the latter were read by Mary Brewster, as recorded in her diary on 18 February 1847 and 26 July 1846, respectively, Logbook 38, MSM.

127. Described in Busch, *Whaling Will Never Do For Me*, 150.

128. Mrs. M. C. Fisher, ca. 1855; Sarah Smith, 3 and 13 May 1883, both quoted in Busch, *Whaling Will Never Do For Me*, 150; Mary Brewster diary, 31 October 1846, Logbook 38, MSM.

129. Eliza Brock diary, e.g., 16 October and 12 November 1853, Logbook 136, NHA; Shubael Norton letter, 2 September 1859, Box 125B, Envelope 22, MVHS.

130. Grimshaw, "New England Missionary Wives, Hawaiian Women, and the 'Cult of True Womanhood.' " For useful discussions of American and European travelers and their ethnocentrism, along with examination of their broader implications for western imperialism, see Pratt, *Imperial Eyes*, and S. Morgan, *Place Matters*.

131. Harriet Allen diary, 21 May 1871, Logbook 401, KWM.

132. See Nantucket fertility studies by Byers, *Nation of Nantucket*, and the conflicting ones by Barbara Logue, "Case for Birth Control before 1850" and "The Whaling Industry and Fertility Decline."

133. Quoted in Busch, *Whaling Will Never Do For Me*, 153.

134. Martha Brown diary, 8 February 1849, in M. Brown, *She Went A-Whaling*.

135. Ibid., 2 March 1848, 29 October 1847, 11 May 1848.

136. Mary Brewster diary, 2 May 1846, Logbook 38, MSM.

137. Martha Brown diary, 9 March 1848, in M. Brown, *She Went A-Whaling*.

138. Shubael Norton letter, 2 September 1859, Box 125B, Envelope 22, MVHS.

139. Mary Lawrence diary, 19 February 1857, in Lawrence, *Captain's Best Mate*.

140. Mary Brewster diary, 26 July 1846, Logbook 38, MSM. Joan Druett identifies the book Brewster cites as written by Sarah Lewis and published initially in 1839; it

was so popular that it went through thirteen editions in ten years. According to Druett, the book defines women as men's spiritual guides and emphasizes the maternal role, generalizing maternal influence to apply to "the poor, the ignorant, the domestic servant" as well as children. See Brewster, *"She Was a Sister Sailor,"* 109.

141. M. Lawrence diary, 22 July 1859, 2 April 1857, in Lawrence, *Captain's Best Mate.*

142. Ibid., 2 January, 22 and 27 April 1857.

143. Creighton, *Rites and Passages,* 92.

144. Elizabeth Stetson diary, quoted in Druett, *Petticoat Whalers,* 169.

145. The story of Charity Norton is related in Whiting and Hough, *Whaling Wives,* 217–18, and repeated in Druett, *Petticoat Whalers,* 168.

146. Martha Brown diary, 1 February 1848, in M. Brown, *She Went A-Whaling.*

147. Many thanks to Alfred Young for suggesting this parallel. See Fox-Genovese, *Within the Plantation Household.*

148. Busch, *Whaling Will Never Do For Me,* 155; Brewster, *"She Was a Sister Sailor,"* 146.

149. Mary Brewster diary, 30 January, 19 February 1847, Logbook 38, MSM (emphasis in original).

150. Ibid., 5 June 1846.

151. Melville, *Moby-Dick,* 114–15.

152. Eliza Williams, "Journal," ca. September 1860.

153. Julia Fisk diary, 5, 7, and 18 February, 6 March, 9 June, 31 May 1859, Silas W. Fisk papers, VFM 1007, MSM.

154. Lydia Hunt Sigourney to Julia Fisk, 6 September 1855, Silas W. Fisk Papers, VFM 1007, MSM.

155. By 1884, the Presbyterian Board of Publication had made this idea the basis for one of their tracts, "A Good Catch; or, Mrs. Emerson's Whaling-Cruise," by Mrs. Helen E. Brown, which was based on the experiences of Mary Chipman Lawrence on the whaler *Addison* in 1856–60. Much of the tract is only thinly fictionalized, except for the main evangelical point: the influence of "Mrs. Emerson" in saving the soul of a reprobate crew member. While her diary makes clear that Mary Lawrence certainly began her voyage with evangelical goals like these in mind, by the end of the voyage its profitability (after poor seasons of whaling) was topmost among her concerns.

156. Julia Fisk diary, 25, 27 and 30 November, 25 December 1859, 1 January 1860, Silas W. Fisk Papers, VFM 1007, MSM.

157. Eliza Brock diary, 16 April 1855, Logbook 136, NHA.

158. Ryan, *Empire of the Mother,* 98, 114.

159. Maritime literary scholar Haskell Springer has written of the whaling and merchant captains' wives' "narrowly limited, simultaneously privileged and deprived lives at sea." He suggests that their story is "one of repeated contradictions": "Freedom from the shore meant confinement at sea; achieving traditional ends required using nontraditional means. . . . While all around them was in motion, they sat; while everyone else worked, they watched. . . . but to say all this is to say no more, really, than that they were, in the ways we see all too clearly now, the second sex." Springer, "The Captain's Wife at Sea," 93, 117.

CONCLUSION

1. Eliza Brock diary, February 1855, Logbook 136, NHA.
2. Eliza Williams, "Journal," 2 February 1860.
3. In addition to the relevant entries in Eliza Brock's diary, see also Joan Druett's account in *Petticoat Whalers*, 109.
4. My sense of this aspect of Victorian gender roles is particularly influenced by Pierre Bourdieu's concept of habitus, as developed in *Outline of a Theory of Practice*; see also the sources cited in the Introduction, note 9.
5. Libby Spooner to Caleb Spooner, 3 December 1858, CC; Susan McKenzie diary, 2 November 1869, Susan Stimson McKenzie File, NBFPL.
6. Springer and Robillard, "Herman Melville," 135.

Cromwell, Peter. Papers, Box 96B

Marchant Family Papers, MV F. No. 225

Norton, Richard E., and Jane Ann Cottle Norton. Correspondence, Box 50B,
Envelope 2

Norton, Shubael Hawes, and Susan Maria Colt Norton. Papers, Box 125B,
Envelope 22

Falmouth, Mass.

Falmouth Historical Society

Gifford Family Collection, Papers of Henry F. Gifford, ca. 1846–1866

Haverford, Penn.

The Quaker Collection, Haverford College

Churchman, George. Journal, 10 vols., 1759–1813

Mattapoisett, Mass.

Mattapoisett Historical Society

Taber, William Loring. Papers

Weeks, Ansel, and Betsy Hiller Weeks. Correspondence

Mystic, Conn.

G. W. Blunt White Library, Mystic Seaport Museum

American Seamen's Friend Society. Records, Coll. 158

Ashbey, Henry. Papers, 1834–1862, Coll. 39

Bates, L. C. Correspondence, VFM 1352

Billings, Noyes & William W. Account Book, 1828–1830, Misc. Vol. 227

Brewster, Mary. Diary, 1845–48, Logbook 38

Church, Walter. Papers, 1864–1869, VFM 1558

Crapo, Lucy Hix. Journal, 1866–1867, Logbook 899

The Day [New London, Conn.]. Newspaper clipping re: Captain Parker
Hempstead Smith, 8 February 1936, George Comer Collection, Coll. 102

Farnsworth, Mary Emma Weaver. "Life Story," Misc. Vols. 155, 156

Fisk, Julia. Diary, 1855–56, 1859–61, VFM 1007

Fisk, Silas W. Papers, VFM 1007

Gates, George W. Collection, 1853–1880, Coll. 153

Holmes, Josiah. Collection, Coll. 46

Hotchkiss, Levi J. Letterbook, 1858–1862, Coll. 89, Vol. 5

Howard, Benjamin B. Account Book, Misc. Vol. 118

Morgan, Charles Waln. Collection, Mss. 27

New Bedford Ship *Hope*. Papers, 1851–1857, VFM 1066

Stark, Mary Rathbun. Letters/Diary 1855–1856, VFM 196

Tripp, Lemuel. Papers, Misc. Vol. 125

Waterman Family Collection, 1797–1869, Coll. 141

Wilcox and Richmond Papers, VFM 1066

Nantucket, Mass.

Nantucket Atheneum, Special Collections

Folger, Judith Burnell. Letter, 1768

Folger, Peleg. Journal, 1751–54

Swain, Eunice. Journal/Poetry, 1776–1788

Wyer, Joseph, and Margaret Wyer. Letters and Misc. Papers, 1791–1804

Nantucket Historical Association, Edouard A. Stackpole Research Center

Anonymous. Diary, ca. 1821–1832, Mss. 28, Book 7

Barney, Eliza. Genealogical Records, Mss. 186, Vols. 1–3

Brock, Eliza Spencer. Sea Journal, 1853–1856, Logbook 136

Bunker, Hepsabeth Russell. Diary, Mss. 159, Folder 1

Bunker, Sarah West. Letters and Pocket-Book Diary, 1850, 1858, Mss. 13, Folders 15–17

Carey, Betsy. Account Book, 1816–1829, Mss. 10, AB 536

Cash, Azubah. Sea Journal, 1850–1853, Logbook 312

Census, Nantucket 1800. Mss. 122, Book 1, Folder 2

"Cent Schools" Clippings and Notes. Vertical Files "C"

Coffin, Charles G. & Henry. Business Papers, Mss. 152

————. Business Papers, Carlisle Collection, Mss. 334

Coffin, Hiram. Letter, Mss. 150, Folder 33

Coffin, John. Account Book, 1786–1820, Mss. 10, AB 518

Coffin, Micajah. Papers, Congdon Collection, Mss. 36

Coffin, Zenas. Store Book, 1806–1827, Mss. 334, Folder 6

Coleman Family Papers, Mss. 107

Fanning, Kezia Coffin. Diary, 1775–1800, Typescript Notes and Extracts, Mss. 2, Folder 4

Folger Family Papers, Mss. 118

Folger, Walter. Account Book, 1764–1810, Mss. 10, AB 150

Folger, William C. Genealogical Notes, Mss. 118, Book 8

Gardner Family Papers, Mss. 87

Joy, Francis. Ledger, 1787–1799, Mss. 10, AB 194

Keeper of Asylum [unidentified]. Journal, 1826–27, Mss. 127, Folder 39

Macy, Caleb. Account Book, Mss 10, AB 99

Macy Family Papers, Mss. 96

Macy Family Papers, Cloyes Collection, Mss. 119

Macy, Judith. Day Book, 1783–1807, Mss. 10, AB 37

Macy, Obed. "Obed Macy's Book: Family Mirror," Mss. 119, Folder 3

Marshall, Pinkham. Family Papers, Brown Collection, Mss. 283

Mitchell, Eliza. Reminiscences, 1894–1896, Mss. 23

Morey, Elizabeth. Sea Journal, 1853–55. Logbook 207

Nantucket Quaker Monthly Meetings. Records, Mss. 51 and 52

Perry Family Papers, Mss. 210

"Petticoat Row" Clippings and Notes. Vertical Files "P"

Pinkham Family Papers, Mss. 302

Poets and Poetry Collection. Mss. 43, Folder 14

Russell, Mary Hayden, and Forman Marshall Mount. Letter-Journals, 1823–1824, Mss. 83

Russell Family Papers, Mss. 172

Starbuck Family Papers. Mss. 144

Swain, Harriet. Sea Journal, 1852–54, Logbook 33

West, Phebe Hussey. Papers and Correspondence, Mss. 13, Folder 14

Winslow Family Papers, Mss. 166

Worth, Helen Barnard Winslow. Diary, 1855–1861, Mss. 39

Wyer Family Papers, Mss. 145

Young Family Papers, Mss. 190, Folder 1

Nantucket Town and County Building

Proprietary Record Books, 4 vols., 1716–1850, Registry of Deeds

Record Book of the Court of General Sessions and the Inferior Court of
 Common Pleas, Vol. 1, 1721–1785; Vol. 2, 1786–1802, Superior Court Office

Nantucket County, Supreme Judicial Court, Record Books, Vol. 1, 1826–1834,
 Superior Court Office

Probate Records, 1706–1815, Probate Office

Selectmen's Journal, Vol. 1, 1784–1795, Superior Court Office

New Bedford, Mass.

New Bedford City Hall, Tax Assessor's Office

Tax Valuations, 1835, 1840, 1846, 1850, 1859, 1865

New Bedford Free Public Library, Special Collections

Brigham, Lincoln. Notary Public Copybook Record, 1845–1857

Church, C. A. Crew and Agents Accounts, MF 89

Church Pamphlets Collection

Cook & Snow Ledger Book, 1855–1870

Crapo, Henry H. "Memorandum Book of Tax Delinquents," ca. 1838–1840

"Deaths Recorded in The New Bedford Mercury 1845–1874," Vols. 1–3

How, Moses. Diaries, 1813–1882

Index to Crew Lists. Card file

"Marriages Recorded in *The New Bedford Mercury* 1845–1874," Vols. 1–3

McKenzie, Susan Stimson. File

Misc. Mss. Collection

Misc. Whaling Mss. Collection

New-Bedford City Watch, Daily Record Book, 1848–1850

New Bedford Imprints Collection

New Bedford Port Society Collection

Overseers of the Poor Collection

Pease, Zephaniah W. "Historical Address," ca. 1930

Potter, Rev. William J. Sermons

Temperance Collection

Tucker & Cummings. Agent and Crew Accounts

Tucker, C. R. Crew Accounts

Tucker, John F., Vice Consul of Portugal in New Bedford. Correspondence,
 1867 (copies), in back of the Logbook for the Ship *Hibernia*, 1865–1869

Wing, J., & W. R. Wing. Day Book, ca. 1853, MF 112

Old Dartmouth Historical Society–New Bedford Whaling Museum Library

Barker, James. Journal, Mss. 64, Series B, Subseries 12

Barlow, Seth. Papers, Mss. 64, Series B, Subseries 16

Bourne, Jonathan, Jr. Business Records, Mss. 18, Series G, Subseries 2

Burgess, Ann and Paul. Papers, Mss. 94, Subgroup 1, Series A and
    Subgroup 2, Series A

Chapman, John A. Letter, 3 October 1888, Mss. 56, Series C, Subseries 8

Cory, Alexander. Papers, Dead Letter Collection, Mss. 80, Subgroup 3,
    Series K, Subseries 1, Folders 1–20

Cory Family Papers, Mss. 80, Subgroups 1 and 3

Crapo, Lucy Ann Hix. Letters, 1878–80, Mss. 56, Series M, Subseries 32

Cummings, Charles Smith, Papers, Mss. 51, Subgroup 6, Series D

Dallman, Thomas. Letters, 1849, Mss. 56, Series D, Subseries 1

Dartmouth, Town of. Records of the Overseers of the Poor, Mss. 53,
    Subgroup 1, Series B, Subseries 1

Davenport, Lydia. Diary, 1853–1868, Mss. 64, Series D, Subseries 4

Delano Family Papers, Mss. B84-36

Gifford, Charles H. Correspondence, Mss. 56, Series G, Subseries 7

Gifford, David Lewis. Papers, Mss. 56, Series G, Subseries 8

Gifford, Leonard S. and Lucy. Papers, Mss. 98, Subgroup 1, Series A and
    Subgroup 2, Series A

Hawes Family Papers, Mss. 11, Subgroups 1 and 2

Hicks, Andrew. Papers, Mss. 105

Howland Family Papers, Mss. 7

Knowles Family Business Records, Mss. 55

Ladies' Branch of the New Bedford Port Society. Archives, on long-term
    deposit

Local History Collection, Mss. 77

Morgan, Charles Waln. Financial Records, Mss. 41, Subgroup 1, Series V

New Bedford Cordage Company. Ledger Book, 1846–1864, Mss. 1

New Bedford Orphan's Home. Uncat. Mss.

New Bedford Port Society. Archives, on long-term deposit

Oakman, Thomas R. Correspondence, Mss. 56, Series O, Subseries 2

Outfitters Association of New Bedford. Record Book 1859–71, Mss 56,
    Series O, Subseries 5, Vol. 1

Peirce, Charles. Papers, Mss. B85-41.1

Pickens Family Papers, Mss. 24

Ricketson, Annie Holmes. Diary, 1865–1866, Logbook 943

Rodman Family Papers, Mss. 4

Russell, William Tallman. Papers, Mss. 6, Series A, C, E

Seabury, Jason. Papers, Mss. 62, Subgroup 6, Series A and B

Seamen's Bethel Registers, on long-term deposit

Sowle, Ruth Grinnell. Letter, Mss. 56, Series S, Subseries 24

Spooner Family Papers, Mss. 64, Series S, Subseries 63

Stickney, Mary J. Diary, 1879–1880, Mss. 95, Subgroup 2, Series A

Swift & Allen Records, Mss. 5, Subgroup 3

Swift, Eliza Perry. Diary, 1865–1869, Mss. 64, Series S, Subseries 82

Weeks, Charles W. Logbook (includes Diary of Eliza Cushman Weeks, 1861–1862), LB88-10, Vol. 15, on long-term loan from Mattapoisett Historical Society

Whelden, Clara Kingman. Letters, Mss. 56, Series W, Subseries 12

Winsor, Zenas, Jr., and Lucia Russell Allen Winsor. Letters, Mss. 56, Series W, Subseries 40; Mss. 80, Series K, Subseries 4

Newport, R.I.

Newport Historical Society

Deblois Family Papers, Library Special Collections

Providence, R.I.

Brown University, John Carter Brown Library

Nicholas Brown & Company Records, 1762–1782

Providence Public Library, Nicholson Whaling Collection

Beetle Family Papers, Henry Beetle Hough Collection

Rhode Island Historical Society

New England Yearly Meeting of Friends Collection

Rochester, Mass.

Tax Assessor's Office, Rochester Town Hall

Tax Valuations, 1855, 1860, 1870, 1880

Salem, Mass.

Phillips Library, Peabody Essex Museum

Almy, Lydia. Diary, 1797–1799, typescript

Putnam, Rachel Hurd. Diary, 1855–56

Sandwich, Mass.

Sandwich Historical Society

Burgess, Hannah Rebecca. Papers and diaries

Sharon, Mass.

Kendall Whaling Museum

Allen, Harriet. Diary, 1863–67, Logbook 401-A

———. Sea Journal, 1868–72, Logbook 401

Braley, Samuel Tripp. "Journal Kept on Board Ship *Arab* of Fairhaven, 1845–49," Logbook 255

———. "Journal Kept on Board Ship *Arab* of Fairhaven, 1850–1853," Logbook 258

———. "Journal Kept on Board the Ship *Harrison* of New Bedford, 1854–1857," Logbook 261

Conner, Satira. Diary, 1854–1859, Logbook 401-B

Howland, Philip. Family Papers

Marble Family Papers

Weeks, Charles. Letter, 24 November 1829

Taunton, Mass.

Bristol County Probate Office

Bristol County Probate Records

Waltham, Mass.

Federal Records Center, National Archives, New England Region

Crew Lists, 1822–1830, Customs Districts of New London and Stonington, Conn.

Washington, D.C.

U.S. Census Office

Seventh Decennial Census of the United States, 1850. "Population Schedules . . . Bristol County, Mass." Microfilm, Rolls 307, 308, 309

Worcester, Mass.

American Antiquarian Society

Drew, Abigail Gardner. Diary and Reminiscences, 1799–1818, Octavo Vols. "D"

Gardner, Jared M. Correspondence, Gardner Family Papers

Pinkham-Gardner Family Correspondence, 1794–1826, Misc. Mss. Boxes "P"

Privately Owned Collections

Acushnet, Mass.

Ashley Family Papers

Chapel Hill, N.C.

Diman, Martha J. Diary, 1841–55

Fairhaven, Mass.

Blackmer, Seth. Correspondence

New Bedford, Mass.

Gifford, Susan Snow. Diary, 1859–60, on long-term deposit at the Old Dartmouth Historical Society, Whaling Museum Library

Leonard, John, and Sylvia Tucker Leonard. Family Papers

Published Primary Sources

Anthony, Joseph R. *Life in New Bedford a Hundred Years Ago*. Edited by Zephaniah Pease. New Bedford: Old Dartmouth Historical Society, 1922.

Blackmer, Seth. Letters. Published in *My Dear Husband: Being a Collection of Heretofore Unpublished Letters of the Whaling Era*, compiled by Genevieve Darden. New Bedford: The Descendants of Whaling Masters, Inc., 1980.

Blackstone, William. *Commentaries on the Laws of England*. Oxford, England: Clarendon, 1765–69.

Boston Port Society. *Twentieth Annual Report of the Boston Port Society for the Year 1848–49*. Boston, 1849.

Brewster, Mary. *"She Was a Sister Sailor": Mary Brewster's Whaling Journals, 1845–1851*. Edited by Joan Druett. Mystic, Conn.: Mystic Seaport Museum, 1992.

Brown, Andrew. *A Sermon, on the Dangers and Duties of the Seafaring Life*. Boston, 1793.

Brown, Martha. *She Went A-Whaling, 1847–49*. Edited by Anne MacKay. Orient, N.Y.: Oysterponds Historical Society, 1993.

Caulkins, Frances Manwaring. *History of New London, Connecticut, from the First Survey of the Coast in 1612 to 1852*. New London, Conn.: the author, 1852.

Chase, Elijah. "Letter to 'mother,' [10 December 1842]." Quoted in Kendall Whaling Museum *KWM Newsletter* 8, no. 1 (Spring 1990): 8.

Crapo, Henry H. *The New-Bedford Directory and Town Register*. New Bedford, 1836, 1841, 1845, 1849, 1856, 1865.

Crapo, William W. *Centennial in New Bedford: Historical Address by William W. Crapo, delivered on the occasion of the celebration in New Bedford of the Fourth of July, 1876; to which are added an account of the celebration and an appendix*. New Bedford: E. Anthony & Sons, 1876.

Crevecoeur, J. Hector St. John de. *Letters From An American Farmer*. Originally published 1782; reprint, New York: Penguin Classics, 1987.

Dall, Caroline. *The College, the Market and the Court*. Boston, 1867.

Denison, Rev. Frederic. *Illustrated New Bedford, Martha's Vineyard, and Nantucket*. Providence: J. A. & R. A. Reid, 1879.

"A Description of Duke's County." *Collections of the Massachusetts Historical Society*, 2d ser., 3 (1815): 38–94.

Flavel, John. *Navigation Spiritualiz'd*. London, 1671.

Folger, Walter, Jr. "A Topographical Description of Nantucket." Originally published 1791. Reprinted in *Nantucket in Print*, edited by Everett U. Crosby, 96–98. Nantucket: Tetaukimmo Press, 1946.

Franklin, Benjamin. "Letter to Kezia Coffin, London, 29 August 1769." Reprinted in *Historic Nantucket* 27:4 (April 1980): 27.

Freeman, James. "Notes on Nantucket." *Collections of the Massachusetts Historical Society*, 2d ser., 3 (August 1807): 19–38.

The Friend [Honolulu, Hawaii], 8 November 1858.

Gulick, Luther. "To My Personal Friends." Ascension Island [Ponape], privately published, 1859. Copy held at Old Dartmouth Historical Society–New Bedford Whaling Museum Library, New Bedford, Mass., Pam BI-524.

Hale, Sarah Josepha. *Harry Guy, the Widow's Son: A Story of the Sea*. Boston: 1848.

———. *Woman's Record, or Sketches of All Distinguished Women from the Creation to A.D. 1854*. Originally published 1855; reprint, New York: Source Book Press, 1970.

Hart, Joseph C. *Miriam Coffin; or, The Whale-fishermen*. Originally published 1834; reprint, New York: MSS Information Corporation, 1969.

Hawes, Mrs. Elizabeth. *The Harp of Accushnet: Poems*. Boston, 1838.

The Holy Bible, containing the Old and New Testaments: Translated out of the Original Tongues: and with the Former Translations Diligently compared and revised. Trenton, N.J., 1795.

"Homeward Bound," *Godey's Ladies' Book* 15 (1838): 71–72.

Howland, Llewellyn. *The Middle Road*. Quoted in "Nineteenth-Century New Bedford," unpublished typescript by William Weinraub and Stuart Frank. Mystic Seaport Museum, G. W. Blunt White Library, ca. 1975.

Kelley, Jesse F. *History of the Churches of New Bedford*. New Bedford, 1869.

Lawrence, Mary Chipman. *The Captain's Best Mate: The Journal of Mary Chipman Lawrence on the Whaler Addison, 1856–60*. Edited by Stanton Gardner. Hanover: University Press of New England, 1966.

Macy, Obed. *The History of Nantucket*, 2d ed. Mansfield, Mass.: Macy & Pratt, 1880.

Mather, Cotton. *The Religious Marriner.* Boston, 1700.

———. *The Sailour's Companion and Counsellour.* Boston, 1709.

Melville, Herman. *Moby-Dick; or, The Whale.* Originally published 1851; reprint, New York: New American Library, 1980.

Nelson, Maud Mendall. *New Bedford Fifty Years Ago: Recollections.* N.p., 1914.

New Bedford Daily Mercury, 1 April 1852.

New-Bedford Port Society for the Moral Improvement of Seamen. *Annual Report* (1st–40th). New Bedford: various printers, 1831–1870.

New York Marine Register: A Standard of Classification of American Vessels. New York: R. C. Root, Anthony & Co., 1858.

Parkman, Ebenezer. *Zebulun Advised.* Newport, 1738.

Phillips, Catharine. "The Life of Catharine Phillips." In *The Friends' Library: Comprising Journals, Doctrinal Treatises, and Other Writings of Members of the Religious Society of Friends*, edited by William Evans and Thomas Evans, 11: 188–287. Philadelphia, 1848.

Ricketson, Annie Holmes. *The Journal of Annie Holmes Ricketson on the Whaleship A. R. Tucker 1871–1874.* Edited by Philip Purrington. New Bedford, Mass.: Old Dartmouth Historical Society, 1958.

Ricketson, Daniel. *The History of New Bedford.* New Bedford, 1858.

Rodman, Samuel. *The Diary of Samuel Rodman, 1821–1859.* Edited by Zephaniah W. Pease. New Bedford: Reynolds Printing Co., 1927.

———. *Samuel Rodman Diary of 1827.* Edited by Bradford Fuller Swan. New Bedford, Mass.: Reynolds Printing, 1935.

Rotch, William. *Memorandum Written in the Eightieth Year of His Age.* N.p., 1916.

Routh, Martha. "Memoir of Martha Routh." In *The Friends' Library: Comprising Journals, Doctrinal Treatises, and Other Writings of Members of the Religious Society of Friends*, edited by William Evans and Thomas Evans, 12:413–77. Philadelphia, 1848.

The Sailor's Magazine and Naval Journal [monthly]. Vols 1–40 (1828–1867). New York: American Seaman's Friend Society.

Sansom, Joseph. "A Description of Nantucket." Originally published in *The Port Folio*, Vol. 5, Philadelphia, 1811. Reprinted in *Nantucket in Print*, edited by Everett U. Crosby, 137–48. Nantucket: Tetaukimmo Press, 1946.

Sigourney, Lydia Hunt. *Poems for the Sea.* Hartford, Conn., 1850.

———. *The Sea and the Sailor*, 4th ed. Hartford, Conn., 1857.

Smith, Thomas. *A Practical Discourse to Sea-faring Men.* Boston, 1771.

Strother, D. H. "A Summer in New England." *Harper's New Monthly Magazine* 21 (1860): 1–19, 442–61, 745–63.

Thomas, Benjamin F. *The Town Officer, a Digest of the Laws of Massachusetts in Relation to the Powers, Duties, and Liabilities of Towns.* Worcester, Mass.: Warren Lazell, 1845.

"A Topographical Description of New Bedford." *Collections of the Massachusetts Historical Society*, 1st ser., 4 (1795): 232–37.

Truair, John. *A Call from the Ocean.* New York, 1826.

United States Census Office. *Seventh Census of the United-States, 1850.* Washington, D.C.: Robert Armstrong, 1853.

———. *Eighth Decennial Census of the United-States, 1860.* Washington, D.C.: Robert Armstrong, 1864.

Wayland, Francis. *The Claims of Whalemen on Christian Benevolence.* New Bedford, 1843.

Weiss, John. "The Claims of Seamen." Boston, 1849.

The Whaleman's Shipping List and Merchant's Transcript [weekly newspaper], New Bedford, 1843–1914. Years consulted: 1843–1870.

Williams, Eliza Azelia. "Journal of a Whaleing Voyage to the Indian and Pacific Oceans, kept on board the Ship Florida, T. W. Williams, Master, Commencing September 7th, 1858." In *One Whaling Family,* edited by Harold Williams, 3–204. Cambridge, Mass.: Riverside, 1964.

Woolman, John. *The Journal and Major Essays of John Woolman.* Edited by Philip J. Moulton. New York: Oxford University Press, 1971.

SECONDARY SOURCES

Albion, Robert G., William A. Baker, and Benjamin W. Labaree. *New England and the Sea.* Mystic, Conn.: Mystic Seaport Museum, 1972.

Allen, Everett S. *Children of the Light: The Rise and Fall of New Bedford Whaling and the Death of the Arctic Fleet.* Boston: Little, Brown, 1973.

Almy, Charles, Jr., and Horace W. Fuller. *The Law of Married Women in Massachusetts.* Boston: George B. Reed, 1878.

Alpern, Stanley B. *Amazons of Black Sparta: The Women Warriors of Dahomey.* New York: New York University Press, 1998.

Armstrong, Nancy. *Desire and Domestic Fiction.* New York: Oxford University Press, 1987.

Arnold, Allan A. "Merchants in the Forecastle: The Private Ventures of New England Mariners." *American Neptune* 41 (July 1981): 165–87.

Bacon, Margaret Hope. *Mothers of Feminism: The Story of Quaker Women in America.* San Francisco: Harper & Row, 1986.

Baker, Margaret. *Folklore of the Sea.* North Pomfret, Vt.: n.p., 1979.

Basch, Norma. "Equity vs. Equality: Emerging Concepts of Women's Political Status in the Age of Jackson." *Journal of the Early Republic* 3 (1983): 297–318.

———. "Invisible Women: The Legal Fiction of Marital Unity in Nineteenth-Century America." *Feminist Studies* 5, no. 2 (Summer 1979): 346–66.

Battick, John. "The Searsport Thirty-Six: Seafaring Wives of a Maine Community in 1880." *American Neptune* 44 (1984): 149–54.

Baym, Nina. *Novels, Readers, and Reviewers: Responses to Fiction in Antebellum America.* Ithaca: Cornell University Press, 1984.

———. *Woman's Fiction: A Guide to Novels by and about Women in America, 1820–1870.* Ithaca, N.Y.: Cornell University Press, 1978.

Bender, Thomas. *Community and Social Change in America*. New Brunswick, N.J.: Rutgers University Press, 1978.

Bennholdt-Thomsen, Veronika. "Towards a Theory of the Sexual Division of Labor." In *Households and the World Economy*, edited by Joan Smith, Immanuel Wallerstein, and Hans-Dieter Evers, 252–71. Beverly Hills, Calif.: Sage, 1984.

Bercaw, Mary K. *Melville's Sources*. Evanston, Ill.: Northwestern University Press, 1987.

Blecki, Catherine La Courreye, and Karin A. Wulf, eds. *Milcah Martha Moore's Book: A Commonplace Book from Revolutionary America*. University Park: Pennsylvania State University Press, 1997.

Blewett, Mary H. *Men, Women, and Work: Class, Gender and Protest in the New England Shoe Industry, 1780–1910*. Urbana: University of Illinois Press, 1988.

Bloch, Ruth H. "American Feminine Ideals in Transition: The Rise of the Moral Mother, 1785–1815." *Feminist Studies* 4 (1978): 101–26.

———. "The Gendered Meanings of Virtue in Revolutionary America." *Signs* 13, no. 1 (Autumn 1987): 37–58.

———. "Religion, Literary Sentimentalism, and Popular Revolutionary Ideology." In *Religion in a Revolutionary Age*, edited by Ronald Hoffman and Peter J. Albert, 308–30. Charlottesville: University Press of Virginia, 1994.

———. "Untangling the Roots of Modern Sex Roles: A Survey of Four Centuries of Change." *Signs* 4 (1978): 237–52.

Blumin, Stuart M. *The Emergence of the Middle Class: Social Experience in the American City, 1760–1900*. Cambridge, U.K.: Cambridge University Press, 1989.

———. "Rip Van Winkle's Grandchildren: Family and Household in the Hudson Valley, 1800–1860." In *Family and Kin in Urban Communities, 1700–1930*, edited by Tamara K. Hareven, 100–121. New York: New Viewpoints, 1977.

Bolles, Edmund Blair. *Remembering and Forgetting: An Inquiry into the Nature of Memory*. New York: Walker, 1988.

Bolster, W. Jeffrey. *Black Jacks: African American Seamen in the Age of Sail*. Cambridge, Mass.: Harvard University Press, 1997.

———. " 'To Feel Like a Man': Black Seamen in the Northern States, 1800–1860," *Journal of American History* 76 (March 1990): 1173–99.

Bonham, Julia C. "Feminist and Victorian: The Paradox of the American Seafaring Woman of the Nineteenth Century." *American Neptune* 37:3 (July 1977): 203–18.

Bourdieu, Pierre. *Outline of a Theory of Practice*. Translated by Richard Nice. Cambridge, U.K.: Cambridge University Press, 1977.

Bowles, Dorothy A. "Lydia H. Sigourney." *Dictionary of Literary Biography*, 73:264–74. Detroit, Mich.: Gale Research, 1988.

Boydston, Jeanne. *Home and Work: Housework, Wages, and the Ideology of Labor in the Early Republic*. Oxford: Oxford University Press, 1990.

———. "To Earn Her Daily Bread: Housework and Antebellum Working-Class Subsistence." *Radical History Review* 35 (1986): 7–25.

Boylan, Anne M. "Women in Groups: An Analysis of Women's Benevolent Organizations in New York and Boston, 1797–1840." *Journal of American History* 71, no. 3 (December 1984): 497–523.

Bratt, James D. "The Reorientation of American Protestantism, 1835–1845." *Church History* 67, no. 1 (March 1998): 52–82.

Breen, T. H. "An Empire of Goods: The Anglicization of Colonial America, 1690–1776." *Journal of British Studies* 25 (October 1986): 467–99.

———. "Narratives of Commercial Life: Consumption, Ideology, and Community on the Eve of the American Revolution." *William & Mary Quarterly* 50, no. 3 (July 1993): 471–501.

Bridges, Amy. "Becoming American: The Working Classes in the United States before the Civil War." In *Working-Class Formation: Nineteenth-Century Patterns in Western Europe and the United States*, edited by Ira Katznelson and Aristide R. Zolberg, 157–96. Princeton: Princeton University Press, 1986.

Brodhead, Richard H. *Cultures of Letters: Scenes of Reading and Writing in Nineteenth-Century America*. Chicago: University of Chicago Press, 1993.

———, ed. *New Essays on Moby-Dick*. New York: Cambridge University Press, 1986.

Brown, Kathleen M. *Good Wives, Nasty Wenches, and Anxious Patriarchs: Gender, Race, and Power in Colonial Virginia*. Chapel Hill: University of North Carolina Press, 1996.

Brown, Richard D. "The Emergence of Urban Society in Rural Massachusetts, 1760–1820." *Journal of American History* 61 (1974): 29–51.

———. *Knowledge is Power: The Diffusion of Information in Early America, 1700–1865*. New York: Oxford University Press, 1989.

———. *Modernization*. New York: 1975.

Brownstein, Rachel M. *Becoming a Heroine: Reading about Women in Novels*. New York: Penguin, 1984.

Brumberg, Joan Jacob. "Zenanas and Girlless Villages: The Ethnology of American Evangelical Women, 1870–1910." *Journal of American History* 69 (September 1982): 347–71.

Busch, Briton Cooper. *"Whaling Will Never Do for Me": The American Whaleman in the Nineteenth Century*. Lexington: University of Kentucky Press, 1994.

Bushman, Richard L. *The Refinement of America: Persons, Houses, Cities*. New York: Vintage, 1992.

Butler, Judith P. *Gender Trouble: Feminism and the Subversion of Identity*. New York: Routledge, 1990.

Butler, Martin Joseph. "J. & W. R. Wing of New Bedford: A Study of the Impact of a Declining Industry upon an American Whaling Agency." Ph.D. diss., Pennsylvania State University, 1973.

Byers, Edward. "Fertility Transition in a New England Commercial Center: Nantucket, Massachusetts, 1680–1840." *Journal of Interdisciplinary History* 13, no. 1 (Summer 1982): 17–40.

———. *The Nation of Nantucket: Society and Politics in an Early American Commercial Center, 1660–1820*. Boston: Northeastern University Press, 1987.

———. "Putting the History Back in Historical Demography: Nantucket Reexamined." *Journal of Interdisciplinary History* 16 (1986): 683–90.

Cadbury, Henry J. "Nantucket and Its Quakers in 1722." *Proceedings of the Nantucket Historical Association* (1946): 18–19.

————. "An Off-islander's Impressions, June 1781." *Proceedings of the Nantucket Historical Association* (1949): 47–50.

Campbell, George Duncan. "The Sailor's Home." *American Neptune* 37, no. 3 (July 1977): 171–84.

Cancian, Francesca M. *Love in America*. Cambridge, U.K.: Cambridge University Press, 1987.

Carpenter, Charles H., Jr., and Mary Grace Carpenter. *The Decorative Arts and Crafts of Nantucket*. New York: Dodd, Mead, 1987.

Carroll, Kenneth L. "Early Quakers and 'Going Naked as a Sign.'" *Quaker History* 67, no. 2 (Autumn 1978): 69–78.

Carson, Cary, Ronald Hoffman, and Peter J. Albert, eds. *Of Consuming Interests: The Style of Life in the Eighteenth Century*. Charlottesville: University Press of Virginia, 1994.

Chambers-Schiller, Lee Virginia. *"Liberty, A Better Husband": Single Women in America: The Generations of 1780–1840*. New Haven: Yale University Press, 1984.

Chandler, Alfred D. *The Visible Hand: The Managerial Revolution in American Business*. Cambridge, Mass.: Belknap, 1977.

Chudacoff, Howard P. "Newlyweds and Family Extension: The First Stages of the Family Cycle in Providence, Rhode Island, 1864–1865 and 1879–1880." In *Family and Population in Nineteenth-Century America*, edited by Tamara K. Hareven and Maris A. Vinovskis, 179–205. Princeton: Princeton University Press, 1978.

Cleary, Patricia A. "'She Merchants' of Colonial America: Women and Commerce on the Eve of the Revolution." Ph.D. diss., Northwestern University, 1989.

Coffin, Louis, ed. *The Coffin Family*. Nantucket: Nantucket Historical Association, 1962.

Colby, Barnard L. *For Oil and Buggy Whips*. Mystic, Conn.: Mystic Seaport Museum, 1990.

Collier, Jane, and Sylvia Yanagisako, eds. *Gender and Kinship: Essays Toward a Unified Analysis*. Stanford: Stanford University Press, 1987.

Conningham, Frederic A. *Currier & Ives Prints: An Illustrated Check List*. Rev. ed. New York: Crown Publishers, 1970.

Coontz, Stephanie. *The Social Origins of Private Life*. London: Verso, 1988.

Cott, Nancy F. *The Bonds of Womanhood: "Woman's Sphere" in New England, 1780–1835*. 2d ed. New Haven: Yale University Press, 1997.

————. "Domesticity." In *A Companion to American Thought*, edited by Richard Wightman Fox and James T. Klopenberg, 181–83. Oxford: Blackwell, 1995.

Crane, Elaine Forman. *A Dependent People*. New York: Fordham University Press, 1985.

————. *Ebb Tide in New England: Women, Seaports, and Social Change, 1630–1800*. Boston: Northeastern University Press, 1998.

Creighton, Margaret S. "American Mariners and the Rites of Manhood, 1830–1870." In *Jack Tar in History: Essays in the History of Maritime Life and Labour*, edited by Colin Howell and Richard J. Twomey, 143–63. Fredericton, N.B.: Acadiensis, 1991.

————. *Dogwatch and Liberty Days: Seafaring Life in the Nineteenth Century*. Salem, Mass.: Peabody Museum, 1982.

————. "Fraternity in the American Forecastle, 1830–1870." *New England Quarterly* 63 (December 1990): 531–37.

————. *Rites and Passages: The Experience of American Whaling, 1830–1870*. Cambridge, U.K.: Cambridge University Press, 1995.

Creighton, Margaret S., and Lisa Norling, eds. *Iron Men, Wooden Women: Gender and Seafaring in the Atlantic World, 1700–1920*. London: Johns Hopkins University Press, 1996.

Crosby, Everett U., ed. *Nantucket in Print*. Nantucket, Mass.: Tetaukimmo Press, 1946.

Culley, Margo, ed. *American Women's Autobiography: Fea(s)ts of Memory*. Madison: University of Wisconsin Press, 1992.

D'Andrade, Roy. "Cultural Meaning Systems." In *Culture Theory: Essays on Mind, Self, and Emotion*, edited by Richard A. Shweder and Robert A. LeVine, 88–119. Cambridge, U.K.: Cambridge University Press, 1984.

Darden, Genevieve M., ed. and comp. *My Dear Husband: Being a Collection of Heretofore Unpublished Letters of the Whaling Era*. New Bedford: The Descendants of Whaling Masters, Inc., 1980.

Darrah, William C. *Cartes de Visite in Nineteenth-Century Photography*. Gettysburg, Pa.: W. C. Darrah, Publisher, 1981.

Davidoff, Leonore, and Catherine Hall. *Family Fortunes: Men and Women of the English Middle Class, 1780–1850*. Chicago: University of Chicago Press, 1987.

Davidson, Cathy N. *Revolution and the Word: The Rise of the Novel in America*. New York: Oxford University Press, 1986.

Davis, Lance E., Robert E. Gallman, and Karin Gleiter. *In Pursuit of Leviathan: Technology, Institutions, Productivity, and Profits in American Whaling, 1816–1906*. Chicago: University of Chicago Press, 1997.

Davis, Lance E., Robert E. Gallman, and Teresa D. Hutchins. "Risk Sharing, Crew Quality, Labor Shares and Wages in the Nineteenth Century American Whaling Industry." Working Paper No. 13. National Bureau of Economic Research, Cambridge, Mass., 1990.

————. "The Structure of the Capital Stock in Economic Growth and Decline: The New Bedford Whaling Fleet in the Nineteenth Century." In *Quantity & Quiddity: Essays in U.S. Economic History*, edited by Peter Kilby, 336–98. Middletown, Conn.: Wesleyan University Press, 1987.

de Leonardo, Micaela. "The Female World of Cards and Holidays: Women, Families and the Work of Kinship." *Signs* 11, no. 3 (1987): 440–53.

de Pauw, Linda Grant. *Seafaring Women*. Boston: Houghton Mifflin, 1982.

Decker, Robert Owen. *The Whaling City: A History of New London*. Chester, Conn.: Pequot Press, 1976.

Dell, Burnham N. "Quakerism on Nantucket," *Proceedings of the Nantucket Historical Association*, Vol. 3, Bulletin No. 2 (January 1955): 3–26.

D'Emilio, John, and Estelle B. Freedman. *Intimate Matters: A History of Sexuality in America*. New York: Harper & Row, 1988.

Demos, John. *A Little Commonwealth: Family Life in Plymouth Colony.* Oxford: Oxford University Press, 1970.

Dening, Greg. *Mr. Bligh's Bad Language: Passion, Power, and Theater on the Bounty.* Cambridge, U.K.: Cambridge University Press, 1992.

Dexter, Elisabeth Anthony. *Career Women of America, 1776–1840.* Francestown, N.H.: Marshall Jones Co., 1950.

———. *Colonial Women of Affairs: Women in Business and the Professions Before 1776.* 2d ed., rev. New York: A. M. Kelly, 1972 (1931).

Dimock, Wai-Chee. *Empire for Liberty: Melville and the Poetics of Individualism.* Princeton: Princeton University Press, 1989.

Ditz, Toby L. *Property and Kinship: Inheritance in Early Connecticut, 1750–1820.* Princeton: Princeton University Press, 1986.

Douglas, Ann. *The Feminization of American Culture.* New York: Anchor, 1988.

Downey, Judith M., and Virginia M. Adams, eds. *Whaling Logbooks and Journals, 1613–1927: An Inventory of Manuscript Records in Public Collections.* Rev. ed. New York: Garland, 1986.

Druett, Joan. *Hen Frigates: Wives of Merchant Captains Under Sail.* New York: Simon & Schuster, 1998.

———. "More Decency and Order: Women and Whalemen in the Pacific." *Log of Mystic Seaport* 39, no. 2 (Summer 1987): 65–74.

———. *Petticoat Whalers: Whaling Wives at Sea, 1820–1920.* Auckland: Collins, 1991.

———. "Those Female Journals." *Log of Mystic Seaport* 40, no. 4 (Winter 1989): 115–25.

Druett, Joan, and Mary Anne Wallace. *The Sailing Circle: 19th Century Seafaring Women from New York.* East Setauket, N.Y.: Three Village Historical Society and Cold Spring Harbor Whaling Museum, 1995.

Duban, James. *Melville's Major Fiction: Politics, Theology, and Imagination.* DeKalb: Northern Illinois University Press, 1983.

Dublin, Thomas. *Transforming Women's Work: New England Lives in the Industrial Revolution.* Ithaca: Cornell University Press, 1994.

———. "Women and Outwork in a Nineteenth-Century New England Town: Fitzwilliam, New Hampshire 1830–1850." In *The Countryside in the Age of Capitalist Transformation,* edited by Steven Hahn and Jonathan Prude, 51–69. Chapel Hill: University of North Carolina Press, 1985.

Dubois, Ellen, Mari Jo Buhle, Temma Kaplan, Gerda Lerner, and Carroll Smith-Rosenberg. "Politics and Culture in Women's History: A Symposium." *Feminist Studies* 6 (1980): 26–64.

Dunn, Mary Maples. "Latest Light on Women of Light." In *Witnesses for Change: Quaker Women over Three Centuries,* edited by Elisabeth Potts Brown and Susan Mosher Stuard, 71–85. New Brunswick, N.J.: Rutgers University Press, 1989.

———. "Women of Light." In *Women of America: A History,* edited by Carol R. Berkin and Mary Beth Norton, 114–33. Boston: Houghton Mifflin, 1979.

Dye, Ira. "Early American Merchant Seafarers." *Proceedings of the American Philosophical Society* 120 (October 1976): 331–60.

Eden, Trudy. "The Turks and the American Woman: The Cultural Meaning of

Opium in Eighteenth-Century America." Unpublished paper dated 22 December 1993, in author's possession.

Ellis, Leonard Bolles. *History of New Bedford and Its Vicinity, 1602–1892*. Syracuse, 1892.

Ellis, Richard. *Men and Whales*. New York: Knopf, 1991.

Erickson, Amy Louise. *Women and Property in Early Modern England*. London: Routledge, 1993.

Faragher, John Mack. *Sugar Creek: Life on the Illinois Prairie*. New Haven: Yale University Press, 1986.

———. *Women and Men on the Overland Trail*. New Haven: Yale University Press, 1979.

Farber, Bernard. *Guardians of Virtue: Salem Families in 1800*. New York: Basic, 1972.

Farrell, James J. *Inventing the American Way of Death*. Philadelphia: Temple University Press, 1980.

Federal Writers' Project of the Works Project Administration of Massachusetts. *Whaling Masters*. New Bedford, Mass.: Old Dartmouth Historical Society, 1938.

Fingard, Judith. *Jack in Port: Sailortowns of Eastern Canada*. Toronto: University of Toronto Press, 1982.

Finley, Ruth E. *The Lady of Godey's: Sarah Josepha Hale*. Philadelphia: J. B. Lippincott Co., 1931.

Flayderman, E. Norman. *Scrimshaw and Scrimshanders: Whales and Whalemen*. New Milford, Conn.: N. Flayderman, 1972.

Fliegelman, Jay. *Prodigals and Pilgrims: The American Revolution against Patriarchal Authority 1750–1800*. Cambridge, U.K.: Cambridge University Press, 1982.

Folbre, Nancy. "Patriarchy in Colonial New England." *Review of Radical Political Economics* 12, no. 2 (Summer 1980): 4–13.

Folbre, Nancy, and Marjorie Abel. "Women's Work and Women's Households: Gender Bias in the U.S. Census." *Social Research* 56, no. 3 (Autumn 1989): 545–69.

Forbes, Susan S. "Quaker Tribalism." In *Friends and Neighbors: Group Life in America's First Plural Society*, edited by Michael Zuckerman, 145–73. Philadelphia: Temple University Press, 1982.

Fox-Genovese, Elizabeth. *Within the Plantation Household: Black and White Women of the Old South*. Chapel Hill: University of North Carolina Press, 1988.

Frank, Stuart M. "The Seamen's Friend." *Log of Mystic Seaport* 29 (1977): 52–58.

Frost, J. William. *The Quaker Family in Colonial America*. New York: St. Martin's, 1973.

Fuller, Wayne E. *The American Mail: Enlarger of the Common Life*. Chicago: University of Chicago Press, 1972.

Geertz, Clifford. *The Interpretation of Cultures*. New York: Basic, 1973.

Gillis, John R. *A World of Their Own Making: Myth, Ritual and the Quest for Family Values*. New York: Basic, 1996.

Gilmore, William, J. *Reading Becomes a Necessity of Life: Material and Cultural Life in Rural New England, 1780–1835*. Knoxville: University of Tennessee Press, 1989.

Ginsberg, Lori. *Women and the Work of Benevolence*. New Haven: Yale University Press, 1990.

and Private in Women's History: Essays from the Seventh Berkshire Conference on the History of Women. Ithaca: Cornell University Press, 1992.

Henretta, James A. "Families and Farms: *Mentalité* in Pre-Industrial America." *William & Mary Quarterly*, 3d ser., 35 (1978): 3–32.

Herndon, Ruth Wallis. "The Domestic Cost of Seafaring: Town Leaders and Seamen's Families in Eighteenth-Century Rhode Island." In *Iron Men, Wooden Women: Gender and Seafaring in the Atlantic World, 1700–1920*, edited by Margaret S. Creighton and Lisa Norling, 55–69. Baltimore: Johns Hopkins University Press, 1996.

Heyrman, Christine Leigh. *Commerce and Culture: the Maritime Communities of Colonial Massachusetts, 1690–1750*. New York: W. W. Norton, 1984.

Hoffman, Ronald, Mechal Sobel, and Fredrika J. Teute, eds. *Through a Glass Darkly: Reflections on Personal Identity in Early America*. Chapel Hill: University of North Carolina Press for the Omohundro Institute of Early American History and Culture, 1997.

Hohman, Elmo Paul. *The American Whaleman: A Study of Life and Labor in the Whaling Industry*. New York: Longmans, Green & Co., 1928.

Hood, Adrienne D. "The Material World of Cloth: Production and Use in Eighteenth-Century Rural Pennsylvania." *William & Mary Quarterly*, 3d ser., 53, no. 1 (January 1996): 43–66.

Horton, James Oliver. "Freedom's Yoke: Gender Conventions Among Antebellum Free Blacks." *Feminist Studies* 12, no. 1 (Spring 1986): 51–76.

Howell, Colin, and Richard Twomey, eds. *Jack Tar in History: Essays in the History of Maritime Life and Labour*. Fredericton, N.B.: Acadiensis, 1991.

Howland, Franklyn. *A Brief Genealogical and Biographical History of Arthur, Henry, and John Howland, and Their Descendants*. New Bedford: the author, 1885.

Hurd, D. Hamilton. *History of Bristol County, Massachusetts*. Philadelphia, 1883.

Jackman, Eugene T. "Efforts Made Before 1825 to Ameliorate the Lot of the American Seaman, With Emphasis on His Moral Regeneration." *American Neptune* 24 (1964): 109–18.

Jehle, Michael A. *From Brant Point to the Boca Tigris: Nantucket and the China Trade*. Nantucket: Nantucket Historical Association, 1994.

Jensen, Joan. *Loosening the Bonds: Mid-Atlantic Farm Women, 1750–1850*. New Haven: Yale University Press, 1986.

John, Richard R., Jr. "Managing the Mails: The Postal System, Public Policy, and American Political Culture, 1823–1836." Ph.D. diss., Harvard University, 1989.

Jones, Richard Michael. "Stonington Borough: A Connecticut Seaport in the Nineteenth Century." Ph.D. diss., City University of New York, 1976.

Kelley, Mary. *Private Woman, Public Stage*. Oxford: Oxford University Press, 1984.

———, ed. *The Power of Her Sympathy: The Autobiography and Journal of Catharine Maria Sedgwick*. Boston: Massachusetts Historical Society; distributed by Northeastern University Press, 1993.

———ny, Robert W. "Yankee Whalers at the Bay of Islands." *American Neptune* 12 (1952): 22–44.

Gleason, Philip. "Identifying Identity: A Semantic History." *Journal of American History* 69, no. 4 (March 1983): 910–30.

Glenn, Myra. "The Naval Reform Campaign Against Flogging: A Case Study in Changing Attitudes Toward Capital Punishment, 1830–1850." *American Quarterly* 35 (Fall 1983): 408–25.

Goffman, Erving. *The Presentation of Self in Everyday Life*. Garden City, N.J.: Doubleday, 1959.

Gordinier, Glenn S. "Evangelists, Landsharks, and the Character of Seamen's Benevolence in Nineteenth-Century America." *Log of Mystic Seaport* 43, no. 2 (Summer 1991): 31–37.

Greenhill, Basil, and Ann Giffard. *Women Under Sail: Letters and Journals Concerning Eight Women Travelling or Working in Sail Vessels Between 1829 and 1949*. New York: Great Albion, 1971.

Grigg, Susan. "Toward a Theory of Remarriage: A Case Study of Newburyport at the Beginning of the Nineteenth Century." *Journal of Interdisciplinary History* 8, no. 2 (Autumn 1977): 183–220.

Grimshaw, Patricia. "New England Missionary Wives, Hawaiian Women, and the 'Cult of True Womanhood.'" *Hawaiian Journal of History* 19 (1985): 71–100.

Gutman, Herbert. "Work, Culture, and Society in Industrializing America, 1815–1919." In *Work, Culture, and Society in Industrializing America: Essays in American Working-Class and Social History*, 3–78. New York: Pantheon, 1977.

Hajnal, John. "European Marriage Patterns in Perspective." In *Population in History: Essays in Historical Demography*, edited by D. V. Glass and D. E. C. Eversley, 103–43. London: E. Arnold, 1965.

Hall, Peter Dobkin. "Family Structure and Economic Organization: Massachusetts Merchants, 1700–1850." In *Family and Kin in Urban Communities, 1700–1930*, edited by Tamara K. Hareven, 38–61. New York: New Viewpoints, 1977.

———. "Marital Selection and Business in Massachusetts Merchant Families, 1700–1900." In *The Family: Its Structures and Functions*, 2d ed., edited by Rose Laub Coser, 226–40. New York: St. Martin's, 1974.

Halttunen, Karen. *Confidence Men and Painted Women: A Study of Middle-Class Cultu in America, 1830–1870*. New Haven: Yale University Press, 1982.

Hansen, Karen V. *A Very Social Time: Crafting Community in Antebellum New En* Berkeley: University of California Press, 1994.

Hegarty, Reginald B., comp. *Addendum to "Starbuck" and "Whaling Masters Bedford Customs District*. New Bedford, Mass.: New Bedford Free Pub 1964.

———. *Returns of Whaling Vessels Sailing From American Ports: A Co Alexander Starbuck's "History of the American Whalefishery," 187? Bedford, Mass.: Old Dartmouth Historical Society, 1959.

Heller, Thomas C., Morton Sosna, and David E. Wellbery, e* *Individualism: Autonomy, Individuality, and the Self in We?* Calif.: Stanford University Press, 1986.

Helly, Dorothy O., and Susan M. Reverby, eds. *Gender*

Kerber, Linda K. "Separate Spheres, Female Worlds, Woman's Place: The Rhetoric of Women's History." *Journal of American History* 75 (June 1988): 9–39.

———. *Women of the Republic: Intellect and Ideology in Revolutionary America*. New York: W. W. Norton, 1986.

Kerber, Linda K., Nancy F. Cott, Robert Gross, Lynn Hunt, Carroll Smith-Rosenberg, and Christine M. Stansell. "Forum: Beyond Roles, Beyond Spheres: Thinking about Gender in the Early Republic." *William & Mary Quarterly*, 3d ser., 46, no. 3 (July 1989): 565–85.

Kessler-Harris, Alice. *Out to Work: A History of Wage-Earning Women in the United States*. Oxford: Oxford University Press, 1982.

Keyssar, Alexander. "Widowhood in Eighteenth-Century Massachusetts: A Problem in the History of the Family." *Perspectives in American History* 8 (1974): 107–9.

Kolodny, Annette. "Turning the Lens on 'The Panther Captivity': A Feminist Exercise in Practical Criticism." In *Writing and Sexual Difference*, edited by Elizabeth Abel, 159–75. Chicago: University of Chicago Press, 1982.

Kverndal, Roald. *Seamen's Missions: Their Origin and Early Growth*. Pasadena: William Carey Library, 1986.

Labaree, Benjamin W., William M. Fowler Jr., John B. Hattendorf, Jeffrey J. Safford, Edward W. Sloan, and Andrew W. German. *America and the Sea: A Maritime History*. Mystic, Conn.: Mystic Seaport Museum, 1998.

Lancaster, Clay. *The Architecture of Historic Nantucket*. New York: McGraw-Hill, 1972.

Langley, Harold. *Social Reform in the United States Navy, 1798–1862*. Urbana: University of Illinois Press, 1967.

Laqueur, Thomas Walter. *Making Sex: Body and Gender from the Greeks to Freud*. Cambridge, Mass.: Harvard University Press, 1990.

Laslett, Barbara, and Johanna Brenner. "Gender and Social Reproduction: Historical Perspectives." *Annual Review of Sociology* 15 (1989): 381–404.

Lasser, Carol. " 'Let Us Be Sisters Forever': The Sororal Model of Nineteenth-Century Female Friendship." *Signs* 14, no. 1 (Autumn 1988): 158–81.

Leach, Robert J. "The Hicksite Separation on Nantucket." *Quaker History* 71, no. 1 (Spring 1982): 31–53.

Leach, Robert J., and Peter Gow. *Quaker Nantucket: The Religious Community Behind the Whaling Empire*. Nantucket: Mill Hill Press, 1997.

Lebsock, Suzanne. *The Free Women of Petersburg: Status and Culture in a Southern Town, 1784–1860*. New York: W. W. Norton, 1984.

Lemisch, Jesse. "Jack Tar in the Streets: Merchant Seamen in the Politics of Revolutionary America." *William & Mary Quarterly*, 3d ser., 25, no 3 (July 1968): 371–407.

Levenduski, Cristine. *Peculiar Power: A Quaker Woman Preacher in Eighteenth-Century America*. Washington, D.C.: Smithsonian Institution Press, 1996.

LeVine, Robert A. *Culture, Behavior, and Personality: An Introduction to the Comparative Study of Psychosocial Adaptation*. 2d ed. New York: Aldine, 1982.

Levy, Barry. "The Birth of the 'Modern Family.' " In *Friends and Neighbors: Group Life in America's First Plural Society*, edited by Michael Zuckerman, 26–64. Philadelphia: Temple University Press, 1982.

————. *Quakers and the American Family: British Settlement in the Delaware Valley.* New
    York: Oxford University Press, 1988.
Lewis, Jan. "The Republican Wife: Virtue and Seduction in the Early Republic."
    William & Mary Quarterly 44 (1987): 689–721.
Logue, Barbara. "The Case for Birth Control before 1850: Nantucket Reexamined."
    Journal of Interdisciplinary History 15 (1985): 371–91.
————. "The Whaling Industry and Fertility Decline: Nantucket, Massachusetts,
    1660–1850." *Social Science History* 12 (1983): 427–56.
Lystra, Karen. *Searching the Heart: Women, Men, and Romantic Love in
    Nineteenth-Century America.* Oxford: Oxford University Press, 1989.
McCusker, John J., and Russell R. Menard. *The Economy of British America,
    1607–1789.* Chapel Hill: University of North Carolina Press, 1985.
McDannell, Colleen. *The Christian Home in Victorian America, 1840–1900.*
    Bloomington: Indiana University Press, 1986.
McDevitt, Joseph Lawrence, Jr. *The House of Rotch: Massachusetts Whaling Merchants,
    1734–1828.* New York: Garland, 1986.
————. "The House of Rotch: Whaling Merchants of Massachusetts, 1734–1828."
    Ph.D. diss., American University, 1978.
Mack, Phyllis. "Gender and Spirituality in Early English Quakerism, 1650–1665." In
    Witnesses for Change: Quaker Women over Three Centuries, edited by Elisabeth Potts
    Brown and Susan Mosher Stuard, 31–63. New Brunswick, N.J.: Rutgers
    University Press, 1989.
————. *Visionary Women.* Berkeley: University of California Press, 1992.
McKee, Christopher. "Fantasies of Mutiny and Murder: A Suggested Psycho-History
    of the Seaman in the United States Navy, 1798–1815." *Armed Forces and Society* 4,
    no. 2 (February 1978): 293–304.
McMullin, Thomas Austin. "Industrialization and Social Change in a Nineteenth-
    Century Port City: New Bedford, Massachusetts, 1865–1900." Ph.D. diss.,
    University of Wisconsin–Madison, 1976.
Macy, Silvanus J. *Genealogy of the Macy Family from 1635–1868.* Albany, 1868.
Macy, William F. "Hon. Walter Folger Jr." *Nantucket Historical Association Proceedings*
    (20 July 1920): 47–55.
————, ed. *The Nantucket Scrap Basket.* 2d ed., published 1930; reprint, Cambridge,
    Mass.: Riverside, 1984.
Maloney, Linda M. "Doxies at Dockside: Prostitution and American Maritime
    Society, 1800–1900." In *Ships, Seafaring and Society,* edited by Timothy Runyan,
    217–25. Detroit: Wayne State University Press, 1987.
————. "Women in Maritime America: The Nineteenth Century." In *Seamen in
    Society,* edited by Paul Adam, Part 3, 113–21. Bucharest: International Commission
    of Maritime History, 1980.
Marietta, Jack D. *The Reformation of American Quakerism, 1748–1783.* Philadelphia:
    University of Pennsylvania Press, 1984.
Marsh, Peter. "Identity: An Ethogenic Perspective." In *Persons in Groups: Social
    Behavior as Identity Formation in Medieval and Renaissance Europe,* edited by

Richard C. Trexler, 17–30. Binghamton, N.Y.: Medieval and Renaissance Texts and Studies, 1985.

Medick, Hans, and David Warren Sabean, eds. *Interest and Emotion. Essays on the Study of Family and Kinship.* Cambridge, U.K.: Cambridge University Press, 1984.

Mellor, Anne K. *Romanticism and Gender.* New York: Routledge, 1993.

Miller, Jean Baker. "The Development of Women's Sense of Self." Working Paper No. 12, Stone Center for Developmental Services and Studies, Wellesley College, Wellesley, Mass., 1984.

―――. *Toward a New Psychology of Women.* Boston: Beacon, 1976.

Miller, Pamela. Unpublished typescript biography of Samuel T. Braley, untitled, ca. 1982. On deposit at Kendall Whaling Museum, Sharon, Mass.

―――. "Captain Samuel Tripp Braley: Life at Home, Life at Sea." *Essex Institute Historical Collections* 119 (1983): 5–17.

Mintz, Steven. *A Prison of Expectations: The Family in Victorian Culture.* New York: New York University Press, 1983.

Modell, John, and Tamara K. Hareven. "Urbanization and the Malleable Household: An Examination of Boarding and Lodging in American Families." *Journal of Marriage and the Family* (August 1973): 467–79.

Moment, David. "The Business of Whaling in America in the 1850s." *Business History Review* 31, no. 3 (Autumn 1957): 261–91.

Montgomery, David. "The Working Classes of the Pre-Industrial American City, 1780–1830." *Labor History* 9 (1968): 3–22.

Moorehead, Alan. *The Fatal Impact: The Invasion of the South Pacific, 1767–1840.* New York: Harper & Row, 1987.

Morgan, Edmund. *The Puritan Family: Religion and Domestic Relations in Seventeenth-Century New England.* 2d ed. New York: Harper & Row, 1966.

Morgan, Susan. *Place Matters: Gendered Geography in Victorian Women's Travel Books about Southeast Asia.* New Brunswick, N.J.: Rutgers University Press, 1996.

Morison, Samuel Eliot. *The Maritime History of Massachusetts, 1783–1860.* Boston: Northeastern University Press, 1979.

Moseley, Caroline. "Images of Young Women in Nineteenth-Century Songs of the Sea." *Log of Mystic Seaport* 35 (1984): 132–39.

Motz, Marilyn Ferris. "Folk Expression of Time and Place: 19th-Century Midwestern Rural Diaries." *Journal of American Folklore* 100 (1987): 131–47.

―――. *True Sisterhood: Michigan Women and Their Kin, 1820–1920.* Albany: State University of New York Press, 1983.

Nadel-Klein, Jane, and Dona Lee Davis, eds. *To Work and To Weep: Women in Fishing Economies.* St. Johns, N.F.: Institute of Social and Economic Research, Memorial University, 1988.

Newhall, Beaumont. *The History of Photography from 1839 to the Present Day.* 4th ed. New York: Museum of Modern Art, 1978.

Norling, Lisa. "Ahab's Wife: Women and the American Whaling Industry, 1820–1870." In *Iron Men, Wooden Women: Gender and Seafaring in the Atlantic World, 1700–1920,* edited by Margaret S. Creighton and Lisa Norling, 70–91. Baltimore: Johns Hopkins University Press, 1996.

———. "Contrary Dependencies: Whaling Agents and Whalemen's Families, 1830–1870." *Log of Mystic Seaport* 42, no. 1 (Spring 1990): 3–12.

———. " 'How Frought with Sorrow and Heartpangs': Mariners' Wives and the Ideology of Domesticity in New England, 1790–1880." *New England Quarterly* 65, no. 3 (September 1992): 422–46.

———. "Judith Macy and Her Daybook; or, Crevecoeur and the Wives of Sherborn." *Historic Nantucket* 40, no. 4 (Winter 1992): 68–71.

———. "The Sentimentalization of American Seafaring: The Case of the New England Whalefishery." In *Jack Tar in History: Essays in the History of Maritime Life and Labour*, edited by Colin Howell and Richard Twomey, 164–78. Fredericton, N.B.: Acadiensis, 1991.

Norton, Mary Beth. "The Evolution of White Women's Experience in Early America." *American Historical Review* 89:3 (June 1984): 593–619.

———. *Founding Mothers and Fathers: Gendered Power and the Forming of American Society.* New York: Alfred A. Knopf, 1996.

———. *Liberty's Daughters: The Revolutionary Experience of American Women, 1750–1800.* Boston: Little, Brown, 1980.

Nylander, Jane C. *Our Own Snug Fireside: Images of the New England Home, 1760–1860.* New York: Alfred A. Knopf, 1993.

Osterud, Nancy Grey. *Bonds of Community: The Lives of Farm Women in Nineteenth-Century New York.* Ithaca: Cornell University Press, 1991.

Palmer, William R. "The Whaling Port of Sag Harbor." Ph.D. diss., Columbia University, 1959.

Partridge, Eric. *The Penguin Dictionary of Historical Slang.* New York: Penguin, 1972.

Pestana, Carla Gardina. *Quakers and Baptists in Colonial Massachusetts.* Cambridge, U.K.: Cambridge University Press, 1991.

Philbrick, Nathaniel. *Away Off Shore: Nantucket Island and Its People, 1602–1890.* Nantucket, Mass.: Mill Hill Press, 1994.

———. "A House Upon the Sand: Nantucket Island and the Formation of American Literary Culture." Unpublished typescript, ca. 1992, in author's possession.

———. "The Nantucket Sequence in Crevecoeur's *Letters from an American Farmer.*" *New England Quarterly* 64, no. 3 (1991): 414–32.

Poovey, Mary. *The Proper Lady and the Woman Writer: Ideology as Style in the Works of Mary Wollstonecraft, Mary Shelley, and Jane Austen.* Chicago: University of Chicago Press, 1984.

Pratt, Mary Louise. *Imperial Eyes: Travel Writing and Transculturation.* London: Routledge, 1992.

Rabinowitz, Richard. *The Spiritual Self in Everyday Life: The Transformation of Personal Religious Experience in Nineteenth-Century New England.* Boston: Northeastern University Press, 1989.

Radway, Janice A. *Reading the Romance: Women, Patriarchy, and Popular Literature.* Chapel Hill: University of North Carolina Press, 1984.

Rapp, Rayna, Ellen Ross, and Renate Bridenthal. "Examining Family History." In *Sex and Class in Women's History*, edited by Judith L. Newton, Mary P. Ryan, and Judith R. Walkowitz, 232–58. London: Routledge, 1983.

Rediker, Marcus. *Between the Devil and the Deep Blue Sea: Merchant Seamen, Pirates, and the Anglo-American Maritime World, 1700–1750.* Cambridge, U.K.: Cambridge University Press, 1987.

———. "Liberty Beneath the Jolly Roger." In *Iron Men, Wooden Women: Gender and Seafaring in the Atlantic World, 1700–1920,* edited by Margaret S. Creighton and Lisa Norling, 1–33. Baltimore: Johns Hopkins University Press, 1996.

Robertson-Lorant, Laurie. *Melville: A Biography.* Amherst: University of Massachusetts Press, 1996.

Roediger, David R. *Wages of Whiteness: Race and the Making of the American Working Class.* London: Verso, 1991.

Rogers, Sherbrooke. *Sarah Josepha Hale: New England Pioneer, 1788–1879.* Grantham, N.H.: Tompson & Rutter, 1985.

Romero, Lora. *Home Fronts: Domesticity and Its Critics in the Antebellum United States.* Durham, N.C.: Duke University Press, 1997.

Rosaldo, Michelle Z. "Toward an Anthropology of Self and Feeling." In *Culture Theory: Essays on Mind, Self, and Emotion,* edited by Richard A. Shweder and Robert A. LeVine, 137–57. New York: Cambridge University Press, 1984.

Ross, Michael, and Michael Conway. "Remembering One's Own Past: The Construction of Personal Histories." In *Handbook of Motivation and Cognition: Foundations of Social Behavior,* edited by Richard M. Sorrentino and E. Tory Higgins, 122–44. New York: Guilford, 1986.

Rothman, David J. *The Discovery of the Asylum: Social Order and Disorder in the New Republic.* Boston: Little, Brown, 1971.

Rothman, Ellen K. *Hands and Hearts: A History of Courtship in America.* New York: Basic, 1984.

Rotundo, E. Anthony. *American Manhood: Transformations in Masculinity from the Revolution to the Modern Era.* New York: Basic, 1993.

———. "Body and Soul: Changing Ideas of American Middle-Class Manhood, 1770–1920." *Journal of Social History* 16 (Summer 1983): 23–38.

———. "Manhood in America: The Northern Middle Class, 1770–1920." Ph.D. diss., Brandeis University, 1982.

Rubin, Gayle. "The Traffic in Women: Notes on the 'Political Economy' of Sex." Originally published 1975; reprinted in *Feminism and History,* edited by Joan Wallach Scott, 105–51. Oxford, U.K.: Oxford University Press, 1996.

Ruggles, Steven. *Prolonged Connections: The Rise of the Extended Family in Nineteenth-Century England and America.* Madison: University of Wisconsin Press, 1987.

Ryan, Mary. *The Cradle of the Middle Class: The Family in Oneida County, New York, 1790–1865.* Cambridge, U.K.: Cambridge University Press, 1981.

———. *The Empire of the Mother: American Writing About Domesticity, 1830–1860.* New York: Harrington Park, 1985.

Sager, Eric W. *Seafaring Labour: The Merchant Marine of Atlantic Canada, 1820–1914.* Montreal: McGill-Queen's University Press, 1989.

Salmon, Marylynn. *Women and the Law of Property in Early America.* Chapel Hill: University of North Carolina Press, 1986.

Saum, Lewis O. "Death in the Popular Mind of Pre–Civil War America." In *Death in America*, edited by David E. Stannard, 30–48. Philadelphia: University of Pennsylvania Press, 1975.

———. *The Popular Mood of Pre-Civil War America*. Westport, Conn.: Greenwood, 1980.

Schneider, David M. *American Kinship: A Cultural Account*. Englewood Cliffs, N.J.: Prentice-Hall, 1980.

Schuetz, Alfred. "The Homecomer." *American Journal of Sociology* 30 (1944–45): 369–76.

Scott, Joan Wallach. "Gender: A Useful Category of Historical Analysis." In *Gender and the Politics of History*, 28–50. New York: Columbia University Press, 1988.

Scranton, Philip. "Varieties of Paternalism: Industrial Structures and the Social Relations of Production in American Textiles." *American Quarterly* 36 (1984): 235–57.

Seeler, Katherine. "Phebe Folger's Watercolors." *Historic Nantucket* 14 (2): 13–8.

Seidman, Steven. *Romantic Longings: Love in America, 1830–1980*. New York: Routledge, 1991.

Sellers, Charles. *The Market Revolution: Jacksonian America, 1815–1846*. New York: Oxford University Press, 1991.

Sewell, Edward H., Jr. "Sarah Josepha Hale." In *Dictionary of Literary Biography*, 73:159–67. Detroit, Mich.: Gale Research, ca. 1988.

Seymour, Jack M. *Ships, Sailors and Samaritans: The Women's Seamen's Friend Society of Connecticut, 1859–1976*. New Haven, Conn.: Easton, 1976.

Shammas, Carole. "Anglo-American Household Government in Comparative Perspective." *William & Mary Quarterly*, 3d ser., 52 (1995): 104–44.

Shammas, Carole, Marylynn Salmon, and Michel Dahlin. *Inheritance in America: From Colonial Times to the Present*. New Brunswick, N.J.: Rutgers University Press, 1987.

Sherman, Stuart C. *The Voice of the Whaleman*. Providence, R.I.: Providence Public Library, 1965.

Shields, David. *Civil Tongues and Polite Letters in British America*. Chapel Hill: University of North Carolina Press, 1997.

Shweder, Richard A., and Robert A. LeVine, eds. *Culture Theory: Essays on Mind, Self and Emotion*. Cambridge, U.K.: Cambridge University Press, 1984.

Sicherman, Barbara. "Sense and Sensibility: A Case Study of Women's Reading in Late-Victorian America." In *Reading in America: Literature and Social History*, edited by Cathy N. Davidson, 201–25. Baltimore: Johns Hopkins University Press, 1989.

Sklar, Kathryn Kish. *Catharine Beecher: A Study in American Domesticity*. New Haven: Yale University Press, 1973.

Smith, Daniel Scott. "Family Limitation, Sexual Control, and Domestic Feminism in Victorian America." *Feminist Studies* 1 (1973): 40–57.

———. "Parental Power and Marriage Patterns: An Analysis of Historical Trends in Hingham, Massachusetts." *Journal of Marriage and the Family* 35 (1973): 419–28.

Smith, Sidonie. *A Poetics of Women's Autobiography: Marginality and the Fictions of Self-Representation*. Bloomington: Indiana University Press, 1987.

Smith-Rosenberg, Carroll. *Disorderly Conduct: Visions of Gender in Victorian America.* Oxford: Oxford University Press, 1985.

Snow, Edward Rowe. *Women of the Sea.* New York: Dodd, Mead, 1962.

Soderlund, Jean R. "Women's Authority in Pennsylvania and New Jersey Quaker Meetings, 1680–1760." *William & Mary Quarterly,* 3d ser., 44 (1987): 722–49.

Sprague, Stuart Seely. "The Whaling Ports: A Study of Ninety Years of Rivalry, 1784–1875." *American Neptune* 33 (1973): 120–30.

Springer, Haskell. "The Captain's Wife at Sea." In *Iron Men, Wooden Women: Gender and Seafaring in the Atlantic World, 1700–1920,* edited by Margaret S. Creighton and Lisa Norling, 92–117. Baltimore: Johns Hopkins University Press, 1996.

Springer, Haskell, and Douglas Robillard, "Herman Melville." In *America and the Sea: A Literary History,* edited by Haskell Springer, 127–145. Athens: University of Georgia Press, 1995.

Stackpole, Edouard A. *Nantucket in the American Revolution.* Falmouth, Mass.: Kendall Printing Co. for the Nantucket Historical Association, 1976.

———. *The Sea-Hunters: The New England Whalemen During Two Centuries, 1635–1835.* Philadelphia: J. B. Lippincott, 1953.

———. *Whales and Destiny: The Rivalry between America, France, and Britain for Control of the Southern Whale Fishery, 1785–1825.* Amherst: University of Massachusetts Press, 1972.

Stanley, Amy Dru. *From Bondage to Contract: Wage Labor, Marriage, and the Market in the Age of Slave Emancipation.* Cambridge, U.K.: Cambridge University Press, 1998.

———. "Home Life and the Morality of the Market." In *The Market Revolution in America: Social, Political, and Religious Expressions, 1800–1880,* edited by Melvyn Stokes and Stephen Conway, 74–96. Charlottesville: University of Virginia Press, 1996.

Stansell, Christine. *City of Women: Sex and Class in New York, 1789–1860.* New York: Alfred A. Knopf, 1986.

Starbuck, Alexander. *The History of Nantucket: County, Island and Town, Including Genealogies of First Settlers.* Boston: C. E. Goodspeed & Co., 1924.

———. *History of the American Whale Fishery.* Originally published 1876; reprint, Secaucus, N.J.: Castle, 1989.

Stark, Suzanne J. "The Adventures of Two Women Whalers." *American Neptune* 44 (1984): 22–4.

Stein, Roger B. *Seascape and the American Imagination.* New York: C. N. Potter; distributed by Crown, 1975.

Sten, Christopher. *Sounding the Whale: Moby-Dick as Epic Novel.* Kent, Ohio: Kent State University Press, 1996.

Stowe, Steven. *Intimacy and Power in the Old South: Ritual in the Lives of the Planters.* Baltimore: Johns Hopkins University Press, 1987.

Stuard, Susan Mosher. "Women's Witnessing: A New Departure." In *Witnesses for Change: Quaker Women over Three Centuries,* edited by Elisabeth Potts Brown and Susan Mosher Stuard, 3–25. New Brunswick, N.J.: Rutgers University Press, 1989.

Surrey, Janet L. "Self-in-Relation: A Theory of Women's Development." Working
Paper No. 13, Stone Center for Developmental Services and Studies, Wellesley
College, Wellesley, Mass., 1985.

Taylor, Charles. *Sources of the Self: The Making of Modern Identity*. Cambridge, Mass.:
Harvard University Press, 1989.

Theriot, Nancy M. *Mothers and Daughters in Nineteenth-Century America: The Biosocial
Construction of Femininity*. Rev. ed. Lexington: University Press of Kentucky, 1996.

Thompson, E. P. "Time, Work-Discipline, and Industrial Capitalism." *Past and Present*
38 (December 1967): 56–97.

Thompson, Paul, with Tony Wailey and Trevor Lummis. *Living the Fishing*. London:
Routledge & Kegan Paul, 1983.

Thornton, Tamara Plakins. *Handwriting in America: A Cultural History*. New Haven:
Yale University Press, 1996.

Tolles, Frederick. *Quakers and the Atlantic Culture*. New York: Macmillan, 1960.

Ulrich, Laurel Thatcher. *Good Wives: Image and Reality in the Lives of Women in
Northern New England, 1650–1750*. New York: Alfred A. Knopf, 1982.

———. "Housewife and Gadder: Themes of Self-Sufficiency and Community in
Eighteenth-Century New England." In *"To Toil the Livelong Day": America's
Women at Work, 1780–1980*, edited by Carol Groneman and Mary Beth Norton,
21–34. Ithaca: Cornell University Press, 1987.

———. *A Midwife's Tale: The Life of Martha Ballard, Based on Her Diary, 1785–1812*.
New York: Alfred A. Knopf, 1990.

———. "Wheels, Looms, and the Gender Division of Labor in Eighteenth-Century
New England." *William & Mary Quarterly* 55, no. 1 (January 1998): 3–38.

van de Wetering, Maxine. "The Popular Concept of 'Home' in Nineteenth-Century
America." *Journal of American Studies* 18 (1984): 5–28.

Vicinus, Martha, ed. *Suffer and Be Still: Women in the Victorian Age*. Bloomington:
Indiana University Press, 1972.

Vickers, Daniel. "Competency and Competition: Economic Culture in Early
America." *William & Mary Quarterly*, 3d ser., 47, no. 1 (January 1990): 3–29.

———. *Farmers and Fishermen: Two Centuries of Work in Essex County, Massachusetts,
1630–1850*. Chapel Hill: University of North Carolina Press, 1994.

———. "The First Whalemen of Nantucket." *William & Mary Quarterly*, 3d ser., 40
(1983): 560–83.

———. "Maritime Labor in Colonial Massachusetts: A Case Study of the Essex
County Cod Fishery and the Whaling Industry of Nantucket, 1630–1775." Ph.D.
diss., Princeton University, 1981.

———. "Nantucket Whalemen in the Deep-Sea Fishery: The Changing Anatomy of
an Early American Labor Force." *Journal of American History* 72, no. 2 (September
1985): 277–96.

Villier, Alan. *Of Ships and Men: A Personal Anthology*. New York: Arco Publishing Co.,
1964.

Vital Records of Dartmouth, Massachusetts, to the Year 1850. Vols. 1–3. Boston: New
England Historic Genealogical Society, 1929–30.

Vital Records of Edgartown, Massachusetts, to the Year 1850. Boston: New England
    Historic Genealogical Society, 1906.
Vital Records of Nantucket, Massachusetts, to the Year 1850. Vols. 1–5. Boston: New
    England Historic Genealogical Society, 1925–28.
Vital Records of New Bedford, Massachusetts, to the Year 1850. Vols. 1–3. Boston: New
    England Historic Genealogical Society, 1932–41.
Vital Records of Rochester, Massachusetts, to the Year 1850. Vols. 1–2. Boston: New
    England Historic Genealogical Society, 1914.
Vital Records of Westport, Massachusetts, to the Year 1850. Boston: New England Historic
    Genealogical Society, 1918.
Wallace, Frederick William. *Wooden Ships and Iron Men.* London: Hodder and
    Stoughton, 1924.
Ward, Geoff, ed. *Romantic Literature from 1790 to 1830.* London: Bloomsbury, 1993.
Weeks, Emily. "Women of Nantucket." *Nantucket Historical Proceedings* (1912): 31–47.
Weinraub, William, and Stuart Frank. "Nineteenth-Century New Bedford."
    Unpublished typescript, Mystic Seaport Museum, G. W. Blunt White Library,
    ca. 1975.
Wells, Robert V. *The Population of the British Colonies in America before 1776.*
    Princeton: Princeton University Press, 1975.
———. "Quaker Marriage Patterns in a Colonial Perspective." *William & Mary
    Quarterly,* 3d ser., 29 (1972): 415–42.
Welter, Barbara. "The Cult of True Womanhood: 1820–1860." *American Quarterly* 18
    (Summer 1966): 151–74.
Whiting, Emma Mayhew, and Henry Beetle Hough. *Whaling Wives.* Cambridge,
    Mass.: Riverside, 1953.
Wilentz, Sean. *Chants Democratic: New York City and the Rise of the American Working
    Class, 1788–1850.* New York: Oxford University Press, 1984.
Wilson, Lisa. *Life After Death: Widows in Pennsylvania, 1750–1850.* Philadelphia:
    Temple University Press, 1992.
Worrall, Arthur J. *Quakers in the Colonial Northeast.* Hanover, N.H.: University Press
    of New England, 1980.
Worth, Henry Barnard. "Nantucket Lands and Land Owners." *Nantucket Historical
    Society Proceedings* 2, no. 4 (1904).
Zuckerman, Michael. "The Fabrication of Identity in Early America." *William &
    Mary Quarterly,* 3d ser., 34 (1977): 183–214.

INDEX

Baleen. *See* Whale oil and bone

Ballard, Martha, 297 (n. 86)

Ball, Selena, 175

Baptists, 54, 63, 121, 122

Barker, Sarah Coffin, 100, 104

Barnard, Eunice Swain, 301 (n. 75)

Barney, Abiel, 39

Barney, Eliza, 41

Barney, Sarah, 87, 88

Bates, Ambrose, 233–34

Baym, Nina, 323 (n. 88)

Beetle, Eliza, 148, 162–63

Beetle, Henry, 141, 148, 162–63

Bender, Thomas, 283 (n. 14)

Bible, 80, 110, 219, 251, 256–57, 297
(n. 93). *See also* Religion

Blackmer, Hannah, 159, 233

Blackmer, Seth, 170, 196, 233

Blacks. *See* African Americans

Blackstone, Sir William, 33

Bloch, Ruth, 104, 301 (n. 74)

Boarding and boardinghouses: and
women's employment, 38, 44, 158, 159,
226, 288 (n. 68), 309 (n. 102); and maritime residential patterns, 73–74, 77,
224, 228, 237; catering to sailors, 131,
220, 318 (n. 17). *See also* Households

Boomer, Nathan H., 304 (n. 29)

Boston, Mass., 91, 96, 98, 134, 219, 221,
293 (n. 22), 318 (n. 17)

Bourdieu, Pierre, 327 (n. 4)

Bowman, George, 141, 186

Boydston, Jeanne, 156

Braley, Mary Ann, 154, 159, 184, 191,
200, 201, 226

Braley, Samuel, 142, 154, 155, 184, 191,
193, 200, 201

Brewster, Mary, 238, 239–40, 242, 246,
247, 249–50, 253, 255–59, 323 (n. 90),
325 (n. 139)

Brewster, William, 243

Briggs, Abram, 247–48, 254

Brightman, Henry, 160–61

Brock, Eliza, 193, 209, 212, 249, 250, 253,
260, 262–64, 323 (n. 90)

Brown, Helen E., 326 (n. 155)

Brown, Martha, 247, 251, 254, 255, 257–
58, 323 (n. 90)

Brown, Sallee, 180

Brown, Sophia, 145

Brownell, Mary Ann, 158

Bunker, Hepsabeth Russell, 217–18

Bunker, Priscilla, 61, 293–94 (n. 35)

Bunker, Rachael, 41

Bunker, Samuel, 294 (n. 35)

Bunker, Sarah West, 312 (n. 42)

Burgess, Hannah, 223, 312 (n. 42)

Burgess, Paul and Ann, 184

Burke, Edmund, 91, 117–18

Businesses. *See* Merchants; Whalefishery;
Whaling agents; Work, women's

Byers, Edward, 34, 46, 52, 65, 86, 88, 284
(n. 6), 293 (n. 22), 294 (nn. 39, 48)

Cape Cod, Mass., 11, 17, 21, 24, 92, 123,
192

"Cape Horn widows," 116, 168, 190, 192,
194–95, 216, 266; defined, 310 (n. 4)

Carpenter, Charles, Jr., 63, 98, 288 (n. 67)

Carpenter, Mary Grace, 63, 98, 288
(n. 67)

Case, Lydia Ann, 173

Cash, Azubah, 247, 323 (n. 90)

Chapman, John, 198, 234, 235

Chapman, Laura, 234

Chase, Captain, 241

Chase, Elijah, 178

Chase, Mrs. J. E., 151

Chase, Ruth Macy, 290 (n. 88)

Childbirth, 39, 41, 228, 241, 254–55, 321
(n. 53). *See also* Pregnancy

Children: poverty of, in Nantucket,
34–35; education of, 37–38, 40; death
of, 40, 197, 227, 290 (n. 89); care of, in
eighteenth-century Nantucket, 40–41,
289 (n. 77); illegitimate, 41; Crevecoeur
on, 52; of Quakers, 62, 101–2; and
American Revolution, 94; pictures
of, for absent fathers, 155, 186–88;
maritime mothers's difficulties with,
161–62; fathers' relationships with,
190–92; illnesses of, 227, 228; at sea

Davenport, Lydia, 178, 312 (n. 42)

Davidson, Cathy, 103–4

Davol, Edward and William, 180

Death: of whalemen, 35, 135, 192, 194–95, 208, 216, 219, 225, 250; of maritime women, 35, 196–97, 199, 215, 225, 227, 241, 244; of infants and children, 40, 197, 227, 290 (n. 89); sentimental attitudes toward, 194–95; of maritime wife at sea, 241, 244. *See also* Widowhood

Deblois, Henrietta, 205, 244–46

Deblois, John, 205

Delany, Daniel A., 146

Denison, Rev. Frederic, 130–31

"Deputy husbands." *See* Work, women's

Desertion of whalemen, 120, 134, 135, 137, 147

Devol, Samuel, 173

Diaries, 181–83, 184–86, 312 (n. 42), 321 (n. 51)

Dillingham, Paul, 286 (n. 35)

Dimon, Martha J., 312 (n. 42)

Discipline at sea, 28, 120, 137, 151, 155–56, 256, 257–58

Diseases. *See* Illnesses

Divorce, 202–3

Domesticity: of maritime women generally, 3–4, 6–7, 116, 121; and gender roles, 3–7, 116, 121, 166–71, 199, 209–12, 265–70, 312–13 (n. 44); definition of, 4–5; and separate spheres, 4–5, 7, 48, 109, 120–21, 138, 164, 209–12, 216, 222, 244–48, 250, 260–61, 265, 268–70; scholarship on, 5–6, 282 (n. 8); reasons for emergence of, 5–6, 120–21, 265–66; tensions between maritime life and, 7, 167–68, 197–203, 214–18, 265–70; and "home" as center of emotional life, 109, 172, 205, 208, 215–16, 218–23, 233–34, 235–39; and passionate love, 140–42, 164, 165–75; and motherhood, 160–62, 190–92; romantic conventions and ideal of femininity in nineteenth century, 165–75, 199, 209, 212, 217–18, 266–67, 312–13 (n. 44);

and women's religiosity, 170–72, 194–95, 219, 253, 311 (n. 13); and suffering of women, 193, 314 (n. 71); and mourning, 194–95, 197; and marital sexual fidelity, 201–3, 258–59; and emotional costs of separation of husbands and wives, 203–13; and wife as light of home, 217–18; Hale on, 218, 219; Sigourney on, 218–19; and sea-going wives, 238–64. *See also* Authority; Gender; Maritime wives; Marriage

Dress. *See* Clothing

Drew, Abigail ("Nabby") Gardner, 40, 72–74, 104, 107–10, 114, 116, 295 (n. 76), 312 (n. 42)

Drew, Gershom, Jr., 72–74, 107–10, 116, 302 (n. 83)

Drew, Polly, 73

Druett, Joan, 323 (nn. 90–91), 325–26 (n. 139)

Drummond, Mary, 84

Drunkenness of whalemen, 131, 241, 257, 258

Dyer, Mary, 57

Easton, Mrs. Frederick A., 152

Eden, Trudy, 297 (n. 86)

Education: of boys on Nantucket, 26–27, 52, 285 (n. 24); women as teachers, 37–38, 111, 113, 158; of girls on Nantucket, 52, 83–84, 103–4

Ellis, Leonard, 122

Embargo Act of 1807, 96, 122

Emerson, Everett, 283–84 (n. 3)

Enos, John, 180

Fairhaven, Mass., 11, 123, 133, 303 (n. 8)

Families: whalemen's absences from, 6–7, 16, 24, 48, 49, 68, 74, 76–81, 113–14, 123, 167–68, 197–213, 214–17, 233–38; system of labor, 26, 38, 42, 48, 132–33, 164, 324 (n. 115); credit and cash advances for, 28–33, 131–33, 144–47, 306 (n. 57); maritime paternalism for, 28–36, 132–33, 138, 143–47, 285 (n. 32); legal status of wives in

relations of, 310 (n. 122). *See also* Boarding and boardinghouses; Domesticity; Families

Houston, Orlando H., 146

Howes, Lizzie, 204

Howland, Hannah, 198

Howland, Jennie, 233

Howland, Llewellyn, 127–28

Howland, Matthew, 143, 241, 244

Howland, Patience Potter, 152, 196, 199–200, 214–16, 226, 241

Howland, Philip, 143, 149, 152, 196, 199–200, 204, 208, 214–17, 241, 307 (n. 64), 317 (nn. 2, 4)

Howland, Sarah, 198, 204, 214–18, 317 (n. 4)

Hudson, N.Y., 94, 113, 114, 302 (n. 90)

Humphrey, David, 111

Hussey, Benjamin, 28

Hussey, Christopher, 21

Hussey, Eunice Swain, 104–7, 110, 114, 301 (n. 75)

Hussey, George, 301 (n. 75)

Hussey, Hephzibah, 61, 87

Hussey, James, 104, 301 (n. 75)

Hussey, Sylvanus, 293 (n. 35)

Hutchinson, Elizabeth, 289 (n. 84)

Illegitimacy, 41

Illnesses, 142–43, 145, 227, 228, 230, 236, 237, 241, 251

Indians. *See* Native Americans

Infants. *See* Childbirth; Children

Jackson, Caroline, 209

Jackson, William, 209

Jarwood, Nancy, 74

Jefferson, Thomas, 96, 122

Jewett, Sarah Orne, 3

Jones, E. C., 146

Joy, Elizabeth, 295 (n. 78)

Joy, Francis, 31, 295–96 (n. 78)

Keen, Amelia, 152–53

Keith, Marshall, 186, 247

Kelley, Daniel, 31, 32

Ketcham, Jonathan W., 139

King, Almeda, 158

King, Betsey (mother and daughter), 161, 190–91

King, James, Jr., 161, 190–91

King, James, III, 161

King, Matilda, 161

Kingsley, Charles, 314 (n. 71)

Knowles (Thomas) & Co., 143, 241

Kolodny, Annette, 282 (n. 4)

Labor, gender division of, 1–2, 7, 38–39, 41–49, 68, 94, 118–19, 120–21, 140–64, 192–94, 248–53, 262–70, 287 (n. 55)

"Land sharks," 137, 155

Lapham, Isaac, 38, 41, 77, 289 (n. 77)

Lawrence, Mary Chipman, 249–51, 256–58, 323 (n. 90), 326 (n. 155)

Lawrence, Minnie, 256–57

Lay system of wages. *See* Whaling

Leach, Robert, 293 (n. 22)

Leonard, John, 147, 154, 179, 186, 190, 191, 198, 204

Leonard, Sylvia Tucker, 147, 149, 154, 179, 186–88, 190, 191, 194, 198, 204

Letters, emotional importance of, 13, 78–79, 151–54, 165–67, 169, 173–77, 183–86, 188, 229–30, 307–8 (n. 83). *See also* Mail and mail service

Letters from an American Farmer. See Crevecoeur, John de

Lévi-Strauss, Claude, 306–7 (n. 61)

Lewis, Eliza, 150

Lewis, Sarah, 325–26 (n. 139)

Linton, Sarah ("Sallie"), 229–30, 239

Literacy rates, 104, 169

Literature. *See* Novels; Reading; *and specific authors*

Loneliness: of whalemen, 155, 157, 184, 205, 208, 233–34; of maritime women, 181, 183–84, 209, 212, 223, 227, 229, 232, 233, 236–37, 269, 320 (n. 34); of maritime wives at sea, 244, 247–49, 253, 259–61, 263, 269

Long, Elizabeth, 74

Long Island, N.Y., 8, 10, 17, 21, 24, 92

Love: eighteenth-century conjugal, 66, 77–79; of maritime women for husbands, 77–79, 183–86, 230, 239–40; subordination of, to faith, 79–81; and Romanticism, 84, 103–14, 116, 120–21, 195, 265; separation of lovers due to parental tyranny, 104–5; reinforced by faith, 105–6, 111, 114, 195; and suffering, 105–6, 172, 181, 183–84, 192–95; and courtship, 107–8, 172, 173–81; passionate love in nineteenth century, 140–42, 164, 165–75; of whalemen, 140–42, 164, 183–86, 197–203; scrimshaw of marriage proposal, 141; romantic conventions and ideal of femininity in nineteenth century, 165–75, 199, 209, 212, 217–18, 266–67, 312–13 (n. 44); Christianity and romantic love, 170–72, 194–95, 311 (n. 13); poetry associated with, 172; and fear of deceit, 172, 179–80; and premarital sex, 178, 180–81; and loneliness, 181, 183–84, 320 (n. 34); and remarriage, 196–97, 199–200; maintenance of relationships during whalemen's absences, 197–203, 214–17; and reunion of married couples after separation, 198–99; and emotional costs of separation, 203–13; Victorian America's ideal of, for white middle class, 301 (n. 78). *See also* Friendship; Marriage

Lystra, Karen, 173–74, 301 (n. 78), 311 (n. 13), 312–13 (n. 44)

Mack, Phyllis, 68–69, 293 (n. 22)

McKenzie, Susan, 249, 269, 323 (n. 90)

Macy, Barzillai, 44, 290 (n. 89)

Macy, Caleb, 27, 43–45, 290 (n. 96)

Macy, Caleb, Jr., 44, 290 (n. 89)

Macy, Elisha, 44, 290 (n. 89)

Macy, Judith Folger Gardner, 27, 37, 42–45, 48–49, 67–68, 71, 288 (n. 67), 290 (nn. 88, 89, 96, 98)

Macy, Obed, 27, 39, 43–45, 49, 68, 93–94, 96, 97, 290 (n. 89), 295 (n. 75)

Macy, Ruth, 44, 49, 290 (n. 89)

Macy, Silvanus, 44, 49, 290 (n. 89)

Macy, Zaccheus, 292 (n. 14)

Mail and mail service, 122, 143, 150–54, 169, 184–86, 234–35. *See also* Letters

Manchester, Christiana, 175

Manchester, James, 132

Manchester, Rhoda, 175

Manhood. *See* Gender

Marchant, Mrs. Cornelius, 151

Marietta, Jack D., 299 (n. 26), 300 (n. 61)

Mariners' wives. *See* Maritime women

Maritime culture: masculinity of, 1–2, 9, 12, 46, 48, 120, 256, 269; scholarship on, 2–3; historical overview of, 7–9. *See also* Whalefishery

Maritime women: Melville on, 1, 141, 170, 194; stereotypes of, 2; identity as, 2, 3–4, 9, 164, 168, 189–92, 212, 232–33, 238, 262, 266–69; and absences of husbands, 6–7, 16, 24, 34–35, 48, 49, 68, 74, 76–81, 113–14, 167–68, 197–217, 229–38; Crevecoeur on, 16–17, 24, 36, 39, 42, 49–51, 53, 64–65, 68, 74, 114, 118, 119, 152, 296 (n. 86); as "deputy husbands" or surrogates for husbands in business matters, 16–17, 36–37, 43, 48, 133, 148–49, 154, 287 (n. 56); movements around community, 24, 39, 77, 157–58, 226–28, 234–35, 260–61; credit and cash advances for, 28–33, 131–33, 144–47, 306 (n. 57); paternalism for, 28–36, 132–33, 138, 143–47, 285 (n. 32); deaths of, 35, 196–97, 199, 215, 225, 227, 241, 244; and childbirth, 39, 41, 228, 241, 254–55, 321 (n. 53); sociability of, 39–40, 72–74, 77, 78, 107, 151–54, 226–28, 235, 260–61, 321 (n. 51); remarriage of, 43, 195–96, 314 (n. 80), 315 (n. 82); attitudes of, toward whalefishery, 46–47; familiarity with specialized maritime language, 46–47; and patriarchy, 47–50; as Quakers, 53, 64–65, 71–72, 77, 79–81, 264; age at marriage of, 65, 104; courtship of, 66, 107–8,

172–81; residential patterns of, 74–76, 181, 223–26, 234–37, 244–47, 253; love for husbands, 77–79, 183–86, 230, 239–40; religious faith of, 79–81, 170–72, 194–95, 219, 251, 253, 256–57, 259–60, 311 (n. 13); and unhappiness in marriage, 108–10, 200, 235–37, 315 (n. 94); as "Cape Horn widows," 116, 168, 190, 192, 194–95, 216, 266, 310 (n. 4); in Hart's novel *Miriam Coffin*, 118–19; communication with whalemen during voyages, 143, 150–54, 169, 173, 184–86, 188, 234–35, 307–8 (n. 83); illnesses of, 145, 230, 236, 237, 241; as social surrogates for whalemen, 151–54; and furnishings on ship for whalemen, 154–56, 157; loneliness and suffering of, 181, 183–84, 192–95, 209, 212, 223, 227, 229, 232, 233, 236–37, 259, 260, 269, 314 (n. 71), 319 (n. 27), 320 (n. 34); residences of, 181–82, 223–27, 235–36; diaries of, 181–86, 312 (n. 42), 321 (n. 51); pictures of, for absent husbands, 186–87, 197; and marital sexual fidelity, 201–3; divorce of, 202–3; and emotional costs of separation from husbands, 203–13; friendships between, 229–33. *See also* Children; Domesticity; Families; Households; Marriage; Motherhood; Wives at sea; Work, women's

Marriage: and whalemen's absences, 6–7, 16, 24, 48, 49, 68, 74, 76–81, 113–14, 123, 167–68, 197–217, 229–38; Crevecoeur on, 16–17, 49–50, 65–66, 68, 72; legal status of wives in colonial America, 32–33, 37; wives' financial contributions in, 37–38, 41–45, 48–49, 113, 148–49, 157–63, 288–89 (n. 68), 308 (n. 98), 309 (n. 102); remarriage, 43, 195–97, 199–200, 225, 314 (n. 80), 315 (n. 82); Quaker rules on, 62, 67–68, 87–88, 100–103; reasons for, in Nantucket, 65–66; youthful marriages in Nantucket, 65–66; age at, 65–66, 104; of whalemen, 65–66, 140–47, 168,

183–86, 197–203; Quakers' view of, 66–67, 70–71, 264; endogamous marriages, 72, 224, 226, 320 (n. 39), 321 (n. 51); maritime women's love for husbands, 77–79, 183–86, 230, 239–40; breaking of Quaker rules on, 100–103; exogamous marriages, 101–2; and Romanticism, 103–14, 116, 120–21, 195, 265; courtship before, 107–8, 172, 173–81; unhappiness in, 108–10, 200–201, 235–37, 315 (n. 94); and passionate love in nineteenth century, 140–42, 164, 165–75; husbands' financial responsibilities in, 142–43, 154, 164; wives' transition from single to married life, 181–82, 192, 223–24; maintenance of relationships during whalemen's absences, 197–203, 214–17; and reunion following separation, 198–99; whalemen's home life between voyages, 199, 200, 237, 315 (n. 94); sexual fidelity in, 201–3, 258–59; and divorce, 202–3; and emotional costs of separation, 203–13; poetry on, 217–18; and wife as light of home, 217–18; "sibling exchange" marriage, 224, 320 (n. 39). *See also* Families; Gender; Households; Maritime women; Motherhood; Whalemen; Widowhood; Wives at sea

Martha's Vineyard, Mass., 93, 148, 151, 229, 289 (n. 84)

Masculinity. *See* Gender

Mather, Cotton, 287 (n. 56)

Mattapoisett, Mass., 123, 138, 139, 153, 181, 224, 227, 232, 321 (n. 51)

M'Cleave, Eliza Ann, 290 (n. 88)

Melville, Herman, 1, 3, 9, 12, 14, 15, 20, 81–82, 119, 123, 127, 128, 137, 141, 170, 194, 259, 260, 270

Merchants, 29–32, 35, 43, 131–34, 144–47, 306 (n. 57); women as, 35, 42, 44–46, 56, 118–19, 158–59, 288–89 (n. 68), 308 (n. 98), 309 (n. 102). *See also* Whaling agents

Merchant shipping, 26, 36–37, 96, 108,

Nantucket, 54–59, 293 (n. 22); Starbuck's leadership of, 54–61, 70, 87, 89;
persecution of, 57; worship at Quaker
meetings, 58; New England Yearly
Meeting, 59, 62, 91, 294 (n. 39); separate men's and women's monthly meetings for business, 59–60, 63; women's
meeting in Nantucket, 59–61, 65, 67,
68, 87–90, 287 (n. 48); leadership in
women's meeting, 60–61, 82, 87–90,
293–94 (n. 35); family relationships of
leaders of, 61, 87, 88, 293–94 (n. 35);
relationship between men's and wom-
en's meetings, 61, 87–89, 287 (n. 48),
293 (n. 31); leadership in men's meeting, 61, 88; marriage rules of, 62,
67–68, 87–88, 100–103; discipline
of, 62, 73, 86–90, 97–103, 264, 289
(n. 84); meetinghouse for, in Nantucket, 63; number of, in Nantucket,
63, 90, 96; plain style of, 63–64, 97–
100, 102, 294 (n. 48); view on marriage, 66–67, 70–71, 264; gender roles
of, 68–72, 264; familial metaphors for,
72; reform movement in 1770s, 82, 84,
86–90, 96–103, 298–99 (n. 26); and
peace testimony, 86, 91; disownment
by, 88, 90, 91, 97, 98–102, 301 (n. 75);
sex ratio of women to men, 88–89;
and women ministers, 89; decline of,
90, 96–98; and American Revolution,
90–97, 299 (n. 26); and material possessions, 97–99; and music and dancing, 99–100; impact of Romanticism
on, 103–14, 116; school of, 111, 113; in
seventeenth century, 121; in New Bedford, 122, 303 (n. 8)
Quilts and quilting, 40, 155, 157

Race, 9–12, 19, 26, 96, 105, 112–13,
128, 134, 203, 254, 258. See also Class,
socioeconomic; Gender
Rapp, Rayna, 310 (n. 122)
Read, Almira, 203
Read, Captain, 203
Read, T. B., 193, 212

Reading, 83, 100, 103–4, 109–10, 160,
251, 253, 256, 259, 260
Recruitment of whalemen, 26–28, 120,
134, 137, 138–39, 304 (n. 29)
Religion: and women, 79–81, 170–72,
194–95, 219, 251, 253, 256–57, 259–
60, 311 (n. 13); and sailors, 219–20,
251, 253, 256–57, 259–60, 318 (n. 17).
See also Quakers; and other Protestant
denominations
Remarriage, 43, 195–97, 199–200, 225,
314 (n. 80), 315 (n. 82)
Restraining Act of 1775, 91
Revolutionary War. See American
Revolution
Richardson, John, 55–56, 70
Richmond, George, 143–44
Ricketson, Annie, 250, 312 (n. 42), 323
(n. 90)
Roberts, Lucy, 141–42, 144, 310 (n. 4)
Rodman, Samuel, 95
Romanticism, 84, 103–14, 116, 120–21,
195, 265
Romantic love. See Love
Rotch, Francis, 91
Rotch, Joseph, 35, 121
Rotch, William, Jr., 95, 221, 318 (n. 23)
Rotch, William, Sr., 33, 35, 91, 95, 116
Rothman, E. K., 311 (n. 19)
Rothman, Ellen, 176, 180
Routh, Martha, 90, 102
Rubin, Gayle, 307 (n. 61)
Russell, Ann, 197, 227
Russell, Benjamin, 177
Russell, Jane. See Andrews, Jane Russell
Russell, Joseph, 121
Russell, Mary Hayden, 250, 323 (n. 90)
Russell, Reuben, 178–79
Russell, Roland, 169, 175–76
Ryan, Mary, 260, 310 (n. 2)

Sailors: masculine world of, 1–2, 48, 120,
256, 269; as occupational group, 2–3;
peripatetic nature of, 203–9, 233–34;
and religion, 219–20, 251, 253, 256–
57, 259–60, 318 (n. 17); vices of, 220,

241, 257, 258, 319 (n. 27). *See also*
Whalemen
Sailor's Home movement, 221–22, 319
(n. 24)
Sailor's Magazine, 192, 193, 209, 221–22,
240–41, 319 (n. 24)
Sailors' wives. *See* "Cape Horn widows";
Maritime women
Sansom, Joseph, 46
Scranton, Philip, 285 (n. 32)
Scrimshaw, 141, 188–89, 268–69
Seabury, Oliver, 204
Seafaring. *See* Maritime culture; Mar-
itime women; Merchant shipping;
Whalefishery; Whalemen; Wives at
sea
Seidman, Steven, 295 (n. 58)
Separate spheres. *See* Domesticity;
Gender
Sewing, 158–59, 217, 251, 253
Sexual division of labor. *See* Labor, gen-
der division of
Sexuality, 178, 180–81, 201–3, 258–59
"Shanghaiing" of whalemen, 137
Sheep raising, 45–46, 114. *See also* Farms
Ships. *See* Whaling vessels
Shoe manufacturing, 43–44
Sigourney, Lydia, 159, 190, 218–19,
259–60, 263
Sisson, Charley, 173
Sisson, Phebe C., 153–54
Slocum, Maria, 175
Slott, Harriet, 186
Smalley, Orrick, 306 (n. 57)
Smith, Elizabeth Oakes, 193
Smith, Fred, 189
Smith, Mary T., 223–24
Smith, Parker, 223–24
Smith, Sarah, 249, 253
Smith-Rosenberg, Carroll, 229, 296
(n. 81), 310 (n. 2)
Snell, Moses, 224
Snow, Abby, 320 (n. 34)
Snow, Susan. *See* Gifford, Susan Snow
Sociability of maritime women, 39–40,
72–74, 77, 78, 99–100, 107, 151–54,

226–28, 229–33, 235, 253–54, 260–61,
263, 321 (n. 51)
Society of Friends. *See* Quakers
Soderland, Jean, 61, 65
Sowle, James, 157–58, 165–77, 179, 196
Sowle, Ruth Grinnell, 157–58, 165–77,
179, 196, 198
Sowle, Sylvia, 159
Sperm whales, 21–23, 136
Spinning, 44, 288 (n. 67)
Spooner, Caleb, Jr., 224, 233–35, 269, 320
(n. 40)
Spooner, Caleb, Sr., 203–4, 224–25, 320
(n. 40)
Spooner, Elizabeth (wife of Gideon),
224–25
Spooner, Elizabeth (Libby) Hathaway,
203–4, 225, 233–35, 269, 320 (n. 40)
Spooner, Elizabeth (Lizzie) Francis, 225,
233
Spooner, Ella, 225
Spooner, Gideon, 224, 225, 234–35
Spooner, Lydia, 320 (n. 40)
Spooner, Shubael, 224, 225, 233, 268–69
Springer, Haskell, 326 (n. 159)
Stanton, Eliza, 158
Starbuck, Barnabus, 61
Starbuck, Christopher, 28
Starbuck, Dinah, 75–76
Starbuck, Dinah Coffin, 61, 293 (n. 35)
Starbuck, Dorcas Gayer, 61, 87
Starbuck, Hephzibah, 55, 293–94 (n. 35)
Starbuck, Jethro, 61
Starbuck, Kezia, 99
Starbuck, Mary Coffin, 54–61, 70, 87, 89,
292 (n. 15)
Starbuck, Mary (mother of Nathaniel), 56
Starbuck, Nathaniel, 55, 56, 292 (n. 15)
Starbuck, Nathaniel, Jr., 59, 61, 292
(n. 15), 293 (n. 35)
Starbuck, Thomas, 75–76
Stark, Mary, 323 (n. 90)
Stetson, Captain, 199, 257
Stetson, Elizabeth, 251, 257
Stickney, Mary, 323 (n. 90)
Stokes, Jane, 57, 293 (n. 22)

husbands" for, in business matters, 16–17, 36–37, 43, 48, 133, 148–49, 154, 287 (n. 56); age at beginning of career, 27, 138, 167, 224, 285 (n. 24); wages of, 28, 135; debts of, 35; deaths of, 35, 135, 192, 194–95, 208, 215, 219, 225, 250; age at marriage, 65; marriage of, 65–66, 140–47, 168, 183–86, 197–203; courtship of, 107–8, 172, 173–81; "home" as center of emotional life of, 109, 172, 205, 208, 215–16, 218–23, 233–34; Burke on, 117–18; in Hart's novel *Miriam Coffin*, 118; drunkenness of, 131, 241, 257, 258; and "land sharks," 137, 155; heirs' claims on, 139, 305 (n. 33); families' requests for information about young sailors, 139–40; illnesses of, 142–43; financial responsibilities of, for families, 142–43, 145–46, 154, 164; communication with families during voyages, 143, 150–54, 169, 173, 184–86, 188, 234–35, 307–8 (n. 83); residence of, 149, 224–26, 320 (n. 32); families' responsibilities for, during absences of, 149–50; wives as social surrogates for, 151–54; clothing for, 154, 155, 158–59; furnishings on ship for, 154–56, 157; loneliness of, 155, 157, 184, 205, 208, 233–34; pictures of family members for, 155, 186–88, 197; home cake for, 186; pictures of, 187, 190–91; scrimshaw carving by, 188–89, 268–69; children's relationship with, 190–92; remarriage of, 195, 196–97, 199–200, 225, 314 (n. 80), 315 (n. 82); home life of, between voyages, 199, 200, 224, 237, 315 (n. 94); marital sexual fidelity of, 201–3, 258–59; divorce of, 202–3; and emotional costs of separation from wives, 203–13; decision to stay at home, 205, 208–9, 234; career switching by, 208, 237; length of time on shore, 224. *See also* Families; Gender; Maritime women; Marriage; Whaling, work of; Wives at sea

Whale oil and bone, 8, 19, 21, 28, 41, 96, 123, 128, 130, 136–37, 249, 250, 251, 260, 311 (n. 15). *See also* Whaling, work of

Whaling, work of: length of voyages, 6–7, 24, 123, 137, 140, 142, 148, 157, 164, 167, 178, 181; class relations in, 9–12, 26–28, 120, 134–40, 247–48; role of career whalemen, 12, 26–27, 120, 134–35, 138–39, 224, 266, 285 (n. 24); capture and processing of whales, 21–24, 135–36, 248–50; dangers of, 22–24, 69–70, 135–37, 192, 250; composition of crew, 26, 134–35, 138–39; training of officers, 26–27; recruitment, 26–28, 120, 134, 137, 138–39, 304 (n. 29); age at beginning of career, 27, 138, 167, 224, 285 (n. 24); social relations of work in, 27–28, 151–54; discipline, 28, 120, 137, 151, 155–56, 256, 257–58; lay system of wages, 28, 135; paternalism, 28–36, 132–33, 138, 143–47, 285 (n. 32); masculine world of, 46, 48, 120, 256, 269; desertion, 120, 134, 135, 137, 147; immigrant and foreign labor in, 134, 137; parental permission for young seamen, 138–39, 304 (n. 29); push-pull rhythm of, 140–42, 203–9 passim, 233–34, 262, 265, 269; on the Sabbath, 259. *See also* Maritime women; Whalefishery; Whalemen; Whaling agents; Whaling grounds; Whaling vessels; Wives at sea

Whaling agents, 137–40, 143–47, 149–50, 323 (n. 86)

Whaling grounds: overview, 8–9; eighteenth-century, 24–25 (map), 96; nineteenth-century, 120, 123, 124–25 (map), 137

Whaling ports, 7–8, 10–11, 96, 137, 155, 252, 253–55, 263, 269. *See also specific cities*

Whaling vessels, 8, 9, 19, 21–22, 26, 120, 123, 132, 244–48

Whelden, Clara Kingman, 248, 323 (n. 90), 324 (n. 114)

Widowhood, 34–35, 94, 192, 194–95, 197. *See also* "Cape Horn widows"; Remarriage

Wilkey, Alden and Sarah, 160

Wilkinson, Elizabeth, 98

Williams, Eliza, 244, 246, 249, 259, 263, 323 (n. 90)

Wilson, Benny, 152

Winslow, Cornelia, 233

Wives at sea: letter writing by, 151, 229; benefits of, 151, 240–41; journals and diaries of, 209, 212, 262–63, 323 (n. 90); and maternal responsibilities, 215, 255, 260, 261; shipowners' objections to, 216, 240, 241; and romantic friendships with women, 229, 230; happiness of, 237–38, 324 (n. 114); unhappiness of, 238, 253, 263, 323 (n. 91); love and duty as motivations for voyage, 238–40, 255, 261; and domesticity, 238–64; death of, 241, 244; and childbirth, 241, 254–55; isolation of, 244, 247, 248, 249, 253, 260, 261, 263, 264, 269, 326 (n. 159); shipboard living spaces for, 244–48; seasickness of, 246, 247, 248, 259; crews' reactions to, 247–49, 254, 324 (n. 113); and whale capture and processing, 248–50; activities of, 251, 253; religiosity of, 251, 253, 256–57, 259–60; temporary homes of, in foreign ports of call, 252, 253–55, 263, 269; limited influence of, 256–59, 261; in merchant shipping, 324–25 (n. 115). *See also* Maritime women

Women. *See* Gender; Maritime women; Wives at sea

Wood, John and Sally, 208

Woolman, John, 63, 71–72, 97, 294 (n. 48)

Wool production on Nantucket, 45–46

Work, men's. *See* Labor, gender division of; Merchant shipping; Whaling

Work, women's: as "deputy husbands" or surrogates for husbands in business, 16–17, 36–37, 43, 48, 133, 148–49, 154, 287 (n. 56); community sustenance as, 24, 35–36, 65–76, 151–54, 287 (n. 55); income-producing, 37–38, 39, 41–45, 94, 113, 148–49, 157–63, 288–89 (n. 68), 308 (n. 98), 309 (n. 102); eighteenth-century concepts of, 38–39, 47–49, 264; traditional responsibilities and housewifery, 38–41, 44, 68, 154–60 passim, 224–28, 290 (n. 96); illicit, 41, 158, 308 (n. 100); entrepreneurial, 41–45, 118–19, 158–59, 308 (n. 98); nineteenth-century concepts of, 155–56, 161–64, 265–66; "pastorialization" of, 155–56, 266; and ideas about manual labor, 162–63; suffering as, 192–94; at sea, 239–40, 246, 250–53, 255–56. *See also* Labor, gender division of

Worth, Benjamin, 27

Worth, Christopher, 68

Worth, Elisabeth Ann, 233

Wright, Ebenezer, 320 (n. 40)

Wright, Lydia Spooner, 320 (n. 40)

Wright, Martha Coffin, 53

Wyer, Joseph and Margaret, 40

Wyer, John, 32

GENDER AND AMERICAN CULTURE

Delinquent Daughters: Protecting and Policing Adolescent Female Sexuality
in the United States, 1885–1920
by Mary E. Odem (1995)

U.S. History as Women's History: New Feminist Essays,
edited by Linda K. Kerber, Alice Kessler-Harris, and Kathryn Kish Sklar (1995)

Common Sense and a Little Fire: Women and Working-Class Politics
in the United States, 1900–1965
by Annelise Orleck (1995)

How Am I to Be Heard?: Letters of Lillian Smith,
edited by Margaret Rose Gladney (1993)

Entitled to Power: Farm Women and Technology, 1913–1963
by Katherine Jellison (1993)

Revising Life: Sylvia Plath's Ariel Poems
by Susan R. Van Dyne (1993)

Made From This Earth: American Women and Nature
by Vera Norwood (1993)

Unruly Women: The Politics of Social and Sexual Control in the Old South
by Victoria E. Bynum (1992)

The Work of Self-Representation: Lyric Poetry in Colonial New England
by Ivy Schweitzer (1991)

Labor and Desire: Women's Revolutionary Fiction in Depression America
by Paula Rabinowitz (1991)

Community of Suffering and Struggle: Women, Men, and the Labor Movement
in Minneapolis, 1915–1945
by Elizabeth Faue (1991)

All That Hollywood Allows: Re-reading Gender in 1950s Melodrama
by Jackie Byars (1991)

Doing Literary Business: American Women Writers in the Nineteenth Century
by Susan Coultrap-McQuin (1990)

Ladies, Women, and Wenches: Choice and Constraint in Antebellum
Charleston and Boston
by Jane H. Pease and William H. Pease (1990)

The Secret Eye: The Journal of Ella Gertrude Clanton Thomas, 1848–1889,
edited by Virginia Ingraham Burr, with an introduction by Nell Irvin Painter (1990)

Second Stories: The Politics of Language, Form, and Gender
in Early American Fictions
by Cynthia S. Jordan (1989)